The Korean Frontier in America

The Korean Frontier in America

IMMIGRATION TO HAWAII, 1896-1910

WAYNE PATTERSON

 University of Hawaii Press • Honolulu

Library of Congress Cataloging-in-Publication Data

Patterson, Wayne.
    The Korean frontier in America : immigration to Hawaii, 1896–1910
    Wayne Patterson.
        p.   cm.
    Bibliography: p.
    Includes index.
    ISBN 0–8248–1090–2
    1. Koreans—Hawaii—History. 2. Immigrants—Hawaii—History.
3. Hawaii—Emigration and immigration. 4. United States—Emigration
and immigration—Government policy. 5. Immigrants—Government
policy—United States. 6. United States—Foreign relations—Korea.
7. Korea—Foreign relations—United States. I. Title.
DU624.7.K67P37   1988   88–1163
996.9'004957—dc19   CIP

To my mother
Marjorie Kief Patterson

CONTENTS

MAPS

PREFACE

MUCH has been written about immigration to the United States from many parts of the world including East Asia. But while Japanese and Chinese immigration have received quite a bit of attention, the same has not been true for Korean immigration. The little material that does exist, in both Korean and English, tends to be little more than brief remarks at the beginning of longer treatises on the subject of Koreans in America. Thus, one reason for this study is to help correct the imbalance that exists in the study of Asian immigration to the United States. Moreover, a study of Korean immigration to United States not only fills a gap in the literature of the peopling of America, but it also gives important insights into several key issues in international relations of the turn of the century.

One of these issues is the role of American policy in Korea during the heyday of dollar diplomacy. What was the role of Horace Allen, the American minister to Korea, in Korean immigration? Were his actions in keeping with American policy toward Korea at the time?

A second issue concerns the methods and policies followed by sugar planters in fostering Korean immigration to Hawaii and what effects they had in Honolulu, Washington, Tokyo, and Seoul.

A third issue is the decline of Yi dynasty (1392–1910) Korea. Because Korean immigration to the United States occurred during the last years of the dynasty, a study of it can provide additional information on late Yi institutions, leaders, politics, and decision making.

A closely related and fourth focus of this study is the Japanese seizure of Korea. An examination of Korean immigration can clarify not only some of the reasons for Japan's actions but also the implementation of Japan's foreign policy toward the peninsula.

Finally, this study looks at Japanese-American relations at the turn of the century. Relations between the two nations were entering a new and more complicated phase, and the heretofore unknown role of Korean immigration can help shed new light on this relationship.

Thus, in addition to presenting a history of the early immigration of Koreans to America, this study addresses itself to key issues in Korean-American relations, Hawaiian history, late Yi Korean history and politics, Japanese-Korean relations, and Japanese-American relations at the advent of the twentieth century.

This project began as research for a doctoral dissertation at the University of Pennsylvania in the 1970s, and I am indebted to a number of people and institutions for help along the way: to Hilary Conroy, who first suggested the topic and who became my dissertation supervisor; to Chong-Sik Lee, Allyn Rickett, and Norman Palmer, who served on my dissertation committee; to the University of Pennsylvania, which granted me language-study funds to go to Korea in 1972 and a Penfield Fellowship to work in Korea, Japan, and Hawaii in 1973; to Agnes Conrad, Janet Azama, and Mary Ann Aoka of the Hawaii State Archives; to Edward Beechert, Frances Jackson, Donald Johnson, Andrew Lind, Bernard Hormann, Nobuo Masuda, Michael Macmillan, Theresa Chaesoon Youngs, the late Tae-Sook Kwon, Charlotte Oser, Stanley Schab, Sam-Suk Han, In-Hwan Oh, Deborah Church, Arthur L. Gardner, and Herbert Barringer of the University of Hawaii; to Lela Goodell of the Hawaiian Mission Children's Society; to Robert L. Cushing and Mary Matsuoka of the Hawaiian Sugar Planters' Association; to Mrs. James P. Morgan and Francis Morgan for allowing me to use the diary of their father/grandfather; to the Reverend Samuel A. Moffett for allowing me to use his personal papers in Seoul; to Robert Hyung-Chan Kim; to Rhoda Komuro for allowing me to use her grandfather's papers; to John Keating Sands for permission to use his father's correspondence; to Andrew H. N. Kim for the use of his article on his parents; to Western Michigan University, Fairleigh Dickinson University Press, ABC-Clio Press, the Korean Oral History Project, the Hawaiian Mission Children's Society, and the Society for Historians of American Foreign Relations for the use of their material, both published and unpublished; to Bong-Youn Choy; to the National History Compilation Committee in Seoul; to the Social Science Research Council of the American Council of Learned Societies for a postdoctoral grant with research funds provided by the Ford Foundation; to the Saint Norbert College Personnel Committee for sabbatical leave and a grant from the Faculty Improvement Fund; to Edward Wagner for inviting me to the Korea Institute, Fairbank Center for East Asian Research, Harvard University, in 1984; to Michael Rogers, John Jamieson, and Robert Scalapino for inviting me to the Center for Korean Studies, Institute of East

Asian Studies, University of California at Berkeley, in 1984; to Dae-Sook Suh for inviting me to the Center for Korean Studies, University of Hawaii, in 1985; and to Lew Young-Ick and Han Sung-Joo for inviting me to the Asiatic Research Center, Korea University, in 1985. I would also like to thank Yur-Bok Lee and Robert Swartout, Jr., for their well-founded suggestions and comments. Finally, I thank Damaris A. Kirchhofer for her stewardship of this book.

Research was carried out at the following libraries and research collections: Harvard-Yenching Library; New York Public Library; Hoover Institution of War, Peace, and Revolution; Hawaiian Sugar Planters' Association library; Bernice P. Bishop Museum in Honolulu; Seoul National University library; Korea University library; *Gaimushō gaikō shiryōkan* [Diplomatic Records Office] in Tokyo; East Asiatic Library at the University of California at Berkeley; Hamilton Library and the library of the Center for Korean Studies at the University of Hawaii; Hawaiian Mission Children's Society Library; Hawaii State Archives; the National Archives in Washington, D.C.; Ohio State Historical Society in Columbus; Presbyterian Historical Society in Philadelphia; and the University of Southern California library.

A NOTE ON NAMES AND
THEIR SPELLINGS

For Japanese names and places, romanization is based upon the modified Hepburn system, with the exception of Kobe and Tokyo, with surnames placed before given names as is the practice in Japan. For Korean names and places, romanization is based upon the McCune-Reischauer system, with the exception of Seoul, and surnames are placed before given names, as is the practice in Korea. There are, however, a number of Koreans in the United States who have chosen alternate spellings of their names and who give their surnames last, in the Western style. There are other Korean names written in English whose Chinese characters are unknown to the writer, making it impossible to create the McCune-Reischauer spellings. In such cases, Korean names will sometimes appear at variance with the McCune-Reischauer system, and given names will sometimes precede surnames.

1

The Setting

THE arrival in Hawaii of seven thousand Koreans between 1903 and 1905 was the culmination of processes that had been developing during the last half of the nineteenth century in both Korea and Hawaii. In Korea, the decline of the Yi dynasty (1392–1910) and the "opening" of the country by Japan in 1876 and the United States in 1882 set into motion a series of events which caused Koreans to seek a more stable and prosperous environment abroad. In Hawaii, the needs of the sugar industry and the predominance of Japanese workers there made the sugar planters look to Korea to solve their labor problems. These two processes developed independently of each other for several decades before they joined together shortly after the turn of the century.

Emigration from one country to another is a universal phenomenon of recorded history; Korea has been no exception. Thousands of Koreans went to Japan before the eighth century, taking with them the more advanced civilization of the continent.[1] In China, the Japanese monk Ennin recorded the existence of entire Korean communities in the ninth century.[2] For the next millennium there was no significant emigration of Koreans until the middle of the nineteenth century when the Yenpien section of Manchuria and the Maritime Provinces of Russia became the destination for many Koreans. That migration northward is indicative of some of the features that would characterize the migration of Koreans to Hawaii in the early twentieth century, and thus a brief outline of this earlier experience will be helpful.

Emigration to the area near Vladivostok began in the early 1860s, and by 1868 the number of immigrants reached 2,000. A famine in northern Korea in the following year caused an additional 4,500 to emigrate. As word spread of the advantages in Russia and as conditions in Korea deteriorated, more and more Koreans moved north. Alarmed at the exodus, the Korean government attempted to stem the tide by stricter controls at the northern border. After all, emigration was technically illegal, as it had been in China and Japan. Nevertheless, by the end of the century there were 23,000 Koreans living in the Maritime Provinces of Russia.[3]

What were the motives of the emigrants and how did they fare in their new environment? From all accounts, the emigrants were motivated to leave their homeland by natural disaster, poverty, high taxes, and government oppression in general and by reports of good prospects abroad. Once they had arrived in Russia they tended to exhibit three characteristics. First, they acculturated quickly to their new surroundings, including rapidly acquiring the Russian language, customs, and religion. Second, Koreans abroad projected an image of clean, hard-working people of good character who quickly became successful and prosperous in their new home. Third, they tended to be permanent settlers rather than sojourners.[4]

Conditions in Korea continued to deteriorate in the final decades of the nineteenth century—a phenomenon that will be examined in greater detail later—and more people became uprooted. In Hawaii, meanwhile, economic and social forces were operating which would soon lead to an invitation to Koreans. When the opportunity to go to Hawaii presented itself at the turn of the century, many Koreans chose that option, having had four decades of experience with emigration to the area north of Korea.

After the first European contact was made with Hawaii by Britain's Captain Cook in 1778, the islands quickly became a new frontier for American missionaries, whalers, coffee growers, and sugar planters. By 1835, sugar had replaced coffee as the main crop, a transformation that began with the formation of Koloa Plantation on the island of Kauai. From that time forward, sugar was king, transforming the nature of the Hawaiian economy into large-scale, labor-intensive plantations.

At first, the white sugar planters employed native Hawaiians on a contract-labor basis to work the sugarcane fields. Because the demand for sugar was low in those early years, the growers were able to obtain enough workers. As time passed, however, a decline in the population of native Hawaiians and their general reluctance to perform plantation work combined with an increase in demand for sugar to produce a labor shortage.[5] This shortage, sometimes real and sometimes contrived, was destined to last for more than a century and to become a key factor in the social, economic, and political history of Hawaii. The search for additional sources of labor extended to other countries, with the result that more than 400,000 immigrant laborers were eventually recruited from thirty-three countries.[6] The 7,000 Koreans who arrived between 1903 and 1905 were part of this larger phenomenon.

By mid-century the realization of a labor shortage brought together the sugar planters and the Hawaiian government in a concerted effort to obtain foreign workers.[7] In 1850 the planters formed the Royal Hawaiian Agricultural Society to investigate outside sources of labor and promote plantation interests. In that same year the legal system was brought into line with the planters' wishes when the contract-labor system was extended to foreigners who might enter Hawaii under contract to the sugar planters. The law provided that contracts made in a foreign country for service in Hawaii were binding and that prison sentences could be imposed for failure to fulfill a contract.[8] This made contract labor similar to indentured servitude in colonial America. With these developments, the sugar planters became the single most powerful economic group in Hawaii—a status that continued even after annexation to the United States in 1898, when contract labor became illegal—and were to leave a legacy of a century of economic, political, and social domination of Asian immigrants by white plantation owners.

Although the sugar planters and the government arranged for the first immigrant laborers in 1852, when 293 Chinese from the Canton area arrived, serious searching for workers abroad did not begin until 1864 when an Act to Provide for the Importation of Laborers and for the Encouragement of Immigration was passed.[9] This act created a Board of Immigration signifying governmental supervision of immigration.

In 1865 Chinese laborers in small numbers began arriving in Hawaii. In general, the planters were pleased with them, calling them "quiet, able and willing men."[10] The influx of Chinese remained relatively slight until 1876 when the Kingdom of Hawaii signed a reciprocity treaty with the United States permitting Hawaii to export sugar duty free to a previously tariff-protected American market. The treaty gave sugar its biggest boost, expanding production tenfold in the following decade.[11] With the new demand for sugar came an increased call from the planters for laborers, and the decade between 1876 and 1885 witnessed the greatest influx of Chinese laborers. By the time annexation occurred, a total of nearly 50,000 Chinese had immigrated to Hawaii.[12]

The arrival of the Chinese marked the beginning of cycles of plantation labor in Hawaii that were to continue as each new racial group arrived as immigrants. For example, the Chinese received favorable comment initially but later became targets for criticism. As their three-year contracts expired, many of them moved into the cities seeking work at low wages, and tradespeople began to complain of unfair competition. That the Chinese and subsequent immigrants failed to renew their contracts is not surprising. Sugar plantations in Hawaii operated much like independent fiefdoms and were notorious for unfavorable working conditions: low wages, long workdays, lack of opportunity for promotion, poor treatment by foremen, and in general, discipline that denied the worker a reasonable amount of freedom.[13]

From the planter point of view, a system of controls was necessary to keep the worker docile and to ensure the continuous performance of monotonous and physically exhausting labor. Accepting employment in a land several thousand miles from home and among aliens left the new immigrant laborer in a dependent state. In addition to language difficulties, immigrants faced ethnic segregation on the plantation, which hindered acculturation. Thus the economic interest of planters in keeping immigrants on the plantations coincided with the natural inclinations of the immigrants to stick together.[14] So in the early years, the immigrants' racial traits were extolled and their critics were few. But once the immigrants discovered the opportunities that lay in other lines of work, the plantation became associated with inferior status and they began to leave the cane fields for the city.

As the Chinese moved to the cities they became more visible to the urban middle class, which saw them as competitors willing to work for low wages. As a result townspeople began to complain to the government that the Chinese were not doing what they had been brought to Hawaii to do, that is, to work on the plantations. They also complained that the Chinese were too different racially to assimilate, that they smoked opium, that they were disease-ridden, that the ratio of men to women was too high for ease of mind, and that there were simply too many of them. By 1882 only 5,000 of the 14,000 Chinese in Hawaii still worked on plantations, and Chinese constituted nearly one-quarter of the total population of the kingdom.[15]

Despite the tendency of the Chinese to leave the plantations, the planters were still generally happy with these docile laborers. Moreover, transportation costs were low and a worker's wages amounted to only ten dollars per month at that time. Naturally, the planters wished that the Chinese would stay on the plantations, which would mitigate adverse public pressure, but their main concern was that exclusive reliance on Chinese might result in a labor monopoly.[16]

The political elite in Hawaii also had its doubts about Chinese, and their convictions were strengthened when the United States passed the Chinese Exclusion Act in 1882 as a result of anti-Chinese agitation in California. Certainly the planters also saw how closely their interests were tied to their biggest market. Thus, when the first legislative restriction limiting the number of Chinese allowed to enter was passed in Hawaii in 1883, the pressure mounted on the planters and the government to find another source of inexpensive plantation labor. To that end the sugar planters organized the Planters' Labor and Supply Company, the predecessor of the Hawaiian Sugar Planters' Association, to act as a pressure group pushing the Hawaiian government to allow for the introduction of a sufficient supply of inexpensive plantation labor.

In 1878, Pacific Islanders were imported, but they did not take to plantation work. Six hundred Norwegians arrived in 1881 and 300 Germans came between 1882 and 1885, but both groups proved too expensive to transport and recruit. The most promising non-Oriental laborers seemed to be the Portuguese, who first arrived in 1878 and eventually numbered about 14,000. Yet the Portuguese also proved to be expensive to transport, demanded higher wages, and seldom renewed their contracts.[17] For these reasons, the planters were not satisfied with Portuguese immigration, but those seeking annexation and Americanization saw the Portuguese workers as a means for peopling the Islands with white labor. Thus began the long-standing friction between the government and public opinion on the one hand, which desired expensive white labor (or at least "cognate" races from the Pacific islands), and the planters on the other hand, who desired inexpensive Asian labor.

With legislative limitations placed on the number of Chinese permitted to immigrate to Hawaii and with the Portuguese temporarily out of the running because of the expense involved, the planters, encouraged by King Kalakaua, turned to the Japanese as the most suitable race to offset the Chinese. This was the beginning of planter policy to mix the races on the plantations to prevent any one racial group from achieving a labor monopoly.[18] Later, the Koreans would be used in a similar role to offset the Japanese.

The first systematic immigration from Japan began in 1885 and by the early 1890s surpassed the Chinese as the largest immigrant labor group in the Islands.[19] Like the Chinese before them, most of the Japanese originally intended to make money in Hawaii and then return home after a short sojourn abroad. Yet, like the Chinese, many Japanese stayed on in Hawaii because of weakening home ties, the pleasant climate, and the difficulty of saving enough for the return passage.[20] Also like the Chinese, the Japanese left the plantations and went into other trades even more quickly than the Chinese had.[21] As Japanese laborers moved to the cities, the townspeople now began to complain anew about foreign competition.[22]

The planters also became critical of the Japanese, too, but for different reasons. Unlike the patient and docile Chinese, the Japanese were a proud and nationalistic people who would not be pushed around. Consequently, Japanese laborers were quick to take offense at plantation injustices. Even sympathetic accounts of plantation life acknowledge the abuses of the system:

> [T]he employer furnished housing, food, a limited amount of furniture and medical attention. The housing was usually in barracks-like buildings and the food was of the plainest sort. If the laborer deserted his work he was likely to be hauled before a police magistrate and fined or imprisoned. On many plantations the laborers were treated with some degree of kindness and consideration, but at best plantation work under the contract system did not attract the better type of laborers nor did it keep them after their contracts had expired. The labor at Koloa Plantation with its military-trained German overseers did not have an easy time and desertions were many and frequent.[23]

The Japanese soon acquired the reputation of difficult and unreliable workers. One manifestation of this reputation was a new phenomenon on the scene—strikes. Although under the contract-labor system strikes were illegal, work stoppages occurred from time to time as the Japanese workers began to act collectively. Between 1890 and 1897 there were twenty-nine Japanese-inspired work stoppages,[24] and the rate of desertion reached 6 percent by 1895.[25]

While the Japanese represented cheap labor, the strikes and rising desertion rates were a source of consternation to the planters. By the late 1890s the Japanese bid fair to achieve their own labor monopoly and this partly explained their unreliability from the point of view of the planters. Their solution was to mix races, as they had done earlier, to prevent any one race from achieving a labor monopoly:

> The tendency to strike and desert, which their [Japanese] wellnigh full possession of the labor market fosters, has shown Planters the great importance of having a percentage of their laborers of other nationalities. . . . [The Japanese] seize on the smallest grievance, of a real or imaginary nature, to revolt and leave work. . . . For this tendency to strike the only remedy possible is the introduction of some other class of labor to supplement the Japanese.[26]

In addition to complaints from the planters, adverse public opinion forced the government to take notice of the problem. As the numbers of Japanese in Hawaii grew, the Hawaiian government became aware of the power of Japan, which was strong enough to make demands and protest vigorously in defense of its subjects in Hawaii—a role which the weaker Chinese government had been unable to fulfill. Rumors that Japan wanted to annex Hawaii began to circulate.

The large and growing Japanese population was also a threat to the political dominance of the white propertied class in Hawaii, which made its move for supremacy in the late 1880s and early 1890s. To this end, barriers to Japanese political participation were maintained, though the Japanese government suggested strongly in 1894 that the Japanese in Hawaii be given voting rights and more holidays. With the powerful Japanese navy lurking in the background, tensions rose, providing grist for the mill of those who urged annexation as the only course to ward off the Japanese threat. The white middle class and the annexationists had made their biggest move in 1887 when they forced the Hawaiian royalty to accept constitutional amendments limiting the power of the monarchy. Six years later, in 1893, the monarchy was overthrown and the Republic of Hawaii was inaugurated with Sanford B. Dole as president.

The change in government did not alter the problems faced by the planters and the new government concerning the Japanese immigrants, which paralleled the problems faced a decade earlier with the Chinese. That is, the government wanted to promote the importation of (more expensive) white labor and also to decrease the number of new Japanese immigrants. The planters were wary of any plan that would deny them access to inexpensive Asian labor. Yet they were not entirely satisfied with the obstreperous Japanese workers and sought to lessen their tendency to strike by importing another race of inexpensive laborers. Moreover, the greater the supply of labor, the easier it was to keep wages low. The solution worked out by the government and the planters was to augment the immigration of Chinese, who had never really stopped coming, while at the same time attempting to induce more white labor to come to Hawaii.

In reopening Chinese immigration, the government and the planters were treading on thin ice. While the planters retained a certain nostalgia for the patient and industrious Chinese, especially in light of their experiences with Japanese workers, political considerations made the renewed immigration of Chinese labor risky at best. For one, annexation was almost a certainty by the mid-1890s and this meant that, barring a special dispensation for Hawaii, the Chinese Exclusion Act would prohibit Chinese from entering Hawaii. Second, public opinion in Hawaii was not at all in favor of renewed Chinese immigration. "Fort Street will come to resemble the business quarter of Amoy, Foochow, or Canton, and white civilization will be submerged," read an 1895 editorial.[27] Third, by advocating Chinese immigration the Hawaiian government undermined its own political support since the American Union Party, which was naturally pro-annexation like the government, had inserted an anti-Oriental immigration plank into its party platform.[28]

Finally, statutory obstacles presented problems since an 1892 law limited the number of Chinese immigrants to 5,000 a year.

It was becoming clear that the use of Chinese to counterbalance the more numerous Japanese had only lukewarm support of the government. It was also clear that from the point of view of the planters, renewed Chinese immigration would be only a temporary filip prior to annexation. The planters, without much enthusiasm, did try to placate the government by agreeing to import one white worker for every ten Chinese or Japanese they imported. To this end the planters offered inducements to white Americans, Germans, Italians, and Portuguese, but without notable success.[29] For the planters, the ideal answer to the Japanese problem was another inexpensive Asian race other than Chinese. It was in this context that the first mention of Koreans as laborers surfaced.

The first proposal from the planters to import Korean laborers came in the fall of 1896 as a way to avoid importing more expensive white labor. Since the planters had agreed earlier that year that at least 10 percent of their imported labor would be other than Chinese or Japanese, why not observe (unobtrusively) the letter, if not the intent, of the agreement by suggesting that the 10 percent be (inexpensive) Koreans? The government was not fooled, however. When the proposal was first made at a meeting of the Hawaii government Executive Council in November 1896 by H. Hackfeld and Company (one of the Big Five and later known as Amfac), President Sanford Dole and his other cabinet officers, Finance Minister Samuel M. Damon and Attorney General William O. Smith, approved the importation of Koreans but lumped them with Chinese and Japanese, which meant that the planters would still have to import white labor.[30] Not surprisingly, Hackfeld forwarded no applications for Koreans.[31]

While nothing came of this initial proposal, it did make a favorable impression on the two most influential members of the Hawaiian government, President Dole and Attorney General Smith. In a meeting on immigration with the planters (who had reorganized into the Hawaiian Sugar Planters' Association in 1895) in the summer of the following year (1897), both men spoke favorably of promoting Korean immigration.[32] These favorable attitudes were important since both officials would retain their leadership positions in the government of the Territory of Hawaii after annexation to the United States.

During the remainder of 1897 and the first half of 1898 there was no further mention of importing Koreans. Annexation occurred in the summer of 1898, but the laws of the United States would not begin to apply to Hawaii until passage of the Organic Act in June 1900. This meant that Hawaii still had two years to import immigrant labor under contract. Since the planters were unsure what the attitude of the U. S. Congress would be toward the continued immigration of Asians, either free or under contract, they determined to "get in all the labor we could whilst we had the opportunity."[33] With this intention of loading up on labor came the second proposal to import Koreans.

In September 1898, a circular appeared on the desks of the planters under the heading "COREAN LABORERS." It came from an emigration agent in Manchuria promising to supply no fewer than seven hundred Koreans to the planters for three-year contracts at $12.50 per month, with the planters paying $50.00 in passage money for each immigrant.[34] At least two of the planters were interested. Walter M. Giffard, Vice-President and Manager of the William C. Irwin Company, which controlled a number of sugar plantations, noting the need to offset the Japanese and the uncertain attitude of Congress toward continued Chinese immigration, asked the manager of the Hutchinson Plantation on the island of Hawaii whether he would be interested in having Korean laborers. The response was positive, with the manager ordering twenty-five Koreans.[35] And the manager of Laupahoehoe Plantation, J. M. Lydgate, agreed to try Koreans "if there were no great expense involved."[36]

Despite this second initiative to bring Koreans to Hawaii, the effort came to nothing. While the reason was that the agent did not receive the requisite number of orders (700), it is clear that the idea was still premature. There was still plenty of labor, and so the need for Koreans was not an urgent and pressing issue. In fact, a period of three years was to elapse before the subject was to be raised again, in 1901. During these three intervening years events and conditions would make Koreans seem indispensable to the planters.

While efforts to organize a systematic immigration to Hawaii proved to be unsuccessful initially, at the same time a few Koreans began to arrive in the Islands on their own initiative. To be sure, a number of Korean students and diplomats had passed through Hawaii since 1883 on their way to the mainland United States. Included among these were Sŏ Chae-p'il [Philip Jaisohn], Sŏ Kwang-bŏm, Yu Kil-jun, Yun Ch'i-ho, An Ch'ang-ho, Min Yŏng-hwan, and Kim Kyu-sik. The first record of Koreans disembarking in Hawaii is that of the arrival in May 1896 of two men with the surname "Kum," who listed their occupations as "merchants." They were probably ginseng merchants from China, which would account for the variant rendering of the "Kim" surname. A third Korean merchant, with the name of Pack [Pak] (age 38), arrived two years later in 1898. Four Korean "grocers" with surnames Kam

Korean cities where recruiting offices were located

(age 29), Kam (32), Kam (51), and Chung (22) arrived from Hong Kong in 1899, followed two weeks later by three "druggists" named Tsu (51), Chang (36), and Chin (20). Two Koreans named Kam (31) and Leong (34) from Neuchang (near Mukden) arrived in 1900, followed four days later by three Korean druggists named Hung (31), Hung (45), and Chin (34) from Hong Kong. A single Korean by the name of Yu arrived in January 1901, followed by four others between July 1, 1900, and June 30, 1901. And twelve male Koreans arrived between July 1, 1901, and June 30, 1902.[37]

Thus, in the six years between 1896 and 1902 about twenty Koreans, mostly ginseng merchants from China, arrived in Hawaii, probably to ply their trade among the numerous Chinese and Japanese immigrants on the plantations in Hawaii. They would soon be joined by thousands of their countrymen whose immigration would be systematically organized by the sugar planters.

2

The Planning Begins

THE sugar planters had supported annexation to the United States because it would mean increased demand for their product. At the same time they recognized that annexation could create difficulties in the realm of immigrant labor, and they had tried, without success, to elicit a guarantee that American laws would not interfere with the importation of laborers for the plantations.[1] That is, after annexation, Chinese would be prohibited from coming to Hawaii, strikes would be legal, contracts already in force would be voided, no new contracts could be offered, it would be illegal to prepay transportation or otherwise to assist immigrants, and immigrants in Hawaii would be now free to move to the mainland United States. It was in this new climate that Koreans once more became the topic of serious consideration.

In any given year before annexation the planters had usually imported between five and seven thousand immigrant laborers. But in the uncertain climate of 1898–1899, 40,000 Japanese were brought in as a cushion against a possible labor shortage after passage of the Organic Act of 1900 and as a means for keeping the wage rate down.[2] By 1900 a total of 65,000 Japanese were in Hawaii, more than double the number of any other population group.[3] And they continued to arrive as 1901 saw the arrival of more than 7,000 and twice as many arriving the following year.[4]

This influx increased the ambivalence with which the planters viewed the Japanese. On the one hand, they were dependent upon this inexpensive and reliable source of labor. On the other hand, the rising number of Japanese increased their fear that the Japanese were consolidating a labor monopoly. This fear was based upon a number of observable trends.

One of these trends was evident in the dramatic increase in the number of strikes (now legal) involving Japanese. In the last six months of 1900 alone there were twenty-three strikes involving 7,000 Japanese workers.[5] A second trend was an increasing unreliability of Japanese workers. Even before annexation the Japanese desertion rate, which had been 6 percent in 1895, jumped to 16 percent in 1898 when such action was still illegal.[6] After annexation, many Japanese workers began shifting from plantation to plantation seeking better working conditions, and those plantations where laborers were ill-treated had great difficulty in keeping their workers.[7]

Others began an exodus to California to work for the railroads or fruit orchards. Since labor was now legally free to sell itself to the highest bidder, the blandishments of wages which on the mainland often reached $1.50 per day, as compared with 70 cents a day in Hawaii, constituted a powerful drawing factor. In 1902 almost a thousand Japanese left for the West Coast; two years later saw the departure of 6,000; and in 1905 more than 10,000 left for California.[8]

Still others left the plantations and moved to the towns and villages in the Islands, a movement that worked to the detriment of the planters because it not only deprived them of needed labor but also aroused the ire of the white middle-class tradespeople in Hawaii against Japanese immigration and increased pressure on the planters.[9] Pressure also came from Washington which wanted the "Americanization" of the Islands and deplored the large and increasing numbers of Japanese immigrants. This put now-Governor Dole in somewhat of a predicament, causing him to state (not altogether truthfully) in a letter to President McKinley that "the labor immigrants do not form a permanent addition to the population of this country, as there is a constant return immigration of this class to their own country."[10]

The large number of Japanese who came to Hawaii between 1898 and 1902 served to exacerbate the problems perceived by the planters, who more than ever saw the need to find another race to offset the Japanese, and by the government and the general public in Hawaii and the United States as a whole, which were becoming even more troubled about Japanese immigration especially now that the Chinese were excluded. For these reasons, then, the need for Koreans seemed all the more pressing, and it was at this time that the subject of Korean labor was once again broached after a three-year lapse.

At their annual meeting in November 1900, the Hawaiian Sugar Planters Association (HSPA) decided that the individual plantations would be assessed according to their sugar production for expenses incurred in recruiting foreign labor.[11] In this recruitment drive one of the trustees of the HSPA, E. Faxon Bishop, of whom we shall hear more later, returned from New York with a few hundred Negroes, Portuguese, Italians, and Puerto Ricans. Of these, the Puerto Ricans appeared at first to be the most promising as a counterbalance to the Japanese; so in December of that year and continuing through most of 1901 some 6,000 were brought to Hawaii. Unfortunately for the planters, the results were far from satisfactory.[12] The *Planters Monthly* reported:

> The Porto Ricans, when they arrived, gave the least promise, either as citizens or laborers, of any immigrants that ever disembarked at Honolulu. The men had been carelessly recruited at a time when the laboring population of Porto Rico was in a condition of acute distress. It is probable that few of them were in a physical condition to make a long voyage when they went on shipboard. . . . They were half-starved, anemic, and, in some cases, diseased. A considerable number of petty criminals, wharf rats, and prostitutes from Ponce and other coast towns accompanied them. They were not so much representatives of the people of Porto Rico as of famine and misery in the abstract when they arrived in Honolulu.[13]

Despite this negative report, there was one important salutory effect of the importation of Puerto Ricans, which was not lost on the planters in their concern to offset the Japanese:

> From the planters' point of view an important result of the Porto Rican immigration was the moral effect that their arrival had on the Japanese. The latter had begun to fancy that with the enforcement of the Federal Chinese Exclusion and contract laws after the annexation they were complete masters of the labor situation in Hawaii. They formed temporary combinations for the purpose of striking at critical periods of the planting and grinding seasons, and in this way had succeeded in forcing up wages. The regular arrival of monthly expeditions of Porto Rican laboring people throughout an entire year largely disabused them of this sense of monopoly and made them much more reasonable in their relations with their employers.[14]

The lessons learned by the planters from the Puerto Rican immigration were twofold. First, greater care was necessary in the recruitment process in order to obtain reasonably satisfactory cane field workers. Second, another race of laborers was needed to offset the majority Japanese since the Puerto Ricans obviously would not do. Remembering the patient and docile Chinese, especially when compared with the Japanese, as well as the fact that the Chinese constituted inexpensive Asian labor, the planters convinced the Hawaiian government to ask federal officials once again for an exemption from the Chinese Exclusion Act. To that end, in the summer of 1901 Henry E.

Cooper, former foreign minister of the Republic and now secretary of the Territory of Hawaii, traveled to Washington. Cooper was rebuffed in the attempt to have Chinese again come to Hawaii, but taking a fallback position, he then asked whether Koreans were also subject to the Chinese Exclusion Act and was told they were not.[15]

The planters were disappointed but realistic about their chances of obtaining Chinese, one planter stating: "Naturally, could we have got in some Chinese to have mixed the labor races on the plantations, it would have been better, but from present appearances it would simply be futile to make any attempt to stem the tide of public opinion on the exclusion question."[16]

Now that it was clear that Chinese could not be used as an offset to the Japanese, Koreans assumed more importance in the minds of the planters. But, while Koreans might serve satisfactorily in that respect, would they be good workers? The two concepts were joined: the better the workers, the more effective an offset they would provide. After all, the Puerto Ricans had offset the Japanese only slightly because they were unsatisfactory workers. Second-hand information from Korea that was available at the time gave preliminary indications that Koreans would indeed be good workers:

> The officers of the [mining] company speak in the highest terms of their gentle behavior and industry. The Koreans work more steadily and endure fatigue much better than the average Japanese. . . . It is reported that a Korean coolie can dig more coal in one day than a Japanese coolie in one and a half days; besides, the Korean coolies are more obedient and respectful to their employers than the same class of Japanese.[17]

> They are poor, dreadfully poor. I know of no poorer people. But they are amenable to the proper discipline, willing and not difficult to manage. I have talked with many of them. . . . The Korean men of the laboring classes are bigger men than the Japanese and have not the conceit and deceit of the Japanese. They would make good field workers and would not want a homestead or any inducement to come here other than a fair wage.[18]

> Hear the testimony even of the foreign mining companies, who avow the Koreans are the best workmen of any nationality they have employed.[19]

> As a matter of fact the Korean is the pick of all the Orientals as a workman. I have worked Chinese, Japanese and Koreans during the past seven years and I have not the slightest hesitation in saying that the Korean is decidedly the best.[20]

Whether or not the planters were aware of any of these opinions or reports about hard-working Koreans, their primary concern remained that of offsetting the Japanese. This had become critical now that Chinese were prohibited by law and the Puerto Ricans had proved unsuitable. One planter wrote: "The fact that the recruiting of Porto Rican laborers has practically stopped, and also the fact of there being no offset to the large preponderance of Japanese on all plantations, has made the latter about as independent as they were a year ago."[21] Another stated flatly, "The reason we would like to get Koreans here is that some of the planters fear that getting so many Japs here as we have, they will combine against us in strikes."[22]

The planters began their discussions about the Koreans in secret, and these discussions occurred within the framework of continued importation of Japanese labor and the labor needs of the plantations. In fact, the Labor Committee of the HSPA suggested that there was currently a labor shortage because 5,000 more Asians (Chinese and Japanese) had departed the plantations than had entered since 1900 and concluded that more than 9,000 additional workers were necessary to put the plantations "in a state of efficiency."[23] This necessitated an increase in the number of Japanese immigrants which, if made public, could cause serious problems and perhaps lead to Japanese exclusion. One planter noted that this "should be kept absolutely confidential."[24]

The need to import Koreans while at the same time increasing the number of Japanese immigrants was viewed by the planters as an urgent matter which should be undertaken as soon as possible. One reason for the urgency was the attitude of Washington. The planters were hopeful: "It seems to be the desire of the administration not to cripple the Island industries, and consequently I do not think we will have any trouble in getting such labor of any description, outside of Chinese, as we may wish."[25] At the same time, the HSPA trustees realized that this favorable attitude might be only temporary: "We feel that the present is a golden opportunity to not only get in all the Koreans we can, but also Japanese, as there is no knowing whether a change in officials or administration at Washington might give us considerable opposition and undo all that the present ones have promised." Since Cooper's visit to Washington, Gifford wrote, "both the Collector of Customs and the Inspector of Immigration have been privately instructed from Washington in these matters [concerning Koreans], and the assurances are very favorable, at least for the present."[26] Moreover, the planters had received additional assurances that Koreans would not be interfered with by federal officers "providing they are able bodied men and able to obtain employment *after* arrival, *and also providing that no contract, written or implied, be made with them prior to their departure from Korea.*"[27]

Thus the planters had at least a temporary go-ahead from Washington as long as they conducted the recruitment of immigrants within the confines of American law.

As a result of Washington's favorable attitude toward importation of Koreans, the subject of Korean labor became "the principal topic under discussion at meetings of the HSPA trustees."[28] Walter M. Giffard wrote that "the whole of the planting interests here . . . have strongly urged the Trustees to act *at once* in the matter, and to send a committee to Korea with power to act in event of their being able to arrange an immigration at rates satisfactory to the Association."[29] William G. Irwin, based in San Francisco, thought the suggestion to send someone to Korea "a good one."[30] It was now a question of whom to send.

It was important to select a capable person to go to Korea. In Giffard's "opinion nobody but men of sound judgment and the best of executive ability should be sent on a mission of this kind." He was cautious because "we certainly do not want a second edition of the Porto Rican matter."[31] "Several names were proposed" but no agreement was reached and the matter was temporarily postponed.[32] In the following week the name of E. Faxon Bishop was proposed, but illness prevented his going.[33] The planters next turned to C. M. Cooke who replied that someone from Alexander and Baldwin should make the trip.[34] H. P. Baldwin then proposed that William O. Smith make the trip, and William G. Irwin in turn suggested F. M. Swanzy.[35] It was clear that the planters were having difficulty in finding someone to send in that November of 1901, and were thus forced "to let the matter lay over for a short season."[36] Perhaps it was not surprising that Honolulu-based businessmen were unwilling to go to Korea, which was "now practically impenetrable on account of the severe winters encountered there."[37] Whether because of the lack of availability of the right person or because of considerations of climate, it was clear that a new approach was needed.

Because the planters initially could find no one to go to Korea, it was decided to write to Korea for information. The first letter was written by F. M. Swanzy to Leigh Hunt, who had interests in the Seoul-Inch'ŏn railroad with James R. Morse and in the Unsan Gold Mines in northern Korea. Swanzy's letter contained "a long list of questions [with] particular emphasis . . . placed upon the name of a firm being given to the Association, so that it might be engaged in the future to conduct any immigration which we might engage in."[38] Hunt wrote back to suggest that the planters contact Walter D. Townsend, head of the American Trading Company, in Inch'ŏn.[39] Accordingly, the planters "made up a large number of questions" for Townsend, whose reply to those questions "the Trustees consider very satisfactory." So satisfactory was Townsend's reply that the planters intended "opening up further the question of Korean immigration to these islands at a very early date."[40]

So the planters in effect marked time until the spring when one of their more competent members could make the journey to Korea to initiate immigration. Into the breach stepped the American Minister to Korea, Horace N. Allen, whose timely intervention was to stamp his imprimatur upon the Korean project.

3

Enter Horace Allen

Horace Allen, the American minister to Korea, and his wife had left Korea on October 15, 1901, for home leave in Toledo, Ohio, where they stayed with Allen's sister Jennie and her husband, Clayton Everett.[1] As Allen was about to begin his return journey to Korea in February 1902, William G. Irwin in San Francisco was informed by Jacob Sloat Fassett that Allen would be passing through San Francisco.[2] Fassett was Congressman from Elmira, New York, and co-owner with Leigh Hunt of the Unsan Gold Mines. Naturally, Irwin was interested and arranged to meet Allen's train when it arrived in Oakland.[3] The meeting between these two men was to affect significantly the search for Korean workers for the plantations in Hawaii and in the process would have profound implications for Korean-American relations, Japanese-American relations, and Japanese-Korean relations over the next five years.

Horace Allen had been one of the first Americans to arrive in Korea after its opening by Japan in 1876 and the ratification of the Shufeldt Treaty between Korea and the United States in 1883. His arrival in 1884 as a medical missionary for the Presbyterians led to almost immediate involvement with the Korean government when he was called upon to bind up the wounds of an important official injured during a coup attempt in 1884. His medical skill in saving the injured minister's life earned him entry into the highest councils of the government. Soon Allen found politics more interesting than medicine and eagerly accepted the post of secretary to the American legation in 1890—an appointment made at the request of King Kojong (reign 1864-1907).[4] During the seven years he served in that position Allen dominated the legation because of his intimacy with the king. Allen cemented his friendship to Kojong in 1896 when he helped him escape from the Japanese to the Russian legation.[5] In the following year, when Allen was being considered for promotion to minister, Kojong asked that the appointment go to Allen, "an old and thoroughly valued friend to himself [Kojong] and to Korea."[6]

From the beginning of his diplomatic career, Allen had always endeavored to secure for American business as many franchises or concessions as possible in Korea. By doing this he hoped that the United States government would take a greater political and diplomatic interest in a land in which Americans were increasing their economic presence. In essence, Allen was not dissimilar to other diplomats at the turn of the century who felt that the flag should and would follow the dollar. Allen's practice of "dollar diplomacy" was combined with a political campaign pressing the State Department for an active involvement in Korea—a policy that was firmly resisted. Allen felt that the cautious attitude of Washington put him at a disadvantage in attempting to deal with the more aggressive maneuverings of China, Russia, and Japan. Ironically, Kojong, like Allen, also favored an active American policy in Korea, as Kojong (elevated to emperor in 1897) felt that he could "trust a people so lacking in foreign aggressiveness."[7]

Allen's dollar diplomacy was instrumental in benefiting American businessmen in Korea as well as increasing the American presence and, Allen hoped, political interest in the peninsular empire. In 1887, for example, Kojong had asked Allen how Korea could "interest the U.S. government and people in Korea and secure our help in keeping off China." Allen's quick answer was to "give the gold mining franchise to an American company."[8] Eight years later the gold mining franchise again came up and Kojong wanted to give it to Allen himself, but on the latter's advice the franchise was granted to an American businessman. The grant caused Allen to write to the secretary of state that Kojong's "confidence in America and Americans has just been unmistakeably manifested in the granting of a very valuable mining right."[9] Yet the granting of this first concession to an American was as much a favor to Allen as a vote of confidence in the United States. Following the gold mining franchise came additional grants to Americans: for the Inch'ŏn railway, steamship lines, water and electric systems, coal mines, and a trolley system for Seoul—all on the advice of Horace Allen.[10]

Kojong desired Allen's counsel. At times he called Allen in every day, consulted him on everything, and "always" took his advice.[11] Allen himself wrote, "It makes no difference which one [Japan or Russia] gets the most influence in the Palace . . . the Emperor always turns to me and the more they scare him the more eager he is to turn everything over to the Americans."[12] So Kojong's relationship with the United States was built around his friendship with Allen, his unofficial adviser; and his friendship with Allen was built around his trust in the nonaggressive policy of the United States. It was this background that accompanied Allen as his train rolled westward toward San Francisco and his first meeting with the planters.

"Dr. Allen spent an afternoon at my house," Irwin wrote to his associate Walter Giffard in Honolulu, "and I went into the matter of Korean labor very fully with him." Allen was a useful man to talk to because he was "in touch with the government and people there" and because his position "makes his services and advice additionally valuable." Continuing, Irwin wrote that Allen had "kindly consented to meet" with the HSPA, and he "will give you an idea of the value of the labor in question, the possible difficulties in arranging it to come here, and he would also use his own influence with the Washington government to prevent obstacles in that direction." In return, Irwin wanted the planters "to supply him with all the data he requires as to cost of living and matters of that nature . . . to receive him and place carriages at his disposal, and in fact do anything . . . to make his stay there pleasant." He added, "It is very important that the Trustees should do all they can for this gentleman, as it is very kind and considerate of him, considering the position he occupies, to consent to the trouble he is going to in having this interview." Irwin concluded his letter by emphasizing that this unique opportunity should not be wasted: "I trust there will be no misunderstanding about meeting Dr. Allen."[13] With the letter to Giffard Irwin enclosed a letter of introduction for Allen addressed to F. M. Swanzy, at that time president of the HSPA.[14]

Irwin's brief but important encounter with Allen in San Francisco convinced him that the planters had found a solution to their labor problems, for two weeks later he wrote: "I have no doubt the information which he could give would be very important, and perhaps do away with the necessity of sending anybody especially to Korea to investigate that class of labor. I shall look with interest for news regarding your interview with Dr. Allen."[15]

Allen was also excited by the prospect and had the *Nippon Maru* run at extra speed to give him more time in Honolulu to consult with the HSPA.[16] Allen's enthusiasm was hardly surprising, as his entire diplomatic career in Korea had been devoted to obtaining franchises for American businessmen. As he sailed for Hawaii and his meeting with the planters, it is not difficult to imagine the picture he would paint of Korean workers, being on record as comparing them favorably with Indians and Negroes[17] and insisting that they were superior to other Orientals.[18]

The Allens arrived in Honolulu harbor late in the evening of March 3, 1902. Stormy weather and the late hour made it impossible for the planters to do anything for them that evening. After breakfast the next morning, HSPA president F. M. Swanzy visited Allen on board ship and personally escorted him to the meeting with the assembled HSPA trustees. After the meeting Allen met briefly with Governor Sanford B. Dole and then took lunch at the Pacific Club with Swanzy. Because of the heavy rain that afternoon, Giffard wrote, "It will be impossible for the Trustees to do very much for the Doctor," but "he will be taken care of by one or two members of the Association during the afternoon so far as the weather will permit."[19]

It is evident that the planters did their utmost to accommodate Allen during his brief stay, as Irwin had suggested. The key event, though, was the meeting that morning between Allen and the planters. The minutes of the meeting reveal that Allen "discussed at length with the Trustees the practicability of Korean immigration, the capacity of the Koreans for work, and the conditions existing in Korea."[20] Swanzy's diary entry for that day recorded, "[Allen] will help us all he can to get Korean laborers and he gave invaluable information and some good advice."[21]

A more detailed version is contained in a letter from Giffard to Irwin. Unlike the rather innocuous versions in the HSPA minutes and Swanzy's diary, the letter reveals the startling information that Allen not only agreed to help by acting as liaison between the planters and the Korean government but also, and more important, that in doing so he would be engaged in questionable actions. Specifically, Giffard wrote that the meeting "was very satisfactory to the Planters" as "the Doctor gave us considerable details regarding the Koreans *and* also suggested valuable ideas to the Trustees." Moreover, Allen would "look into matters further so far as the Korean Government is concerned." Allen anticipated that the question of propriety would arise if he were linked with the project. This consideration caused Giffard to write that Allen would "*of course prefer that anything that he may have to say to us will come though some other source than his own letters,* and he suggested that Mr. Townsend was the proper man to attend to such matters, as he was a thoroughly reliable and responsible party."[22] It was clear that the project was somehow tainted.

A letter written by Allen himself sheds further light on the meeting and reveals that the planters had been engaged in systematic violations of American immigration laws. He "could not give them any assurance about the importation" because, he wrote, "*I don't quite see how they can make it fit with the immigration laws against contract labor. They said they do it successfully with the Japanese and can do the same for Koreans, but that is their matter.*" Brushing aside the fact that the whole thing was apparently illegal, Allen concluded that "the

Koreans would go I think and they would be good workers and they are not Chinese."[23]

And so Allen departed Honolulu on the *Nippon Maru* on the evening of March 4. As we shall soon discover, he was prepared to assist the planters in four ways: first, by obtaining the approval of the Korean government and emperor; second, by selecting a recruiter; third, by intervening on behalf of the planters in Washington; and fourth, by helping the planters evade the immigration laws of the United States. To obtain yet another franchise for American business in Korea, Allen, who was sworn to uphold the laws of the United States, had suggested "valuable ideas" to the HSPA for getting around the law. Allen's ideas would soon be put into operation. Moreover, knowing that the project involved not only the violation of American laws but also the violation of his instructions not to meddle in the internal affairs of Korea, Allen even arranged that his correspondence with the planters would be "laundered" through an intermediary. It is clear that the sugar planters in Hawaii had been systematically violating the law against contract labor in importing Japanese workers since the Organic Act of 1900 had become law and that Allen, far from washing his hands of the affair, had agreed to assist the planters to do the same with Koreans.

Before it was outlawed in 1885, contract labor as it was practiced in the United States was a system in which a worker, usually an immigrant, was indentured to an employer for a period of (usually seven) years at wages lower than those paid to American citizens. In return, the immigrant worker, before leaving the homeland, was guaranteed a job and one-way passage to the United States. The contract between the worker and his employer had the force of law, so that a worker could be jailed if he left his job before the end of the stipulated period. Toward the end of the nineteenth century, however, the growing strength of the trade union movement resulted in the passage of an act in 1885 outlawing contract labor. The aims of this act were to protect American labor from foreign competition, raise the standards for the admission of immigrants, and prevent a decline in wage rates. Thus, after 1885 in the continental United States and after 1900 in the Territory of Hawaii, it was illegal to offer a contract to an immigrant before he or she arrived in the United States, and it was also illegal for an employer to pay transportation to the United States for the immigrant.

The planters were heartened by the successful outcome of the meeting with Allen,[24] but their enthusiasm was dampened almost at once by a disappointing letter from Townsend, which arrived just after Allen's departure. Townsend was unaware that he was Allen's initial choice for recruiter; Giffard wrote that he "does not seem at all favorable" to the project. In effect, Townsend told the planters he would not act as a recruiter or as an intermediary for Allen's incriminating letters to the planters because, as we shall see later, he felt (correctly) that the immigration of Koreans to Hawaii would involve breaking American immigration laws regarding contract labor. This was unfortunate to the planters because Townsend was "the gentleman to whom we wrote previous to our interview with Dr. Allen and whom the latter stated was a very responsible and reliable individual to take up the matter of Korean labor for the Association."[25]

Clearly this was bad news for the planters. Moreover, by the end of April, nearly two months after the Honolulu meeting, there had been no word from Allen and the planters began to worry that something had gone wrong.[26] So concerned was Irwin that in early May he returned to Honolulu to "take up Korean immigration and start private correspondence with Dr. Allen and find out definitely just how matters stand at the present time."[27]

The planters were worried that their Korean initiative would be stillborn; if so, this would jeopardize their plans to use the Koreans as an offset to the Japanese. This concern was placed in clear perspective by Giffard who, as president of the HSPA's labor committee, reminded Irwin that the Japanese were and would remain for the forseeable future the mainstay of plantation labor and that the planters "do not think that what has been expended for the introduction of Japanese has been at all excessive, as it has saved the day so far as labor conditions are concerned on all the plantations in the group, and wages would have been one-third higher than they are now." Since the Japanese would remain the primary source for plantation labor, "still it will be necessary in the interests of all plantations to have Portuguese or Koreans introduced so that the Japanese laborers will not be so independent in their relations with their managers and bosses."[28] So the planters in the spring of 1902 entertained no thoughts of terminating Japanese immigration in favor of Korean immigration. Rather the Koreans were desired *in addition* to the Japanese for their offsetting value. At the moment, though, the Korean initiative seemed in doubt.

While the planters in Honolulu faced the uncertainty which the lack of news on their Korean initiative had aroused, Horace Allen in the meantime had arrived in Korea at the end of March unaware that Townsend had already rejected any role for himself in recruiting Koreans.[29] Since Townsend had just left for Japan on business, Allen turned first to the necessary task of convincing Emperor Kojong of the merits of sending Koreans to Hawaii.[30] Given the degree of centralization of power in late Yi Korea, the consent of the palace was a sine qua non to earn the approval of the Korean government.

On the very afternoon of his arrival Allen had an audience with Kojong where the subject was presumably first broached.[31] Allen's strategy was an ingenious one, playing to the emperor's pride, because soon after the audience Allen "was visited by an official from the emperor to ask if it were true that Chinese could not enter the United States while Koreans might do so." Allen replied that it was true and "took occasion to explain the nature of our laws regarding Chinese exclusion and contract laborers."[32] Within a month Allen was so convinced that Kojong had been persuaded that he concluded, "There will be no great difficulty with Koreans; they seem to like the idea of being able to send their emigrants where the Chinese are not allowed to go."[33]

With the approval of the Korean emperor in hand, Allen turned next to the task of selecting a recruiter. Walter D. Townsend, the "responsible party" who had corresponded with the planters a few months earlier and whom Allen had in mind for recruiting emigrants and laundering his correspondence with the planters, had been in Japan for over a month, and it was thus not until early May that Allen had a chance to see him in Korea. In a letter to Jacob Sloat Fassett, Allen wrote that Townsend "has now been up to see me and we have talked over the matter." During that talk Allen discovered what the planters had known for over a month: "[Townsend] is not at all inclined to go into it as he thinks the danger of action for violation of the contract labor laws is too great." While Allen entered a pro forma disclaimer, "I could not have anything to do with the matter in strict conformity with my instructions," in the next breath he disclosed the strategy he would pursue: "Yet with an emigration bureau organized by the Koreans themselves after the manner of the same institutions in Japan, I should think the matter might be as simple as it is in Japan."[34] Allen had, in effect, just admitted that what he was about to do would violate his instructions from the State Department not to meddle in the internal affairs of Korea. He had also once again acknowledged that he would participate in the violation of American immigration laws by sending Koreans to Hawaii on the same (illegal) basis that Japanese were currently being sent.

Allen's strategy was set, but he still needed someone to serve as recruiter—someone whose desire for gain overrode any scruples about violating American laws. Allen chose David W. Deshler who was "willing to take it up if the Planters can give [him] the necessary assurance in regard to the laws."

Allen also needed a "launderer" for his incriminating letters to the planters and eased Congressman Fassett (the recipient of this letter) into the role of intermediary with the words: "I don't care to correspond with the Planters on the subject but if you care to suggest to them that they correspond with Deshler I think the matter may be fully investigated."[35]

This letter to Fassett in Elmira, New York, was written exactly two months after Allen's meeting with the HSPA in Honolulu and represented the first (albeit indirect) news from Allen to the planters. (From Fassett in New York, Allen's letters would then be sent to Irwin in San Francisco and from there to Giffard in Honolulu.) Because of the distances involved in these postal circumventions, the planters did not get the news from Allen via Fassett until early July, four months after the meeting. Soon afterward, Irwin, now in Honolulu, wrote directly to Allen and in mid-August received replies from both Deshler and Allen. (Allen this time ignored his vow not to write directly to the planters.) Allen's letter endorsed Deshler ("You could not have a better man to attend to your matters") and spoke of his own future role: "I shall do all I can consistent with my official duties to assist Mr. Deshler who will, I think, experience no difficulty here in this matter." He concluded with the warning, "The chief thing as I see it will be to see that the U.S. laws are not violated."[36] Allen had told the planters, in effect, not to get caught.

Thus, by the end of the summer of 1902, Allen had gone a long way toward constructing the preliminary apparatus necessary to begin Korean immigration to Hawaii. Before proceeding further, it is fitting to consider briefly the relationship between Allen and Deshler.

Horace Allen and David Deshler first met in Korea during the first week of June 1896. Deshler was in the Orient looking for concessions for his financial backers in his hometown of Columbus, Ohio. At that time Allen, who was also from Ohio, was secretary to the American legation in Seoul, a post he had held since 1890.

Upon his arrival in Korea, Deshler looked up Allen and, indicating that he represented a sizeable amount of money, expressed an interest in obtaining a banking concession as well as part of the interest in the Seoul-Inch'ŏn railway which Allen had obtained for James R. Morse, a New York businessman. Because Deshler came with letters of reference from, among others, William McKinley, the Republican contender for president in that election year, Allen wrote to Morse and Leigh Hunt with the suggestion that they include Deshler in their plans since he could provide some of the capital necessary to finance the railroad project.[37]

While Allen was trying to interest Morse and Hunt in Deshler, a third friend of Allen's, Walter Townsend, offered Deshler a partnership in the American Trading Company, which dealt in general merchandise and whose head office was managed by Morse in New York with branch offices in Inch'ŏn, Korea, and in Kobe, Japan. Allen's brother-in-law, Clayton Everett, a Toledo businessman, also had an interest in this business venture.[38]

Before accepting Townsend's offer, Deshler left Korea in July for New York to meet with Hunt and Morse. When he returned to Korea that September, Deshler decided to throw in with Townsend and the American Trading Company and attempted to obtain a mining concession near Pusan.[39] Because the Germans had been trying hard to acquire the Pusan mining concession and because the Korean government had been resisting their proposal for a very long time, Allen could not help him very much.[40] Deshler was later able to obtain a part interest with Leigh Hunt in the Unsan Gold Mine concession.

Although Deshler's trip to the United States in the summer of 1896 was primarily for business reasons, it had political overtones that were to overshadow, at least temporarily, the business aspects of his relationship with Allen and to alter permanently their personal relations. During his sojourn in Korea, Deshler had become aware of Allen's political ambition to become the American minister to Korea. As it would be good for business to have a friend occupy the top diplomatic post in Korea, Deshler decided to assist Allen. Since his family had important political connections in Ohio, Deshler was in a unique position to help Allen attain his goal.

David W. Deshler came from a distinguished banking family in Columbus, Ohio. The first Deshler in Columbus, David W. Deshler, arrived there in 1817 from Easton, Pennsylvania, with his wife, Betsey Green. He bought the Clinton Bank and some land on which was later erected the Deshler Hotel. Deshler's son, William Green Deshler, was born in 1827. A financial wizard, William became the wealthiest man in Franklin County, Ohio. One of his tellers was his nephew, William K. Deshler, the father of our protagonist.

William K. Deshler had a son in 1872 whom he named David W. after his own grandfather, and a daughter whom he named Louise. William K. Deshler died in 1880 and his widow was remarried two years later to George Kilbron Nash. In 1886 she also died, and ten years after her death, David's and Louise's half sister, Mary Nash, died. The death of his wife and daughter almost crushed George Nash, and now David and Louise, his stepson and stepdaughter, were the only family remaining to him.[41]

George Nash was a prominent Ohio politician. He had been appointed to the Ohio Supreme Court by the then Governor Charles Foster. At that time Nash belonged to the Sherman-Hanna-McKinley wing of the Republican Party which was at odds with the Joseph Foraker faction. Because of this split, although Judge Nash was Marcus Hanna's choice for governor in 1895, he lost the nomination to Asa Bushnell who was a Foraker man.

It was at this point that Nash's stepson (David Deshler) went to Korea and met Allen, and because Nash's subsequent political career will be of importance in Allen's own position in Korea we will want to take a brief look at Nash's political career after 1896. In 1897, after Hanna had won control of the party machinery, Nash was named chairman of the Republican State Executive Committee. Nash in turn supported Hanna's candidacy for the U.S. Senate in 1898. In the following year, with Hanna's aid and the endorsment of Boss George Cox of Cincinnati, Nash received the Republican nomination for governor and won. He was reelected in 1901. Eight months after leaving the governor's office, on October 28, 1904, Nash died.[42]

When David Deshler returned to Korea in September 1896, he had already convinced his stepfather to lead the fight to secure the post of minister for Allen. Deshler's enthusiasm (Allen wrote to his brother-in-law Clayton Everett who was also helping out in the campaign[43] that Deshler "is most anxious that I should receive the appointment")[44] was matched by Nash's, who also wrote to Everett: "I became interested in Dr. Allen through my stepson, Mr. D. W. Deshler, who is now living in Chemulpo [Inch'ŏn], Korea. . . . On account of my son's request and the fact that I am thoroughly satisfied that Dr. Allen is fit for the position I am determined to do all that I can to help him."[45] Allen was grateful, of course, and wrote to Nash for the first time; David, he said, "has informed me of your kind interest in my case and has suggested that I write you regarding my application." Allen went on to relate his various successes in Korea and indicated that he would have letters of recommendation sent to him.[46]

At this point Nash took over the campaign to secure Allen's appointment as American minister to Korea. In January 1897, Nash wrote to President-elect William McKinley (who was from Canton, Ohio) suggesting Allen's appointment because of his fitness for the office and "as a great personal favor to myself." Nash was of the opinion that the letter had "the desired effect" and added, "I can say, and I hope you will not think me boastful, that Maj. McKinley and I have been personal friends for twenty years, and I think that he will be inclined to grant any personal request, within reason, which I may make." Moreover, McKinley "also knows Mr. Deshler personally, likes him, and I think will be inclined to assist him." Nash also buttonholed Senator John Sherman, the new secretary of state and a friend for twenty-five years. Saying of Sherman that "one of his characteristics is to remember his friends," Nash added that he had "never asked a personal favor at his hands, but I will do so in the case of Dr. Allen."[47] Nash also noted to

Allen that Sherman "has also been very intimate with the family of Mr. Deshler, and this too will be of service to you."[48] Not unexpectedly, when Nash wrote to Sherman requesting Allen's appointment, Sherman answered by saying, "I will be very glad to do anything I can to meet the wishes of Mr. Deshler."[49]

Recounting his representations to McKinley and Sherman, Nash wrote confidently to Allen, "I do not think that you have cause to worry," and mentioned that he had written a long letter to David regarding his (Allen's) prospects. As a final note, Nash asked Allen to "keep a friendly eye on my boy, and if you see that he is inclined to go into the wrong paths, which I do not anticipate, you for my sake will try to lead him in the right direction."[50]

Allen's candidacy progressed favorably under Nash's guidance and by the end of February Nash had collected all the letters of reference to present to McKinley when he assumed office in March.[51] That spring, three other candidates surfaced but Nash had received word that "the outlook seems good to me."[52] The outlook was even brighter because the current minister, John Sill, was a Democrat who had not supported McKinley.

As Allen's prospects brightened, his friendship with Deshler, personal friend to both President McKinley and Secretary of State Sherman, also grew stronger during the spring of 1897.[53] In mid-June, Deshler telegraphed to Allen, "Have just received telegram. Good prospects. Deshler."[54] A month later, when the appointment finally came, Deshler wired Allen, "My deepest and sincerest congratulations. Have just received the news of your appointment. D. W. Deshler."[55] On that same day, Deshler and his partner, Walter Townsend, drank a toast to Allen's health.[56]

Two days after the appointment, Nash wrote to Allen to congratulate him and noted that he was "very anxious in regard to Dave's future." Referring to the loss of his wife and daughter, Nash added, "There are but two persons left in the world for me to love, and these are Dave and his sister." Continuing, he said, "I do not so much desire that he should be successful in business as that I hope at all times he will be a good man." He concluded by asking Allen "to keep a watchful eye upon him and assist him in the way which is the nearest to my heart."[57]

In the one year since having met, both Allen and Deshler were inextricably linked by mutual favors. Allen felt strongly the obligation he had to Deshler, writing that he owed his "promotion to the post of Minister to David Deshler largely as he got his stepfather, Gov. Nash of Ohio, to intercede with his personal friend President McKinley."[58] Might Allen do something for Deshler in return? Years later, Allen was to lament that he "had not been able to do anything for him in a financial way myself."[59] But Allen did try to help Deshler by securing him employment.[60] Earlier, of course, it had been Allen who had helped him with business contacts which Deshler had parlayed into a partnership with Townsend's American Trading Company. In that business, Deshler's role had developed to the point that he maintained a second home in Kobe, where a branch office of the company was located. Having a residence in Japan would later come in handy when Koreans would transfer to ships bound for Hawaii and undergo physical examinations. In addition to acquiring a Japanese home, Deshler also married a Japanese woman, Hideno Honda, with whom he had lived for some time without benefit of clergy.[61] By 1900 Deshler had also become involved in the Unsan Mines where he worked with Leigh Hunt and came to know the character of Korean workers.[62] So when the emigration franchise became available in the fall of 1902, Allen was able to obtain the concession for the thirty-year-old Deshler who subsequently made a handsome commission as a result. Allen in this way repaid Deshler for all he had done to obtain his appointment as minister to Korea five years earlier.

The meeting between the sugar planters in Hawaii and Horace Allen, the American minister to Korea, initiated an alliance between business interests and political interests which was to have decisive import not only for the immigration of Koreans to the United States but also for the subsequent history of Korea and Hawaii. It served the planters by putting the initial steps of the importation of Korean labor into operation.

It also served Allen not only because he saw immigration to Hawaii as a means of furthering American business interests in Korea but also because he wanted the project to be successful in order to repay the enormous political debt he owed to Deshler and Deshler's stepfather in Ohio. There was every indication that Allen was totally behind the project in the early months of his involvement, which included winning the approval of Emperor Kojong, selecting Deshler as the recruiter, arranging with Fassett to launder his correspondence with the planters, suggesting that the Japanese model be followed in creating an Emigration Bureau, and assuring the planters that he would help them by undertaking actions that would not only violate his instructions but also violate United States law. The stage was now set for the project to move into the next stage: the sending of an HSPA representative to Korea and the establishment of a Bureau of Emigration.

4

Bishop Goes to Korea

THE project of recruiting Korean immigrants had reached the stage where one of the planters could now travel to Korea to meet with Horace Allen and David Deshler and begin preparations for the first shipment of Koreans. For one thing, the weather in Korea was much better in the autumn of 1902 than it had been the previous winter. Furthermore, Allen had laid the necessary groundwork to give the project a good chance of success. So when the planters received Allen's and Deshler's letters in early September stating that everything in Korea was in readiness, the next stage could begin.

On September 5, 1902, the HSPA trustees met and selected E. Faxon Bishop to go to Korea, with $25,000, "to take the necessary steps toward inaugurating the Korean immigration."[1] After receiving the permission of his firm, C. Brewer and Company, and tendering his resignation as secretary of that organization the next day, Bishop was ready to leave for Korea.[2]

At the age of thirty-nine, Eben Faxon Bishop, a cousin of Charles Reed Bishop, had been working for C. Brewer and Company since 1883, rising to the position of secretary in 1891 and assuming also the duties of treasurer in 1893. In addition to his posts with C. Brewer, Bishop was the president of several sugar plantations managed by the company. In the HSPA, Bishop served on the Labor Committee with Giffard and three others.[3] So he was well versed in the needs of the sugar industry in general and the labor situation in particular. During the previous year, Bishop had been the planters' first choice for the important mission to Korea, and he remained their first choice now in 1902.

Bishop and his wife departed Honolulu on September 9 aboard the appropriately named S.S. *Korea* for the ten-day voyage to Yokohama.[4] Bishop's tasks in Japan were twofold. First, following Allen's script, he obtained a copy of Japan's 1894 Emigrant Protection Law. This first task was easily accomplished. The second task was to arrange passage for Korean immigrants on Japan's trans-Pacific steamship service. This proved to be a bit more troublesome.

In two letters from Japan to the HSPA trustees, Bishop asked for permission to arrange for a chartered boat to go directly from Korea to Hawaii in the event that he was unable to arrange for the Koreans to book passage on the regularly scheduled lines. After discussing the issue in two separate meetings, the trustees decided that Bishop was "not to attempt direct shipments by chartered vessels" but rather "to make every reasonable effort to arrange for shipments of small numbers of Korean laborers by regular mail boats." Failing that, the trustees wrote to Bishop, he should return to Honolulu.[5]

How had such a seemingly minor matter assumed such importance for the planters? What difference did it make whether Koreans came by charter from Korea or aboard the regularly scheduled Pacific Mail steamers from Japan? The answers lay first in the fact that the planters intended to bring in the Koreans illegally, as they had been doing successfully for two years with the Japanese. A charter from Korea would focus unwelcome attention on the (illegal) immigration of Koreans and invite an investigation, while a small number of Koreans arriving on the regular sailings might not. Second, the planters wanted to avoid any fanfare associated with the initiation of Korean immigration because of the antipathy it would arouse among the anti-Asian public. Among the HSPA trustees "the prevailing opinion was that it would be suicidal for us to make such a charter as the attention of all Labor Unions and newspapers generally would be called to the fact and the same be referred to as importation of Coolie labor throughout the United States."[6] The planters, in short, wanted to avoid criminal charges against themselves as well as complete exclusion of Japanese and Korean laborers.

Luckily for the planters, Bishop was able to arrange for the Koreans to take passage on the regular steamers even as the above instructions from the trustees were en route to him. His two tasks in Japan having been accomplished, the Bishops sailed from Yokohama to Korea during the first week of October.[7] When they arrived in Inch'ŏn, the Bishops stayed at Deshler's home, as the single hotel in the city was of poor quality.[8] Immediately, Bishop made contact with Horace Allen, and the three men quickly reached a meeting of minds, allowing Allen to report to the planters (via Fassett in New York), "Deshler says everything is proceeding nicely and I think they will do things in a manner to allow of my sending a favorable report on the matter."[9] The favorable progress was confirmed by a letter from Bishop to the trustees who, upon reading the letter, unanimously adopted a resolution "approving of the steps already taken by him on behalf of the Association providing for the immigration of Korean laborers."[10] Bishop had not only attended to sending the Koreans aboard the regular steamers but had also made preliminary arrangements for an initial trial shipment of Korean laborers.[11] So pleased were the trustees that they ordered four additional lots of fifty men and not more than twenty-five women and ten children above the age of two.[12]

Although the initial negotiations had gone well, the planters were still worried about their violation of the immigration laws. Accordingly, their order for the four additional lots was conditional: "provided the first lot is allowed by the immigration authorities to land."[13] This concern was echoed by C. M. Cooke who wrote to one of the plantation managers, "[Bishop's] last letter was quite encouraging, but of course, we do not feel sure that these people will be permitted to land."[14]

To protect themselves, the trustees informed Bishop that in subsequent negotiations with Deshler the planters would insist on two conditions. First, the HSPA could suspend the immigration at any time "if from any cause the people cannot land or if they prove unsatisfactory as working people." This would not only prevent a repetition of the Puerto Rican fiasco of the previous year but would also allow the planters to halt the process immediately if the federal inspectors discovered the truth about the Korean immigrants, thus minimizing the troubles that might be visited upon them. Second, the planters insisted that Deshler "shall assume the liability for return passages of immigrants in case they are refused landing at Honolulu after the first lot." In effect, what the trustees were saying was that they would take responsibility for getting Koreans through the first time, but thereafter Deshler would be responsible for maintaining the conditions that would allow Koreans to be admitted. It would be up to Deshler, therefore, to make sure that the interpreters whom he sent with each load were well coached. If Deshler would agree to these two conditions, Bishop was authorized to sign an agreement for one year.[15]

After Bishop concluded the initial discussions with Deshler and Allen in Korea, he left for China to give Allen room to operate. In a remarkably detailed letter from Shanghai to his boss at C. Brewer and Company, C. M. Cooke, Bishop wrote, "I did all that I could before leaving [for China] even to drawing up the Regulations governing the proposed Bureau of Emigration and the Edict itself." Having done that, Bishop "saw the people who have the project in hand [Allen] and watched it closely to the point of its submission to the Emperor [by Allen], after which it was a case of political pull [Allen's] and there was nothing that I could do to help matters."

Even during his relatively short stay in Korea, Bishop had seen and learned enough about corruption in the government to know that only someone with Allen's political pull could successfully shepherd the immigration project through to completion. The immigration measure, like "all measures proposed in Korea are viewed by Government officials from the standpoint of gain, and there is great jealousy among the various factions and one will block the other if he can unless he is promised something out of what is to be made out of the proposed measure." As an example, Bishop related an incident which had occurred while he had been a guest at Deshler's home in Inch'ŏn: Emperor Kojong was desirous of purchasing Deshler's home and sent a messenger asking the selling price, so Deshler put a "big figure" on the property and "from that time on almost every day some official or other from Seoul came down to call on Deshler and find out what he was to get out of it if the deal went through."

"I mention this," Bishop continued, "to show what the Korean character is and what one has to contend with when anything of any official nature is sought to be accomplished." Given this situation, "Mr. Deshler was of the opinion that it would be better to have me out of the way for the time in order to discourage any rivalry among factions all of whom are on the make." Bishop agreed that "there was no use in my doing this waiting at Chemulpo, as it was a process that everything that has to have Government sanction has to go through and it is sometimes a tedious process that takes months to accomplish."

As a result, Bishop and his wife left for Peking where he heard from Deshler that nothing had happened yet, and so the couple proceeded to Shanghai where they were "waiting to hear that the Imperial Edict has been promulgated permitting emigration which will be wired me as soon as it takes place." Despite the waiting, he was optimistic because his "last advice from Korea indicates that matters are progressing favorably, but what with petty interferences and general procrastination one has to possess their soul with patience and wait."

While waiting in Shanghai for the news from Deshler, Bishop sought to reassure the trustees on a couple of issues. The first was that his colleagues in Honolulu might "think I am not attending to business by leaving Chemulpo." To allay any fears of his leaving the job unfinished, Bishop convincingly reminded them that "the success or non-success of this venture has some bearing on my personal ability" and reminded them that "a Portuguese venture was left too soon by the Planters Agent some years ago and the result was rather disastrous, and I don't want a repetition of this sort of thing to my credit on the HSPA Ledger if I can help." In other words, Bishop did not want to be accused of carelessness in the Korean project.[16]

The second issue on which Bishop sought to reassure the trustees was the quality of the Koreans as workers. It will be remembered that while the planters desired the Koreans primarily for their value in offsetting the Japanese, it was also necessary that they be reasonably competent workers, unlike the Puerto Ricans who had been imported the previous year. Naturally, the better the Koreans were as workers, the greater the counterbalance they would provide against the Japanese. Moreover, the planters were becoming increasingly distressed over the tendency of the Japanese to leave the plantations for the towns or for California. The concern of the planters on these issues was exemplified by C. M. Cooke who wrote to Bishop, "I trust from what you have seen of the people in the fields as you have passed through the country you have gained a favorable impression that they will make good laborers for our plantations."[17]

On these issues of the suitability of Korean workers Bishop was unequivocal. "I feel as confident as I can without positively knowing, that the Koreans will prove good laborers if we can get them to the Islands," wrote Bishop. Moreover, the Koreans "are lusty strong fellows and physically much the superior of the Japs," and "in rice culture and mining work they excel any other nationality."

Bishop also addressed himself to the problem of instability with which the planters had been plagued by the Japanese. The Koreans, Bishop felt, would be superior in this regard because of the operation of two factors, both negative ones. The first was the deterioration of late Yi Korea: "I feel . . . that as compared with the Japs they will be more permanent as they should have no home ties or at least should have none considering the way they are ground down at home, and the advantages they would enjoy in the Islands as compared with what they have at home should tend to make them a fixture." The second factor was what he identified as a trait common to Koreans who, he said, "are not thrifty and it is doubtful if they would be saving enough to lay by a competence to return home with."

Bishop concluded this lengthy letter from Shanghai with unbridled optimism mixed, as usual, with the uncertainty over federal detection of immigration law violations: "I can't for the life of me see how it is possible for them to prove other than good laborers for us and I am so imbued with this idea that it is almost a conviction and by long odds the most favorable proposition that the HSPA has up for consideration, and I hope that . . . the first shipment passes the Immigration officer without trouble."[18]

The trustees in Honolulu were pleased with Bishop's report when they received it in early December. C. M. Cooke opined that with the arrival of the Koreans "our plantations will be greatly benefited." Like everyone else, though, he worried about the chance of getting caught by federal authorities: "We look forward with much interest to the first shipment but have some fear that there may be difficulties in store in regards to passing the United States authorities here."[19] Cooke also assured Bishop that he had done well, adding, "I think you have not left a stone unturned to accomplish the business in the most acceptable manner and you have done far better than any Commission that I know of who have endeavored to get laborers here."[20]

Meanwhile, in mid-November, the Korean emperor had issued the long-awaited imperial edict authorizing Deshler to send emigrants to Hawaii, and Deshler wired the news to Bishop in Shanghai. After receiving the wire, Bishop returned to Korea and concluded the arrangements with Deshler by the end of the month. Bishop was then able to write again to the trustees to inform them that the first shipment was due to arrive in Honolulu in mid-January 1903 and that additional shipments would follow, as Giffard observed, "providing the first one is admitted into the country without trouble."[21]

By the end of 1902, then, the long-term success of Korean immigration rested upon four considerations. The first, as we have repeatedly seen, was whether the Koreans could slip by the immigration officials. By now there was no doubt that risky business was involved. Walter Giffard, for example, sent Irwin copies of one of Bishop's letters to the trustees as well as a letter from Bishop to Deshler "which will give you considerable information regarding the terms upon which these emigrants are to come here." That these letters revealed illegal activities is clear in Giffard's closing words: "Please consider these letters confidential and see that they do not in any way slip out of your hands."[22]

A second consideration remained whether the Koreans would turn out to be good plantation workers. Bishop had already pronounced them to be excellent workers, but the proof of this assertion would of necessity take place in the sugarcane fields. To that end Giffard noted that "as a matter of course, this Korean immigration is as yet an experiment and will remain so until the three shipments above noted have been tried and proved satisfactory."

The third consideration crucial to the long-term success of Korean immigration was the reliability of the Korean government. Bishop had already noted that corruption was rife in Seoul and the trustees feared the government could cause them many problems. This fear was reflected in Giffard's statement that "the Korean question is and will continue for many months to be an experiment only, as we never know but what it may be cut off by the Korean Government whenever its officials feel like it."[23]

A fourth consideration was the attitude of the Japanese government toward Korean immigration to Hawaii. The initiation of Korean immigration would not only lessen the demand for Japanese and cut into the profits of the Japanese emigration companies but would also keep the wages of Japanese laborers low because of the offsetting value of the Korean laborers. William G. Irwin reiterated the value of the Koreans vis-à-vis the Japanese when he told Giffard that if the Koreans "cost more, even, than the Japanese it will pay the planters to import a few, so as to let the Japanese understand that they are not the 'only pebbles on the beach.' "[24] The planters had informed the Japanese consul in Honolulu, Saitō Miki, privately of Bishop's mission. Nonetheless, Cooke said he would "not be surprised if you find strong opposition from the Japanese government."[25]

What the planters could not foresee during that Christmas season of 1902 was that all four of these potential obstacles to the long-term success of Korean immigration to Hawaii would arise to vex their well-laid plans. For now, though, the planters were congratulating themselves and Bishop over the initiative. Bishop, his mission accomplished, left Korea for a ten-day vacation in Japan writing before he left, "Everything is lined up to carry out the 'Gaelic' program and I feel confident it will go all right unless some snag is encountered at Nagasaki, and as Mr. Deshler will accompany the party to Nagasaki and see them off I feel pretty certain it will go all right."[26] While Bishop vacationed in Japan, the first group of Koreans left their native land for Hawaii on December 22. On Christmas Eve Bishop once again boarded the S.S. *Korea* and arrived in Honolulu on January 2 "in fine spirits."[27] Upon his arrival Bishop received the accolades of the HSPA trustees[28] as well as his own company, C. Brewer.[29]

5

Allen Deals with Seoul and Washington

HAVING examined the attitudes and actions of David Deshler, Faxon Bishop, and the planters, it is fitting that we now turn our attention to perhaps the most important figure in the entire process—Horace Allen. The emigration franchise or concession could be used by Allen to accomplish three purposes. First, as we have seen, by granting it to Deshler he could help repay the political debt owed to Deshler and his stepfather, Governor Nash of Ohio. Second, it would be yet another franchise for American business that Allen could land to further his hope that through dollar diplomacy the United States would be forced to take a more active political role in Korea. Third, Allen, noticing the "amazing increase of Japanese influence" after 1900, could counter any attempt by Japan to control concessions and therefore the economy and government of Korea.[1] In 1902 England and Japan had concluded an alliance that had the effect of increasing Japan's freedom of action vis-à-vis Russia in Korea, and both Allen and Kojong feared that Korean independence was threatened.

Since Allen's policy followed the pattern of opposing any country (other than the United States) that attempted to dominate Korea, the Japanese became Allen's latest target.[2] In this way the emigration franchise was not only a plus for American business and therefore American influence in Korea, but it also represented one fewer franchise that the Japanese could claim for themselves. Allen's anti-Japanese policy conflicted with President Roosevelt's policy, however. And, in addition, there remained for Allen domestic obstacles to overcome before Korean emigration could become an American concession.

The first of these obstacles was the traditional stigma attached to the act of emigrating. Similar in nature to attitudes in traditional China and Tokugawa Japan, it found voice in laws prohibiting emigration, although enforcement was spotty at best.[3] The law prohibiting emigration was based on the norms of Confucian propriety which saw such an act as unfilial behavior. How could one possibly honor one's parents and ancestors while living thousands of miles away? True, thousands of Koreans had emigrated overland illegally to China and Russia without proper papers, but a move to an island in the middle of the Pacific Ocean was a different matter. Allen recognized the heavy weight of tradition on this subject, noting that "heretofore it has been somewhat difficult for Koreans to get permission to leave their country, without which permission emigration would be attended with trouble on returning to their native land."[4] More specifically, he wrote, "It is not always easy for them to leave their country, since if they steal away without proper papers they are liable to suspicion on the charge of treason, which would make it dangerous for them to return."[5] In a bureaucracy still dominated by traditionalists, Allen could expect significant opposition to legal and organized emigration.

A second obstacle to emigration was also a function of Korea's conservative heritage. Because of the isolation of the "Hermit Kingdom," the handful of intellectuals who had ventured abroad to Japan or the United States for study, travel, or on diplomatic missions had come under the "pernicious" influence of Western liberal ideas. Kim Okkyun, for example, the leader of the 1884 coup, had studied under the progressive Japanese reformer Fukuzawa Yukichi. Others like Sŏ Chaep'il (Philip Jaisohn) and Yun Ch'i-ho had studied in the United States and returned to become thorns in the side of Korea's conservative bureaucracy with the establishment of the Independence Club in 1896 and *The Independent* [*Tongnip sinmun*] which advocated reform along Western lines.[6] The possibility existed, therefore, that returning emigrants with a Western education might attain positions of influence in the government and undermine the position of conservatives and their ideology. In the eyes of the sizeable conservative faction in the government, approval of emigration could lead to upheaval down the road.

A third obstacle to emigration was the generally negative public opinion associated with the act. At the popular level, emigration and kidnapping were almost synonymous—if we can believe an incident that occurred in the summer of 1888. At that time, rumors circulated in Seoul and Inch'ŏn that Japanese living in Korea were kidnapping Korean children to sell abroad. These rumors created such an atmosphere of terror that stones were thrown at Japanese homes and the Japanese consul in Seoul was forced to warn Japanese residents there to take precautions.[7] At the elite level, emigration was associated with illtreatment and discrimination abroad. In an article in the fall of 1897 on the recent departure of 200 Koreans to work in the coal mines in Japan,

The Independent editorialized: "We do not mean to discourage the employment of a reasonable number of Korean coolies by the Japanese corporations, but it must be carried on fairly and justly for all sides, so that the coolies will not in the future receive the same kind of treatment at the hands of the Japanese as the Japanese have from the Hawaiians or the Chinese from Americans."[8] It appears then that emigration did not enjoy a particularly favorable reputation across the spectrum of Korean society before 1902. It is also interesting that at least some intellectuals in Korea were fairly well posted concerning racism in America and the harsh treatment of workers on the Hawaiian plantations.

A fourth obstacle to emigration which Horace Allen had to overcome was the lack of a regularized system of issuing passports. Undoubtedly, this state of affairs was related to the first two obstacles just described. It has already been noted that the emigrants to Russia and China had gone without passports; so no special government machinery was involved in this technically illegal movement. It also appears that Koreans who traveled to Japan might not need passports either, since Japan did not require them for Japanese traveling to Korea.[9] Actually, the issuing of passports was usually left to the discretion of the *kamni* (local port official) at the docks where departures took place.[10] In the fall of 1900, for example, the Korean Foreign Office instructed the *kamni* to issue passports only if the intending emigrant was vouched for by a person agreeing to take responsibility. Three months later, passport forms were sent from the Foreign Office to all *kamni*. The *kamni* were also in charge of collecting the passport fees, which amounted to 500 (Chinese copper) cash, of which 200 went to the *kamni* office and 300 to the Foreign Office.[11] So before 1902 passports, when issued at all, were mainly in the hands of *kamni*. The lack of central control and experience with passports could be partly overcome by creation of a department of immigration, as Allen suggested, based on the Japanese model. But the Japanese had already had several decades of experience with emigration and passports, and its institutions naturally reflected the sophistication which attended this longer experience. And the lack of Korean experience in organizing and operating government agencies did not augur well for the long-term success of an imported institution.

The fifth and final obstacle to emigration which Allen faced was the corruption that permeated Korean politics in late Yi Korea. Official corruption and self-interest so dominated the landscape that even at the lowest level, an intending immigrant would have difficulty purchasing a passport, "chiefly," in Allen's words, "since a native having sufficient funds on which to emigrate would be liable to such a system of 'squeezing' that before he could obtain the necessary documents providing for his departure he would probably have exhausted his small capital."[12] As we shall see, Allen would turn this self-interest to his own advantage.

So in the fall of 1902, while Bishop and Deshler waited for permission from the Korean government to begin formal emigration of Korean laborers to Hawaii on a legal basis, the man to whom they had entrusted the very survival of the project had to deal with all these obstacles. Fortunately for Allen, who had promised the planters that he would intervene in their favor with the Korean government, he had in addition to his twenty-year friendship with Emperor Kojong a veritable arsenal of arguments at his disposal. Given the extreme centralization of power in the Korean government, it was the emperor only who needed to be convinced of the merits of granting the emigration franchise to David Deshler.

The first argument Allen used was a renewed appeal to the emperor's pride. Just as he had "softened up" Kojong the previous spring, Allen once again in November of 1902 reminded him of the Chinese Exclusion Act. As a result, Allen noted, "it is probable . . . that the pride of the Emperor in learning that his people might go where the great Chinese are excluded had much to do with the matter."[13]

A second argument in favor of granting the emigration franchise was Deshler's state of origin—Ohio. Allen, of course, was from Ohio, which was also the home state of President William McKinley and Secretary of State John Sherman. Dr. Louis Severance, who founded the only Western hospital in Korea, was also from Ohio. Ohio Wesleyan University was the institution attended not only by Mrs. Allen but also at that time by Kojong's son, Prince Ŭihwa (Eui Wha). So, Allen argued, his Ohioan friend Deshler could surely be trusted with the emigration franchise. A year later, Deshler purchased a steamer to transport immigrants and goods between Korea and Japan. He christened it the good ship *Ohio*.

Allen also argued that emigration to Hawaii would mitigate some of the suffering caused by a recent series of natural disasters and earn Kojong the reputation of a benevolent monarch. Droughts, floods, and the resulting famine in many parts of Korea in 1901–1902 had caused Kojong to forbid hoarding, suspend the export of rice, and import rice from Annam (Vietnam). In October 1901 he had set up a relief office for the starving in imitation of King Injo (r. 1623–1649) and two months later he established the *Hyeminwŏn*. This welfare office, which literally means "Bureau to benefit the people," was charged with distributing rice and other grains to the needy and was funded not only by taxes but also by a 20,000-*wŏn* donation from the royal family and reductions of one-fifth to one-third of the stipends of all government officials, according to their position, for the six-month period December 1901 to May 1902. Yet the Korean government was inconsistent when it came to providing for the welfare of its people, for the *Hyeminwŏn* received but 6,446 *wŏn* out of a total governmental expenditure of 7,585,877 *wŏn* for the year 1902.[14] The famine was not over and people were still starving in the fall of 1902 and well into 1903,[15] but it was expensive to give away rice and the bureau ceased to exist. Permitting emigration was an easier and less expensive means of dealing with the famine. On this subject Allen wrote, "The severe famine of the past winter [in which] the Government had to import large quantities of rice to feed the starving seems to have turned the attention of the officials favorably to the subject of emigration."[16] And it is perhaps no coincidence that the Chinese characters for *Yuminwŏn* (Department of Emigration), established in 1902, had the same meaning as *Hyeminwŏn*, the welfare office which had been set up to assist starving people the year before.

A fourth factor was the greed and self-interest of Korean officials surrounding the emperor and possibly the emperor himself. We have already noted Bishop's rather caustic comments on corruption in the upper reaches of the Korean bureaucracy. While this factor was cited earlier as a possible obstacle, Allen was able to turn it to his advantage. To do this, Allen suggested that the proposed Department of Emigration be situated not within the Foreign Office where it logically belonged, but rather in the Imperial Household Department *(Kungnaebu)*, "the vulture of Korea," according to Yun Ch'i-ho, an official who had studied at Vanderbilt University. The proceeds from the selling of passports would then not go, as before, to the Foreign Office, but, as Yun aptly wrote, "The proceeds of the sale will go to the Emperor's pocket which like Solomon's horse-leech cries 'Give.' It is a pity that this bottomless pocket was unknown to Solomon when he enumerated the three things, yea four things that say not 'It is enough!' "[17] Later, one of the planters would observe that the emperor "only went into this thing for all that he could make out of it."[18] Moreover, permitting emigration would give Korean officials the opportunity to take a percentage of remittances or taxing emigrants upon their return.[19]

The fifth and perhaps most important argument in Allen's arsenal in favor of granting the emigration franchise to Deshler was Allen's ability to play to Kojong's desire for closer ties with the United States. Granting this concession would increase America's economic and, therefore, political stake in Korea, something that both the emperor and Allen had long desired. Allen could point out that such a move would be fitting and proper according to "treaty rights" spelled out in Articles Six and Eleven of the 1882 Treaty of Amity and Commerce (the

Shufeldt Treaty) between the two nations.[20] As Japanese influence and pressure on Korea continued to grow, Kojong increasingly sought solace in this document, which provided for American "good offices" (Article One) in the event that a country should "deal unjustly with" Korea.[21] So granting the franchise would serve to give the treaty even more force.

With the Korean monarch relying increasingly upon the American government, there are indications that Allen was able to take advantage of the situation by representing Deshler to the emperor as an official connected with the government of Hawaii. This was not true, of course, but Allen knew that Kojong would not be the wiser.[22] This understanding, though false, helped convince the emperor that an agreement was being reached with a branch of the American government, rather than simply an American businessman, thereby increasing America's stake in Korea's independence.

So, while Deshler was occupied in Inch'ŏn and Bishop waited nervously in Shanghai, Allen plied the emperor with arguments on the merits of granting the emigration franchise—arguments of pride, profit, famine relief, and closer ties with the United States—at the same time drawing upon his not inconsiderable capital as Kojong's friend and trusted adviser for nearly two decades. In the process, he was not above lying to the emperor, nor was he shy about creating almost single-handedly a new branch of the Korean government, despite instructions from Washington to avoid interfering in Korea's internal affairs.

Allen's arguments were enough to sway the emperor. On November 15, 1902, Kojong granted the emigration franchise to David Deshler, conferring upon him a seal which read, in translation: "The control of the laborers of Great Korea to be employed abroad is hereby given to Deshler, an American citizen."[23] In theory at least, Deshler now had a legal monopoly on the recruitment of emigrants.

On the following day, the Imperial Edict which had been drawn up by Bishop was issued. The first part of the edict established the *Yuminwŏn* or Department of Emigration, although the literal translation was "People-easing bureau," and described its organization.[24] The second part of the edict was entitled "Imperial Rules and Regulations of the Department of Emigration of the Empire of Korea," consisting of twenty-one articles and borrowed directly from the 1894 Emigrant Protection Law of Japan.[25] Two days later Min Yŏng-hwan was appointed president of the new department.[26] As Allen had suggested, the new department was located within the Imperial Household Department (Kungnaebu).[27] Because of the importance of this placement on subsequent events, it is necessary to examine briefly the Household Department and its relationship to Kojong.

The head of the Household Department was one Yi Yong-ik,

although he was temporarily in eclipse in the fall of 1902 when the new department was added to his bailiwick. He returned to his position in early 1903 undiminished in influence. As head of the Imperial Household Department, Yi "control[led] all the revenues of the country" and was "now practically Emperor" according to William Sands, the American adviser to that department.[28] Moreover, his department was *primus inter pares*, "the 'inner' department controlling all the rest." The Household Department "was the principal channel through which the emperor communicated with the outside world." As a result, "it was impossible to bring order out of the chaos which passed in Korea for government [because] the Emperor was supreme and absolute in all things. He stood above the law,—or, to be more exact, perhaps, he was the law personified."[29] Thus any concession granted to a foreign power that needed imperial approval had to be approached with one eye on the attitude of the powerful Yi Yong-ik, the trusted adviser to the emperor and head of the powerful Imperial Household Department.

By mid-December 1902, then, Deshler had been granted the franchise, the *Yuminwŏn* had been created, Bishop was en route back to Honolulu, and the first group of Korean emigrants was about to depart. Allen had been successful in bringing all of this about. It was now time for him to fulfill his promise to the planters to lobby Washington in defense of this new initiative to prevent a new round of Asian exclusion laws aimed at Japanese and Koreans. At the same time Allen felt the need to insulate himself from charges that he had interfered in the internal affairs of Korea in violation of his instructions. He accomplished both objectives with a letter to Secretary of State John Hay. The letter was a masterpiece of deception and circumlocution which, if taken at face value, as it was in Washington, placed the immigration of Koreans in the best possible light and gave no indication of the leading role Allen had played and Deshler was about to play in the process.

The first item of interest in Allen's letter was his complete disassociation from the project. "Lately Koreans have become interested in the Hawaiian Islands where large numbers of Chinese and Japanese reside," Allen intoned, adding innocently, "I hear that a number of Koreans have banded themselves together with the intention of going to Honolulu during the coming winter," and "some of them will take their families it is said." He continued that "there had been talk of organizing an emigration bureau ever since last winter," and "I understand that the recently issued regulations were modeled after the emigration laws of Japan." The use of the passive voice and of phrases such as "I hear," "it is said," "I understand," and "there had been talk" was a clever subterfuge to create the impression that he had had no part in establishing the newly created *Yuminwŏn*. And with good reason, for had his superiors in Washington learned that he had once again interfered in internal Korean affairs, Allen would have risked dismissal.[30]

A second theme in Allen's letter to Hay was an attempt to counter potential objections in Washington to a new wave of yet another group of Asian immigrants—by minimizing the numbers involved, maximizing the laudable traits of the Korean people, and stressing that no precedent was being set. To the first point he wrote that the number of immigrants would never be large because Korea was not overcrowded and because the government "would probably take alarm at anything like a great exodus and withhold the necessary passports." Turning to the second point, Allen wrote that the Koreans "are a docile, good-natured, patient and hard working race" who "differ from the Chinese in being able to take on our ways rather easily." In addition, "ages of subjection to their superiors make them law abiding and easy to govern; at the same time they seem able to absorb ideas of liberty and equality very readily." To the third point, Allen wrote that no precedent was being set because "there are quite a number of Koreans residing in the United States, whither they have gone chiefly in quest of an education, the desire for which is so strong that genteel Koreans have taken up menial callings to that end," and "Koreans have become naturalized American citizens and are a credit to us." By praising the Korean character, soft-pedaling the numbers involved, and stressing that no precedent was being set, Allen tried to allay fears of a new "yellow peril"—a label that was currently being applied to Japanese immigrants.

A third theme in Allen's letter was intended to prepare Washington psychologically for additional shipments of Koreans. He noted the benefits that would accrue to the sugar plantations and stressed the voluntary aspects of the movement, rather than the fact that they were being actively recruited for the plantations: "It would seem that if these people actually go to our islands and make a report that will lead others to follow, and if the Korean Government allows them to go, they may help to solve the labor question in these islands."

Fourth and finally, Allen's letter attempted to draw off any suspicion that he and the planters were engaged in providing illegal assistance to the immigrants, writing that he was "satisfied that the Korean Government is not engaged in assisting these people to emigrate by advancing them funds." Noting that "most of these people will undoubtedly be too poor to be able to raise the necessary funds," Allen suggested that "their neighbors and friends [would] contribute to assist them with the hope of being able to follow later on with funds sent by these pioneers."[31] This coverup letter to Hay also provided a forum for Allen to argue the planters' case in Washington as he had promised.

Hay wrote back acknowledging the letter and enclosed a letter from the secretary of the treasury, whose office administered the immigration laws.[32] In that letter, Secretary of the Treasury L. M. Shaw wrote, "Koreans are admissable thereto, provided they are not found, upon arrival, to belong to any of the classes coming within the prohibition of the immigration laws and those relating to importation of contract laborers."[33] It still remained to be seen whether the Korean immigrants would conform to these regulations.

Allen also sent a letter to Governor Sanford B. Dole, whom he had met during his stopover in Honolulu in March. This letter covered many of the same points as the letter to Hay and was thus similarly intended to keep the governor unaware of the conspiracy to break immigration laws. Unlike the State Department, though, Dole knew of the planters' initiatives in this matter and was favorably inclined toward them, judging from his positive comments made five years earlier. Therefore, in a section obviously meant for the planters, Allen wrote to Dole that the Koreans "are a patient, hard working, docile race, easy to control from their long habit of obedience," and certainly "a more teachable race than the Chinese." Allen was sure that the planters would be interested to hear that "if Koreans do get to the Islands in any number it will be a Godsend to them (Koreans) and I imagine they will be found to be unobjectionable and of good service as laborers." Finally, Allen added for the benefit of planters worried about worker instability, "Those who are accompanied by their families may not care to return if the conditions are favorable to their residence abroad."[34] Dole wrote back to Allen thanking him for the letter and indicating that the letter would "be placed before the parties most interested in the subject."[35] Allen was thus assured that the planters would get his message.

By the end of the year 1902, then, both Bishop and Allen had completed successfully their respective tasks. The venture would not be complete, though, until Deshler had shown that he could be counted on to carry out his part of the bargain. Only then would all parties be assured that emigrants could be recruited in Korea and slip in undetected. We must now turn to Deshler in his role as a recruiter and learn the fate of the great scheme.

6
Deshler Begins to Recruit

As we have already seen, between his arrival in 1896 and 1902, David Deshler had embarked upon several business ventures. One of these was with Walter D. Townsend, James R. Morse, and the American Trading Company. Another was with Leigh Hunt, J. Sloat Fassett, and the Unsan Gold Mines. It is not surprising to find that Deshler, a member of a prominent Ohio banking family, was also manager of the Inch'ŏn branch of the Hong Kong and Shanghai Banking Corporation (known in Korea as the P'ungguk Bank).[1] All of these activities were carried out at the Deshler Foreign Business House located in Nae-dong in Inch'ŏn.[2]

In the spring of 1902, Allen had selected Deshler to be the recruiter for the Hawaiian sugar planters and during the summer that followed, the two men had extensive discussions about the project. When Deshler wrote to Irwin in August that everything was in readiness, E. Faxon Bishop was dispatched to Korea to negotiate the details with him. With Allen's aid, Deshler was granted the exclusive franchise to recruit emigrants and the *Yuminwŏn* was created to assist in the process. By the end of November 1902 it was now time for Deshler to begin the recruiting process.

Deshler's first step was to create two organizations to manage the process. The first was the *Tongsŏ kaebal hoesa* or East-West Development Company, which was to handle the recruiting.[3] The second newly created organization was the Deshler Bank, with operating capital of $25,000 provided by Bishop, to handle the financial aspects of the operation.[4] As both the Deshler Bank and the East-West Development Company were located in the same building, with a sign outside in both Korean and English, it is clear that this separation of functions was more apparent than real.[5]

Second, Deshler had to find assistants and interpreters. He had found his first interpreter, Chŏng In-su, through his connection with the Unsan Gold Mines. Chŏng "was one of those ambitious young men who wanted to learn to speak English with the idea that he was coming to America some day. So he had come to the Hard Learning Club in Pyeng Yang [P'yŏngyang] one evening and told Choi Yong-wha [Ch'oe Yŏng-hwa], the English teacher, that he was going to learn English from him. And Choi was said to have said to him that it would be impossible for him to speak English because his lips were too thick. As a matter of fact, his lips were not at all any thicker than anybody else's. . . . Well, Jung [Chŏng] was not discouraged by Choi's joking remark. On the contrary, he had determined more than ever to learn to speak English some day better than Choi did himself. So he did. He had gone to an American gold mining camp in the north and working as a flunky to the American engineers there, he had learned to speak English well enough to be the Korean interpreter."[6]

But Deshler needed more than one interpreter, and beginning on December 6 and for the next ten days, he advertised in the *Hwangsŏng sinmun* for "honest young men of good character" who could read, write, and speak English to work in the bank.[7] One of the applicants was one Hyŏn Sun who, after job-hunting unsuccessfully, learned through the newspaper that the Deshler Bank was looking for English-speakers. After walking around Inch'ŏn he found the office with its signboard, "East-West Development Co."; he met with Deshler who accepted his application and told Hyŏn that he would go to Hawaii as an interpreter. Hyŏn stayed the night and met with Ahn Chung-soo [An Chŏng-su], another interpreter hired by Deshler, who told him more about the East-West Development Company.[8] Deshler's advertisements yielded a total of eight men.[9] He and his assistants could now begin recruiting.

This third step of actually going out and recruiting emigrants was to prove more difficult. Deshler had already begun advertising emigration in the local newspapers, "for the purposes of education, observation and engagement in commerce, industry and agriculture."[10] To supplement these newspaper notices, Deshler and his assistants traveled to several seaport cities to put up notices about the need for laborers in Hawaii, about the type of work offered there, and that payment of wages would be in American money.[11] Although the recruiters spoke in glowing terms of the opportunity, the Koreans were initially suspicious and "believed only a fraction" of what they heard, with the result that no one was signing up to emigrate to Hawaii.[12] For some, fear of the unknown was an inhibiting factor, most having never been far from home.[13] Others hesitated because they thought ill of leaving their relatives and deserting the graves of their ancestors.[14] Still others feared the distances involved; it was one thing to emigrate north to the Vladivostok area but quite another to cross several thousand miles of the Pacific Ocean, perhaps never to return.[15] If Deshler could get one group to go, to break the ice, then perhaps subsequent groups would not be so difficult to recruit.

This initial snag was solved by the timely intervention of the Reverend George Heber Jones of the Methodist Episcopal church of Inch'ŏn and a personal friend of Horace Allen. Hyŏn Sun, a parishoner in Jones' Yong-dong church, recalls that Jones, "who could speak the Korean language very fluently, . . . advised his church members to join the emigrants to Hawaii."[16] He told them that the weather and scenery in Hawaii were very agreeable and furthermore, as Christians, they could set up a church there and evangelize.[17] That he was able to convince some of his parishioners to be the first to go to Hawaii is not surprising, given the Methodists' description of Jones as an excellent organizer who "possessed the magnetic power and eloquence to move the masses."[18] Even Horace Allen at one time remarked, "This Bishop Jones over here keeps me busy keeping him out of jail for undue influence; the Koreans all want to go to Heaven in his chariot."[19] Jones was clearly doing a favor for Horace Allen, and may even have been in contact with Min Yŏng-hwan, the head of the *Yuminwŏn* in the process.[20] While some other American missionaries in Korea would soon come to oppose emigration to Hawaii, it is clear that Jones genuinely approved of the idea partly for the emigrants' own advantage and partly in the belief that mission work would be more successful away from the home country.[21]

As a result of Jones' "explanation, his followers, more than fifty Christian men and women, and twenty workers in Inch'ŏn harbor volunteered to go abroad."[22] As they were awaiting departure from Inch'ŏn, Jones "held large tent meetings in order to inspire them with laudable ambitions and prepare them for the strange experiences so soon to overtake them." In addition, he "supplied them with a liberal amount of good literature" and "also handed a few of the leaders among them letters of introduction to the Superintendent of Methodist Missions in Hawaii."[23] Jones had performed his part admirably.

The first group, primarily from Inch'ŏn, Suwŏn and Pup'yŏng,[24] and numbering slightly over one hundred, had undergone a cursory physical examination[25] and were now ready to depart. Deshler had already paid their passage to Honolulu, given each fifty dollars in pocket money to show to the immigration inspectors, and had signed them to three-year "work agreements" on the plantations—all of this illegal. On Monday, December 22, 1902, "wiping tears,"[26] the first group boarded the *Genkai Maru*[27] of the Shosen Steamship Company[28] for the two-day trip to Japan. On board was David Deshler[29] and two interpreters, An Chŏng-su and Chŏng In-su, who would become interpreters for the HSPA and for the first group in the fields, respectively.[30] After arriving in Nagasaki on Christmas Eve, they underwent a second physical examination and received their vaccinations. The remaining 102 immigrants—56 men, 21 women (wives), 13 children, and 12 infants—boarded the Oriental and Occidental Steamship Company's *Gaelic* soon after New Years Day 1903 for the ten-day voyage to Hawaii.[31] So pervasive was the Christian influence among this first group that during this pioneer voyage they "organized a prayer-meeting in the steerage of their ship and carried on Christian work among their fellow emigrants, so that when they landed under the Stars and Stripes they had a Methodist Episcopal Church organized and fifty-eight of the company were members."[32] Indeed, the Christian influence was to characterize Korean immigration to Hawaii for the duration of the movement.

After "a pleasant and uneventful trip from the Orient," the *Gaelic* arrived off the port of Honolulu at midnight on Tuesday, January 12, 1903, where it remained until 3:30 the next morning when it came into the harbor and docked at the quarantine wharf.[33] Awaiting the first group was the Reverend George L. Pearson, to whom Jones' letters of introduction had been addressed. Pearson, "wielding a wide influence was able to do a great deal for the new arrivals,"[34] arranging for Inspector Stackable to inspect the Koreans on board ship rather at the customary place on Quarantine Island.[35] At the medical inspection by a Dr. Hoffman, eight men were refused landing because of trachoma (a contagious conjunctivitis), along with their five wives and three children.[36] The remaining 86 immigrants—48 men, 16 women, and 22 children— then boarded the narrow-gauge railway to Waialua Plantation on the north shore of Oahu, where they were housed in the Mokuleia Camp. Waialua Plantation had been selected because the manager, William W. Goodale, had offered to take the first lot of Koreans,[37] and because, in the words of C. M. Cooke, "Mr. Goodale will doubtless treat them so well that they will want their friends to follow them."[38]

First impressions are important, of course, and both parties seemed pleased. The Koreans "were full of praise for everything in connection with the voyage,"[39] while the planters "were favorably impressed with their appearance and also with the fact that when they landed they had no tale of woe to pour into [their] ears and no complaints to make. They seem to have gotten along splendidly on the voyage and were well treated by everyone."[40] Even the newspapers, which were generally critical of Asian immigration, ran a story that was not unfavorable. Since the reporters of course did not know that the planters had paid their way or that the Koreans had already signed work agreements before leaving Korea, the *Evening Bulletin's* story read, "That an attempt will be made to secure the men for the plantations goes without saying for the mission of Mr. Bishop was for the express purpose of seeking plantation labor to relieve the cessation of the immigration of Chinese into the country." Labeling the first group "experimental," the article concluded, [If the Koreans] are found to be good laborers on the plantation and take kindly to the country, there is no question whatever that each steamer from the Orient will see a large company of these people."[41]

What was most important for the planters, of course, was that the Koreans had passed Inspector-General Brown's and Immigration Inspector Stackable's examinations. The two interpreters had been well coached by Deshler to state falsely that the pocket money and passage had been paid by the immigrants themselves and that they had made no prior work commitments. Months of worrying on both sides of the Pacific immediately subsided. Naturally, the planters were pleased because this allowed them to authorize a continuation of Korean immigration. To that end, Bishop wired Deshler giving him the green light to proceed with the recruiting of additional groups.[42] Deshler shared the news immediately with his mentor, Horace Allen, who was pleased that his "valuable ideas" for getting around the law had proven to be a success: "A telegram came here a few days ago over the new Pacific cable from Honolulu to San Francisco and across saying they had entered all right. It will be a great thing for them and for the Islands if they continue to go and are not stopped by this [Korean] Government."[43] Bishop also wrote to Min Yŏng-hwan to tell him of the successful arrival of the first group of immigrants and Min forwarded Bishop's letter to Deshler who in turn forwarded it to Allen.[44] Finally, Giffard wrote to Irwin that "the first consignment of Koreans had been admitted into the country without objections from the Inspector."[45] There seemed to be no clouds on the horizon, as all doubts about their landing had been erased. Korean immigration bid fair to continue uninterrupted.

Once the first group of Koreans had been recruited, had left Korea, and arrived in Hawaii without any apparent problems, it was much easier for David Deshler to gather more emigrants. After seeing off the *Gaelic* from Japan, Deshler returned to Korea in mid-January to begin recruiting anew. Aiding him were photographs "showing views of plantations and work thereon," which he had the planters send him in early January.[46] By the first week of February, the recruiting was going so well that he cabled the trustees that he had gathered three additional groups.[47]

The second group of Koreans, numbering 90, left Inch'ŏn on

February 10 aboard the *Kiso Maru*[48] and transferred to the *Coptic* at Nagasaki, arriving in Honolulu on March 2.[49] The interpreter with the second group was Hyŏn Sun, whose autobiography reveals that when it was his turn to go to Hawaii he asked his wife to go with him and she agreed to go. When he asked for permission from his father and grandmother, however, they were less enthusiastic. Nonetheless, Hyŏn and his wife left, and when they reached Honolulu, they remained in quarantine for two days before An Chŏng-su guided this second group aboard the train to the Kahuku Plantation on the north shore of Oahu, where they were welcomed by the manager, Andrew Adams. After being entertained in a large dining hall, Adams told them to purchase what they needed on credit at the plantation store. He also told them what their wages would be: $16 a month for field labor and $30 a month for interpreters. Their camp was composed of twenty small cottages with bunks, with married couples allowed one room while single men were housed three or four to a room.[50]

As this second group was about to leave Korea, Deshler exuded confidence in the continued success of the operation, noting in a letter to Allen that "the men are coming in rapidly for early shipment." Moreover, he added, the eight men from the first shipment arrived back "in good spirits," and three of them "begged to be allowed to return as soon as they are cured of their eye sickness which is a good indication of how they feel." As a result, Deshler concluded, "all this is very gratifying and the return of these men will not have a bad effect on the enterprise—on the contrary I believe it will assist us." That Deshler still depended heavily upon Allen's advice and assistance with the emigration venture was made apparent in the final sentence of Deshler's letter, which read: "I hope to get up to see you soon as I am anxious to complete our conversation on this work that started last summer in your house at Sopple and shall take the first opportunity of getting away."[51]

As the East-West Development "Company's affairs became very busy,"[52] it became necessary to expand operations by hiring more employees and opening branch offices. By employing a Mr. Hannen from Holme, Ringer and Company, as well as a Mr. Remedios, to accompany the emigrants from Korea to Japan, and by hiring a Japanese, Kanatani Kaichi of Osaka, to assist in Yokohama, Deshler would be able to stay in Korea and "look after the innumerable details that are constantly coming up for decision." In addition, preparations were begun for opening branch offices in Seoul, P'yŏngyang, Wŏnsan, Pusan, Kunsan, and Chinnamp'o.[53]

With an increasing number of clients, additional offices, and personnel, and, of course, a desire to make more money, Deshler, an astute businessman, decided to take advantage of the situation. He did so by seeking permission to increase the flow of immigrants. The planters agreed to his request,[54] noting, "There seem to be no impediments in the way of future immigration from that source."[55]

Only one day after the decision was made to increase the number of Korean immigrants, the third group of 77 men, 4 women, and 2 children left Inch'ŏn on March 1.[56] Sailing aboard the *Kyouki Maru*, they arrived at Nagasaki on the third, where they were housed and vaccinated before going aboard the *Korea* on the fifth. After a stop at Kobe on the sixth, the *Korea* arrived at Yokohama on the eighth, where the immigrants underwent an inspection lasting over an hour. During that inspection a three-year-old immigrant child was discovered to have a mild case of smallpox which had gone undetected by the ship's doctor; Deshler's assistant, Kanatani, arranged for treatment at a local hospital. Finally, the immigrants departed at noon on the tenth,[57] and arrived in Honolulu on March 19.[58]

In similar fashion, subsequent groups of emigrants departed as the pace began to quicken, reflecting the desire of Deshler and the planters to increase the number of Koreans moving to Hawaii. For instance, only two days after the third group had departed Korea, a fourth group consisting of 124 emigrants, of whom 107 were men, left on March 3[59] and arrived aboard the *Gaelic*.[60] A fifth group of 73 emigrants, of whom 67 were men, left Korea on March 24.[61] A sixth group of 61 left on April 21[62] from Chinnamp'o aboard the *Suma Maru*.[63] On May 3,[64] a seventh group of 36 left, also aboard the *Suma Maru*.[65] Business was picking up for Deshler and the prognosis was good, as a newspaper report in early May indicated that the "the number [of applicants for emigration] is large."[66]

In summary, by the end of the first six months of 1903 there were nearly 600 Koreans in Hawaii. While accounts differ as to the exact number (there are four different sources), figures provided by Deshler himself—450 men, 60 women, and 60 children—appear closest to the mark.[67] During this first half-year period, since no major obstacles loomed on the horizon, the planters could concentrate on refining, protecting, consolidating, and taking stock of the process which had begun as an experiment but had quickly established itself as a venture with long-term potential.

During the first six months of 1903, the planters had an opportunity to assess the experiment on which they had embarked with the arrival of the *Gaelic* in mid-January. Indeed, only three weeks after the *Gaelic* arrived in port, Giffard reaffirmed that if they proved to be good workers, "the Korean immigration scheme which has been inaugurated will in due course give us an element which will go far towards not only assisting labor requirements but will be of great service in counteracting the evil effects in the labor market caused by too great a preponderance of Japanese."[68]

In fact, the Koreans not only imparted a good first impression, as we have already seen, but also continued to receive rave reviews from the planters. Just two weeks after the arrival of the *Gaelic*, C. M. Cooke wrote that the Koreans "seem to be just what our Plantations need." And on the following day, Giffard wrote to Irwin, who had initiated the project in San Francisco, that he was "pleased to state that the reports received so far from the Koreans lately arrived in this country have been quite favorable and that there are hopes that they will be a satisfactory class of labor for the Islands." Two months later he was able to write that the Koreans were "doing well as laborers." Goodale, to whom the first group of Koreans had been sent, stated that they were "doing good work" and later wrote that they were "a steady lot of men, accustomed to farm work. They begin well and appear contented and willing." Kahuku plantation, where the second shipment had been sent, reported that the Koreans were "giving very good satisfaction and the Company would like to have many more come." On Maui, Korean labor was "proving satisfactory so far," wrote a local newspaper. On the island of Hawaii, the manager of the Hilo Sugar Company asked to be sent a few Koreans, and John Sherman, the manager of the Hawaiian Agricultural Company plantation in Pahala, was "very pleased with the Koreans as field laborers. He has built them new quarters and they seem contented." E. Faxon Bishop, who had gone to Korea six months earlier, wrote that he wished "that we (C. B. and Co.) could get all the Koreans that are coming in as, while they are 'green' in a sense, they soon take hold and when they go to a plantation they stay there, whereas the new Japanese begin to dwindle away from the day they arrive." That the greater stability of the Koreans was generally perceived by other sugar men was noted by Bishop who wrote, "I think that others realize this advantage as the call for Koreans is quite general. . . . everybody speaks well of the Koreans from the Manager down to the Luna in charge of them." Finally, Horace Allen, on his way back to Korea after having spent the summer in Ohio on home leave wrote in his diary: "The Koreans are proving to be excellent laborers and are greatly desired. They also seem to like the work and their surroundings."[69] In short, the Koreans were more than fulfilling the role the planters had mapped out for them as a credible offset to the more numerous Japanese. This valuable asset needed to be nurtured and protected and the planters undertook four measures to accomplish this end.

Immigrants from Korea and Japan naturally did not cross the Pacific in first-class cabins, but as steerage passengers. And since their fare was being paid (illegally) by the HSPA, it was in the interest of the planters to insure that they received the lowest possible rates. Reasoning like any other businessmen, the planters felt that they should get a discounted rate because of the large volume of business they provided for the steamship companies plying the route between Japan and Hawaii. The planters complained, for instance, that they were "not being fairly dealt with" by the Toyo Kisen Kaisha [Oriental Steamship Company], which charged $30 per person, and wrote, "In view of the large numbers of Japanese, and possibly Koreans, that are wanted on our plantations, we should think they would be willing to meet us more than half way in bringing men here."[70] Cooke, for one, thought the fares should be $12 or $15.[71] The HSPA also complained about the Pacific Mail Steamship Line, noting that its "emigrant steerage rates are higher from Yokohama to Hawaii than from Yokohama to San Francisco." Terming this fare structure "outrageous," the planters threatened to boycott the line by having "both Korean and Japanese [laborers] come by some other line of steamers."[72] Irwin in San Francisco was assigned to put pressure on the company's representative there,[73] while another representative was despatched to the East Coast offices of the companies on a similar mission.[74] Since there was no additional correspondence on the matter, the planters presumably got the fare structure they wanted. The economic power of the planters was enormous, and as we have seen before, they were not hesitant to use that power to their advantage.

In addition to insuring that they got the best rates on trans-Pacific steerage fares, the planters also wanted to make sure that they were not being double-billed. That is, they had evidence that "the Planters' Association are paying for the passage of men who have already paid for their own tickets." It was especially galling given the fact that Japanese and, later, Koreans often did not work on the plantations for the full three-year term of their work agreement: "This paying of fifty dollars for each man and then having others leave the Islands makes a terrible expense to the Islands and many of the Plantations are beginning to feel it." The planters planned to "confer" with the agents of the Japanese Emigration Company to straighten out the matter.[75]

This account of the planters' fears of being overcharged and double-billed by the steamship companies is instructive because it not only reaffirms the evidence that the planters were bringing in Koreans and Japanese illegally by paying their passage but also provides additional detail about the actual expenses incurred in circumventing the law in their quest for inexpensive Asian labor.

A second campaign launched by the planters during the first months of Korean immigration to protect their latest venture was to oppose an "objectionable" educational amendment to an Immigration

Law currently before Congress which would mandate that all immigrants be literate in their own languages. Passage of the amendment "would not only exclude all Asiatics but also the lower class Europeans, all of which latter are not any more able to read and write in their own language than the Japanese and Koreans in theirs."[76] The effect would be to "shut out not only Japanese and Chinese, but also Portuguese and Koreans."[77] The proposed amendment thus had very real potential for foiling the newly initiated Korean immigration arrangements as well as scuttling the relatively more important and well established Japanese immigration upon which the planters depended. As luck would have it for the planters, the education clause did not become part of the new immigration law that was passed in March 1903, and the HSPA could breathe a sigh of relief. What the planters could not foresee was that there was another part of this new law which bid fair to bring Korean immigration to a screeching halt later in the spring.

A third campaign undertaken by the planters to protect the newly inaugurated Korean immigration was to encourage a limited renewal of Portuguese immigration. It will be recalled that the planters in years past never really desired Portuguese for their own sake, since their importation represented a substantial expense. Rather, they were desired because, as white labor, they could demonstrate to a skeptical public, including labor unions, critical newspapers, and nervous politicians that the planters were indeed sincere in importing labor eligible for American citizenship. It had now become even more important for the planters to demonstrate this sincerity because they had just begun importing yet another Asian group ineligible for citizenship—Koreans.

One target of this campaign was the immigration authorities, both locally and in Washington. At a meeting of the HSPA trustees it was noted that the planters had promised Inspector General J. D. Brown "to do all they could in the way of getting some other labor here to counteract the large number of Asiatics constantly arriving." It was clear that Brown and his superiors in Washington were even willing to bend the rules to encourage white immigrants because "on his last trip to Washington, he made a point of receiving instructions from his Department to allow the introduction of Portuguese into this country, even though assisted by the planters in the way of passage, etc., but providing that they did not come under any contract expressed or implied." The planters concluded that "as Brown has been particularly friendly in the matter of passing Japanese and Koreans alike, the Trustees are at present of the opinion that it would be well to show him, as well as the authorities at Washington, that we *are* endeavoring to get other labor than Asiatic by importing a load or two of Portuguese immigrants."[78]

A second target of this "token" use of Portuguese labor was the anti-Asian labor unions. The planters "appreciate the fact that in order to quiet the Federated Unions of Labor in the United States in the matter of continued importations of Asiatics to Hawaii and more particularly to prevent undue action by the Unions as to the Korean question it is absolutely necessary to show them that the Planters are also doing all in their power to introduce Europeans or Americans." The unions were a powerful political force that might come out for a complete exclusion of Asians. Therefore, if the planters could "show the Unions that we are recruiting from Europe it may defer action by them this next Congress, we having been assured that a big fight is in contemplation against the introduction of more Japanese into the United States, which of course includes Hawaii; any favorable action in this direction would also, of course, include Koreans."[79]

Thus the proposed symbolic importation of a few of the "more expensive," white Portuguese laborers continued to follow the pattern of making the plantations safe for multitudes of less expensive, Asian laborers. As Giffard cynically remarked, "You may rest assured that there is not a single Trustee in the Association who is in any way thirsting for unnecessary introduction of any European immigration whatever at the present time."[80]

And finally, the planters did everything they could to make sure that knowledge of the mechanics of Korean immigration remained behind closed doors. The measures taken were similar to those used in defense of Japanese immigration matters as well as earlier initiatives on the Korean question, and those involved were well versed in these tactics. For example, the matter of the increase in rate of Korean immigration was something that by experience the planters would want to keep from the eyes of the public, for indeed any increase in Asian immigration would invite renewed calls for a total exclusion of Asians. Thus when C. M. Cooke wrote a letter referring to the increase, he cautioned the recipient to "keep this as a profound secret as I only tell you as a stockholder what is being done on these lines."[81] And it was equally important that the wrong people not discover that the planters were violating the immigration laws in bringing in Koreans. Horace Allen, long practiced at the art of deception, thus concluded a letter to Fassett with a warning: "As to the Hawaiian matter, I send you a letter just received from Deshler. Regard it confidentially and destroy it after reading."[82]

By the late spring of 1903, Korean immigration was apparently well on its way to becoming a regularized and systematic movement, much like the much better established immigration from Japan. For this to occur, however, Deshler and the planters would have to continue to ensure that federal investigators in Honolulu did not discover that the immigration of Korean workers violated the law. And in Korea, Deshler and Allen would have to insure that no objections were raised from that quarter either. Unfortunately for all concerned, in the spring and summer of 1903 would arise troubles in both Hawaii and Korea, any one of which could doom the project in its infancy.

When Sanford B. Dole was sworn in as governor of the newly created Territory of Hawaii, the annexation resulted in the Chinese Exclusion Act being extended to include Hawaii. The planters thus had to turn from Chinese to Koreans to offset the more numerous Japanese immigrants. Hawaii State Archives Photograph.

BISHOP   COOKE   IRWIN

The Hawaiian sugar planters, including such men as C. M. Cooke and William G. Irwin, persuaded E. Faxon Bishop to go to Korea in late 1902 to begin the recruitment process. Hawaii State Archives Photographs.

The first boatload of Koreans, which arrived on January 13, 1903, was sent to the Waialua plantation, managed by William W. Goodale *(above, right)*. Hawaii State Archives Photograph.

Judge Morris Estee *(right)* presided over the trial testing the legality of Korean immigrant arrivals and was bribed by the planters to obtain a favorable ruling. Hawaii State Archives Photograph.

F. M. Swanzy *(above)* went to Japan in the summer of 1905 in a desperate and ultimately unsuccessful attempt to restart Korean immigration to Hawaii. Hawaii State Archives Photograph.

Horace Allen *(top, left)*, U.S. minister to Korea, acted as the intermediary between the planters and the Korean government and was particularly close to Emperor Kojong *(top, right)*. Photographs courtesy of *Kuksa p'yŏnch'an wiwŏnhoe* [National History Compilation Committee of Korea].

Kojong appointed the pro-American Min Yŏng-hwan *(bottom, left)* to head Korea's newly established Department of Emigration, but Yi Yong-ik *(bottom, right)* disapproved of emigration and persuaded Kojong to abolish this department. As a result, the passport forms had to be altered. Photographs courtesy *Kuksa p'yŏnch'an wiwŏnhoe;* photograph of Yi Yong-ik portrait from Korea University.

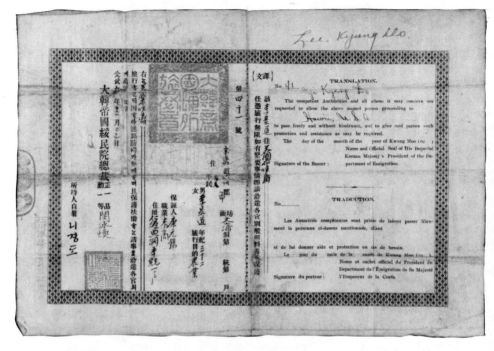

Top: Passport of Yi Kyŏng-do (Lee Kyung Do) issued by the Department of Emigration *(Yuminwŏn)*, headed by Min Yŏng-hwan in December 1902. Photograph courtesy of Bishop Museum, Honolulu.

Bottom: Passport of Ŏm Si-mun (Eum Shi Moon) issued by the Korean Foreign Office in December 1904. By this time the *Yuminwŏn* (Department of Emigration) had been legislated out of existence. Courtesy of Nancy Eum Rogers.

These Pacific Mail Steamships brought Japanese and Koreans to Hawaii, usually departing from Nagasaki, Kobe, or Yokohama. Hawaii State Archives Photograph.

Vanderbilt University-educated Yun Ch'i-ho *(left)* visited Hawaii in the fall of 1905 to investigate the condition of Koreans on the plantations. Photograph courtesy *Kuksa p'yŏnch'an wiwŏnhoe*.

Morioka Makoto was one of the Japanese emigration company owners who disapproved of Korean immigration to Hawaii. Photograph by Yoshitami Tasaka.

Morioka Makoto pressured Japanese Foreign Minister Komura Jutarō *(bottom, right)* and his staff at the Japanese Foreign Ministry to bring Korean immigration to a halt. Photographs of Komūra and Foreign Ministry courtesy Gaimishō gaikō shiryōkan.

Megata Tanetarō *(above, left)* was the Japanese advisor to the Korean Finance Office who vetoed the expenditure which would have allowed Yun Ch'i-ho to go to Mexico to investigate the condition of Koreans there. Photograph courtesy family of Megata Tanetarō.

Itō Hirobumi *(left)* became the resident-general of Korea in 1906 and
was responsible for continuing the
ban on Koreans going to Hawaii. As
a result, no further Koreans came to
work in the Hawaiian sugarcane
field. Photograph of Itō courtesy
Gaimushō gaikō shiryōkan. Sugarcane workers photograph courtesy
Hawaii State Archives.

The final resting place of recruiter
Deshler and his wife, Hideno Honda
Deshler, in the foreigners' cemetery in
Yokohama. Photograph by Andō
Torazō.

7

Troubles in Korea

JUST as Korean immigration was moving out of the experimental stage to become what promised to be a highly satisfactory venture with long-term potential, the worst fears of the planters came true. Six obstacles that Allen and the planters thought they had surmounted surfaced almost simultaneously in both Korea and Hawaii. Taken either singly or in combination, each one held the possibility that Korean immigration would have to be terminated in its infancy. It was once again up to the planters and Horace Allen to rescue the project which both had been working on for over a year.

The first obstacle surfaced in the form of Japanese opposition to Korean emigration to Hawaii. The planters, it will be remembered, were of the opinion that they would "not be surprised [to] find strong opposition from the Japanese government," and tried to cover their bases with the Japanese by informing the Japanese Consulate as well as the representatives of the Japanese emigration companies in Honolulu about their impending Korean initiative.[1] In fact, the tactic of informing the Japanese was probably one of Allen's "valuable ideas," since Allen himself would soon employ the same methods in dealing with the Japanese representatives in Korea.

This strategy initially appeared to work, at least with the Japanese emigration companies, who "continue to assure us that they look upon Korean immigration favorably in that it makes the Japanese already brought here . . . work better on the plantations to have another class of laborers pitted against them." But would it also work for the Japanese diplomatic community?

After the Japanese diplomatic community in Honolulu was informed of the Korean initiative, the planters believed that it was viewed "as favorably as the immigration people do and we look for no trouble unless it is from the Foreign Office in Japan where they are not so well posted regarding the effect that a mixed class of laborers has upon their subjects upon these Islands." It was clear that the planters were most worried about Tokyo, and hoped that the Japanese consul in Honolulu and the emigration companies would explain to Tokyo "that there is no intention of stopping the emigration of Japanese to these Islands but that the only desire of the Planters in getting Koreans was to mix the laboring classes on the plantations so as to have the Japanese work better than they have been doing for the past year or so."[2] What the planters did not know was that the emigration companies made no such representation to the Foreign Office in Tokyo,[3] and that the despatch from Vice-Consul Okabe to Tokyo was factual and noncommittal.[4]

Meanwhile in Korea, Allen visited with the Japanese chargé d'affaires in Korea, Hagiwara Shuichi (Hayashi Gonsuke, the Japanese minister to Korea, was in Japan for the New Year), on January 16 in Seoul, just three days after the *Gaelic* had docked in Honolulu. In that meeting, Allen informed Hagiwara that the project was undertaken "experimentally" and offered the opinion that since the Koreans loved their homeland, the emigrants would not make Hawaii their permanent home. Clearly, Allen was doing his best to downplay the significance of Korean immigration to Hawaii. Hagiwara in reply promised that the Japanese government would not interfere with the project "so long as our [Japanese] emigrants' vested rights were not infringed upon."[5] Allen's tactic appeared to have worked because Hagiwara's accompanying despatch to the Japanese foreign minister was a simple, straightforward account of the departure of the first group of Korean emigrants the month before.[6]

Thus far, neither Okabe in Honolulu, Hagiwara in Seoul, nor Komura in Tokyo had expressed any hostility toward Korean immigration to Hawaii. Rather, they were simply carrying out their duty to report on significant events occurring within their areas of responsibility. The first hint of concern seems to have emanated from the Japanese consul in Inch'ŏn, Katō Motoshirō.

Just as Allen had voluntarily met with Hagiwara in Seoul and had had the planters meet with the Japanese consulate and emigration companies in Honolulu, just so Allen had Deshler in Inch'ŏn meet with the Japanese consul there to head off any opposition from that source. While the planters and Allen had been relatively successful in explaining away any objections from the Japanese, Deshler's meeting with Consul Katō in Inch'ŏn achieved only mixed results. Although Deshler told Katō about the experimental nature of the project, Katō's despatch to Komura reveals that Katō had strong opinions about Korean emigration to Hawaii. In Katō's view, "the competition of the Korean emigrants will adversely affect the position of our Japanese emigrants." He argued that (1) relatively more Koreans tended to take their families with them, with the result that they were more likely to remain permanently in Hawaii; (2) since the Koreans were accustomed to political and social pressure they would be more obedient than Japanese workers; and (3) since the living standard of the Koreans was lower, the planters could decrease wages.

Katō also revealed himself to be strongly disparaging of the Korean government and the Korean people in general. For example, he claimed that the Koreans were lazy, dirty, unskillful, heavy smokers, and did not live orderly lives, making their worth as competition somewhat limited. Averring that there was "no question" but that Korean workers have less ability than the Japanese and that "in work that needs some mechanical knowledge as in manufacturing, it is almost impossible to employ Koreans," Katō reasoned that employers would necessarily have to pay the Koreans lower wages. In discussing the reasons why Koreans were willing to emigrate, he cited in addition to the poor harvests of the previous year the oppression of the government. Katō concluded his despatch by saying that while the plan was a bold one, he doubted it would succeed and that the Japanese government should not worry about competition from Koreans.[7]

By the beginning of February, then, barely one month after the beginning of Korean immigration to Hawaii, only one Japanese official, Consul Katō in Inch'ŏn, had anything negative to say about the project, and even he concluded that it was not worth worrying about. Moreover, it is apparent that his superiors in the Japanese Foreign Ministry in Tokyo agreed, because no response or initiative was made by Foreign Minister Komura. Where then did the opposition come from? It came from the Japanese minister to Korea, Hayashi Gonsuke.

Hayashi had been in Tokyo when the reports from Okabe in Honolulu, from Hagiwara in Seoul, and from Katō in Inch'ŏn, arrived on Komura's desk. So Hayashi was already well posted on the issue when he returned aboard a Japanese warship to his post in Seoul in mid-February, and he had formed a definite opinion on the subject. Upon his arrival he immediately asked for an audience with the Korean emperor to discuss "urgent business between Japan and Korea."[8] During that audience, Hayashi "informally notified the Korean Government that their emigration to Hawaii is interfering with Japanese emigrants and he therefore looks upon it as unfriendly."[9] At this point we need to look at three related questions: What was the reaction of the planters? Was Hayashi correct in his allegations? Did Hayashi have hidden motives?

The planters had always been aware of the influence that the Japanese government exercised over the Korean government. Bishop, for one, felt "some anxiety, for while the Korean Government at heart despises the Japanese, they are at the same time afraid of them, and in a frame of mind to be easily intimidated."[10] Giffard noted that there was "a great possibility of the Japanese Government making complications in this Korean immigration matter."[11] Irwin, in San Francisco, acknowledged that the Japanese "naturally have a large pull on that country"[12] and "presume[d] they can make a good deal of trouble." He defiantly stated, "It is probably showing them that we are not satisfied with the manner in which their labor is brought to Honolulu by us at a great expense and then they simply endeavor to skip over to the mainland when an opportunity occurs."[13] Clearly, the threat from Japan was to be taken seriously.

The planters had learned about Hayashi's opposition in mid-March when Bishop received two letters from Deshler concerning the Japanese minister's actions. This was a serious matter, and the HSPA trustees called a meeting to decide how to respond. But the planters in Honolulu found themselves to be relatively helpless in the affair, and besides authorizing Bishop to write a letter to Deshler, they could do little.[14] They were once again reminded how valuable Horace Allen, on the scene at Seoul, was to the continuation of their project.

No one knew this better than William Irwin in San Francisco, who one year earlier had met Allen for the first time to ask his assistance in promoting Korean immigration to Hawaii. Now that it appeared that the planters would once again have to make use of Allen's services, Irwin determined "to write to Dr. Allen at Korea myself and find out whether or not the Japanese influence is powerful enough there to stop this immigration which we have started." But what Irwin wanted was intervention rather than information, since Allen represented "a powerful factor in connection with this matter. His long residence in Korea has given him great influence with the King and his Court."[15] Indeed, the planters were assured that Allen was doing his "best to overcome this opposition in our behalf in Korea."[16]

Knowing that Allen had already gone far beyond the limits of his official duties as America's senior diplomatic representative in Korea to help the planters, and was doing so again, Irwin proposed that the HSPA bribe Allen to "keep his good will and favor." Noting that "we will certainly also have to do something towards giving him something more than *thanks*," Irwin suggested to Giffard, "I do not presume for a moment that he would accept a bribe, or anything of that nature, but we can put it in such a shape that it might come within his official capacity to accept some remuneration for the great services which he has rendered to us."[17] While there is no evidence that Allen ever received or was offered a bribe from the planters, their trump card was their economic power, and they were never hesitant to use it.

Whether through the efforts of Allen or the reluctance of Hayashi to press the issue, or both, the crisis seemed to abate somewhat, especially after a reassuring communication from Deshler, and the flow of immigrants continued.[18] It was now also apparent that Hayashi's opposition was not the result of policy made in Tokyo but rather something of his own doing. Before leaving this subject, though, it is necessary to explore the relationship between Japanese and Korean immigration in a bit more detail to determine whether Hayashi's charge of "interfering with Japanese emigrants" was in any way accurate.

The relationship between Korean and Japanese immigration began to be developed by the HSPA even before the first group of Koreans arrived. A month before the docking of the *Gaelic*, the HSPA's Labor Committee recommended a reduction of Japanese immigrants from 1,500 per month to 1,000 per month, with one third of that number to be women. While the high proportion of Japanese women was sought on the assumption that a man with a wife and possibly children would be more stable and thus more apt to stay in Hawaii, the reduction in total number was recommended because the Labor Committee "thought that the Association could very well afford to reduce the number of men, particularly as the Korean question was turning out so satisfactorily."[19] In addition, the planters planned a cut in wages to begin in March, two months after the beginning of Korean immigration.[20]

Hayashi was thus correct when he complained to the Korean government that Korean immigration to Hawaii would interfere with Japanese emigration. It would result in limited opportunity for Japanese to emigrate to Hawaii, reduced profits for Japanese emigration companies, and also a lowered standard of living for the Japanese in Hawaii. This explains why the positive statements of the emigration agents and the consulate to the planters were not mirrored in their private correspondence to Tokyo.

On the other hand, it must be remembered that although the planters had complaints about the effectiveness and stability of the Japanese workers, they were never prepared to abandon Japanese immigration altogether in favor of the fledgling Korean immigration. As the first group of Koreans was en route to Honolulu, the planters reiterated their view that Japanese immigration was "the only reliable immigration to be counted on for some time to come."[21] Even after two months of the apparently successful immigration of Koreans, Giffard concluded in a letter to Irwin marked "confidential," that Japan remained "the only source upon which we may permanently depend for a continual labor supply and whilst our demands from that country must from now on be necessarily less so long as we get Koreans or others, still it is absolutely necessary to keep the ponderous machinery which has been set up for this immigration business."[22]

Finally, evidence suggests that Hayashi had more in mind than the welfare of Japanese emigrants when he announced his opposition to Korean immigration to Hawaii. The Japanese minister was opposed to any American concessions in Korea. Concessions were important in late Yi Korea because if substantial interests in Korea were granted to a particular country, then that country would have a valid reason for protecting the granting power (Korea). And Hayashi was particularly concerned about American concessions. After all, Americans had snared the Seoul-Inch'ŏn railway, the Unsan Gold Mines, the Seoul trolley system, water works, telephone, and electric light plant. One American official, in hindsight, wrote that "every move that Hayashi made was consistent with a policy of ultimate annexation" in a "constant drive against the development of any foreign business that might constitute an interest to be protected."[23] And the emigration franchise was definitely an American concession, with the only authorized recruiter being an American introduced to the court by the American minister and the head of the *Yuminwŏn* being the pro-American Min Yŏng-hwan.[24]

Thus, Hayashi was engaged in the same tug-of-war in Korea over concessions that Horace Allen was in trying to garner concessions for Americans. That is, Horace Allen was using concessions to increase the American stake in Korea, while Hayashi Gonsuke sought to increase Japanese influence by limiting the number of concessions granted by the Korean government to other countries. In less than a year, Japan would go to war with Russia over the question of whose interests in Korea would be predominant. Yet Korean emigration to Hawaii continued because Hayashi as yet had no support in Tokyo. Since he was acting on his own, he could do nothing to stop the process. But Hayashi remained an opponent of the project, and his continued opposition would become an important element in the development of Japanese imperialism in Korea. Two years hence, his influence was to be decisive, and he would no longer be alone in his opposition.

A second source of opposition to Korean emigration to Hawaii that arose almost simultaneously with the Japanese challenge was to be found among a group of American Presbyterian missionaries based in P'yŏngyang. While some missionaries, like George Heber Jones, approved of the project, others began to voice their opposition, which posed a double danger to the project. For one thing, interested workers might be dissuaded from making the move to Hawaii. And, more important, native foes of emigration might seize upon this opposition to add legitimacy to their own opposition. Such opposition might cause the Korean government to withdraw its approval and suspend the movement of Koreans to Hawaii altogether. Once again Horace Allen was forced to intervene to save the project.

There were four reasons for missionary opposition to Korean emigration to Hawaii. The first complaint, raised by Rev. Samuel H. Moffett in P'yŏngyang, was that the Koreans went as contract laborers and therefore were unwitting participants in the violation of the immigration laws of the United States. The charge was true, of course, since the emigrants did sign work "agreements" in Korea stipulating hours, wages, and working conditions—a practice that was illegal. Moffett's opposition extended to the point where he actually talked some would-be emigrants out of going.

How had the missionaries learned that work agreements were signed prior to departure? While the information may well have come from individual Koreans who were about to depart for Hawaii or from Walter D. Townsend who had originally declined the offer to be the recruiter because he did not want to become involved in violating American laws, it is more likely that the missionaries learned the truth from Homer Hulbert's *Korea Review*. While Hulbert had reported in the January 1903 issue that "no contract is made with these men before leaving Korea. They are not required to promise to stay any specified length of time,"[25] the February issue inadvertently reported them to be "under contract for three years."[26] It is clear that Hulbert had not meant to harm the project. In fact, a reading of his January issue shows him to be in complete favor of Korean emigration to Hawaii, citing the advantages to be gained—compulsory education, religious opportunity, comparatively short working hours, and the opportunity to learn "valuable" lessons.[27] The missionaries, however, had read all they needed.

It was important for Allen to counter Hulbert's unfortunate report, not only because it might result in harm to the project but also because it reflected on his own character as the diplomatic representative of the United States in Korea and a former Presbyterian missionary. Allen thus felt obliged to write to Moffett in P'yŏngyang to suggest that he had "acted from a lack of information on the subject," and added, "If I had ten minutes in which to talk to you I am sure I could show you your errors." "I have made particular effort," Allen reassured Moffett, "to see that the immigration laws of the United States, especially the contract labor laws, are not violated."[28] Of course, what Allen had really done was to make particular effort to see that the immigration laws were circumvented.

Allen followed up this letter by enlisting his friend, Homer

Hulbert, in the campaign to counter missionary criticism that the contract labor laws were being violated. And Hulbert was glad to oblige. The August 1903 issue of the *Korea Review* carried an article that began: "There is a mistaken impression on the part of a few of the foreign residents in Korea that the work which is being conducted by Mr. D. W. Deshler in sending Koreans to work in the sugar fields of Hawaii is contrary to U.S. law." Rebutting this charge, Hulbert said "There is a clause in these laws which permits any state or Territory to advertise the advantages of and solicit immigration to that place." Moreover, "the Legislature of Hawaii has appropriated a considerable sum of money for the printing of literature soliciting immigrants, in conformity to the United States laws, and a portion of this literature is being circulated in Korea."[29] It is interesting to note that Allen and Hulbert waited six months before "going public" with this defense. The reason, as we shall see later, lay in the fact that journalist Homer Hulbert could not have made such a statement any earlier than August.

A second reason for missionary criticism, again raised by Moffett, was that the Korean emigrants to Hawaii would be "liable to suffer ill usage or be demoralized." Allen was quick to counter that charge by pointing out that "the move on their part seems to be one that you of all men would be glad to encourage." For "as to the particularly Christian side of the matter, the chief men of the islands are Christians—sons of missionaries, and the sabbath is kept and church going is encouraged." Moreover, "as the movement is one that seems to be desired by our own people and most beneficial in every way for the Koreans, I ask you to withhold judgment until you are better informed."[30] Hulbert contributed to this theme also by writing, again in the August issue of his journal, that "those Koreans who have been in Hawaii for some time seem, so far as the letters we have seen convey intelligence on this point, to be getting along very well, and their children are within reach of modern schools and advantages."[31] Of course, whether the Koreans who went to Hawaii were better or worse off is a question that cannot be answered here. Moreover, the answer would probably be different for different people. All we can say with certainty is that those Koreans who left believed that they would be better off in Hawaii than in Korea.

A third reason for missionary criticism by the P'yŏngyang Presbyterians was that it took promising young men away from Christian work in Korea. While acknowledging that "in a country as wretchedly ruled as this there is beginning to be much restlessness and a desire to get out of it is not to be wondered at," Rev. William Baird's report in the Monthly Station Letter argued that the sugar plantations of Hawaii are "not the best place for the development of the Korean Christians; and the only hope for their country is for those who are Christians to stay here and help to overcome the wrongs here."

Baird's report also criticized benevolent work among religious groups in the United States for luring his pupils away. He related an incident in which a young man who had recently gone to San Francisco had written back to other students in Korea inviting them to leave and giving the impression that they would be able to support themselves by work furnished by the schools there run by Christians. The result of that letter, claims Baird, "was to discredit all I had said to the pupils against their going to America." Another common expectation was that young Korean students could find support from "idiotic rich men" (*miryŏnhan pujadŭl*). Others had resorted to theft and lies in order to get to America, according to Baird. To prevent an exodus, Baird recommended against an "unwise expenditure of benevolence" on the part of American-based denominational groups which are "putting irresistible temptations" in front of his young men and "filling with discontent and restless longings the minds of many."[32] While this report refers mainly to Koreans who wanted to go to the mainland United States, at least some of those who would leave would go to Hawaii.

Another voice on this subject was that of the wife of the missionary William L. Swallen who reported, "We have never known such unrest among the Koreans due to the excitement of so many going to the Hawaiian Islands to work on sugar plantations, and the dreadful hard times. . . ." She admitted that "we can't blame them for wanting to go to America and yet we do not encourage their going." Instead, "we would rather the Christian people would remain here and do what they can."[33]

More than a year later, the P'yŏngyang Presbyterians were still opposed to the emigration of Koreans. William Baird was still complaining that emigration was taking his Christian students and that the missionaries were forced to dissuade some from leaving. In one case in which the students left he wrote, "We very much deplored their going because they were promising boys of some Christian experience and we needed them here." They were needed as teachers, "especially since we find it hard to get a sufficient force of foreign teachers" and "native trained men could do invaluable work."[34] And Charles Bernheisel complained in his diary that three baptized persons and four catechumens had gone to Hawaii under the influence of an evangelist from the Ch'ŏndohoe, whose "influence has been very detrimental to this group where he spent a good deal of time that should have been given to preaching to the heathen."[35]

By this time it was becoming clear that there was nothing they could do to stem the tide, so they did the next best thing and tried to elicit promises from the intending emigrants that they would return to Korea. Consider the following scene played out between Rev. Samuel Moffett and one would-be-emigrant to Hawaii: "Of course, I didn't forget to say goodbye to the Reverend Moffett who baptised me and who was the first American who came to Pyeng Yang. When I went over to his home that evening and told him I was on my way to America, he said, 'Oh, how nice, Easurk! I'm glad, and I wish you all the success from your trip.' Then he asked me what I intended to learn in America. When I told him that I intended to learn to be a doctor and return as a medical missionary from America, he was delighted and said, 'That's just fine. We need more doctors, especially Korean doctors for the Korean people. May God bless you and keep you until your return as a Christian doctor.' "[36]

Horace Allen did not have to address missionary complaints that their best students were leaving for Hawaii because there were many others in the American Christian community in Korea who would oppose the view that going to America was bad for Korean Christians. We have already seen, for example, that George Heber Jones, who had helped round up the first group, remained enthusiastic about emigration to Hawaii, writing in his book, "The Koreans are by nature an industrious and sturdy people as proved by their recent conduct as laborers in Hawaii."[37] Presbyterian missionary S. F. Moore also thought the idea a good one according to an article published in Hulbert's *Korea Review* at the end of 1903 entitled "One Night With the Koreans in Hawaii." In that article he recounted a visit to Kahuku Plantation, where the second group of Koreans had gone earlier that year, and concluded that the Koreans were well treated.[38] A third positive voice appeared in the very next issue of the *Korea Review*. The article, written by Rev. G. L. Pearson in Hawaii, concluded that the Koreans "have received good treatment and they generally are well pleased with their homes, advantages and prospects."[39] Kind words about their treatment also came from missionary Lillias Horton Underwood in her book on Korea.[40] Even Rev. Henry G. Appenzeller before his death had made the connection between Christianity and the good life in the United States, leading one of his Korean students to ask rhetorically, "Was it not worth the while of any timid, downtrodden Korean laborer to make the attempt of reaching this haven of peace and plenty?"[41] Finally, Deshler himself wrote that Korean emigration to Hawaii "had the approval of . . . the majority of the missionaries, who saw in the work an opportunity for Koreans to improve their condition and to acquire useful knowledge and to better themselves financially."[42]

The fourth and final complaint made by the Presbyterian missionaries in P'yŏngyang was centered on denominational jealousies and jurisdictional disputes. While this objection had perhaps the least merit of the four, it was nonetheless a real issue to those who argued it. Moffett wrote to his superiors in New York noting that of those who had emigrated "a far larger number of men less advanced and of less hopeful character have gone to Hawaii." He continued that these men were members of the Presbyterian church and that some of them will no doubt return to Korea to assume responsible positions. Unfortunately, "we [Presbyterians] have no work in Hawaii" and "the result is likely to be a transfer of their allegiance to the Methodist Church," and "we ought not to lose them."[43] One way not to lose them, of course, was not to let them go at all.

So the American missionaries in Korea were not of one mind. The Presbyterian missionaries in P'yŏngyang argued against Koreans going to Hawaii, while most others favored it. Once again Allen had come to the rescue and once again his view had prevailed. Deshler still had plenty of applicants for emigration to Hawaii. Moreover, there was as yet no direct evidence that this dispute had come to the attention of those in the Korean government who might oppose emigration to Hawaii. If it did, it would add fuel to the arguments of those who might argue for a suspension of emigration to Hawaii. And that is just what happened.

The third source of opposition, which arose almost simultaneously with the first two, was one that the planters had feared for some time—opposition from the Korean government. And as the planters had been warned, this opposition arose less from philosophical disagreements with emigration per se, than from the corruption that characterized the final years of the Yi dynasty.

The first hint of opposition to Deshler's enterprise came as a result of an entirely unrelated matter. It will be remembered that while Bishop had been staying with Deshler a few months earlier, the emperor had expressed interest in purchasing his home in Inch'ŏn. Bishop had been so appalled by the maneuverings of the Korean officials who were trying to get a piece of the action that he cited this as an example of a thoroughly corrupt government. Deshler finally agreed to sell the property to Kojong and entrusted Allen and Min Yŏng-hwan to handle the details while he accompanied the first boatload of Koreans to Japan. Allen noted, though, that "when the time came, Koreans whom Deshler had failed to 'fix,' namely the kamni at Chemulpo [Ha Sang-gi], put in such an unfavorable report that HM would not have the property as a gift."[44] Apparently Ha had "brought up such trivial arguments as the fact that in owning such property HM would have to pay rent to the Municipal Council, which hurt his pride."[45]

By failing to bribe the *kamni*, Deshler had ruined his chances of selling his house to the emperor, but more important, he had made an enemy within Korean officialdom who had the ear of the emperor, who had earlier been characterized as "erratic." The *kamni*, Ha Sang-gi, soon began to focus on emigration, and Horace Allen hastened to Deshler's defense: "I understand the Kamni of Chemulpo has been making some adverse remarks about the emigration matter which I have had to reply to."[46] Deshler began to feel the heat and cited as one reason for opening up branch offices of the East-West Development Company in other parts of Korea the need to "get the work away from Chemulpo [Inch'ŏn] as I think we are too near the capital for our own good."[47]

Had the opposition been confined to Ha Sang-gi, this minor incident would have blown over with no consequences for the emigration project. But Allen soon learned that the opposition within the Korean government was much more widespread than he had thought and that his efforts in defense of Deshler and the planters would have to be increased.

He became aware that opposition had reached to the very top of the Korean government when messengers from Emperor Kojong visited him several times requesting suspension of emigration. "[The Korean government] identifies this emigration with the slave trade and thinks that emigration should be prohibited," wrote Allen, who felt that the Korean government held this opinion because they believed the "misconceptions and false articles of the Japanese newspapers about emigration" and because some Japanese in Korea (perhaps Consul Katō Motoshirō of Inch'ŏn or Minister Hayashi Gonsuke) had been circulating these opinions. The locus of the opposition within the Korean government was the Foreign Office whose vice-minister, Pak Yong-hwa, had conveyed the slavery rumors to the emperor[48] and which started making inquiries about the Deshler Bank.[49] This was a serious development because it indicated that now several sources of opposition were linked: Japanese opposition was beginning to fuel Korean opposition, and the arguments were similar to those held by the P'yŏngyang Presbyterians who also opposed Korean emigration to Hawaii.

Allen, the defender of the project, was again called into action. He first asked Japanese Chargé d'Affaires Hagiwara if he knew anything about these Japanese-inspired stories. When he said he knew nothing about them, Allen was convinced that Hagiwara was not opposed to emigration and decided to use him to counter the rumors of slavery that were being circulated by the unnamed Japanese. Accordingly, Hagiwara wrote that Allen asked "in friendship for me [Hagiwara] to convey to Vice-Minister Pak [Allen's] explanation, especially the fact that the Korean emigrants were given their proper rights as emigrants and were not treated as slaves either in the ships or on arrival at their destination, and I accepted this task willingly."[50] By cleverly using a Japanese to counter the Japanese, Allen had once again demonstrated his remarkable ability to manipulate the Korean government to his own ends. And his ploy seems to have worked, at least temporarily, because no more messengers from the emperor arrived asking for a halt to emigration.

The slavery issue did not die, however. It was resurrected a few months later by Yi Yong-ik, the rabidly anti-American head of the Imperial Household Department. Allen first met Yi in 1884 when he was sweeping floors for a living. Soon afterward Yi became a Russian agent, and by a combination of shrewdness and a total lack of scruple, became Kojong's financial counselor and the "most enduring personality" at the imperial court.[51] His anti-Americanism was enough to cause Allen to write in 1903, [Yi] has the idea that whatever is done to the Americans will not be resented . . . and his advice always opposes us so that even the most trivial matters of routine cannot be put through."[52] Yi organized anti-trolley riots (a Collbran and Bostwick franchise) and had American businessmen (such as Deshler) denounced as typical representatives of "countries that eat the flesh of the weak."[53] Naturally, he was opposed to Allen's policy of obtaining franchises for Americans and allied himself with one of the Americans in Korea who disliked Allen to foil the minister's efforts.[54] All this had Allen lamenting that "things here are going from bad to worse" because "Ye Yong Ik is able to run things, and he has made everything as disagreeable for Americans as he can."[55] Thus, one reason for Yi's opposition to the emigration of Koreans to Hawaii was the fact that it represented an American concession. And while Yi's opposition to emigration appeared to run parallel to that of the Japanese, the latter also considered Yi their enemy because he opposed their concession hunting as well and were searching for ways to oust him from power.[56]

Yi was notoriously corrupt, so corrupt in fact that in spite of his position as one of the emperor's favorites, he was temporarily forced from his office as the head of the Imperial Household Department as a result of a petition from other officials in November 1902, at the same time that the *Yuminwŏn* was being created within his supposed bailiwick. As the nominal head of the country's finances, his policies resulted in the collection of "money that he bled from the veins of the people."[57] So a second reason why Yi opposed emigration may have been that he would not profit substantially from it.

Whatever his motives, even while temporarily out of office in the winter of 1902–1903, Yi was no doubt aware of the obnoxious existence of the *Yuminwŏn* within his own department and also of the initial charges of slavery which had been bandied about by unnamed Japanese, the vice-minister of foreign affairs, and perhaps even the emperor himself. Allen had smoothed things over, of course, but he had not yet had to deal with Yi. When Yi returned to his former position in the spring of 1903, he moved quietly at first to disable and then to dismantle the *Yuminwŏn*. He was able to do so because he had never lost the ear of the emperor. He first saw to it that the government budget for the year 1903 appropriated no money for the *Yuminwŏn*.[58] Next, in early April, Yi had the emperor order that passports carry not only the signature of the president of the *Yuminwŏn* (Min Yŏng-hwan), but also the signature of the foreign minister.[59] This had the effect of undercutting the authority of the Department of Emigration by beginning to shift passporting functions away from that agency and to the Foreign Office.

Yi did not challenge Allen and Deshler directly until May, when a critical editorial entitled "People Go to Hawaii" appeared in the May 12, 1903, issue of *Cheguk sinmun* describing the emigrants as slaves and urging the suspension of emigration. Americans, the editorial proclaimed, "lured stupid Koreans with honeyed words and many Koreans have crossed the sea." Because it was "lamentable that our brothers and sisters have become slaves like African Negroes in a strange land," the writer urged everyone to "tell each other how miserable the life is there in the strange land so that we may not hear the sad story again."[60] Allen immediately saw the hand of Yi Yong-ik behind the editorial and, knowing the influence Yi had with Emperor Kojong, moved quickly to head off disaster. In a two-hour meeting with Foreign Minister Yi Chi-yong, Allen complained that the editorial had appeared in a newspaper "under official patronage" and "explained the nature of our immigration laws and how manifestly absurd and unjust" the slavery charges were. In addition, Allen suggested to the foreign minister that the favor was to the Korean government because the American government was "not interested in having these people go to the islands" and "might feel bound to prevent the coming of any large numbers," just as they had the Chinese.

Allen suggested that future imbroglios could be prevented by the appointment of a consul in Honolulu to "report on conditions there affecting Korean immigrants" and, appealing once again to the greed of the Korean officials, "to draw some revenue from visaing passports." This was the first, and would certainly not be the last, suggestion to the Korean government to establish a Korean consulate in Honolulu. In a lapse that would ultimately prove disastrous to Korea and Korean immigration to Hawaii, the Korean government did not respond positively to Allen's suggestion.

Having convinced the foreign minister that there was no slavery involved and having in addition suggested a remedy, Allen then attempted to pinpoint the origin of the report. The foreign minister, Allen wrote, "endeavored to assure me that the damaging reports did not emanate from his office, but they seem to be in accordance with a general attempt on the part of Korean officials headed by the notorious Ye Yong Ik to do everything possible to annoy Americans." That greed as well as anti-Americanism was involved was suggested when the foreign minister "frankly told me that the real objection to the movement was that it removed these people from the operations of the Korean tax collectors [headed by Yi Yong-ik]; in other words they were supposed to be leaving in order to avoid the 'squeeze' and official oppression generally." "Just think of that from a Foreign Minister," Allen remarked caustically, adding, "The Koreans are merely regarded as legitimate prey by their miserable officials." Allen tried a counterattack against Yi by suggesting to the foreign minister that "the people who made trouble for the Seoul Electric Company [which operated Seoul's trolley system and which was headed by Collbran and Bostwick] should be punished severely."[61] This was, of course, an obvious reference to Yi Yong-ik.

Allen felt obligated to inform the planters of the threat and his actions to head it off, doing so by writing to his liaison, J. Sloat Fassett, in Elmira, New York. He also informed his superior, Secretary of State Hay, remembering his promise to the planters to enlist help in Washington and also remembering to conceal his intimate involvement with Korean immigration to Hawaii. As a result, Allen's letter to Washington used the same type of innocent and laudatory phrasing as he had previously employed, writing, "I understand that about one thousand Koreans have gone to Hawaii," and, "I hear from reports from Hawaii that the Koreans find ready employment as farmers, and that they are considered a desirable set of workers, being patient and docile, and a good offset to the Japanese and Chinese."

At first blush, it appeared that Allen once again had bested the opposition. The emperor did not order a halt to emigration despite the opposition of his right-hand man, Yi Yong-ik. Nor did the episode dampen public opinion concerning emigration, for Allen noted that "while the newspaper reports have not been corrected, no similar ones have appeared, and I am informed by some of our missionaries that the people generally do not credit the reports."[62] Moreover, to reinforce his apparent victory, Allen once again turned to Homer Hulbert for assistance. In the May 1903 issue of his *Korea Review*, an item appeared which began by noting, "The interest of the Koreans in the emigration to Hawaii continues," and "an absurd suggestion has been made that they would be subject to slavery on going to the United States, but only the most ignorant people would credit such a report." Hulbert dutifully concluded, "Nothing approaching slavery or enforced contracts is allowed in the United States or its possessions and the government exercises the closest supervision over the emigrants both as to the conditions under which they enter and the treatment they receive."[63]

Having successfully foiled Yi's plans to halt Korean emigration to Hawaii, Allen could now relax and felt free to go on home leave once again, departing for America in early June 1903 and returning to Korea in late November after stops in San Francisco and Honolulu.[64] Yi simply bided his time and waited until Allen departed before completing his work. Although he was unable to convince the emperor to halt emigration, he was able to convince the emperor to cancel the imperial edict which had created the *Yuminwŏn* and provided the rules and regulations protecting emigrants.[65] Accordingly, the newspapers reported the "voluntary resignations" of all but the two top officials of that bureau.[66] Even before this time, it had become apparent that the *Yuminwŏn* was a dead letter, since its head, Min Yŏng-hwan, had been appointed chief of the Bureau of Ceremonies four months earlier.[67] Yi had thus successfully legislated the Department of Emigration and its accompanying rules and regulations out of existence.

Immigration still continued, although now under the shared aegis of the Privy Council [Chungch'uwŏn], the Ministry of Agriculture, Commerce and Industry, and the Foreign Office. As for Yi Yong-ik, his influence was soon to end. Having provoked the increasingly powerful Japanese once too often, the Japanese finally forced him from office in early 1904. In words that would prove prophetic, Homer Hulbert commented, "The country is thus rid of a man who though possessed of a certain degree of ability has done very much to bring the Korean government into difficulties. He was detested by the common people and hated by officials."[68] But he had done grave damage to Korean immigration to Hawaii and unwittingly allowed an opening wedge for Japanese imperialism in the matter.

Korean immigration to Hawaii had so far survived three sources of opposition in Korea: the Japanese Minister to Korea, Hayashi Gonsuke and other unnamed Japanese in Korea; American Presbyterian missionaries in P'yŏngyang; and the Korean bureaucracy, including the Inch'ŏn *kamni*, the vice-minister of Foreign Affairs (Pak Yong-hwa), Yi Yong-ik (the head of the Imperial Household Department) and, at times, even Emperor Kojong himself, who, as we have seen earlier in this chapter, vacillated over his earlier decision to permit emigration. In all three instances Horace Allen was able to intervene successfully, and his worth to the planters had been so valuable that at least one of the planters proposed to remunerate him for his troubles on their behalf.

Allen's protection did not extend to Hawaii, however, where opposition arose also in the spring and summer of 1903. The planters had to deal with these troubles directly on their own turf.

8

Troubles in Hawaii

EVER since the arrival of the *Gaelic* in mid-January, Koreans had been admitted into the country as legal immigrants although they had signed contracts in Korea to work on the plantations and the planters had paid their boat passage for them. That they were being admitted was due in part to luck, the friendly attitude of Immigration Inspector Brown, and the "correct" answers given by the accompanying interpreters. What the planters did not know was that Washington had recently been made aware of violations of the immigration laws when the American consul at Yokohama informed the State Department that the emigration of Japanese to Hawaii was being conducted illegally.[1] Already under pressure from public opinion, especially the voice of organized labor represented by the American Federation of Labor, to limit Asian immigration, this revelation resulted in a hardening of the American government's attitude toward possible violations of immigration laws. In the case of Korean immigration, the planters fell victim to this new vigilance and, on April 30, 1903, their luck ran out.

When the *Nippon Maru* arrived at two in the afternoon on that last day in April, it was carrying 142 Korean immigrants (of whom 113 were adults). Because of the imminent arrival of U.S. Immigration Inspector-General J. P. Sargent in Hawaii, the immigration inspection was stricter than usual, lasting over three hours before the vessel was finally allowed to proceed to Bishop Wharf.[2] During this meticulous examination, the accompanying interpreter, Kang Tae-gun, became flustered and forgot the answers Deshler had had him memorize and told the truth instead. What Kang ("a d . . . fool" according to Giffard) said was that "he had been sent here to interpret for the men who were to receive $15 a month wages and that his compensation was to be $25 per month."[3] As a result, the Koreans were detained for further investigation on Quarantine Island where immigration officers concluded that the Koreans had not only been assisted but that they had also already signed contracts before leaving Korea.[4] The entire episode "set the inspectors about our ears," wrote Giffard, and even though Brown "had been spoken to in regard to the matter," Bishop was forced to admit to Brown that "it was believed that the laborers were assisted," although Bishop would not admit that they had come under an implied contract. The charges were serious enough to warrant the convening of a Board of Special Inquiry to look into the matter. After cabling Deshler to suspend any further emigration activity, the planters prepared to take their case to the board.[5]

At the "annoying" inquiry, the planters "had a bad quarter of an hour during the period of the investigation, not from any personal fear of results but for fear that the whole Korean immigration matter would be jeopardized by the result of the Board's investigation." They "were obliged to prove that as a matter of fact these men came into the country perfectly free and under no contract whatever to work for any particular plantation or individual. Also that they were free to land and find employment for themselves if they so wished."[6] That the planters had mobilized their not inconsiderable clout to influence the board's decision became apparent when on May 6 the Koreans were determined to be legal immigrants and were immediately assigned to Waiakea and Wainaku plantations on the island of Hawaii.[7] The planters admitted that the episode had been "a close shave" and knew that they were still far from being in the clear; they again cabled Deshler to continue the suspension of operation. They were in continuing trouble, they felt, because Immigration Inspector-General Sargent was due any day from Washington and would undoubtedly hear of the case.[8]

Sargent arrived on the *City of Peking* on May 8 apparently with an open mind on the question, being quoted as saying that he had "not come down here to raise any row nor to attempt to create any kind of a sensation." Rather, he recognized that "there is a serious labor problem here." After expressing an interest in meeting the planters and the laborers, he said he would "go to the sugar plantations and see the work that is to be done there, and the men who do it and how they do it."[9]

There was no doubt that Sargent "would have to be handled very gingerly" because there was no telling where he stood on the issue of Asian immigration.[10] In one interview, he appeared to be sympathetic to the planters, calling the labor situation "serious" and lamenting that because the Japanese "will not stay on the plantation" the planters want the law amended to allow Chinese to come in under contract.[11] In another interview, though, he appeared to be anti-planter. Citing "returns of 67% on their investment," he concluded that "there seems to be little doubt that the Planters could afford to pay a reasonable consideration for a good class of labor and still get adequate returns on their investment."[12]

Irwin, in San Francisco, suggested that the best strategy to handle Sargent was to show him that the immigrants were working under good conditions on the plantations and to demonstrate that it was "utterly impossible for white men to work in the cane fields." Moreover, he wrote, "it will be silly to try and hoodwink him regarding the people we are now importing," especially since "such facts are public property." Rather, it would be necessary to show him that such immigration must continue and that "we are in no way attempting to evade the laws other than to introduce what is absolutely necessary for the plantations' welfare." He should also be insulated from the "busy-bodies around Honolulu who will fill him full of false reports."[13] Indeed the planters were so concerned about the threat that Sargent posed to the continued importation of Koreans that they convened a trustees meeting to determine how to deal with him. Because the planters "expected that Mr. Sargent will make an investigation of the [*Nippon Maru*] matter and possibly call upon some of the Trustees for explanations in this regard," especially "the matter of the notes given by the Koreans to the Deshler Bank for the amount of the passage money to Honolulu," it was decided that "it would be better to have the matter in the hands of a committee, rather than that individual Trustees should make statements which might not correspond." Bishop and Smith were chosen to be the committee.[14]

The HSPA's strategy succeeded. Sargent concluded, despite clear evidence to the contrary, that there had been no violation of the law and that he would not instruct the district attorney (R. C. Breckons) to bring charges.[15] His reasoning was that "the Planters had done what they had in perfect good faith and under the impression that the present laws allowed them to solicit immigrants abroad to work here."[16] He was also favorably impressed with the laboring conditions on the plantations.[17] But he warned the planters "most emphatically" that "soliciting of laborers to come here under the assistance of the Planters or their Agents *must stop and that at once.*"[18]

As a result of the investigation and Sargent's visit, which "has been raising the d . . . . down here with our systems of immigration," the planters faced the prospect of having to revamp the system under which Koreans were imported.[19] The change would be along these lines: "Deshler will have to have an Agent here, in the same way that the Japanese people have, he taking all the responsibility in sending immigrants who shall come perfectly free and with no understanding whatever, we to recruit from the consignments as they arrive in the same manner as we do with the Japanese at the present time."[20] Consequently, a man named Hague was employed to "sign up" Koreans as they disembarked in Honolulu, his salary being paid half by Deshler and half by the HSPA. In 1904 Hague was replaced by J. D. Julian.

As the planters began to restructure Korean immigration to satisfy half the legal requirements with a view toward restarting the flow of laborers from that country, they were faced with a third problem, which came on the very heels of the crises they had just weathered over the investigations of the Board of Special Inquiry and Inspector-General Sargent.

Just when the planters thought their troubles with the immigration laws were finally over, they discovered to their chagrin that E. Faxon Bishop was being sued in federal court for $113,000 for violation of the immigration laws against contract labor.[21] The suit was brought by Frederick V. Berger, a law clerk in the Honolulu firm of Lewers and Cooke, who was taking advantage of a recent law enacted on March 3, 1903, allowing private citizens to sue for the amount of $1,000 for each immigrant found to have entered illegally. (There had been 113 adult Korean immigrants aboard the *Nippon Maru* which had docked on April 30.) This new law had been introduced by Senator Henry Cabot Lodge in an effort to crack down on illegal immigration.[22]

The planters responded quickly to the threat posed by this "miserable law," convening two special meetings of the HSPA trustees where it was "decided to fight this blackmailing case to the bitter end." They also cabled Deshler in Korea not to resume recruiting. The planters then set about to identify their adversary and develop a countering strategy.

From their investigations, it soon became apparent to the HSPA that Berger was merely the point man for a "blackmailing hui" (this term is an adaptation from the Chinese character meaning group or association). Moreover, they discovered, this hui included several federal officials "interested in the spoils." One of these was Assistant District Attorney Dunn, who "is well known to be antagonistic."[23]

Another suspected member of the hui was none other than Inspector-General Sargent who was fingered by Irwin in San Francisco. Having received information from a close colleague of Sargent's, Irwin wrote to Giffard telling what the informant had to say about Sargent: "He gives that gentleman a very hard reputation and seems to be of the opinion that while he will talk very favorably to your face, he will stab you in the back when an opportunity offers, and that under the circumstances he is up for the boodle."[24]

The biggest adversary facing the planters, however, was federal judge Morris M. Estee, who would try the case. The judge was an elderly man who held strong opinions about Asian immigration. In fact, earlier in the month he had made an address entitled "The Future of Hawaii," which a local newspaper summarized in the words, "The Small Farmer Must Be Had to Americanize the Islands and Fit Them for the Dignity of Statehood."[25] Clearly, here was a judge with little sympathy for the planters and their questionable immigration practices. To make matters worse, the planters "all know here that Estee is in cahoots with Dunn and will favor any case he is mixed up in."[26]

In fact, the only "friendly" official was District Attorney R. C. Breckons, "who acts as a kind of break as it were." But Breckons could not "stand in the breach at all times and in this particular case, being the District Attorney, he cannot interfere one way or the other. He must as a matter of course remain neutral."[27]

With the assistant district attorney, the immigration inspector-general, and the judge against them, and the friendly district attorney unable to help, the planters were pessimistic about their chances for renewing immigration from Korea. After all, the planters had admitted their guilt during the investigations of the Board of Special Inquiry and that of Inspector-General Sargent. Irwin was sadly forced to conclude, "I am very sorry to say that I cannot view the future of labor in a very satisfactory way. This attempt to blackmail us in regard to the Koreans is a serious matter."[28]

On the other hand, the planters had a great deal of economic and political clout in their arsenal and had never let scruples stand in the way of achieving their objectives. One tactic might be to get some of the unfavorably disposed officials removed. Indeed, Giffard speculated, "Cannot some influence be brought to bear by the Spreckels [a large financial concern] on these officials in getting some of them turned down? Life is getting to be miserable here with such a gang of blackmailers and grafters."[29] There is no record as to whether this suggestion was ever acted upon. Needless to say, though, it gave an indication of the lengths to which the planters were willing to go to resolve this case in their favor. And since it was now before the court, the planters turned their attention on the sixty-nine-year-old Judge Estee.

Giffard had come to the conclusion that "justice cannot be obtained under such conditions in the Federal Court and the sooner Estee and some of his menials are fired the better it will be for all having anything to do with his Court."[30] Irwin agreed with Giffard, writing, "It is certainly most unfortunate that with the important cases that are now rapidly coming up against immigration and plantation interests that such a man as Estee should be on the bench." But he advised caution: "I do not see, however, how we are going to have him replaced. It is no easy matter to get a judge removed from the bench unless there is some specific charge brought against him."[31] Even the vast power of the planters had limits.

So in early June when the case went to court, it appeared that the planters had been unable to use any of their influence to sway either the members of the hui or Judge Estee. And because the facts of the case seemed to militate against the planters, their situation looked grim. Moreover, their prospects continued to deteriorate when the judge dismissed the planters' claim that because the Board of Special Inquiry had already declared the Koreans to be legal immigrants, the court had no jurisdiction.[32] Things were beginning to look hopeless for the planters and Korean immigration, and the HSPA doubted "whether it was good policy on the part of the Trustees to reduce the number of incoming Japanese in view of the stoppage of the Korean immigration."[33] .

The planters were not about to give up, however, and they continued to concentrate on influencing the judge, even if they had to break the law and resort to bribery. That bribery was part of their repertoire should not be surprising considering that earlier the planters had contemplated giving Horace Allen "something more than *thanks.*" Bribing a federal judge was serious business, of course, but the planters were accustomed to operating outside the law. In fact, the idea itself originated with their "ally" in the court system, District Attorney Breckons. As Giffard recounted the incident, Breckons, "who by the way has proved to be an exceedingly good friend not only to our firm but of the planters generally, called on me yesterday in regard to securing a pass for Judge Estee and wife by next trip of the 'Alameda.' " Giffard, in turn, "took the opportunity of giving Breckons one or two ideas that I had in my mind regarding our old friend Estee, in which he to a great extent coincided." That Giffard was willing to go ahead with bribing Estee was revealed when he wrote to Irwin, "We must not forget that as long as that Korean case is before him, it is well to keep him in good humor and do what we can for him."[34] Since the HSPA was part of the larger conglomerate known later as The Big Five, which acted, among other things, as agent for the Pacific Mail Steamship Line, securing the pass for the judge and his wife was no problem.

While the planters went about obtaining the pass for Estee behind the scenes, the opposition showed that it too was not above bribery in an attempt to obtain a favorable ruling in the courts. Unlike the planters, however, they lacked the sophistication needed to pull off the manuever in secret. This is the story: A Korean by the name of Choy Tong Soon [Ch'oe Tong-sun?] arrived in Hilo with a large sum of money and went to the Wainaku Sugar Plantation where some of the Koreans who had arrived aboard the *Nippon Maru* were working. After an unsuccessful attempt to bribe the Korean interpreter there with $200, he went to the Waiakea Sugar Plantation, where the rest of the *Nippon Maru* Koreans were working. Entering the homes of some of the Koreans, Choy offered the sum of $1,000 to any Korean who would furnish evidence that he had come to work under a contract. Unfortunately for Choy, he was discovered by the plantation manager, who pressed charges for practicing medicine without a license when Choy lamely claimed that he was a physician. Choy went to jail and the failed bribery attempt became public knowledge. That public opinion, at least, was favorable to the planters' case was evident when the newspaper report of the incident concluded by saying, "The suit is being pressed by prominent and well known officials, who hope to share in 'divvy' in case they can prove the law to have been violated."[35]

Thus, the attempts at influence-peddling by the two adversaries had radically different results. While the planters had markedly improved their chances for a favorable outcome in the court case, their antagonists had been thrown on the defensive. Wasting no time, the planters seized the initiative in the courtroom, arguing that the Koreans aboard the *Nippon Maru* had been recruited before the law that allowed Berger to sue for damages had been enacted.[36] This argument, coming as it did just before Judge Estee and his wife departed for California (with passage provided by the planters), left the planters optimistic that Estee would rule in their favor when the new court term began in September. In the meantime, the confident planters undertook initiatives outside the courtroom with a view toward restarting Korean immigration, which had been suspended since May.

The planters began by virtually running Berger out of town. Indeed, Berger departed for Victoria at the end of July vowing to return in time for the reopening of the court session.[37] He never returned. A visiting official of the American Federation of Labor, which endorsed the suit as a means of halting Asian immigration, was "glad to see that two young lawyers here have the nerve to buck the capitalists' interests," but ruefully noted that Berger "was practically blacklisted out of the country."[38]

Even before getting rid of Berger, the planters had resorted to politics to restore Korean immigration. While it was illegal for the HSPA and Deshler to recruit Koreans for work on sugar plantations in Hawaii, it was legal for the Territory of Hawaii to recruit them, if the immigrants came unassisted and free to work as they pleased, that is, not under contract. Consequently, the planters had "all been working to get a special item in the Appropriations Bill . . . providing for expenses of such solicitation."[39] They also lobbied successfully for the creation of a commissioner of immigration, a proposal that received favorable reaction in the local newspaper.[40] By the end of July, with Berger gone and the court adjourned, it was announced that Theodore F. Lansing, former treasurer of the Territory of Hawaii, had been appointed commissioner of immigration.[41] The planters had succeeded politically, and were confident that they would succeed legally.

It soon became clear that Lansing and the planters were working hand-in-hand to restore Korean immigration to Hawaii even before Judge Estee announced his decision. In his first newspaper interview in mid-August, Lansing indicated that he had prepared advertising material to be distributed in Korea to obtain labor for the sugar plantations.[42] And in a second interview two weeks later, he indicated how closely his aims and those of the planters coincided: "The Korean proposition gives great promise and I would not be at all surprised if this would be our salvation. There are some of these men working in Hilo and down the road and from all I have heard, they have given the very best of satisfaction. We are working actively along these lines now and hope to meet with success in our efforts. A Korean will work for $15 a month and will be perfectly satisfied with his lot. A Japanese wants more than this."[43]

Judge Estee returned in mid-September from California aboard the *Alameda* and two weeks later ruled in favor of the planters. Throwing out Berger's suit, Estee found that the violations had occurred before passage of the March 3 law.[44] In a sense, the planters had won on a technicality, and had taken steps to protect themselves from further nuisances of this type by arranging for the appointment of a commissioner of immigration to avoid charges that they were "signing up" immigrants before they left Korea. They had no intention, however, of stopping their illegal practice of paying the passage of Korean immigrants.

By the end of September 1903, therefore, all political and legal hurdles had been removed and Korean immigration could be resumed. In fact, 131 Koreans left Korea at the end of August, the first in nearly four months.[45] By chance, Horace Allen was passing through the islands on his way back to Korea after several months of home leave and commented in his diary that, although "some briefless young lawyers brought suit against Mr. Bishop," the courts had ruled in favor of the planters. As a result, he noted with satisfaction, "It seems as though the only way in which the labor agitation in America can prevent the Koreans from coming to Hawaii will be by including them under the Chinese Act."[46] Allen also reassured Governor Nash in Ohio that while his stepson David Deshler at first was "sailing very close to the wind in his immigration matters," the court ruling meant that "Dave was placed in the proper light." Clearly proud of his role in initiating Korean immigration, he concluded his letter to the governor on a positive note: "You see it is a regular God-send to these people to be given that opportunity, while it is a great thing for the Islands. They cannot get Chinese and Japanese are a curse to them. These folk come in as quiet, industrious, largely Christian laborers, and more than meet the best expectations."[47]

In sum, Korean immigration had overcome six obstacles within the first nine months of its existence. In Korea, Horace Allen had deflected opposition from Japanese diplomats, members of Korean officialdom, and American Presbyterian missionaries in P'yŏngyang. In Hawaii, the HSPA had survived investigations by a Board of Special Inquiry and the inspector-general of immigration and a lawsuit in federal court. As a result of these successful manuevers by Allen and the planters, immigration from Korea to Hawaii was able to continue unhindered for another year and a half. With Korean immigration proceeding in a systematic fashion, we can now consider the mechanics of the operation and take a closer look at the Korean immigrants themselves.

9
Systematic Immigration Is Established

During the first six months of Korean immigration to Hawaii, from December 1902 to May 1903, nearly 600 Koreans, consisting of 450 men, 60 women, and 60 children, had entered the Islands before legal troubles had caused the temporary suspension described in chapter 8.[1] Now that the problems had been solved, immigration resumed and continued on a systematic basis for the next year and a half. The relative stability of the process from the fall of 1903 until the spring of 1905 will allow us to examine in more detail the characteristics of the movement, which would reach a total of more than 7,000 immigrants.

Before the suspension of immigration during the summer of 1903, Deshler had established branches of his recruiting business, the East-West Development Company [Tongsŏ kaebal hoesa] in Seoul, P'yŏngyang, and various port cities throughout the peninsula. Moreover, as might be expected, the emigration business benefitted from the disasters and troubles that plagued late Yi Korea. Deshler was quick to seize upon these opportunities to expand his recruiting operations still further. For example, during the early months of recruitment, Deshler was able to capitalize on the recent drought and famine in the province of Hwanghae northwest of Seoul to gather emigrants for Hawaii.[2] And in northeastern Korea, where people were accustomed to moving across the border, emigration to Hawaii was not a completely novel idea. Moreover, as the storm clouds of the Russo-Japanese War gathered in late 1903, Koreans who had migrated to Russia began fleeing the Vladivostok area because the Russians were trying to draft them.[3] Taking advantage of this situation, Deshler opened a branch office in Sŏngjin on the northeast coast.[4] Naturally, after the war broke out in February 1904, recruiting became easier.[5] In all, Deshler had nearly a dozen offices scattered throughout Korea by 1905.[6] These offices were part of what had become a multinational corporation with offices in Korea and Japan and employees of various nationalities.[7]

The first and most important task of these offices was, of course, to attract emigrants by advertising the opportunity of going to Hawaii and the benefits of working there. Accordingly, Deshler's employees placed the notices *(kosi)*, which Lansing had drawn up, in the market-places and other key points throughout the cities.[8] Translated into *han'gŭl*, the notices advertised the availability of jobs in Hawaii, a suitable climate, free education, year-round jobs, wages of $15 a month (the equivalent of 30 *yen* or 57 *wŏn*), and free housing, fuel, water, and medical care.[9] The address of the local office of Deshler's company was on the notice as well.

In addition to posting notices, Deshler's employees gave the hard sell to potential emigrants who came to the offices for further information. The recruiting agents "spared no words to paint a highly attractive picture about life on the Hawaiian plantations," described the climate as "delightful throughout the year," and characterized plantation work as "pleasant."[10] Indeed, this picture of work in Hawaii gained currency among the populace in general. One emigrant recalled that his uncle in P'yŏngyang told him: "The work which lasted only six days a week was more like 'taking a nap under a pear tree,' or 'as easy as eating cake lying down,' " while "earning monthly wages in American gold dollars which was equivalent to the annual salary of the governor of Pyeng-an-do."[11]

While it was natural for the staffers of the East-West Development Company to give exaggerated descriptions of conditions in Hawaii in order to fill their quotas, the lack of legal need to adhere to any truth-in-advertising standards combined with the average Korean's lack of knowledge about real conditions in Hawaii, led in many cases to disappointment and disillusionment. A Korean diplomat (Yun Ch'i-ho) who visited the plantations in 1905 noted that "most of the Koreans I have asked tell me that [they] were deceived by the recruiting agent. They seem to have thought that gold dollars were blossoming on every bush in Hawaii so that all they had to do to be rich was to pick the dollars into their pockets."[12] Still, "the wages offered were high to Koreans who as a whole were very poor" and amounted to "a small fortune for many."[13] And Yun noted that "those who do work earn more than he could in Korea."[14]

Deshler's employees not only manned the offices but also went out among the populace to conduct their recruiting face-to-face. Many of Deshler's Korean employees were Christians, and quite naturally they targeted their recruiting efforts toward Korean Christians. We recall Rev. Charles Bernheisel's lament that an evangelist affiliated with the Ch'ŏndohoe in P'yŏngyang had influenced seven of his young

parishioners to go to Hawaii. And certainly, one of Deshler's first recruiters, Hyŏn Sun, was a Christian. Even Rev. George Heber Jones of
Inch'ŏn, perhaps the strongest supporter of emigration to Hawaii, complained of his flock that "a large number have gone to Hawaii, and
some of its strongest members are engaged in the Hawaiian enterprise,
giving their strength and time to it rather than to the interest of the
church."[15]

In addition to the activities of Deshler's employees who posted
advertisements and personally urged emigration to Hawaii, Koreans
could also hear favorable reports from other sources. If they were Christian, for instance, they might hear of the opportunity from American
missionaries, most of whom approved of Deshler's work. Some, like
Jones, would directly urge emigration. Other missionaries probably
spurred emigration indirectly by describing life in America.[16]

Other Koreans might hear about emigration to Hawaii through
word–of–mouth or newspaper accounts of sailings. They might even
hear about the opportunity from the occasional emigrants who returned
to Korea to take their families back with them to Hawaii.[17] Needless to
say, these returnees, by their actions if not their words, would tend to
present a bright picture of emigration.

After making the decision, the intending emigrant would apply
at the nearest office of the East-West Development Company, where he
would be informed of the departure date. In preparation for the trip
many of the males would alter their hairstyle and clothes. While many
of the Christian emigrants had already rid themselves of their topknot,
others now cut it off in preparation for departure, or did so in Japan en
route to Hawaii.[18] Korean men also began to acquire Western clothes in
preparation for the trip. Female emigrants underwent fewer changes in
hairstyle and clothes, though they discarded their winter clothing.[19]

After undergoing a superficial physical examination at one of
Deshler's branch offices,[20] each emigrant was issued a passport. In order
to obtain a passport, the intending emigrant had first to answer questions regarding his or her name, destination, purpose of the trip, and
how much money was being taken.[21] After satisfactorily answering
these questions, the passport was issued, with the fee of two *wŏn* paid
by the East-West Development Company.[22] Before the demise of the
Yuminwŏn, it was apparent that there was a close working relationship
between Deshler's company and this Department of Emigration, whose
job it was to issue passports. So close was the relationship, in which "the
clerks and interpreters of all field offices of the *Kaebal hoesa . . .* were
authorized to even issue Korean passports to those recruits," that "many
Koreans were unable to distinguish between the work of the *Yuminwŏn*
and the *Tongsŏ kaebal hoesa.*"[23] The clear implication is that Deshler's

organization had actually taken over functions reserved solely for the central government of Korea and that this pattern continued after passporting duties became the nominal province of the Foreign Ministry after the demise of the *Yuminwŏn* in 1903. If this is so, it is further evidence of government laxity that characterized late Yi Korea.

After receiving passports, those emigrants who were not from the immediate area were then led to temporary living quarters near the local offices of the East-West Development Company to wait for a ship to take them to Japan.[24] Those from Seoul traveled the twenty-eight miles to Inch'ŏn by train in two and a half hours.[25]

Typically, the emigrants would board Japanese ships, which dominated the traffic between Korea and Japan. These ships might stop at Chinnamp'o, Inch'ŏn, Mokp'o, and Pusan, for instance, before proceeding to Japan, picking up emigrants at each stop.[26] In the spring of 1904 Deshler bought his own ship, christening it *Ohio*, to carry emigrants as well as freight (Deshler still worked for the American Trading Company which had offices in Inch'ŏn and Kobe).[27] In fact, one of Deshler's early passengers on the *Ohio* was Syngman Rhee.[28]

The short trip from Korea to Japan was often rough. One of the emigrants recalled his departure from Chinnamp'o aboard the *Ohio* thus: "As soon as the ship was out in the open sea it began to rock and roll, and I was already getting a dizzy spell. By nightfall, the ship was rounding the Jang-san-got Point, the promontory famous for innumerable shipwrecks. The boat was now rolling violently, tossing around all the movable things in it from side to side. I was one of them. It made me very sick, indeed, and it made everybody else sick."[29]

In Japan, the emigrants usually disembarked at Kobe, where Deshler had offices as well as a residence, although they might also disembark at Nagasaki or Yokohama. Here they underwent a second, more rigorous, physical examination which about 5 percent failed, mostly because they suffered from trachoma. The fees for the examination, inoculations, baggage handling, and other incidental expenses amounted to $1.25, which was paid by the planters.[30] Once these formalities were completed, the Koreans awaited the arrival of the larger trans-Pacific steamers that would take them to Honolulu. In Kobe, this time was spent waiting at an inn which could accommodate about 300 people and which was run by a Portuguese man named Medias who was assisted by Japanese and Korean workers.[31]

The trans-Pacific steamers docked either at Nagasaki, Kobe, and/or Yokohama before starting out on the ten-day voyage to Honolulu. The Korean emigrants boarding these ships rode in steerage—the fare was about $35—passage being paid (illegally, of course) by the planters via Deshler and his "bank."[32] Once on board they experienced a

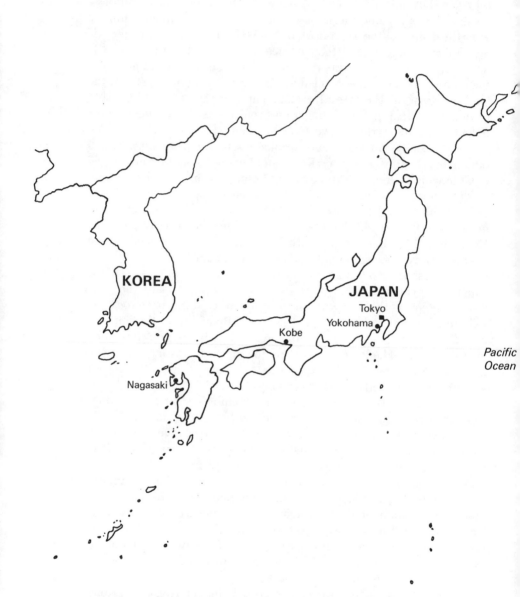

Japanese seaports where the Koreans transferred to trans-Pacific liners. (Tokyo included as a reference point.)

few changes. For example, their food was flavored with Japanese-style shoyu which was too sweet for the Koreans, necessitating the addition of salt. More important, steerage conditions required men and women to occupy the same living area, a marked departure from the mores of a society that maintained the Confucian separation of the sexes.[33]

One of the most important features of the trans-Pacific crossing, however, was the constant intrusion of Christianity. Each boatload of Koreans appeared to have included at least one minister, who took it upon himself to convert his fellow immigrants by telling them that "they were going to America, a Christian country, and that it would be the proper and advantageous thing to become Christians." According to one somewhat exaggerated account, "All the young Koreans were eager to succeed in their venture, so one and all professed to become Christians."[34]

Upon docking in Honolulu the immigrants had to pass still another physical examination and had to show they possessed at least $50 in "pocket money" to guarantee that they would not become public charges. Once having passed the inspection, the immigrants were "signed up" to work on the plantations. As a result of the lawsuits, a Mr. Hague had been employed to sign up Koreans to work on the plantations with half his salary paid by Deshler and the other half by the HSPA.[35] Needless to say, Hague would generally "recruit" all the immigrants from Korea. By 1904, Hague had been replaced by a man named J. D. Julian.[36]

Those whose destinations were on Oahu boarded the railway to take them to their assigned plantations, while those who were assigned to plantations on Maui, Hawaii, or Kauai immediately boarded smaller interisland ships for their final destinations.[37] The arrival of a large group of Koreans to one of the outer islands was usually a newsworthy event.[38]

With each boatload went one interpreter to assist with the immigration inspection at Honolulu and to give the "correct" answer to the inspectors. As we have seen, these interpreters accompanied their groups to their final destinations, where they worked as interpreters at wages of $25 per month, about ten dollars more than the wages of the field workers. On the plantation, the interpreter acted as intermediary between the non-Korean-speaking luna (foreman) and the Korean workers. As Koreans continued to arrive, the need for interpreters on the plantations decreased, with the result that some resigned to go into other lines of work. Hyŏn Sun, for example, resigned to become a minister among the Koreans in Hawaii.[39] Others, finding themselves unemployed, were returned to Korea at the expense of the HSPA.[40]

Once the Koreans had arrived at their respective plantations, they began work in the cane fields with a wage of $15 a month. The work was six days a week, ten hours a day. If the Korean group was large enough, they were given housing in a separate Korean "camp." More often, though, the numbers of Koreans being relatively small, they were assigned houses among those of other immigrants. The managers of the plantations had to accommodate the new arrivals, arranging for rice to be delivered,[41] arranging for their letters to relatives and friends in Korea to be sent to David Deshler who would then mail them in Korea,[42] and assisting the Koreans with their banking needs.[43]

We have already noted that about 600 Koreans had arrived before immigration was temporarily suspended in the summer of 1903. When it was resumed in late August, approximately 600 additional Koreans arrived during the fall for a total of nearly 1,200 arrivals in the year 1903. For that year, the ratio of Japanese to Korean immigrants was about three to one. In 1904 the number of Korean immigrants began to increase, and in the first six months of that year about 1,500 arrivals were recorded. This increase reduced the ratio of Japanese to Korean immigrants to only two to one.[44] And in the last six months of 1904, Korean arrivals increased to 2,000, so that the numbers of Japanese and Korean arrivals were nearly equal. Finally, in the final six months of Korean immigration, from January to June 1905, more than 2,800 arrived, about the same number who came from Japan.[45]

During the period January 1903 to July 1905, Korean immigration totalled slightly more than 7,000 arrivals in sixty-five separate shippings. As we have seen, in these two and a half years immigration rates climbed steadily until, at its height, as many Koreans as Japanese were coming into Hawaii. That was quite an achievement, considering that Japanese immigration had been going on continuously since 1885 whereas the immigration of Koreans was in its infancy. It also indicates that the HSPA trustees were pleased with the Koreans who had been recruited primarily to offset the predominance of Japanese workers on the plantations.

The brief period of Korean immigration to Hawaii was not without its controversies and problems. We have seen that Horace Allen in Korea and the HSPA in Hawaii faced no fewer than six obstacles to immigration from Korea. Now we turn briefly to problems faced by the Korean immigrants themselves during this period.

One problem for would-be Korean immigrants to Hawaii was a result of the suspension of immigration during the investigations and the lawsuit in Hawaii during the summer of 1903. When one group of poor people from Hwanghae-do sold their property and arrived in Inch'ŏn in

May with a view to emigrating to Hawaii, Deshler was unable to accommodate them. Since they could not return to their homes, they were forced to become beggars in Seoul.[46]

For those already "in the pipeline," the suspension of immigration was even more serious and required the personal intervention of David Deshler. Two hundred Koreans in Nagasaki were en route to Hawaii when the suspension was imposed. Deshler wanted to give them return tickets to Korea and the sum of 2 *yen* each. But the Koreans had heard that they would receive over 30 *yen* per month in wages in Hawaii and as a consequence had sold their homes and furniture and had brought their families with them. Since they had no jobs or homes or families to return to in Korea, they demanded that Deshler give each 50 *yen* or else they would refuse to return. When violence threatened, Deshler turned the problem over to a local Japanese employee; he asked the advice of the Japanese Foreign Ministry, which advised the Koreans to return to Korea and then file claims for damages there. As a result, 160 returned to Pusan while the remaining 40 returned to Inch'ŏn.[47]

By far the most serious controversy that affected Korean immigrants to Hawaii during this period was the matter of assisted passage by the planters. In theory, immigrants from Korea would have to pay boat passage from Korea to Japan and from Japan to Hawaii. In addition, they would be responsible for incidental charges such as passports, inoculations, and physical examinations. Finally, they would be required to be in possession of at least $50 in "pocket money" upon arrival in Hawaii. Added up, these expenses would total more than $100. This was a princely sum in Korea at the turn of the century. Even Horace Allen had admitted in his letters to Dole and Hay that most of the emigrants would have to borrow the money.

An analysis of the kind of people who emigrated from Korea will be found in chapter 10. Suffice it to say here that there probably existed an inverse relationship between wealth and the desire to emigrate. Accordingly, we would expect that most of the emigrants were from among the poorer segments of Korean society and therefore unlikely to be able to obtain such a large amount on their own. An examination of the prevailing wage rate in late Yi Korea reinforces this finding. Four independent sources suggest that average wages for workers in Korea at the turn of the century ranged from five to forty cents a day.[48]

Thus most of the emigrants from Korea had to borrow money to go to Hawaii and the institution to which they turned was the Deshler "Bank," the brainchild of Horace Allen. The Deshler Bank was housed in the same building with the East-West Development Company, indicating that its business was intimately associated with the recruiting of immigrants. In fact, the Deshler Bank obtained its first capital from the

$25,000 draft that Bishop had brought with him to Korea in late 1902. Thereafter, Deshler was able to obtain access to planter money to pay passage and provide pocket money by withdrawing money from HSPA accounts maintained in banks in New York and San Francisco.[49] It was in this manner that the bank laundered the illegal passage money provided by the planters. Moreover, the Deshler Bank provided the conduit by which the planters paid Deshler for recruiting. Deshler received a commission of $54 for every man and $41 for every woman.[50]

From the very beginning, then, the Deshler Bank was not an ordinary bank. Its sole depositor was the Hawaiian Sugar Planters Association and the only business the bank seemed to conduct was to lend money to Koreans who were about to emigrate to Hawaii. This was how the planters arranged to conceal the payment of passage and the provision of pocket money. The fact that the planters were able to get away with this illegal practice for the duration of Korean immigration to Hawaii is testimony to their ingenuity.

The activities of the Deshler Bank also signally affected the individual Korean immigrant after arrival in Hawaii. There were, in essence, two sets of money involved: passage money and pocket money. The question of pocket money is rather straightforward. After the immigrant had shown his $50 (in the form of a note drawn on the Deshler Bank), he returned it to Deshler's agent (Hague or Julian) at the dock in Honolulu after signing up for work on the sugar plantations, thus "repaying" his loan.[51] The question of passage money is more complex and there is some question as to whether the Korean immigrants were obligated to repay it (the sum involved was about $50).

Several sources indicate that the passage money was meant to be a loan which must be paid back from the immigrant's plantation wages. This was the information that Deshler gave to the Japanese consul in Inch'ŏn.[52] Hyŏn Sun indicated that the Korean immigrants had ten months in which to pay back the passage money.[53] Rev. S. F. Moore who visited the Koreans in Hawaii said that the Koreans were repaying Deshler at the rate of one dollar a month.[54] One elderly immigrant recalled that he had three years to repay the loan.[55] Another immigrant wrote that they had taken an oath to repay the passage money.[56] The preponderance of evidence, then, seems to suggest that the money which the planters had advanced to the Korean immigrants (via Deshler) would have to be repaid.

Yet it must be remembered that assisting the immigrants from Korea by lending them money for passage (or even paying it outright) was illegal. And monthly deductions from wages would call attention to the fact that the planters had organized a system to assist Korean immigration illegally. Moreover, demands that they repay the money risked raising the ire of Koreans who were unhappy in the sugarcane fields and who might raise an outcry against paying back the passage money—an action that might come to the attention of the legal authorities. Having barely survived the immigration investigations and lawsuit of 1903, the planters wanted to avoid any remaining suspicion that they were involved in breaking the law.

As a result of these considerations, the planters changed their policy midway through the period of Korean immigration. That is, they no longer allowed repayment of passage money to Deshler by means of payroll deduction in order to quell any suspicions of illegal activities.[57] This change in policy seems to have worked to the detriment of Deshler's finances, and in an apparent split with the planters, Deshler made at least one attempt to collect what he felt was due him. In that instance, Deshler sent an associate by the name of A. W. Taylor, with whom he had worked at the Unsan Gold Mines in Korea, to Hawaii in 1904 to link up with his agent in Honolulu, J. D. Julian. Together, the two went to Ewa Plantation on Oahu with a Korean interpreter demanding that the Koreans repay their passage money. So abusive was Taylor's speech and actions that he was assaulted by the Koreans there. In court he stated that he was a (Deshler) bank clerk trying to collect money when he was assaulted by the Koreans. As a result, the judge sentenced eight Koreans to three months at hard labor. For his part, however, Taylor did not attempt to collect any more money and left the Islands.[58]

The planters were concerned that such incidents would eventually arouse suspicion that they were illegally assisting Korean immigration. So, soon after the incident with Taylor, the trustees of the HSPA informed the plantation managers that any repayment of passage money would be accomplished only by Koreans themselves individually writing notes payable to the Deshler Bank.[59] Repayment thus became an individual responsibility rather than an obligation organized and enforced by the planters.

Repayment of passage money also became the first major issue confronting the first nationalist organization of Koreans in Hawaii—the *Sinminhoe* (New Peoples' Association)—and also resulted in the first split in the fledgling Korean community in Hawaii. The *Sinminhoe* was organized in August 1903 by Korean members of the Methodist Church and other educated immigrants with the aim of promoting national unity and the enlightenment and reform of the home government. In December a branch was formed on the island of Kauai. When attempts were made to force the immigrants to repay passage money, the Kyŏng-ju faction of the organization argued that the debt should be forgiven, considering the difficult life of the Koreans in Hawaii, and notified all

Koreans not to pay when people like Taylor and Julian showed up demanding repayment. However, another faction of the *Sinminhoe* which was dominated by non-Christians supported the efforts of Deshler's agents to have the debts repaid. According to Kim Wŏn-yong, this schism led to the dissolution of the organization in April 1904.[60]

As a result of all this confusion, some Korean immigrants wound up repaying some or all of their passage money while others were able to avoid completely any repayment. That Deshler continued to press for repayment even after immigration from Korea ended is suggested by allegations that Deshler himself came to Hawaii with An Chŏng-su in 1906 to collect from the Koreans.[61]

10
Characteristics of the Immigrants and Why They Came

THE Korean immigrants to Hawaii differed significantly from the Japanese and Chinese who came to Hawaii, and they also differed from their Korean countrymen. And the key to these differences lay in large part in their diversity.

Perhaps the most significant characteristic of the 7,000 Koreans who came to Hawaii between 1903 and 1905 was that the great majority came from cities and not from rural districts of Korea. Bernice Kim, who interviewed immigrants in the 1930s stated that "nearly all had been city dwellers" and "very few came from the rural districts."[1] Nearly half came from the Seoul-Inch'ŏn-Suwŏn area, perhaps the most "urbanized" district of Korea at the time, and the other half came from other cities scattered throughout the Korean peninsula.[2] This distribution would be expected because of the locations of the branch offices of the *Tongsŏ kaebal hoesa*. Because many of the immigrants were Christians and because Christians, both foreign missionaries and native converts, were concentrated in the cities, this urban origin is not surprising. That Korean emigrants were primarily from the cities distinguishes them at once from their countrymen, for most Koreans at the turn of the century lived on farms. Moreover, unlike the Korean emigrants, the vast majority of Chinese and Japanese emigrants were from rural areas and came from primarily one part of their respective countries.

It is not surprising, then, that the occupations of the emigrants prior to departure were essentially urban-type, only a small number being farmers.[3] Bernice Kim, for example, concluded that less than one-seventh of the immigrants had been farmers and that the largest proportion had worked as common laborers or coolies. Other occupations included ex-soldiers, minor government clerks, political refugees, students, policemen, miners, woodcutters, household servants, and Buddhist monks.[4] It is very likely that many of the emigrants were under- or unemployed, one immigrant recalling that many were "penniless rakes."[5] This diverse set of occupations indicates that the emigrants differed from the majority of their countrymen. It also distinguishes them from the Japanese and Chinese immigrants, who were primarily farmers.

While most of the Koreans came from cities and had nonfarming occupations, circumstantial evidence suggests that many of the emigrants had not always been city dwellers. Rather, the picture is one of people having been uprooted from homes in the countryside and fleeing to the cities. In the years between 1894 and 1905 no fewer than three major armed conflicts (the Tonghak Rebellion, the Sino-Japanese War, and the Russo-Japanese War) took place on Korean soil. We have already noted that drought and famine had created difficulty for those living in rural Hwanghae Province and elsewhere. Moreover, oppressive taxes, banditry, disease, and other calamities also took their toll, causing some Korean peasants to flee unemployed into the cities, away from their ancestral graveyards and the villages which had been for centuries their families' homes. In a sense, then, many of the emigrants were rootless refugees in their own country and thus had fewer ties to hold them back.[6]

The social characteristics of the Korean immigrants were as diverse as their geographic origins and occupations. It is clear, for example, that many of the immigrants were from the lower fringes of Korean society. The assistant manager of the Unsan mines observed that most of the immigrants "are drafted from the seaport scum."[7] A minister in Hawaii noted that "their habits, brought from their native land, did not contribute to cleanliness."[8] Another cleric identified them as in the "lower" class.[9] Finally, Rev. Moffett in P'yŏngyang had remarked that "a far larger number of men less advanced and of less hopeful character have gone to Hawaii."[10] Certainly this is not surprising—most migrations in history have consisted of people whose opportunities and status in their home countries were marginal.

Yet, while many of the Korean emigrants did come from the lower strata of the Korean social spectrum, the diversity of the group was such that it also included some from relatively more advantaged backgrounds. Such a conclusion can be drawn at least indirectly from the observations of a minister in Hawaii who wrote in obvious reference to upper-class Koreans: "A few have come who are not at all fitted for the work, being unused to hard toil, having too little strength or an enfeebled health. A small number of such characters are dissatisfied and are a burden to the Korean community."[11] The director of a night school for Korean adults in Honolulu reported that "those who have so far come to us have appeared to be a superior class and deeply interested."[12] From a secondary source we learn that 40 percent of the immigrants may have been literate,[13] and this is borne out in part by interview data.[14] Finally, even a few *yangban,* the highest class in Korean society, were numbered among the emigrants.[15] In sum, then, all levels of Korean society were represented among the Korean immigrants to Hawaii. Such was not the case among the Japanese and Chinese immigrants to Hawaii, nor was it typical of the Korean populace in general, which was overwhelmingly rural, farming, homogeneous, and illiterate.

Two characteristics that Korean immigrants had in common with Japanese and Chinese immigrants were age and sex. Using interview data, obituaries, and government documents, we can conclude that most were single young men between the ages of twenty and thirty. There were about ten men for every woman, and children made up less than 7 percent of the total.[16]

The final characteristic of many of the Korean immigrants which distinguished them from their fellow Koreans as well as from Chinese and Japanese immigrants was their connection with Christianity. This relationship is important for understanding, in part, some of the reasons why 7,000 Koreans left Korea for Hawaii.

Just as there were many different kinds of people who left Korea for Hawaii, there were many different reasons for their going. Some reasons were more important than others and, for many, it was no doubt a combination of reasons. In addition, some of the goals and aspirations of the immigrants changed with the passage of time and the circumstances that surrounded them and their native country.

One reason for emigrating was the hope of making a quick fortune in America and then returning to Korea rich and respected. This is the sojourner paradigm which first was identified with early Chinese immigrants who called America *chin-shan* or Gold Mountain.[17] It was also true to some extent among the Japanese immigrants. It is therefore not surprising that the same motivation was present among some of the Korean immigrants to Hawaii. As we have already seen, Deshler's agents tended to exaggerate in describing the advantages of life and work in Hawaii. Moreover, literate Koreans in the cities were exposed to reports in the newspapers which, like the one recounting the presidential election of 1900, stated that the United States was the richest country in the world.[18] A minister who worked closely with the Koreans in Hawaii noted that "many of them were young men ambitious to make their fortunes abroad."[19] And one immigrant recalled that he came to Hawaii at the age of twenty-eight to "make a lot of money and return home to Korea."[20] Even a half-century later, a newspaper reporter in Honolulu wrote: "After fifty years, few have realized the original dream of all immigrants, to return to the land of their birth after amassing a fortune on American soil."[21]

While some of the immigrants from Korea may have had unrealistic hopes about amassing wealth in a short time and then returning home, it is likely that this was not the predominant motivation for the majority of immigrants. Only about one-sixth of the Korean immigrants returned to their homeland, compared with at least half of the Japanese and Chinese immigrants.[22] A large number of Korean immigrants lacked a sojourner mentality because the terrible state of affairs in late Yi Korea did not augur well for a return home. There were also other factors that competed with or supplemented the sojourner impetus for emigration. This is not to say that most of the immigrants were not optimistic about their chances for success abroad. Rather, it suggests that the immigrants who were motivated solely by the prospect of getting rich quickly and then returning were more likely than not to be without a family. Once these fortune-hunters came face-to-face with the reality of wages of 70 cents a day, many of them began to save their money merely to pay for the return passage to Korea. We may conjecture that those who emigrated to make a fortune would be the least likely to remain permanently in Hawaii and probably made up the bulk of those who returned.

A second reason why some of the immigrants left Korea for Hawaii was the opportunity to get a better education for themselves or their children. Horace Allen's letter to Secretary of State Hay mentioned a desire for education "so strong that genteel Koreans have taken up menial callings to that end. . . . The idea of obtaining an education for their children seems to be an incentive as well."[23] The desire for an education was reported as a reason by one researcher interviewing immigrants in the late 1940s,[24] and results from a survey conducted in 1970 showed that 5 percent gave this as a purpose for emigrating.[25] It might also be noted that Yi In-jik's 1906 novel *Hyŏl ŭi nu* [Tears of blood], which was serialized in a daily newspaper and won wide acclaim, portrayed a protagonist who went to study in the United States because he believed that a man with a great sense of mission should not be tied down by concerns for his family if he wished to prepare himself for achieving great things for his country. While the quest for an education was apparently not a major cause for emigration, we can surmise that those who emigrated primarily for this reason would be more likely to become permanent in the United States than the sojourner type.

The desire of Korean Christians for religious freedom was another reason for emigration. To be sure, persecution of those who followed "heterodox" religions had occurred not long before, and the number of Christians (only 100,000 of a total population of 8 million) represented only a small minority breaking with tradition. We have already noted the overwhelming influence of Christianity among many of the Korean immigrants. Thus it is not surprising that a Korean Christian in the 1930s would write: "As the Korean embraced Christianity, he began to look for a place where it might be lived in peace. So when in 1903 the call came for him to emigrate to a country where he could enjoy religious freedom . . . the teachings of the missionary had prepared him for emigration." Yet one must conclude that this was not a major consideration for the majority of the emigrants. In fact, the same writer admitted that "to say that the Christian urge was the greatest among the many that was bringing this strange people from a far-away land to Hawaiian shores would probably not be true."[26]

Another possible reason for emigration may be traced to nationalistic feelings related to reforming the home government or opposing the Japanese takeover of Korea. This is an attractive thesis which is given credence by the fact that Tosan An Ch'ang-ho was at that time involved in setting up the organization that would later become the *Kongnip Hyŏphoe* (Mutual Assistance Association) in San Francisco and also by the fact that the Koreans in Hawaii were soon to become highly politicized in their anti-Japanese nationalistic activities. In addition, the activities of the *Sinminhoe* in Hawaii, discussed earlier in reference to the repayment of passage money, certainly had reform of the home government as one of its aims.[27] It is also quite clear that many Koreans, especially those in the cities, had been aware of the buildup of Japanese power since the signing of the Anglo-Japanese Alliance in 1902. Those who would be directly affected included soldiers, policemen, and government officials. Others would be Christians who had aligned themselves with anti-Japanese missionaries. Even the Japanese government admitted that "among the Koreans resident in Siberia, China, Hawaii and the United States are found not a few who fled the country on account of political disappointment."[28] We can surmise that those emigrants who left for this reason would be the least likely to return to Korea, especially after the establishment of the Protectorate in 1905 and annexation in 1910.

Yet, like the desire for quick riches, an education, or religious freedom, emigration for purely nationalistic purposes must be considered a minor motivation at best, despite the later and somewhat exaggerated claims of some missionaries and nationalist figures.[29] In a survey taken in 1970, for instance, only 13 percent gave fear of Japanese domination as their reason for leaving.[30] While it would not be unfair to say that the decline of the Korean government was a major factor in the decision of many emigrants to leave, it is difficult to translate their departure into active opposition to the government. Moreover, while some emigrants, notably ex-soldiers unemployed when the Korean army was considerably reduced during the Russo-Japanese War, could reasonably blame the Japanese government for their predicament, their removal to sugarcane fields on islands in the middle of the Pacific Ocean seems an unlikely response to Japanese imperialism. Indeed, we must look elsewhere to discover the major reasons for the emigration of 7,000 Koreans to Hawaii.

In attempting to analyze the major causes of the exodus of Koreans to Hawaii it is necessary to consider the indirect influence of Christianity upon many of the immigrants. Because the percentage of Christians in Korea at the time was negligible and because a large proportion of the emigrants were connected with Christianity, it is logical to expect that a brief examination of Korean Christians will yield information about Korean emigrants to the United States.[31]

Most of the American Protestant missionaries at the turn of the century attributed the growth of Christianity in Korea to admiration of Western life.[32] Horace Allen put it this way:

> They admire the comforts . . . of the home life of the strangers. They go home to ponder on the religion which takes hold of the present life of man and makes it more enjoyable. They mark our cheerful faces and our enjoyment of life and wonder at the cause. They listen to the tales of the achievements of Western science. . . . When they realize that all this is the outcome and development of our religion, the practical value of Christianity makes a powerful appeal to them.[33]

This view was echoed by those on the receiving end, as the following statement by the Korean Christian quote earlier attests:

> To the timid, stoical Korean, the message was one of hope and life. Eagerly he asked of its power and a sample of its results. The one was told him by the missionaries, the other was pointed out to him in the advanced life of the United States. Soon the United States was the hope of Korea, for was it not there that the wondrous Cross had brought beneficent results? Was it not there that the pagan ceased from troubling and the Christian could rest? Was it not worth the while of any timid, down-trodden Korean laborer to make the attempt of reaching this haven of peace and plenty?[34]

The desire for a better life along Western lines became the primary reason not only for conversion to Christianity but also for emigration to the United States. Oppression and poverty fell most heavily upon the lower classes of Korean society, and it was at this level in the cities and surrounding towns that American Protestant (mainly Presbyterian) missions carried out their proselytizing activities. Dissatisfaction with their lot in society provided compelling reasons for such Koreans to convert to Christianity. The converts naturally turned to missionaries for advice and assistance.[35]

Because of the favorable comments made by most American missionaries about Deshler's enterprise, there came to be a general association among the Korean populace between missionaries and emigration to the United States. The following passage, in which a missionary recounts the experience of one of his colleagues, amply illustrates this association:

> She says that poverty unquestionably brought the girl to her but not many days had passed before the mother felt it better to brave poverty than to trust her child to a foreigner. The neighbors accused her of being a bad woman and an unnatural mother. They said it might be well for a time. There would be plenty of rice and good clothes but by and by the girl would be carried away to America and what her fate would be no one could tell. An assurance was finally given in writing that the child should never be carried out of the country, which partially satisfied the mother though it was several months before she was really at ease.[36]

What this suggests is that Koreans who were not exposed to American missionaries in the cities would tend to be more reluctant to emigrate than those accustomed to associating with them. Indeed, exposure to missionaries (and perhaps conversion) was but one, albeit important, influence on the decision to emigrate.

The isolation that characterized the "Hermit Kingdom" could not help but produce among the Korean populace a state of mind of provincialism. Isolation, traditionalism, Confucianism, and conservatism characterized the average Korean, especially in the rural areas where most Koreans resided. In the years following the opening of Korea in 1876, foreign influences, confined mainly to the cities, began to make inroads on Korean traditional society. These influences along with revolutions in transportation and communication broadened the horizons of Koreans who came into contact with them, enabling some to consider the possibility of overseas emigration, an idea that would have been almost unthinkable twenty years earlier.

These changes, which occurred over a relatively short time, were limited, of course, but were momentous nonetheless. Diplomats and students regularly traveled to the United States and returned to Korea. Even Emperor Kojong's son, Prince Eui Wha (Ŭihwa), attended school in the United States. One returned student, Philip Jaisohn (Sŏ Chae-p'il), started the first newspaper to be published partly in English. Other newspapers soon appeared, carrying news of foreign places and events. In 1901 the YMCA was established in Seoul and two years later Korea mounted an exhibit at the 1903 World's Fair in St. Louis. In 1900 the first railroad was completed in Korea, linking Seoul and Inch'ŏn. Four years later Seoul and Pusan would be similarly linked. Inside Seoul, electric streetcars built by Americans crisscrossed the city with only an occasional unfortunate accident. In fact, Americans outnumbered all Westerners in Seoul and competed successfully for concessions.

But westernization proceeded selectively in Korea, being confined mainly to Seoul and other large coastal cities. In the countryside, where the majority of Koreans lived, Western influence was muted and change yielded to tradition. Thus while foreign and Western influences elicited a favorable response from a small minority in the cities, for the rest of Korea anything foreign was suspect. Distrust of things foreign extended to missionaries as well as foreign contact in general. Consider the following letter from a worried Korean mother to her son who was at that time a member of a diplomatic mission traveling abroad:

> Dear Boy, I hear that foreigners don't use rice. I can't imagine how anybody could live without eating "pap" three times a day. When I think how hungry you must be on cakes made of some kind of flour, I can neither sleep nor eat. Don't you, even for fun, put on foreign clothes. O how ugly a foreigner appears in tight black trousers looking like a pair of walking stilts. My son, I hear that Korean youths who go abroad contract the bad habit of smoking cigarettes, instead of our long pipes and of loving foreign costume despising the "topknot" and the beautiful Korean dress and hats of liberal dimensions. I cannot explain this change of heart otherwise than by supposing that when a Korean goes abroad, foreigners give him a certain medicine to compass the change. It seems but natural that foreigners should desire us to adopt their modes of dress, because the comeliness of our costume hurts their pride. They say many a foreigner remains a life long bachelor. No wonder. What girl would marry him so badly dressed. Once in the province of Kang-kei, a foreign gentleman came to see your father. He wanted to take our pictures. Because your father insisted on it, I consented to have my picture taken. Seeing me, the foreigner offered to shake hands with me; but I was so scared that I left the hall, photography or no photography, and I was sick four days afterward. Remember all this, my boy, refuse to take the heart changing medicine, and come back to me soon unchanged in taste and dress.[37]

These attitudes would most likely be found in those who were older, who resided in the countryside, whose places of residence were their birthplace, and who were not Christian; in other words, most of the Korean population. Koreans sharing a philosophy like the one exhibited in this letter would probably not be quick to consider emigrating to the United States.

On the other hand, for young men in the cities who were accustomed to missionary and other American influences, the prospect of emigration did not seem so frightening. For some, torn from their traditional habitat by war or poverty, the city was their second home. Rootless, unable to perform the required Confucian rituals at the ancestral graveyard, and dispossessed of farms and perhaps family, they poured into the cities without jobs, becoming primary candidates not only for conversion to Christianity but also for emigration to the United States.

In what can only be described as a classic "push-pull" phenomenon, we must conclude that the overwhelming majority of Korean immigrants left because of a combination of bad conditions in Korea and good prospects in Hawaii. Such a formulation is not surprising as it was the engine of most migratory movements in modern history.

In the Oh Survey of 1970, more than two-thirds of the respondents indicated one of the following four categories as their reason for leaving: "poverty" (17 percent), "poverty and reported good prospects in Hawaii" (16 percent), "reported good prospects in Hawaii" (20 percent), and "reported good earnings in Hawaii" (16 percent).[38] We have already examined the "pull" factors of Hawaii in sections on recruiting and the "sojourner" explanation for emigration. We now examine more closely the "push" factors in Korea.

Accounts of Koreans in Hawaii written not long after the annexation of Korea by Japan uniformly attribute bad economic conditions as the primary reason for emigration. This is true not only of Korean accounts,[39] but also in three separate Japanese accounts.[40]

Among the conditions in Korea which led to poverty among the lower classes was periodic famine, which from time to time afflicted various parts of Korea in the last years of the Yi dynasty. Beginning in 1898, famine hit Hwanghae-do and Chŏlla Namdo. In desperation, Emperor Kojong ordered the government to suspend all civil engineering projects except urgent ones, to stop the export of rice, and to import rice from Annam. In the fall of 1901, Kojong established the *Hyeminwŏn* (People-Assisting Bureau) to help starving people—in imitation of a similar office set up during King Injo's reign—and donated 20,000 *wŏn* for relief. Nonetheless, provincial reports showed an ever-increasing number of needy families and agrarian revolts.[41] That famine and emigration were linked at least briefly is suggested by several scholars[42] and is buttressed by the fact that the Korean name of the Department of Emigration *(Yuminwŏn)* meant "People-easing bureau." This suggests that emigration was perhaps seen initially as a method of easing the people's lives. When emigration to Hawaii finally began, a local Korean newspaper attributed it to famine.[43] And even Horace Allen mentioned "the severe famine of the past winter" in explaining the emigration to Governor Dole of Hawaii.[44]

Famine was not the only "push" factor impelling Koreans to leave for Hawaii at the turn of the century. A cholera epidemic was raging. Banditry in several parts of the country continued unchecked as a result of the recent wars. The counterfeiting of nickel pieces caused inflation and monetary instability. Thus, even if one had a steady job in Korea, times could be difficult. Consider the following passage:

> It has been mentioned above that wages in Korea were nothing. The laborer was worse off than the beggar. His life was but a mere existence just beyond the pale of starvation. To the laboring class in Korea, the call to work where fuel and shelter were assured, with any kind of a cash wage, was a call to the land of abundance, and he came because of this opportunity to earn what to him was a respectable wage.[45]

Apart from natural disasters and general instability must be added the venality of the Korean government. At the end of a long dynastic cycle, late Yi Korea seemed enervated by corruption, high taxes, and general mismanagement, which further added to the discontent of the people. Horace Allen, for example, suggested that "considerable numbers have desired to go to the islands with the hope of bettering their condition and escaping the persistent oppression of their tax collectors."[46] A missionary in P'yŏngyang wrote, "In a country as wretchedly ruled as this there is beginning to be much restlessness and a desire to get out of it is not to be wondered at."[47] Finally, another missionary in P'yŏngyang wrote:

> You will hear of the rumors of war, probably, more than we do. The Koreans are much disturbed and some are already fleeing to the mountains. We can only trust there is nothing in the rumors and that there will be no war. We have never known such unrest among the Koreans due to the excitement of so many going to [the] Hawaiian Islands to work on the sugar plantations, and the dreadful hard times . . . not that the crops here are so poor (there is a famine in other parts of Korea) but everything has gone up so in price and money is simply no good, which makes everything so uncertain. Still the Koreans go on building the palace here at Pyeng Yang in spite of the hardships, squan-

dering so much money, and just squeezing the poor people to death. We can't blame them for wanting to go to America.[48]

It seems clear that the majority of Koreans who left for Hawaii did so not only because of the good reports they had heard about Hawaii but also because they were escaping from poverty, instability, and oppression in Korea. Together, these two factors provided a powerful motivating force in fueling the movement to Hawaii at the turn of the century.

11

Koreans As Workers

BY the spring of 1905, the planters had had more than two years of experience with the Koreans as sugarcane workers. They were now in a position to assess their worth as plantation laborers and, more important, as an offset to the Japanese.

At the end of the first year of immigration, the Koreans were still receiving praise. In his presidential address to the HSPA at the end of 1903, H. A. Isenberg cited the "small number of Coreans, who, so far, have given satisfaction."[1] This led to a decision to double the number of Korean immigrants.[2] And at the plantations themselves, individual managers continued to press their parent body (the HSPA) for additional Korean workers.[3]

Koreans had been desired by the planters primarily as an offset to the majority Japanese and secondarily for their qualities as reliable, stable, inexpensive, and docile workers. Indeed, these two sets of attributes were related. But the Koreans were not quite as docile as the planters had hoped, although they remained more tractable than the Japanese. The first indication of trouble came at the end of 1903 when the HSPA trustees met to consider how to handle some Koreans from Waiakea and Wainaku plantations on the island of Hawaii who had come to Honolulu with complaints of ill-treatment. At the meeting, "it was moved by Mr. Swanzy that the Koreans be informed that the plantations of this Island cannot engage them, and that they must return to Hilo where their services are needed, and in consideration of their consenting to do so, their passage will be paid."[4] One month later, Kilauea Plantation on Kauai reported that "one whole batch of sixty-two Koreans suddenly quit work with a view to coming back to Honolulu," drawing the laconic comment from Giffard, "It is strange that Andrew never can handle his labor the same as other managers do."[5] In the

114

spring of 1904, a "temporary disturbance" among Koreans was noted at Laupahoehoe Plantation (Hawaii) in connection with the discharge of a Korean interpreter.[6] In the summer of that year 200 Koreans on Waipahu Plantation on Oahu mobbed the plantation doctor who, they claimed, killed an ailing Korean worker by kicking him in the stomach.[7] And, finally, in June of 1905, a strike involving 160 Koreans occurred when they protested the firing of 80 of their countrymen for beating a luna at Maui's Paia Plantation. In sympathy, 80 more Koreans at the Kailua camp went on strike, resulting in the arrest of four of the leaders and a near riot.[8] To be sure, a handful of minor incidents over the course of two years does not constitute consistently volatile behavior. In fact, a report at the time concluded, "In the case of Koreans, these troubles have been in nearly all cases entirely among themselves."[9]

More than making up for these minor disturbances among themselves and with the planters was the value of Koreans as strikebreakers to offset the more numerous Japanese. In December of 1904, for example, when half the 2,500 Japanese workers on Waialua Plantation went on strike, the planters collected 250 Koreans from various plantations to take the place temporarily of the striking Japanese.[10] Six months later, when some Japanese went on strike at Wailuku, Maui, the planters rounded up 50 Koreans as substitutes.[11]

And although it is beyond the scope of this study, it should be noted that Koreans were used in similar fashion in the large-scale Japanese-inspired strikes of 1909 and 1920. Their willingness to participate in these two labor actions was determined not only by the greater financial rewards offered to strikebreakers but also by Korean animosity toward the Japanese because of the establishment of the Protectorate in 1905 and annexation of Korea in 1910.

While the Koreans generally got good marks for their greater docility and their utility as strikebreakers, to what extent did they exhibit stability as workers? By 1905, the planters were complaining bitterly about the increasing tendency of Japanese to leave Hawaii for California and the American Northwest in search of higher wages on the railroads and in the orchards. Would the Koreans follow the lead of the Japanese? Although they were relative newcomers to Hawaii, the Korean immigrants indeed began to follow the same pattern as the Japanese, but to a lesser degree.

The first fears in this regard came in the fall of 1904 when C. M. Cooke noted that for laborers accompanied by wives, "It is more difficult for them to leave and they prefer to remain at the plantation where they have families." As a result, Cooke resolved to take the matter up "with Mr. Deshler in reference to Koreans, as it won't be long before

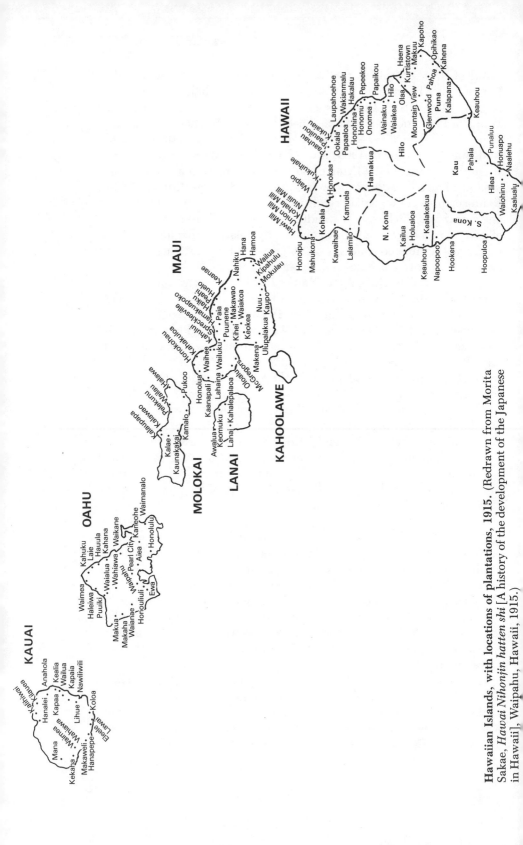

Hawaiian Islands, with locations of plantations, 1915. (Redrawn from Morita Sakae, *Hawai Nihonjin hatten shi* [A history of the development of the Japanese in Hawaii], Waipahu, Hawaii, 1915.)

they will want to go to the Coast, as soon as they get a little ahead in finances."[12] Despite planters' attempts to increase the number of female immigrants, however, the ratio remained approximately one in ten.

It took a while for the Koreans to follow the pattern that the long-established Japanese had developed. Indeed, during the first two years of their residence in Hawaii, only 90 men, 9 women, and 4 children left Hawaii. Not until 1905 did the number of Koreans leaving Hawaii reach significant proportions, when 563 men, 31 women, and 24 children departed—a total of 618. Of this number, 399 (373 men, 16 women, and 10 children) went to California, that is, about two-thirds of the departures for that year, while the remaining one-third, or 219 (190 men, 15 women and 14 children), returned to Korea.[13]

A look at the system developed by the Japanese will provide some insights into the pattern increasingly followed by Korean immigrants to Hawaii. A candid report by the commissioner-general of immigration revealed that a railroad corporation had "cunningly devised" a plan to bring Japanese to the Pacific Northwest: Japanese immigrants to Hawaii went to "hotels" kept by labor agents and "consistently claimed under examination by immigrant inspectors" that they were merely seeking employment in the Islands and that they had made no advance arrangements for employment either in Hawaii or on the mainland. The immigration inspectors had to admit them because they were of robust physique and thus unlikely to become public charges. After being admitted they remained for a few days or weeks and then boarded ship for the Pacific Northwest. Because they were admitted to the United States in Hawaii, their voyage to Seattle or Portland was "coastwise," and thus they could not be examined upon arrival there about a previous contract. The report also noted that Japanese immigration directly to the mainland was negligible while Japanese arrivals from Hawaii had been at the rate of one thousand to three thousand per month. The report concluded, "That several thousand laborers have been imported under this evasion of the law is not doubted."[14]

While the Korean version of this operation was not nearly as sophisticated and did not involve as many Koreans as Japanese, nonetheless in early 1905 there were many similarities. Two representatives (Messrs. Smith and Power) of the Great Northern and the Northern Pacific railroads arrived in Honolulu in February seeking to recruit five thousand workers for railway construction between Seattle and Minneapolis. They established headquarters at the Hansŏng (Seoul) Hotel owned by one Mun Hong-sŏk and offered Koreans daily wages of $1.10 in February, $1.20 in March, $1.30 in April, and $1.50 in May, June, and July.[15] While it is unclear whether the company paid the boat fare of $28.00 between Honolulu and the coast, it was clear that the wages being offered were well in excess of the 70 cents a day being offered in Hawaii.

The same calculations applied to orchards in California. Spurred on by a commission of $10.00 for every recruit, agents for the orchard owners visited plantations, offering the workers daily wages of $1.50 during the fruit season, about double the plantation wage. Naturally, both Japanese and Korean workers responded to such inducements. Cooke, for instance, lamented that "some 800 to 900 Japs and Koreans left on the Manchuria Saturday. There is also a steamer expected to carry away 900." The solution, according to Cooke, was to raise wages $2.00 per month.[16] This was also the solution urged by the Japanese consul-general in Honolulu, Saitō Miki, who wanted a higher standard of living for his people in Hawaii, and who also wanted as well a reduction in the number of Japanese leaving Hawaii for the mainland, where anti-Japanese sentiment was growing.

That the Japanese consul in Honolulu wanted Japanese to remain in Hawaii was not lost on the planters when Koreans began to follow in the footsteps of the Japanese. In March and again in May 1905, HSPA President F. M. Swanzy wrote to Horace Allen in Korea to complain about the increasing exodus of Koreans to the mainland and suggested that Allen persuade the Korean government to appoint "a good Korean consul here who would and could advise these people against going on to California. It is not for their advantage. True, there are a few months in the year when they get wages in excess of those to be earned here, but year in and year out they can do better here than in California."[17] As we shall soon see, Horace Allen had already tried and failed to convince the Korean government to station a consul in Honolulu. Moreover, by the spring of 1905, Horace Allen was no longer in a position to help the planters.

Thus far in looking at the utility of Korean laborers from the perspective of the planters, it is clear that while the Koreans did engage in strikes from time to time and, in addition, showed an increasing propensity to move to the mainland, overall their docility and stability were more pronounced than those of the Japanese. This was important if the Koreans were to be a successful counterbalance to the more numerous Japanese. But how were the Koreans as workers, and how did they compare with the Japanese?

The first source of information on this question is an informal survey taken by the Japanese consul in the spring of 1905 for the Foreign Ministry in Tokyo. Saitō's report quotes the manager of Ewa Plantation as praising the obedient character of the Korean workers. The managers at Waialua and Kahuku praised the Koreans over the Japanese for their

greater stability, while admitting that Japanese workers were more efficient. Another manager acknowledged that Koreans were less valuable
workers than Japanese, but that Koreans were preferable because Japanese workers were unstable, always wanted to leave for the mainland,
and often went on strike over small matters. A manager of a plantation
on Kauai complained that, on an average, only half of his 170 Koreans
worked, most tending to idle away their time. Saitō concluded that
although the Korean immigrants were far worse than Japanese immigrants as workers, they were favorably accepted by the planters because
of their obedient character and their stability.[18]

Before dismissing Saitō's conclusion as the product of Japanese
chauvinism, a look at a second important source of information tends to
confirm the judgment that Koreans on the sugar plantations of Hawaii
were at best mediocre workers. The source is the collection of reports of
plantation managers submitted in early 1905 to the parent body, the
HSPA. Organized by island, these reports cover every plantation in
Hawaii. Because they were meant for internal consumption only, they
are candid and objective assessments of the labor qualities of their
workers. Some of these reports are excerpted below:

Kauai. The 65 Koreans who made up 19 percent of the work
force of Kilauea Sugar Company elicited the comment: "Good workers,
but lose much time." At Makee Plantation where 136 Koreans constituted 15 percent of the labor force, the manager concluded that they
were "inferior to Chinese and unable to do the heavy work the Japs do."
Lihue Plantation's 57 Koreans (4 percent of the total) were characterized as "not quite so good as Chinese and Japanese." The 113 Koreans at
Koloa Plantation (15 percent of the total) were "not so capable or industrious as Japanese." McBryde Plantation's 192 Koreans (16 percent)
"promise well as field laborers, but we have not had enough experience
with them to give any opinion." The manager of the Hawaiian Sugar
Company characterized his 168 Koreans (11 percent) as "our third
choice for field labor; they are not nearly as bright or smart as the Japanese; are industrious enough, but have no initiative." Gay and Robinson's Plantation employed 22 Koreans (12 percent), about whom it was
noted, "being recent arrivals, little experience as regards this class."
Waimea Plantation listed Koreans in third place behind Japanese and
Chinese in preference for field labor and wrote that they "are very little
tried as yet, but seem fairly well adapted for our field work." Kekaha
Plantation's 95 Koreans (11 percent) were listed third in preference for
field labor behind Chinese and Japanese."

Oahu. The Oahu Sugar Company employed 203 Koreans (21
percent) and listed them in third place behind Chinese and Japanese
workers. Ewa Plantation employed 288 Koreans (13 percent), who

were characterized as "a new class of labor not wholly tried. I prefer the Chinese to Koreans." Manager Goodale reported, of the 107 Koreans at Waialua Plantation (8 percent): "[They] have been here so short a time it is hard to say definitely; they promise well." Kahuku Plantation employed 80 Koreans (12 percent of the total work force) where Manager Adams listed them third in preference behind Chinese and Japanese and characterized them as "industrious as field laborers. Excitable, but easily influenced by authority." Honolulu, Apokaa, Waianae, and Waimanalo plantations employed no Koreans.

Maui. Pioneer Mill employed 66 Koreans (5 percent) and reported that "[we] have only lately had this class of laborers, too short a time to form an opinion." Hawaiian Commercial and Sugar Company employed 236 Koreans (10 percent) where the manager, H. P. Baldwin reported that they "have not been in the country long. Not so reliable as Japanese or Chinese." The 31 Koreans at Kihei Plantation (7 percent) were ranked third in preference behind Chinese and Japanese and were described by the manager as "fair workers, with signs of improvement as they become more climatized." Maui Agricultural Company employed 93 Koreans (6 percent) and reported that "some are fairly good, but most are inferior to the Japanese and Chinese." Kipahulu Plantation employed 21 Koreans (10 percent) who were "similar to Japanese (not to be depended on as steady day laborers)." Hana Plantation's 6 Koreans (2 percent) were "not nearly as desirable as Japs or Chinese." Olowalu and Wailuku plantations did not employ Koreans.

Hawaii. Hawaii Mill and Plantation employed 74 Koreans (22 percent) who were listed as fifth in preference behind Hawaiian, Portuguese, Japanese, and Chinese and who were characterized as "good common and field labor." Union Mill employed 17 Koreans (7 percent) but did not comment on their quality. The 86 Koreans employed at Kohala plantation (19 percent) were described as "fairly good, quiet but very slow." The 8 Koreans working at Halawa Plantations (8 percent) were "poor" according to the manager. Pacific Sugar Mill's 49 Koreans (10 percent) were characterized thus: "So far, our experience with Koreans is limited: their capabilities as workmen neither equal the Chinese or Japanese field laborers." Honokaa Plantation employed 59 Koreans (9 percent) who rated the comment, "Rather new in the country; so far very satisfactory for field work." Paauhau Plantation had 40 Koreans (8 percent) but the manager could only say, "Had but few and only a short time. Cannot say." The 39 Koreans at Hamakua Plantation (9 percent) were described as "same as Chinese but inclined to be quarrelsome and intemperate. Not as industrious as Chinese, Portuguese or Japanese." The 3 Koreans on Kukaiau Plantation (2 percent) earned the comment, "So far they have not proven satisfactory to us." The Koreans on Ookala Plantation were praised as "fairly good labor." Laupahoehoe Plantation employed 24 Koreans (6 percent) who were characterized as "fairly good laborers and seem to stand the climatic conditions. We have had but little experience with these." Hilo Plantation's 11 Koreans (2 percent) were "very unreliable." Olaa Plantation employed 267 Koreans (18 percent) and listed them third in preference behind Chinese and Japanese, characterizing them as "unsteady as new men but with tendency to improvement." Hawaiian Agricultural Plantation's 51 Koreans (12 percent) were "fairly good workers, but not so reliable as the Japs or Chinese." The 106 Koreans at Hutchinson Plantation (18 percent) were listed fourth in preference behind Puerto Ricans, Chinese, and Japanese, and "have to be educated to work; are willing enough." On Puako Plantation, the 10 Koreans there (13 percent) were listed fifth in preference behind Hawaii, Portuguese, Japanese and Chinese. Niulii, Hakalau, Honomu, Pepeekeo, Onomea, and Waiakea plantations did not employ Koreans.[19]

The picture that emerges from these two reports is that the abilities of Koreans as sugarcane workers were limited at best. Two questions immediately arise: why were the Koreans such mediocre field workers, and how would the HSPA respond to these less than glowing reports about Korean labor?

The Planters had had high expectations that the Koreans would turn out to be an excellent class of labor. Indeed, when E. Faxon Bishop went to Korea in the fall of 1902, he wrote back: "I feel as confident as I can without positively knowing, that the Koreans will prove good laborers if we can get them to the Islands. . . . They are lusty strong fellows and physically much the superior of the Jap. In rice culture and mining work they excel any other nationality and I can't for the life of me see how it is possible for them to prove other than good laborers for us."[20] How could Bishop have been so wrong?

In fact, Bishop was not necessarily wrong in his glowing report of the average Korean peasant farmer or worker. Rather, Bishop's error was in assuming that the immigrants to Hawaii would be typical Korean peasants. Instead, as we have seen, most of the Korean immigrants were city people, either unemployed or having urban-type employment, and were unaccustomed to agricultural labor. Thus they differed from the majority of their countrymen in Korea as well as from their Chinese and Japanese immigrant counterparts, who were predominantly peasant farmers. Thus it is not surprising that the Koreans would rank lower than Japanese and Chinese workers given their background in Korea.

Another possible explanation for the lackluster performance of Koreans may be found in the racism and discrimination that character-

ized the sugar industry in Hawaii. Why, indeed should one work diligently if there was no opportunity for upward mobility within the
industry? Most of the lunas were European, and upper-level positions
remained closed to all but a few Asians. Effectively barred from the
higher-paying jobs and managerial positions within the sugar industry,
there was little incentive to exert oneself.

Their urban background may also help explain why Koreans
were less likely to strike than were the Japanese on the plantations. It is
probable that many of the Japanese, being farm workers originally and
having no other job skills, planned to spend long years on the plantations in Hawaii. Naturally, they were interested in improving working
conditions and wages in an area of employment in which they saw
themselves engaged for the long term. Koreans on the other hand perhaps did not see themselves as plantation workers in the long run,
because their urban background and job interests did not lend themselves to a future on the sugar plantations. As a result Koreans might
have been more passive and docile in the face of low wages and poor
working conditions which they considered temporary. This perhaps
explains to some extent why the Koreans were mediocre workers and
also more docile than the Japanese.

While it is beyond the scope of this study, it might be appropriate to extrapolate in a tentative way from what we have already learned
about the background of the Korean immigrants and their lackluster
work record during their first two years in Hawaii to get a glimpse of
the future development of the Korean community. Indeed, the Koreans
as a group were destined to leave the sugar plantations faster than any
of the other thirty-three ethnic groups in the cane fields and recorded
one of the highest rates of urbanization in Hawaii. We should not be
surprised at these phenomena given the background of the Korean
immigrants. Nor should we be surprised that this behavior presaged
rapid upward mobility. Familiarity with cities and urban job skills
would stand an immigrant in good stead in an American society that
was rapidly becoming urban oriented, especially in the socio-economic
structure of Hawaii, which made any job outside the plantation the first
upward step on the ladder of success.[21]

The second question we must answer is, What was the reaction
of the planters to the realization that the Koreans were not especially
good plantation workers? It is important to keep in mind the different
levels of responsibility in the sugar industry, as well as the original aims
of the planters in importing Korean labor. At the lower level there is no
doubt that the individual plantation managers were not particularly
enthused with their Korean workers. C. Wolters, the manager of Hutchinson Plantation, for example, replied to a query from the HSPA, "In

the opinion of the writer the wages for Koreans should not be raised."[22] And more than a month later he wrote concerning a two-dollar per month raise: "We wonder if this applies to Koreans as well as Japanese, since the former class is not worth it."[23]

While the individual plantation manager was primarily interested in how much work he could get from his immigrant laborers, the parent body, the Hawaiian Sugar Planters Association, had larger concerns that went beyond mere worker productivity. The HSPA, in short, had to wrestle with immigrant policy in an effort to prevent any one race, in this case the Japanese, from achieving a labor monopoly. Thus the interest of the higher-ups in the sugar industry was less with the Koreans as workers (as long as they were better than the recently imported Puerto Ricans) and more with the Koreans as an offset to the majority Japanese. Since the Korean immigrants seemed to be filling the bill in this respect, the HSPA was willing to overlook the fact that they were not particularly good field workers.

As a result, despite decidedly mixed reviews as workers, and despite the fact that the Koreans were beginning to leave for the mainland in increasing numbers like the Japanese, the relatively greater docility and stability of the Koreans prompted the planters in the spring of 1905 to continue to promote the immigration of Koreans to Hawaii. Their continued interest in doing so would soon become apparent when events in Tokyo and Seoul in the spring of 1905 brought Korean immigration to a halt.

12

Japanese Opposition Resurfaces

EVEN though the Hawaiian Sugar Planters' Association recognized that Korean immigrants were not superior agricultural laborers, their relative docility and stability made them a more than adequate offset to the Japanese, who were better workers but more inclined to strike or leave for the mainland. By the spring of 1905, Koreans had become the second largest group of immigrant workers on the plantations, accounting for 10 percent of the labor force (as compared with the Japanese who comprised 66 percent), surpassing the Chinese who now constituted only 9 percent and who were prohibited from coming by the Chinese Exclusion Act of 1882.[1] Into this picture of seeming tranquility came events with origins in Seoul, Tokyo, Mexico, and Hawaii that would completely shatter the system of Korean immigration to Hawaii and lead to its ultimate demise.

On April 1, 1905, Korean Foreign Minister Yi Ha-yŏng prohibited emigration, notifying all *kamni* to cease issuing passports.[2] Before examining the reasons for the prohibition, let us first look at the reaction of Allen, Deshler, and the planters.

When the prohibition was issued, Deshler was in Japan and thus initially unaware of the order. And because of the time required for mail delivery, the planters remained unaware of it for a month and a half. As usual, then, the burden fell once again upon Horace Allen to intervene on behalf of Deshler and the planters to persuade the Korean government to allow immigration to continue. Allen's interest lay not only in the debt he felt he owed Deshler and in his desire to increase American commercial, and thus political, interest in Korea, but also because after nearly three years of dealings with the planters, a web of reciprocal favors had been established: One of the planters had suggested giving Allen "something more than *thanks*" in the spring of

1903.[3] And when the Allens' ship docked in Honolulu in the fall of that year on his way back to Korea from home leave, he wrote that Bishop "took ùs for a drive during about the whole afternoon." Allen acknowledged that "of course, my cordial reception was due to the great interest in Korean immigration."[4] When Allen returned to Korea in November 1903, he boldly began to correspond directly with Swanzy, no longer making use of his go-between, Fassett, in New York. Allen also sent a Korean chest to Swanzy, who in turn offered "to make things nice for us in Honolulu."[5]

So Allen turned himself to the task at hand. In a letter to Swanzy informing him of the prohibition, Allen said that he was "trying to do what I can for you, and expect Deshler to turn up soon." And because he was a friend of Durham White Stevens, an American appointed by Japan as an adviser to the Korean Foreign Office, Allen opined, "I think Stevens will assist us as far as Hawaii is concerned and we may bring about a better condition of affairs. One lot of would-be emigrants to Honolulu were stopped recently."[6] The bad news was confirmed by Deshler three weeks later when he returned to Inch'ŏn from Japan and informed the planters via his liaison in Honolulu, J. D. Julian, of the order. On the receipt of these two discouraging letters from Korea, the planters convened meetings to discuss the implications, but there was little they could do but await developments in Seoul.[7]

Allen was optimistic that he could alter Korean government policy—after all, he had no compunction against interfering in Korean domestic politics and had certainly done so successfully in the past. But his ability to wield influence stemmed mainly from his powerful position as American minister to Korea. Thus, it came as a double dose of bad news to the planters when Allen also revealed in his letter to Swanzy that he had been replaced as minister to Korea by Edwin V. Morgan.[8]

In early March, Allen had begun to worry aloud about the security of his position as minister, noting, "I have no political influence any more since Governor Nash and President McKinley have left."[9] Not only had Allen lost his friends in Washington, but he had also been arguing against American policy in Korea in a campaign that bordered on insubordination. Indeed, President Roosevelt and his adviser on East Asian affairs, William W. Rockhill, had come to the conclusion that Allen's anti-Japanese position rendered him ineffective as a spokesman for Roosevelt's pro-Japanese views concerning the Korean peninsula.[10] When the news of his dismissal became known on March 20, an outcry arose. Emperor Kojong told President Roosevelt that he was "greatly grieved."[11] Deshler sent a letter of condolence, having read of the dismissal in a Kobe newspaper.[12] A petition by American residents in

Korea to President Roosevelt was circulated; Deshler was one of the signers.[13] Durham White Stevens wrote letters to Rockhill and the Japanese minister in Washington, Takahira Kogorō, requesting that Allen be kept on the job.[14] All this was to no avail. Allen had lost his job and had to prepare to leave Korea.

This political development would have a direct impact on Korean immigration. It meant, for instance, that Allen's ability to influence the Korean government on the issue in the short time that remained to him in Seoul was severely circumscribed. This consequence was not lost on the planters. In his last letter to Allen, Swanzy wrote in mid-May that the planters were "full of regret at this bit of bad news." Labeling his dismissal as "little short of an outrage," Swanzy ruefully noted "that the stoppage of Korean emigration to Hawaii comes at a most unfortunate time," since the planters "thought it was earmarked well likely to float for long." Still in the dark about the reasons behind the "unjust" and "annoying" prohibition, Swanzy complained to Allen that Koreans in Hawaii "are well treated here and regularly paid." Swanzy also suggested, correctly as it turned out, that "there must be something more at the back of this action of the Korean Foreign Minister than meets the eye," since "he must realize the enormous advantage there is in this emigration to the emigrants and their relatives left at home so it cannot be that he does not think it is a good thing from their point of view." He concluded by noting: "I suppose all we can do is to wait for developments."[15] The fears of the planters were justified. Allen's power base in Korea had eroded to such an extent that he was unable to do anything for the planters and the prohibition remained in force.

Allen left Korea on June 9 aboard Deshler's ship the *Ohio*, his friend having given him free passage and freight to Kobe.[16] In Japan, Allen transferred to a trans-Pacific liner. Ironically, one of his fellow passengers was Japanese Foreign Minister Baron Komura Jutarō, who was on his way to the Portsmouth peace talks in New Hampshire and who would be the principal architect of the dissolution of all the efforts to which Allen had devoted himself regarding Korean immigration to Hawaii. In his last letter to Swanzy, Allen wrote, "We will go home by the Northern route to save Mrs. Allen the heat of travel. If we ever get to the islands I will look you up."[17] Arriving back in Ohio, Allen set up medical practice in Toledo. In a final parting shot justifying his efforts to aid Korean immigration to Hawaii and countering the derogatory remarks about the Korean character being made at the time by George Kennan in his article in *Outlook*, "Korea: A Degenerate State," Allen wrote in December 1905 of the Koreans in Hawaii, "[They] are liked much better than the Chinese or Japanese. They are sober, patient, hard working and industrious, and so frugal that in order to have money in [the] bank they are inclined to go without sufficient food. As for being stupid, they learn English faster than either the Chinese or Japanese and are most faithful patrons of any school to which they may obtain entrance."[18]

The planters were alone now, with no intermediary in Seoul to help them. So when Swanzy, Bishop, and Irwin met for dinner at Irwin's Honolulu home in late May "for the purpose of talking over Korean and Japanese immigration matters," they settled upon the same tactic they had used three years earlier when Allen's ship had brought him to Hawaii on the way to Korea: they resolved to meet the incoming minister, Edwin V. Morgan, who had a scheduled layover on his way to Korea in early June.[19] The new minister was already on record as favoring emigration: in an interview with a Korean in Washington he had said, "Korea must bear in mind that she has to . . . dispatch many young men to foreign countries to study modern civilization."[20] And while Morgan was en route from the West Coast, the planters received word that the Japanese fleet had demolished the Russian fleet, virtually insuring Japanese control over Korea.[21] Therefore, any discussion with Morgan concerning Korean immigration to Hawaii would have to address the Japanese attitude toward it.

Morgan arrived in Hawaii on June 2 aboard the *Siberia* and that morning had with the planters "a general discussion of Korean immigration, the relations of the Japanese towards Korea, and the treatment of the Koreans on the plantations." According to the minutes of the meeting, "Morgan expressed himself as favoring Korean immigration to Hawaii, believing that it is a good thing for the Koreans to come here and that they are well treated by the plantations." Prophetically, he stated that "unless the Japanese prohibited it . . . the Koreans if left to their own inclinations would be glad to come to Hawaii."[22] That afternoon, Morgan was escorted to Ewa Plantation by HSPA President Swanzy, where a large number of Korean immigrants were working.[23]

As Morgan sailed from Honolulu for his new post in Korea, the planters were obviously heartened by his positive attitude. But they also knew that he would not have the "clout" that his predecessor Allen had had at the Korean court. What they did not know was that Korean immigration to Hawaii faced obstacles of a much greater magnitude than Allen had ever had to deal with.

On the surface, there were four reasons why the Korean government prohibited emigration. The first, suggested by a comment in the government-sponsored newspaper, was that the Koreans in Hawaii wanted to return to Korea because of the hard labor and their difficulty in adapting to life in Hawaii, but they were unable to return because they could not save enough to purchase a steamship ticket.[24] A second reason, not a new one, was revealed in a Japanese diplomatic message, which noted strong opposition to emigration from the director of the Korean tax office, who felt that emigrants were leaving in order to avoid the "squeeze." Third, the same report referred to "problems" within Korea in carrying out emigration procedures and the fact that there were no Korean diplomats in the receiving countries to protect emigrants.[25]

The fourth ostensible reason for prohibiting emigration stemmed from circumstances surrounding the emigration of 1,033 Koreans aboard a chartered ship to Mexico. The explanation published in the government newspaper referred to these emigrants as being "sold and treated as slaves."[26] It was said that "they were herded like cattle till over a thousand were collected, and friends were not allowed to see them, so that the idea spread that they were being taken as slaves."[27] Actually, just as the ship was to depart Inch'ŏn, one of the emigrants was found to have contracted smallpox, and all the emigrants were forced to disembark and be placed in quarantine in Inch'ŏn. Naturally, when their friends and relatives learned that the ship had not yet sailed and went to see them, they were prohibited from doing so, leading to rumors that they were being sold into slavery.[28]

Before examining these issues in more detail, we should first take a look behind the scenes. If we pull back the curtain, we will find that the real reason for the prohibition of emigration from Korea lay not in Seoul but in Tokyo.

During the period 1904–1905, Japan's main foreign policy concern was, of course, the currently raging Russo-Japanese War which, by the spring of 1905, had turned in favor of Japan. As the outcome of the war became increasingly clear, the Japanese Foreign Ministry headed by Baron Komura Jutarō turned its attention to other pressing foreign policy issues which had necessarily taken a back seat to the prosecution of the war with Russia. One of these issues was the postwar relationship between Japan and Korea; another was the current state of Japanese-American relations. These two issues were related not only in assuring a favorable American attitude toward a possible Japanese protectorate over Korea but also in mollifying the growing anti-Japanese sentiment in California.

Anti-Japanese sentiment in California can be traced in large part to the increasing numbers of Japanese immigrants arriving there after 1900, and secondarily to the demonstrated might of the Japanese military in routing the Russians. While the problem did not reach crisis proportions until 1905, the antagonism began at the turn of the century with the annexation of Hawaii. This action facilitated the movement of Japanese immigrants in Hawaii to the mainland since it constituted movement within the country rather than across international borders. Between 1890 and 1899 only 15,572 Japanese arrived on the West Coast, an average of 1,550 a year. In 1900, however, 12,635 arrived on the West Coast; in 1901 the number was 5,269; in 1902, 14,270 arrived; in 1903, 20,041; in 1904, 14,382; and in 1905, 11,021 Japanese arrived.[29] Most were Japanese from Hawaii, not Japan.

The cause of this migration of Japanese from Hawaii to California was economic. Workers on the sugar plantations were paid about 70 cents per day, while the prevailing wage rates in the orchards and on the railroads on the mainland were approximately twice that. And the only impediment to this eastward movement was the boat fare of approximately $30. In rational economic terms, this migration is not surprising.

Yet as the numbers of Japanese in California increased, political tensions grew. The Democratic party of California, for example, urged that the Chinese Exclusion Act be applied to Japanese, the governor called for the exclusion of Japanese in his speeches, and major newspapers began to editorialize in favor of a Japanese exclusion act. The movement also spread beyond the West Coast when the American Federation of Labor also began to call for the exclusion of the Japanese.[30]

Payson J. Treat, in his classic study of Japanese-American relations during the period 1895 to 1905, characterizes the relationship as an amicable one, noting that President Theodore Roosevelt generally approved of Japanese predominance in Korea. Moreover, Roosevelt and the Japanese saw eye-to-eye on the matter of restrictive legislation against the Japanese in America—they were opposed.[31] Yet nations interact on several levels, and this was true of Japan and the United States in the early years of the twentieth century. Within the administrations of Roosevelt in the United States and Foreign Minister Komura in Japan, forces were at work to prevent racial animosities from rising to the surface. The American side of the story has been ably documented by Roger Daniels and need not be recounted here.[32] It was dramatically illustrated in the October 1906 San Francisco School Board Incident when Japanese children were ordered to join the Chinese in the Oriental school since they were classified as Mongolian, and Roosevelt was forced to intervene to persuade the school board to rescind the order.[33] Needless to say, Roosevelt was adamantly opposed to a Japanese exclusion act. For him it was a matter of realpolitik that a friendly big power not be discriminated against. For Japan, the issue was more complicated and involved not a small measure of national pride and sensitivity.

Ever since the Meiji Restoration in 1868, Japan had struggled to achieve equality with the West. It had successfully thrown off unequal treaties, defeated the Chinese in a war, acquired a colony of its own in Taiwan, and was about to defeat Russia, a major European power, in a war. Clearly, Japan was no longer a second-class nation and would not be treated as one. This was especially true in the matter of racial discrimination and the threat of an exclusion act similar to the Chinese Exclusion Act of 1882. As the Japanese ambassador to the United States put it in 1924 when faced with the imminent prospect of just such an act: "To Japan the question is . . . one . . . of principle. To her the mere fact that a few hundreds or thousands of her nationals will or will not be admitted into domains of other countries is immaterial, so long as no question of national susceptibilities is involved. The important question is whether Japan as a nation is or is not entitled to the proper respect and consideration of other nations. . . . The manifest object of the [exclusion act] is to single out Japanese as a nation, stigmatizing them as unworthy and undesirable in the eyes of the American people."[34] Passage of a Japanese exclusion act would have the effect, like that of the San Francisco School Board Incident the following year, of putting Japan and the Japanese in the same low category as China and the Chinese. Japan by this time saw itself as a nation in the first rank of the world powers and saw China (and Korea, for that matter) sinking lower and lower. Clearly if such an exclusion act were passed, Japan would lose face internationally. It was thus in the national interest of Japan to prevent passage of a Japanese exclusion act by the United States.

By early 1905, from the vantage point of Tokyo, it looked as if the same process that had led to the Chinese Exclusion Act of 1882 was being repeated for the Japanese. Both Komura, a Harvard graduate, and his vice-minister of Foreign Affairs, Chinda Sutemi, had previously been posted in the United States and were thus well acquainted with the anti-Oriental feelings of Americans in general and Californians in particular. Indeed, Chinda, when he was consul in San Francisco in the 1890s, predicted that "the mass migration of lower class Japanese in the future will undoubtedly create a grave situation in the relationship between Japanese and Americans in this country which, sooner or later, will adversely affect the honor and reputation not only of the Japanese in this country but of those in Japan."[35] While Roosevelt was busy twisting arms in California in an effort to reign in the anti-Japanese politicians there, Komura and his subordinates sought to defuse this potentially explosive issue with a series of measures of their own aimed at slowing or halting the flow of Japanese from Hawaii to California, while at the same time preserving the right of Japanese to emigrate to Hawaii.

One such measure was the severe restriction of emigration from Japan to the mainland United States. And those few who were permitted to do so were generally a better class of people than the laborers who went to Hawaii.[36] A second measure was the creation of the Central Japanese League by the Japanese consul-general in Honolulu, Saitō Miki. This organization was formed in 1903 to instill in the Japanese laborers an attachment to their plantations and to promote a feeling of mutual obligation between workers and owners. As an attempt to diminish the number of strikes as well as to prevent workers from going on to California for higher wages, this effort had the enthusiastic support of the planters, who naturally shared with the Japanese government a desire to keep Japanese laborers on the plantations in Hawaii.[37]

A third step taken by Japan was apparently in response to a suggestion by Walter Giffard to the director of one of the Japanese immigration companies that the passports issued to Japanese laborers contain the words "To Hawaii Only." Giffard added that "we have no doubt the bluff would work" because the Japanese were afraid to offend their government.[38] This plan was not only adopted by the Japanese government, but was also supplemented by a verbal warning to each emigrant not to proceed to the mainland United States.[39]

In another move to halt outmigration, Consul-General Saitō Miki adopted the practice of issuing circulars "prohibiting" Japanese from leaving Hawaii for California. The first of these circulars, which of course had no force of law, was issued in 1904 and was reissued from time to time afterward. Like the other measures adopted by the Japanese government, these circulars were ignored by the immigrants, whose noncompliance was duly noted by the Japanese government.[40]

Consul-General Saitō also led a campaign for a hike in wages for plantation workers, reasoning that reducing the disparity in wages between Hawaii and California would lessen the attraction of the mainland. Saitō's efforts in this direction elicited mixed reactions from the planters, some of whom were of the opinion that this would simply help the Japanese pay their boat fare to California. Nonetheless, a two-dollar per month raise went into effect in 1905.[41] Another measure discussed by the planters but never instituted, probably because of its doubtful legality, proposed a five-hundred-dollar licensing fee for labor agents from the West Coast.[42]

Perhaps the most interesting suggestion on how to prevent Japanese from going to the mainland came from Takahira Kogorō, the Japanese ambassador to the United States. It is of interest because it became American policy in March 1907. The ambassador's suggestion to Komura was as follows: "I would submit for your consideration question as to whether Imperial Government will not object if the United States Government take measures to prohibit Japanese or other immigrants of the labouring class to Hawaii or other insular possession to come to the United States proper. I am not certain whether or not the United States Government can take such measure, but if approved, I may propose to the United States Government to take the matter into consideration as a measure to appease people of Pacific Coast."[43] Demonstrating that the Japanese government wanted to prevent any legislation in the United States that would smack of discrimination against Japan and the Japanese, when Roosevelt did issue the executive order to that effect two years later, the then foreign minister, Hayashi Tadasu, complained that it was a distasteful measure, but still preferable to a Japanese exclusion act: "The United States authorities have prohibited this transmigration. We believe that our countrymen can so transmigrate, as once they were in Hawaii they were in American territory, where under treaty rights they have freedom of travel. The Americans refuse to allow this, though by treaty we think that they have no right to do so. On the other hand, if we protest too much, then the United States threaten to close Hawaii to Japanese immigration altogether, which would even be more disadvantageous than the prohibition for Hawaiian Japanese to travel to America."[44]

Thus the Japanese government, at times in concert with the planters, sought ways short of American legislation to prevent its immigrants from moving from Hawaii to California. If these measures proved unsuccessful, then they faced the prospect of a Japanese exclusion act which would besmirch Japan's image as a nation of the first rank. Yet the Japanese government was aware that these measures were not succeeding. As long as there was a significant differential in pay between Hawaii and California, Japanese immigrants in Hawaii would continue to move to the American mainland. And as the Japanese from Hawaii arrived in California at the rate of about a thousand per month, there was increasing pressure from California to pass a Japanese exclusion act. It was at this point that this issue became joined with Korean immigration to Hawaii.

When emigration from Korea to Hawaii first began more than two years earlier, Hayashi Gonsuke, the Japanese minister to Korea, made known his opposition. His position, it will be recalled, was based on the accurate perception that it would be detrimental to Japanese in Hawaii and also limit the opportunity for other Japanese to emigrate. He also opposed it because, as an American concession, it made Japanese control of Korea more difficult. Yet his opposition was his own and did not reflect official policy. Nonetheless, he remained an opponent of Korean immigration to Hawaii.

It was only a matter of time before a second source of opposition to Korean immigration to Hawaii emerged. Predictably, this came from the private Japanese emigration companies who were engaged in sending Japanese to Hawaii. It has already been demonstrated that once Korean immigration was operating on a regular basis, planter demand for Japanese immigrants naturally decreased—by the number of Korean immigrants.[45] This meant reduced profit for the Japanese emigration companies. Despite attempts by the planters to explain that their policy of mixing the races on the plantations was intended to induce the Japanese to work better, and thus ward off opposition from that source, in the summer of 1904 the emigration companies first expressed their opposition in the form of a letter to Foreign Minister Komura. The author of the letter was Morioka Makoto, the director of one of the largest emigration companies.

Morioka's letter began by reviewing the history of Japanese immigration to Hawaii from 1885 and tracing the development of the Japanese community there. As the community grew, Morioka continued, trade, remittances, and donations to Japan increased as well. Emigration, he insisted, was also a boon to the individual emigrant, who traded poverty for prosperity. This success was threatened, contended Morioka, by Korean immigration because the result would be fewer Japanese immigrants in Hawaii and a falling off of trade. Morioka concluded by asking Komura to regulate Korean immigration so that it would not injure what he saw as the national interest of Japan.[46] While Morioka's appeal was couched in terms of Japanese national interest, it is clear that his main concern was the reduced profits for the emigration companies as a result of the successful Korean immigration.

Despite this appeal, there was no response from Komura, and Korean immigration continued unimpeded. Perhaps the lack of a response was due to the fact that the Foreign Office was at that time engaged in more important issues—namely, the successful prosecution of the war with Russia. Or perhaps it was due to the fact that the Japanese Foreign Office respected the sovereign right of Korea to send emigrants wherever it chose. On the other hand, the Emigrant Companies Association of Japan, which consisted of about three dozen emigration concerns, was a powerful economic force with substantial clout.[47] Moreover, the Japanese government was beginning to be concerned about the welfare of its emigrants abroad.[48] In fact, it was not until Korean immigration to Hawaii became linked with the growing deterioration of Japanese-American relations and the prospect of the passage of a Japanese exclusion act that Komura's attitude changed.

The change in Komura's attitude can be traced from February 1905. By this time the outcome of the Russo-Japanese War was no longer in doubt. It was also clear that the various measures undertaken by Japan to prevent its emigrants from moving from Hawaii to California were not having the desired effect, which resulted in increasing sentiment there to exclude Japanese. Into this picture came a second letter of protest from the Japanese emigration companies to Komura. In this second letter, Morioka was joined by two other emigration company directors, Hyūga Terutake and Tomiochi Chūtarō, in calling for the Japanese government to put a halt to Korean immigration to Hawaii. No doubt these men were motivated primarily, as before, by the reduction in their emigration businesses. This time, however, they argued that because the Korean government did not regulate the number of Koreans who left for Hawaii, "the balance between the demand for and the supply of labor has been lost, and the wages of the laborers are falling because of competition." In language reminiscent of Californians complaining about Japanese immigration, the three men continued: "We suppose that Japanese immigrants cannot compete with the Koreans when wages are decreasing, since Korean immigrants do not need the money for sanitation and education, and are satisfied only with sufficient money for food and clothes." They concluded, "As a result, there is a tendency for the number of Japanese emigrants trying to move to the American continent by boat to increase, despite the prohibition law, while the Korean immigrants to Honolulu are increasing."[49]

No doubt aware of the government's anxiety over the large numbers of Japanese arriving in California from Hawaii, these emigration agents were presenting to Komura the reason for the disparity in wages between the two areas: the presence of Koreans as strikebreakers kept the wages for Japanese in Hawaii low, which in turn made the higher wages in California seem all the more attractive to them. They were right, of course, for this was one of the reasons behind planter strategy to mix the races on the plantations. And if Komura had not been aware of the relationship between Korean immigration to Hawaii and Japanese movement to California before, he was certainly aware of it now.

Yet even after receiving this information in mid-February, Komura took no action until he received an urgent cable from Consul Ueno in San Francisco two weeks later. The cable read: "State Senate of California passed March 1st a resolution to call attention of the President and State Department to menace of Japanese immigration and to request that immediate action will be taken by treaty or otherwise to limit and diminish the further immigration of Japanese labourers in the United States. The resolution will probably pass the Assembly today." Later that day, Ueno again cabled to report, "The resolution reported in my telegram eight was passed by the Assembly this morning."[50] This resolution was significant for it was the first time that the state legislature had officially called upon Roosevelt and the U.S. State Department to pass a Japanese exclusion act. Clearly, this greatly increased pressure on Washington to enact a law desired neither by Roosevelt nor by the Japanese.

As a result of this communication, Komura on that day, March third, finally became convinced that Korean immigration to Hawaii must be halted. On that very day he wrote to Consul Saitō in Honolulu asking for information on Korean immigration, reviewing briefly its history, and concluding: "I regret for the sake of our Japanese emigration businesses that Korean emigration has shown this success in such a short time—less than two years. Looking at the future from the situation of today, I think we cannot waste one day and it is necessary to consider measures to prevent Koreans from emigrating to Hawaii."[51]

In this way the issue of Korean immigration to Hawaii became joined with the issue of Japanese immigration to the United States and the necessity of preventing what now seemed increasingly likely—a Japanese exclusion act, passage of which would psychologically catapult Japan from the ranks of a world power. Prohibiting Korean emigration would also produce secondary benefits of appeasing the unhappy emigration companies, assuring a higher standard of living for Japanese in Hawaii, and increasing opportunities for poverty-stricken Japanese farmers to seek prosperity abroad. Komura's determination to halt Korean immigration to Hawaii must thus be seen as yet another, albeit more drastic, step designed to stem the flow of Japanese from Hawaii to California. The reasoning was simple and the Japanese had now had enough experience with capitalism to know how to manipulate the system to their advantage: If Korean immigration to Hawaii were halted, then the Japanese immigrants there would regain their monopoly on labor and as a result would have a better chance of demanding higher wages on the plantations. As wages rose, California would become less attractive economically as the wage gap between the two areas would be narrowed and fewer Japanese would be induced to migrate. As fewer Japanese from Hawaii arrived, anti-Japanese sentiment on the coast would diminish and result in an easing of pressure on Washington to enact a Japanese exclusion act. Ironically, it meant that the Japanese had decided to mount an exclusion campaign against the Koreans in order to prevent their own exclusion from the United States. The right of Korea to send its people abroad would have to be sacrificed to prevent Japan from losing face internationally.

13

Japan Brings Emigration to a Halt

SINCE Japan had a preponderance of power in Korea by the spring of 1905 by virtue of winning the war against the Russians (whose defeat would be sealed by the destruction of their naval fleet in the Tsushima Straits at the end of May) and by agreements signed with the Korean government during the course of the war, it would seem that Japan could easily force Korea to prohibit emigration. Komura, however, chose instead to exploit weaknesses within Korea to achieve his goal. In this connection, a useful paradigm to keep in mind is the traditional Chinese metaphor concerning the relationship between the disease of the body (national weakness) and the disease of the extremity (imperialism). That is, imperialism can be successful by taking advantage of the internal weaknesses of a country.

Komura's first step in his effort to prevent Korean immigration to Hawaii was to gain more information on the subject. On the same day that he wrote to Saitō in Honolulu asking for information and stating his conviction that Korean immigration should be halted, he also wrote to his consuls in Inch'ŏn, Mokp'o, Pusan, and Kunsan, asking them to report on Korean emigration from these cities.[1] Komura then waited for an opportunity to present itself. He had less than one month to wait.

The opportunity came when the Korean government itself temporarily prohibited emigration early in April. Komura first learned about the prohibition when he read about it in the *Hōchi shinbun*. He immediately cabled Hayashi in Seoul to confirm the news.[2] Hayashi replied by cable to confirm the report, citing the lack of Korean diplomats in receiving countries, difficulties surrounding emigration to Mexico, and opposition by tax officials. He added that the prohibition would remain in effect until governmental protection of Korean emigrants abroad could be arranged and legal details clarified.[3] This was the opening Komura had been waiting for.

On the following day he replied to Hayashi that this action on the part of the Korean government was "very convenient" because of the competition between Korean and Japanese workers in Hawaii, and also the numerous cases of infectious diseases among Korean emigrants that Japanese hospitals in Kobe and Yokohama had to deal with. His cable concluded with the statement, "Please consider maintaining the prohibition for some time."[4] The basic outline of subsequent Japanese policy on this issue was beginning to take shape.

Much of the responsibility for implementation of this policy rested with Hayashi Gonsuke in Seoul. For despite the fact that Japan appeared to be reacting to an opportunity created solely by the action of the Korean government, a look behind the scenes reveals that Hayashi, an opponent of Korean immigration to Hawaii from the beginning, had been putting pressure on the Korean government even before receiving instructions from Komura. The first person to learn of these behind-the-scenes maneuverings was David Deshler.

Deshler had been in Japan when he read in the *Kobe Chronicle* that emigration had been temporarily prohibited by the Korean Foreign Office. Upon learning of this action, Deshler immediately returned to Korea and had a talk with the foreign minister, Yi Ha-yŏng. Yi assured Deshler that he was strongly supportive of Korean emigration to Hawaii, noting that the Koreans were treated kindly in Hawaii, and that he had no objection to it. The problem, he continued, lay with the arrival of "a new and irresponsible company" recruiting Koreans for work on sisal plantations in the Yucatan. Since Yi "did not consider Mexico a suitable place" and because "he very much desired to stop the exploiting of Koreans and inducing them to emigrate to undesirable places by irresponsible people," he told Deshler that he had "originally intended to prohibit the emigration of Koreans to Mexico, but that upon consultation with His Excellency the Japanese Minister to Korea, the Japanese Minister [Hayashi Gonsuke] pointed out that it would be unfair to discriminate in favor of any emigration company or country and that if one were stopped all must stop." As a consequence, Yi told Deshler that it would be better "to stop emigration entirely until such a time when laws and regulations could be drawn up and put in operation which would offer emigrants the desired protection."[5] Thus it had been Hayashi, acting on his own, who had pressured the Korean government to extend the prohibition to include Hawaii by arguing that emigration rules and regulations were inadequate. Japanese strategy was becoming clearer: until adequate regulations were drawn up, the prohibition would remain in force.

In Tokyo, Komura began receiving replies to the questions he had posed to the Japanese consuls in Korea and Hawaii concerning Korean emigration to Hawaii. The information he received tended to reinforce his determination to prevent Koreans from going to Hawaii. The Japanese consul in Kunsan, for example, informed Komura that the number of emigrants from his district was increasing.[6] In Mokp'o, the consul stated that Deshler's business was gradually expanding.[7] Katō Motoshirō, in Inch'ŏn, reported that the Koreans were happy with their jobs and were liked by the planters. Katō also reported that the Koreans in Hawaii were able to save goodly amounts of money, referring specifically to postal money orders of 400 *yen* per month in remittances to one family and 60 *yen* for another. He also acknowledged that some workers returned, but usually for the purpose of taking their families back to Hawaii.[8] Katō's report thus contradicted the local newspaper report which attributed the prohibition in part to inability to adjust and difficulty in accumulating enough money for return passage. To Komura it was clear that if Japan did not step in, the problem was going to get worse.

Three obstacles that first presented themselves to Hayashi and Komura in their attempt to make the prohibition on emigration permanent were the prompt appearance of a revised set of emigration regulations, opposition from David Deshler, and difficulty in enforcing the prohibition by the Korean government.

Within two weeks of issuing its order temporarily prohibiting emigration, the Korean Foreign Office submitted a hastily written set of emigration regulations to the Korean government for approval. They were rejected, insuring that the ban would continue.[9] While no explanation was given, we may be reasonably sure that a combination of weak leadership on the part of the Korean foreign minister and continued Japanese diplomatic pressure lay behind the rejection. It was clear that Hayashi had argued that emigration regulations should be systematically drawn up only after adequate research and consultation.

Even though Foreign Minister Yi Ha-yǒng approved of Korean emigration to Hawaii, he had submitted to Hayashi's demand that the ban include Hawaii as well as Mexico. Moreover, he was unable to advocate successfully his own department's revised set of regulations two weeks later. Additionally, Yi appears to have been a reluctant foreign minister. Appointed in April of 1904,[10] he had tried to resign several times, most recently on the day that he had ordered the *kamni* to stop issuing passports. Kojong did not accept his resignations, and so he remained in office.[11] Horace Allen had characterized Yi as follows: "Has exalted idea of his diplomatic ability. Means well. Sometimes unexpectedly stubborn, again as unexpectedly, yielding. Good impulses, easily influenced."[12]

It had been Yi Ha-yŏng to whom Deshler had gone to protest the prohibition. At that interview, Deshler was asked to halt recruitment until emigration rules could be drawn up; he replied that he would and that he would be glad to work under any regulations the government enacted.[13] Deshler's actions show, however, that he had little confidence in Yi's ability to restore emigration, an attitude undoubtedly exacerbated by Yi's unsuccessful attempt to promulgate new rules a few days later. And Deshler continued to recruit as if nothing had happened.[14] Moreover, Deshler began to exert pressure on the Korean government. On April 6 one of Deshler's Japanese employees threatened to sue the *kamni* of Chinnamp'o for damages if he continued to prohibit emigration from his port.[15] The same scene was repeated four days later in Inch'ŏn when the same man threatened the *kamni* there with a 130,000 *wŏn* damage suit.[16] Komura knew of Deshler's actions[17] and, fearing that the Korean government might be cowed by Deshler's threatened lawsuits, asked the Japanese chargé d'affaires in Seoul, Hagiwara Shuichi, to check on the report.[18] Hagiwara cabled back that he could find no evidence that Deshler had carried out his threats.[19] Komura could thus conclude that Deshler was simply bluffing.

While Deshler was busy threatening the Korean government with lawsuits, the Japanese were more concerned with the increasingly apparent inability of the Korean government to enforce its own prohibition. Concern was first raised by Komura himself, who noted that the ship carrying the emigrants to Mexico left on April 4, three days after the prohibition went into force.[20] Hayashi cabled back that they had been collected before the prohibition order.[21] A week later, however, Komura learned that two shiploads of emigrants had passed through Mokp'o after the prohibition had been enacted. The first ship, with 40 emigrants, had departed from Inch'ŏn while the second, carrying 215 emigrants, left Chinnamp'o on April 10.[22] Consequently, Komura fired off messages to the consuls in Inch'ŏn and Chinnamp'o.[23] Fearing the worst—that the Korean government had rescinded the order—Komura cabled Hagiwara to ask if that had occurred.[24] Hagiwara assured Komura that the law was still in force but that the Korean government was allowing those emigrants who had been recruited before the prohibition law had been enacted to depart.[25]

By this time it was clear to Japanese diplomats in Korea that their boss was upset by the continued departures of Koreans for Hawaii more than a month after emigration had been officially prohibited, and the accompanying unspoken assumption was that they should begin putting pressure on the Korean government to tighten up enforcement.

Consequently, Chargé d'Affaires Hagiwara went to the Korean vice-minister of foreign affairs, Yun Ch'i-ho, to complain and to ask Yun to stop the exodus.[26] Yun replied that the emigrants in question had been issued passports before April 1 and that when they had all departed, there would be no more emigration. Perhaps acknowledging that there were some irregularities in enforcement, Yun also assured Hagiwara that henceforth the prohibition would be more strictly enforced.[27] But just two days later, Hagiwara was forced to return to Yun's office to ask specifically about the latest incident, when 92 emigrants departed from Chinnamp'o on May 7, leading Yun to ask the *kamni* in Inch'ŏn whether those emigrants had been collected before or after the prohibition.[28] The reply was such that Hagiwara concluded that Deshler had recruited them after April 1, and he demanded that the Korean Foreign Office punish the *kamni* of Inch'ŏn and Chinnamp'o for dereliction of duty.[29]

It is clear that the need to force the Korean government into compliance with its own law was felt not only at the highest levels of the Japanese diplomatic mission in Seoul, but also at the local level. The vice-consul in Chinnamp'o, for example, in reporting to Komura, found himself having to explain that the aforementioned 92 emigrants (68 men, 11 women, and 13 children) had been recruited in P'yŏngyang before April 1 (according to Deshler's assistant) and that when they were denied passports by the *kamni* at Chinnamp'o, Deshler put them aboard his ship the *Ohio* and brought them to Inch'ŏn without passports. The vice-consul assured Komura that he was "trying to enforce this law."[30] Komura obviously expected that Japanese consuls in all the port cities of Korea would exert similar pressure on the local *kamni*.

In the meantime, Hayashi Gonsuke, who had been in Tokyo briefly, returned to Seoul in mid-May and picked up where Hagiwara had left off in pressuring the Korean government to tighten enforcement of the ban on emigration. When he met with Foreign Minister Yi Ha-yŏng on May 31, for instance, he complained that the *kamni* in Inch'ŏn was still issuing passports and that other Koreans bound for Hawaii were arriving in Japan without passports, and urged Yi once again to enforce his own regulation.[31] So confused was the situation that four days later Yi himself asked Hayashi's assistance in enforcing the ban more strictly.[32] Still, a week later, Hayashi was back to complain to Yi that the *kamni* were still allowing emigrants to depart.[33]

That Deshler continued to operate and that the Korean government was lax in enforcement was also evident when Komura's subordinate, Ishii Kikujirō, checked with Yokohama and Kobe, where Korean emigrants transferred to trans-Pacific steamers. From the governor of Kanagawa Prefecture (where Yokohama is located), Ishii learned that on April 15 the *Coptic* had sailed carrying 175 Koreans, on April 29 the *Siberia* had left with 329 Koreans, and on May 9 the *Mongolia* had departed with 279 Koreans—all bound for Hawaii.[34] When Ishii checked with Kobe,[35] he was told that the flow of Korean emigrants had been halted and that only 32 remained because they were ill and would be sent back to Korea when they recovered.[36]

Finally, by the middle of June, more than two months after the Korean government had prohibited emigration (at the insistence of Japan), the Japanese government was at last convinced that the prohibition was being enforced. Naturally this was due in large part to pressure by Komura on Hayashi, Hagiwara, and the consuls in Korea to force the Korean government to tighten enforcement. They in turn put pressure on Foreign Minister Yi Ha-yŏng, Vice-Foreign Minister Yun Ch'i-ho, and the *kamni* at the port cities to halt the exodus. Of course, the cashiering of Allen had made their efforts to bully the Korean government easier. Now Komura could depart for the Portsmouth peace talks in New Hampshire (with Horace Allen as a fellow passenger) and leave Hayashi in Seoul to convert the temporary ban on emigration into a permanent one. Hayashi was well equipped for this task, for he knew where the Korean government was vulnerable on this issue. Moreover, he would no longer have to brook interference from Horace Allen.

There were three weak points in the Korean government of the time which Japan was able to exploit in the issue of Korean immigration to Hawaii, and Hayashi was prepared to take advantage of every one. They relate to administrative mismanagement and are concrete signs of dynastic decline in the last years of the Yi dynasty. These weaknesses made the course of Japanese imperialism in general and the halting of Korean immigration to Hawaii in particular easier to accomplish.

First was the lack of suitable rules and regulations protecting emigrants. This problem arose because the Korean government had never been of one mind when it came to emigration. When the *Yuminwŏn* (Department of Emigration) had been created by imperial decree in late 1902 and placed in the *Kungnaebu* (Imperial Household Department), it was accompanied by emigration rules and regulations modeled after those of Japan. When Yi Yong-ik, the head of the Imperial Household Department, succeeded in persuading Emperor Kojong to abolish the *Yuminwŏn* by imperial decree in the fall of 1903 while Horace Allen was on home leave, its rules and regulations went too. Emigration still continued under the joint proprietorship of the Foreign Office, which authorized the *kamni* to issue passports, and of the Ministry of Agriculture, Commerce and Industry, under the aegis of the *Chungch'uwŏn* (Privy Council).[37] From this point onward, emigration proceeded on a dubious legal basis, with no rules and regulation protecting emigrants.

Hayashi Gonsuke had followed these events closely. And he confirmed that emigrants were permitted to leave with no regulations in effect when he made a point of asking the Korean government in the summer of 1904 for a copy of its emigration rules and regulations and received no answer.[38]

Of possible explanations for the failure of the Korean government to enact rules and regulations to protect emigrants, the lack of unity of opinion over this issue in the Korean government stands out. On the one hand, there were those who approved, including Yi Ha-yŏng, Yun Ch'i-ho, Min Yŏng-hwan, and, on occasion, Emperor Kojong. At the same time there were opponents to emigration in powerful positions in the Korean government. These included not only Yi Yong-ik, but also the former vice-minister of Foreign Affairs, Pak Yong-hwa, Ha Sang-gi, the *kamni* in Inch'ŏn, tax officials, and, also on occasion, Emperor Kojong. Had recruitment to high office in the final decades of the Yi Dynasty been based on Western training and expertise, these anti-emigration officials would have amounted to a small minority with little support. Officials chosen during this period, however, continued to be primarily men of traditional learning who presumably would hold a negative view toward emigration.[39] That is, Confucian-educated men would naturally tend to look upon emigration as extremely unfilial behavior, as it would prevent one from performing the proper rituals at the graves of one's parents and ancestors.

This stalemate between pro- and anti-emigration figures in the government was the legal limbo into which emigration was thrust when Emperor Kojong, at the behest of Yi Yong-ik, abolished the *Yuminwŏn* and the accompanying rules and regulations. It was not until the spring of 1905 that rumors surrounding the Mexican affair finally spurred the Korean government into belated action to repair the damage. By that time, however, Japanese policy had become one of preventing Korean emigration to Hawaii. Because of Allen's departure and the predominant position that Japan occupied by this time as the result of the Russo-Japanese War, Hayashi Gonsuke could now demand successfully that any new set of rules and regulations enacted by the Korean government be thoroughly researched. Indeed, this requirement was demanded by Hayashi because he was fairly certain that the Korean government was not efficient enough to carry out a thorough investigation of emigration. As a result, Hayashi could accomplish Japan's policy aim of making the temporary ban on emigration a permanent one. He could also use this example of mismanagement to argue that Japan should take control of Korea's foreign affairs generally.

The second weakness of the Korean government exhibited in the issue of Korean immigration to Hawaii, and another example of the mismanagement that characterized late Yi Korea, was the failure to assign consuls to Honolulu and other overseas locations where thousands of Koreans now resided. This area of vulnerability was one which Hayashi was able to use to advance Japan's policy by arguing that the Korean government needed to undergo a complete evaluation of the system of emigration, knowing full well that it was unlikely to do so. He could also use this oversight, as he did in the matter of Korea's lack of emigration rules, to argue that Japan should take overall control of Korea's foreign relations.

It is the responsibility of every nation to dispatch diplomats to areas where large numbers of its emigrants reside, for the purpose of representing their interests to the host country and to safeguard their welfare. On the one hand, perhaps it is not suprising that the Korean government was neglectful in this respect, for its one Western legal adviser, the American Clarence Greathouse, was not conversant in international law and usage. More important, perhaps, was the fact that the Korean government was "ambivalent toward Western international law. Its attitude was the result of adherence to indigenous values as embodied in Confucian precepts." As a result, Korea "did not have a single international lawyer."[40]

On the other hand, the Korean government had had numerous opportunities and proddings to conform to proper international usage. An acceptable alternative to appointing consuls overseas, if budgetary or other considerations made problems, was the practice of appointing a leading citizen of the region as an honorary consul; Korea itself had done so when Bostwick was appointed to that post in San Francisco. That no consul was named at this time, in spite of numerous proddings to do something, and the failure of the government to rectify the situation seem inexcusable and lend support to the view that Korea's government was terribly mismanaged.

The first of these many proddings came only two days after the establishment of the *Yuminwŏn* in the fall of 1902. At that time the Russian chargé d'affaires in Seoul wrote to the Korean Foreign Office to point out that there were tens of thousands of Koreans living in the Vladivostok area and that there was no Korean consul there.[41] The Korean government took no action. And naturally, when the Koreans started arriving in Hawaii in January of 1903 there was no Korean consul to greet them.

The question of a consul specifically for Honolulu was first broached six months after immigration to Hawaii began, and it was Horace Allen, not the Korean government, who initially raised the issue. The first prodding came when Allen went to then Foreign Minister Yi Chi-yong to complain about Yi Yong-ik's charges that the immigrants in Hawaii were treated as slaves. Allen's recourse was to suggest "the appointment of a Korean consul to reside in Hawaii and report on conditions there affecting Korean immigrants."[42] No consul was sent, and a year elapsed before the subject was again raised.

When the issue of a Korean consul in Honolulu was raised for the second time, again it was not at the initiative of the Korean government but rather at the initiative of the planters whose minutes record: "Mr. Smith spoke of the necessity of a Korean Consul at Honolulu and it was voted that Mr. Bishop be requested to write to Mr. Deshler on the subject."[43] Deshler, of course, passed his letter on to Allen who brought it to the attention of Vice-Minister of Foreign Affairs, Yun Ch'i-ho. Thus began the deep involvement of Yun Ch'i-ho in the issue of Korean immigration to Hawaii.

Yun was born into a *yangban* family in 1864 and studied at Emory College in Georgia and Vanderbilt University in Tennessee. An early advocate of reform and progressivism, Yun returned to Korea in 1895 to become a leader of the Independence Club and served as vice-minister of education. In 1902 he was posted to Wŏnsan and in 1903 to Mokp'o as *kamni*. Service at these two port cities from which emigration took place under his aegis made him familiar with Deshler's enterprise. At the beginning of the Russo-Japanese War in 1904, he was appointed vice-minister of Foreign Affairs. Allen characterized Yun thus: "Educated in America. A consistent Christian. A most honorable man. A Patriot. Intelligent and well posted. Timid and somewhat pessimistic."[44]

Indeed, in the summer of 1904 Yun was pessimistic about the abilities of the government for which he worked, writing in June that "Korea has become what she is through the imbecility, corruption and oppression of her own government. Despotism unchecked has ruined the country."[45] Despite his despair over the condition of his country, Yun was nonetheless in favor of emigration and study abroad, having on occasion given boat passage to students intending to go to the United States.[46] So he agreed to meet with Allen three weeks later to discuss the possibility of a Korean consul in Honolulu. At that meeting, which Allen had arranged as a response to the planters' request, Allen told Yun that he had proposed to the Korean government that Yun be appointed consul, and he mentioned that it was likely to be a permanent position no matter what action Japan would take in Korea.[47]

Yun, however, faced opposition from two sources: missionary and family. Shortly after talking with Allen, Yun met with his friend, the Reverend James Scarth Gale, who told him: "If I did not believe there is Providence, I would give up all hope for Korea. But somehow or other I believe there is a better time coming and we need men like you here."[48] Yun received an equally negative reaction from his father: "What for will you go? There is neither honor nor money nor public service nor private profit. We, I and your mother, are getting old. You would have to come home if far away [to perform the proper Confucian rituals at the gravesite]. Will you now go away tens of thousands of li now that you are with us? No, do not think of it."[49] Despite these arguments, Yun allowed Foreign Minister Yi Ha-yŏng to propose his name to the government as Korean consul in Honolulu.[50] But the decision was out of his hands: no consul was appointed. Meanwhile, the number of Korean immigrants there continued to grow.

The third prodding to the Korean government came from Hayashi Gonsuke at the end of the summer of 1904, who added that if it was not prepared to establish a consulate in Honolulu, he would recommend that Japanese Consul Saitō Miki fill the position.[51] Hayashi then started a rumor that Emperor Kojong had actually appointed Saitō to be honorary Korean consul.[52] These maneuverings were actually part of a larger campaign by Hayashi to force the Korean government to recall *all* of its diplomatic missions abroad and replace them with Japanese missions already there.[53] In this way, the issue of Korean immigration to Hawaii was bound up with the overall process of the Japanese takeover of Korea's foreign affairs. Despite these ominous moves by Japan, the Koreans in Hawaii remained without a consul.

The fourth instance of prodding the government for a consul came from an unlikely source—a private citizen in Korea. According to a newspaper report, in November of 1904, one Hyŏng Sŏk-chŏng approached the Ministry of Agriculture, Commerce and Industry, the government agency now supposedly in charge of emigration, and asked for permission to organize a society for the purpose of protecting Koreans residing abroad.[54] This unusual initiative was also unsuccessful: still no consul to Hawaii was named.

A fifth prodding came in December of 1904 from the planters in Honolulu when they wrote to Durham White Stevens, the Japanese-appointed American adviser to the Korean Foreign Office, on the subject of a Korean consul.[55] As before, nothing came of this initiative.

The sixth and final prod to the Korean government to set up a consulate in Honolulu came in January 1905 from the Koreans in Hawaii. In a memorial sent to Kojong requesting that he appoint a Korean consul, the immigrants wrote, "All the other nations have consuls and if it is a question of money the petitioners with other Koreans in

Hawaii will provide the funds for maintaining the consulate."[56] When, once again, no action was taken, the Koreans in Hawaii made the same request to the Korean legation in Washington, with similar results.[57]

Thus, through two years of prodding from different sources, the Korean government consistently refused to appoint a consul in Honolulu to look after the needs of seven thousand immigrants. So when it became Japanese policy to prevent Korean emigration to Hawaii in the spring of 1905, Hayashi was able to argue that emigration should not resume until this deficiency had been rectified. The Japanese solution, of course, was to appoint its own diplomats, enabling Japan to accomplish its larger aim of taking control of Korean foreign relations. The mismanagement of the Korean government had helped Japan's seizure of Korea.

A third weakness which Japanese imperialism was able to exploit was found in the events surrounding the emigration of 1,033 Koreans to Yucatan, Mexico, in the first week of April 1905. Once again, in the handling of this affair, the Korean government demonstrated the incompetence and inefficiency which characterized late Yi Korea.

Emigration to Mexico was clearly illegal. Deshler's imperial charter permitting him to recruit workers for Hawaii consituted the only legal emigration from Korea.[58] To recruit Koreans for work in Mexico required government permission, but this permission was lacking. Nonetheless, a Japanese emigration company called the Continental Colonization Company (*Tairiku shokumin kaisha* in Japanese and *Taeryuk sikmin hoesa* in Korean) arrived in Korea in December 1904 and openly solicited recruits, running an advertisement in the government-sponsored *Hwangsŏng sinmun* continuously for nearly a month.[59] An alert and efficient foreign office should have taken note and put a halt to this solicitation, or at least required the company to seek official permission. It did neither, and the recruitment for Mexico continued.

Furthermore, once recruited, these thousand emigrants for Mexico had no passports. This is not surprising, since the entire enterprise was illegal from the beginning and was conducted outside official channels.[60]

To make matters worse, Korea not only did not have a consulate in the Yucatan to look after the interests of these emigrants, but it did not even have diplomatic relations with Mexico. In fact, a competent foreign office would never have allowed its countrymen to go to a place like the Yucatan where labor conditions were nothing short of terrible. By contrast, the Japanese government had conducted the necessary research and, with the exception of the Enomoto colony of 1896, would not permit its subjects to emigrate to Mexico. Information was generally available, either from Japan or from books on the region, but the Korean government apparently did not avail itself of these sources.[61] Since Korea had no diplomatic relations with Mexico, it was even more incumbent upon the Foreign Office to investigate conditions in the Yucatan. This was not done.

These anomalies became evident when the discovery of a case of smallpox caused the entire shipload to disembark in Inch'ŏn and be held incommunicado in quarantine. Naturally, rumors circulated that these thousand Koreans were being sold into slavery in Mexico. When the Korean government finally reacted by prohibiting emigration, the quarantine had already ended and the ship illegally sailed off to an unknown fate in the Yucatan. Yet the action did provide the opportunity for Hayashi to bully Foreign Minister Yi Ha-yŏng into extending the prohibition to include Hawaii, which had now become one of Japan's foreign policy aims in Korea.

Thus, the lack of emigration rules and regulations, the absence of a Korean consul in Honolulu (as well as Mexico and Vladivostok), and the illegal departure of one thousand emigrants to an uncertain fate in the Yucatan, demonstrated vividly the maladministration which characterized the final years of the Yi dynasty. Much of the blame resides in the Korean Foreign Office and the shortcomings of Yi Ha-yŏng who served as foreign minister for much of the time. Yet perhaps it was too much to expect adequate leadership from a ministry whose top position (despite Yi Ha-yŏng's relatively long tenure) resembled a game of musical chairs, with no fewer than ten foreign ministers serving during the three-year period 1903–1905.[62]

The obvious weakness and ineffectiveness of the Korean government in regard to emigration policies were exploited by Japan within the larger framework of the Japanese control of Korea after the end of hostilities in the Russo-Japanese War. That is, Japan did not have to appear to bully Korea to force it to halt emigration. Rather, Japan could demonstrate to Koreans as well as to other nations, particularly England and the United States, that its actions in forcing Korea to suspend emigration until "adequate" rules and regulations were promulgated showed "humanitarian concern" for the welfare of Korean immigrants. George Trumbull Ladd, the apologist for Japan, could write three years later with some justification, "With regard to all foreign relations with Korea, whether of legitimate business, of commerce, or of emigration, the civilized world is undoubtedly much better off now that their custody is in the hands of the Japanese Residency-General." In a specific reference to the inept Korean Foreign Office, Ladd continued, "Foreign affairs have always been with the Emperor and Court of Korea a particularly favorable but mischievous place for intrigue and intermeddling. . . . The Korean Foreign Minister in 1905 was not an efficient and responsible representative of either the intentions or transactions of his own government."[63] To its own people, Japan could justify its action as guaranteeing greater opportunity for emigration to Hawaii, solicitude for the welfare of Japanese immigrants already there, and concern for the economic well-being of Japanese emigration companies. This latter point was put forward by Hayashi Gonsuke when he met with one of the directors of the Continental Colonization Company.[64] Only Komura and his colleagues in the Japanese Foreign Ministry knew that the main purpose behind Japanese policy to halt Korean immigration to Hawaii was to prevent the United States from enacting a Japanese exclusion act.

The issue of Korean immigration to Hawaii was also intimately bound up with the larger issue of the Japanese takeover of Korea's foreign affairs in 1905. Only a week after the Japanese-forced decision by the Korean government temporarily to ban all emigration, the Japanese government decided upon the contents of a document which would become seven months later the basis for the Protectorate Treaty between Japan and Korea. Beginning with the phrase, "Japan should establish the right to protect Korea and should take charge of all Korean foreign relations in order to accomplish the perfect defense of Japan," the document listed four items that a protection treaty should include, among them a Japanese resident-general to supervise the Korean government, Japanese responsibility for the enforcement of treaties between Korea and foreign countries, and the prevention of Korea from entering into additional direct relations with other countries. Most telling, though, was the first item, which read, "Japan should take charge of Korean foreign relations and the protection of Korean emigrants."[65] In effect, the negligence of the Korean government in the emigration issue provided an important rationale as well as vehicle for the Japanese takeover of Korea's foreign affairs and the subsequent demise of Korea's last dynasty.

14

The Planters and Korea Fight Back

As we have seen, the weaknesses of the Korean government precluded any need for Japan to resort to the distasteful use of overtly strong-arm tactics and instead allowed Japan to argue with some justification that humanitarian concern was the motivation in persuading the Korean government to declare a temporary ban on emigration. Once that had been accomplished, Japan could then argue that it could permit the Korean government to resume emigration only if it promulgated rules and regulations which had been the result of a thorough and careful investigation. Because of the demonstrated weakness of the Korean government, and in particular the Korean Foreign Office, in the summer of 1905, Japan could be reasonably sure that the Korean government was not up to such an effort, thereby insuring Japan's intent to choke off Korean immigration to Hawaii permanently, while at the same time appearing to be Korea's benefactor. Moreover, the issue had become useful to Japan when it argued that Japan should take over the foreign relations of Korea and allow Japanese diplomatic representatives to take care of Korean interests abroad, including the care of Korean emigrants. Japan's paramountcy in the issue was challenged, however, by the planters who still desired Korean immigration and by the Korean government, which came to realize that the issue of emigration was intimately related to its continued sovereignty and independence as a nation state.

Despite the ban on Korean emigration in early April 1905, there were still many Koreans "in the pipeline," as Deshler endeavored to send as many as he could before the Korean government, under pressure from Japan, could clamp down. As a result, the month of May saw the arrival of nearly one-seventh of the entire Korean population in Hawaii, when 1,003 immigrants landed at Honolulu.[1] As enforcement tightened, the number of arrivals from Korea diminished to 92 in June, and 109 (71 men, 21 women, and 17 children) in July—the last arrival of Koreans in significant numbers.[2]

As the number of Korean arrivals dwindled, the planters began to take action to restart the inflow of their most reliable and inexpensive offset to the majority Japanese laborers on the plantations. In early June, for example, they had met with the incoming American minister to Korea, Edwin V. Morgan, hoping that he could persuade the Korean government to allow emigration to resume.[3] But the planters knew that he would not have the clout that Allen had had and also that the locus of decision-making on this issue had now shifted from Seoul to Tokyo. They had to address these changed circumstances, at the same time making sure that federal officials would still be kept in the dark about the illegal assistance the planters were providing Korean immigrants.

Indeed, the planters had a brief scare in mid-June, shortly after Morgan had left for Korea, that their circumvention of the immigration laws had been uncovered. The occasion was once again the arrival of Immigration Commissioner J. P. Sargent who had come to Hawaii "to regulate immigration and probably stop Koreans."[4] To prevent such an occurrence, HSPA President F. M. Swanzy met with Sargent on the afternoon of June 15,[5] and two days later, on the morning of June 17, the assembled HSPA trustees "had long talks" with Sargent.[6] During these talks, the planters discovered that their secret was still intact and that Korean immigration would not face obstacles from Washington. Tokyo was another matter.

An unfounded rumor that one of the individual plantation managers had sent someone to Korea in May to recruit workers may have been the catalyst for the next step taken by the planters.[7] For in early July, the "HSPA Trustees press[ed]" Swanzy "to go to Japan and Korea on labor matters." As president of the HSPA, Swanzy could hardly refuse to go. But he knew that any decision on Korean immigration would be made in Tokyo, not Seoul, so he planned to go only to Japan. By chance, on the day Swanzy was to depart on the *Manchuria*, Secretary of War Taft arrived from California aboard the same ship. He had lunch with Swanzy at the Royal Hawaiian Hotel, where Swanzy no doubt learned that Taft was en route to Japan to give Roosevelt's endorsement of Japan's preeminence in Korea.[8] The ship sailed at five that afternoon, July 14.

The importance of Swanzy's mission was underscored by Cooke, who wrote that "[Swanzy] will endeavor to get the immigration started again. . . . It is very important that we have the Koreans."[9] Three weeks later he noted: "I hope Mr. Swanzy may be successful in opening up the emigration from Korea. . . . It is highly important that something should be done and you can rest assured that no stones will be left unturned so far as we are concerned here in Honolulu."[10] If Swanzy's mission were unsuccessful, the planters would be faced with the prospect of having to import more expensive European labor, a step strongly supported by labor organizations and the territorial government, which preferred white immigrants, but naturally resisted by the planters. To be on the safe side, while Swanzy prepared to leave for Japan, the HSPA sent a representative to New York with $2,000 to recruit Italians and Portuguese.[11] Cooke succinctly summed up the attitude of the planters about this move: "At the same time while most everyone is prejudiced in the same way, so long as they cannot obtain Oriental laborers it seems wise to stare the matter in the face and take a few laborers so as to help out in case the immigration of Koreans and Japanese is stopped. You are not alone in your views as to the introduction of Italians and Portuguese."[12]

Swanzy hoped to meet with Durham White Stevens in Japan. Stevens was an American appointed by Japan as adviser to the Korean Foreign Office, having previously served as the American counselor to the Japanese Legation in Washington. Japan was able to appoint Stevens to that position as a result of the outbreak of the Russo-Japanese War which markedly increased Japanese influence in Korea. Stevens was appointed as a result of a provision that "a foreigner recommended by the Japanese Government [be appointed], as an adviser to the Foreign Office, in order that any important matters relating to foreign affairs will be decided by his advice." In addition to Stevens, the protocol also called for "a Japanese recommended by the Japanese Government, as an adviser to the Finance Department, in order that anything concerning financial matters will be decided by his advice."[13] The person selected to this position was Megata Tanetarō, who will also figure prominently in the issue of Korean immigration.[14]

As Stevens took up his duties as adviser to the Korean Foreign Office in the fall of 1904,[15] there was no doubt that Japan trusted him to view Korean affairs in the same light as did the Japanese Foreign Ministry. Yet Stevens was no mere puppet of Japan. After all, the intensely pro-Korean Horace Allen had initially recommended Stevens for the post some three years earlier,[16] and it was Stevens whom Allen in his last letter to Swanzy suggested might be of some assistance in restarting Korean immigration to Hawaii.[17] So when Swanzy reached Yokohama aboard the *Manchuria* on July 26, 1905,[18] Ozawa, the head of the Japan Emigration Company, informed him that Stevens was in Korea, but would be in Tokyo in about ten days.[19] Swanzy was optimistic that his forthcoming meeting with Stevens would be fruitful.

The confidence that Allen and then Swanzy placed in Stevens' willingness and ability to help restart Korean immigration was apparently well founded. Initially, at least, it seemed that Stevens was either ignorant of, or opposed to, Japan's efforts to prohibit Korean immigration to Hawaii. For on June 15, apparently as a favor to his recently departed friend Horace Allen, he had an audience with Emperor Kojong to suggest that Vice-Foreign Minister Yun Ch'i-ho be sent to Japan and then to Hawaii to investigate the condition of the Koreans there. Kojong agreed, and Stevens then suggested the same idea to Foreign Minister Yi Ha-yǒng, Hayashi, and Megata who "all agreed that it was an excellent idea, but none of them seems particularly anxious to put the proposal into effect."[20] Nonetheless, the acting prime minister, Sin Sang-hun, told Yun, in the presence of Foreign Minister Yi Ha-yǒng, to make the trip, giving him the necessary governmental authorization.[21]

So in mid-July, with the blessings of Kojong and Stevens, Yun arrived in Tokyo on July 22.[22] Stevens followed Yun five days later.[23] Thus, as Swanzy was heading west across the Pacific, Stevens and Yun were heading east across the Straits of Japan. By early August, all three men were in Tokyo.

The first meeting was held, without Yun in attendance, on August 9 at the Imperial Hotel where Swanzy was staying. That Stevens was still not opposed to Korean immigration to Hawaii seems clear from Swanzy's diary entry for that day: "D. W. Stevens called on me at the hotel, he having arrived from Seoul the other day. We had a pleasant, interesting and satisfactory talk about Korean immigration."[24]

On the following day, all three men, Stevens, Swanzy, and Yun, met for lunch at the Tokyo Club. Also in Tokyo was David Deshler who arranged to have dinner that evening with Swanzy, after which the two men talked about Korean immigration until one in the morning.[25] The next afternoon, Yun met with Swanzy at the Imperial Hotel where Swanzy told Yun that the planters liked Korean laborers and were sorry that emigration had been suspended. Yun then informed Swanzy that he would be visiting Hawaii to investigate the situation, and Swanzy offered to pay for the entire trip. Yun, a man of great integrity, declined, telling Swanzy, "Of course it is out of the question that I should accept the offer since that would prejudice the Korean government against any report I may make, if at all favorable to the planters."[26] After this talk, Swanzy met again with Stevens and "had a pleasant chat."[27]

While Yun waited in Tokyo for the ship to take him to Hawaii, he conferred with his Japanese counterparts in the Foreign Ministry. Yun left the meeting convinced that the Japanese government intended to keep Koreans out of Hawaii. Yun believed he had discovered the reason from a conversation he had with an agent of the Continental Colonization Company: "He told me that the Taeryuk [sikmin] hoesa men are opposed to the Korean immigration to the Hawaiian islands as that would interfere with Japan's immigration, and that they would like to see Korean immigration directed to countries—like Mexico for instance—where Japanese are not found. I see from this little talk why the Japanese Legation in Seoul was so anxious to stop the Korean emigration."[28]

Yun was clearly bitter, for his diary records: "Now just think of it. Japan, whose surplus coolies, titled and otherwise, pour into Korea in tens and hundreds of thousands to grab everything in sight, to kick and cuff and cuss the Koreans as ingrates and savages for not being grateful for being kicked, cuffed and cussed. This generous and altruistic Japan grudges the few miserable dollars which the Korean laborers may pick up in the dust and mud of the Hawaiian canefields!"[29]

When Japanese officials learned of Yun's suspicions that Japan's policy was to prevent Koreans from going to Hawaii, Ishii Kikujirō hedged, telling him that the government was not completely against Korean immigration to Hawaii and was willing to allow it to resume, with certain limitations, when the Korean government enacted an emigrant protection law similar to Japan's. Ishii then explained Japan's emigration regulations and Yun agreed to urge the Korean government to enact such regulations upon his return to Seoul. Ishii also told Yun that Japan had no objection to his trip to Hawaii.[30] Despite the decidedly lukewarm attitude of the Japanese government, Yun was still resolved to carry out his mission. All he needed was the money from Seoul.

The money finally arrived on August 27 when Yun received a telegram reading: "Proceed to Hawaii and Mexico. Transmitted 1,000 yen to the Japanese Bank, Seoul."[31] Why had Mexico now been added to Yun's itinerary? Two reasons stand out. First, the rumors of slavery that had surrounded the departure of the ship carrying the thousand Koreans to Mexico in April seemed to have been confirmed by the beginning of August when a letter was received from a Chinese ginseng merchant in Mexico that the Koreans in the Yucatan were treated like slaves.[32] So concerned was Emperor Kojong that he issued an (ineffectual) order that they be returned.[33] Yun was being sent to investigate their fate.

A second reason for the addition of Mexico to Yun's itinerary was tied up with the issue of the resumption of the right of Koreans to emigrate. If Yun were to visit both Hawaii and Mexico and then return to Korea to draw up emigration rules and regulations, this, it was hoped, would satisfy the conditions which Japan had stipulated before emigration could be resumed.

This new development could hardly have been enthusiastically received by the Japanese, because it would not only force them to act in a heavy-handed way (which they wanted to avoid) to keep the prohibition on emigration in force, but it could also complicate and even reverse Japanese efforts to transfer Korean diplomatic missions abroad to the control of Japanese diplomatic missions. That is, it was not inconceivable that Yun's visit to Mexico might result in an attempt to establish diplomatic relations between Korea and Mexico and the posting of Korean diplomats in Mexico City and Merida in the Yucatan. Stevens, who had by now been briefed by the Japanese Foreign Ministry on the whole issue of Korean emigration, was thus decidedly cool when Yun informed him about the addition of Mexico to his mission, saying: "Oh never mind Mexico. Besides, 1,000 yen—only 500 dollars U.S. gold [is] hardly enough for the Hawaiian trip."[34] Now even Stevens was opposed to Yun's trip. Nonetheless, at the end of August, Yun was prepared to depart to carry out his mission to Hawaii and Mexico.

Yun left on the afternoon of August 30 aboard the *Manchuria* for the ten-day voyage to Honolulu.[35] On the same ship went a letter from vice-minister of Foreign Affairs Chinda Sutemi to Consul Saitō in Honolulu asking that he assist Yun in his inspection tour of the Koreans in Hawaii.[36] And Ishii Kikujirō, director of commerce of the Japanese Foreign Ministry, provided Yun with a letter of introduction to Saitō.[37]

Also aboard the *Manchuria* with Yun Ch'i-ho was F. M. Swanzy, who had met several times with Vice-Foreign Minister Chinda, Director of the Commerce Bureau of the Foreign Ministry Ishii, and Prime Minister Katsura Tarō to discuss the Japanese attitude toward Korean immigration to Hawaii. Under instructions to treat Swanzy as warmly as possible while in Tokyo, these officials informed him that they would permit Korean emigration to resume once the Korean government had enacted suitable rules and regulations. Because they were still concerned about anti-Japanese feeling in California, they also told Swanzy that the Japanese government would not protest if the United States enacted a law temporarily prohibiting Japanese from moving from Hawaii to the mainland without the approval of the Japanese consul in Honolulu. Swanzy, in turn, assured them that the HSPA would continue to provide passage for Korean and Japanese immigrants to Hawaii.[38]

Two days before departing, Swanzy met one last time with Stevens at the Japanese Foreign Ministry and "had an hour's talk with him on Korean affairs." Stevens told him that "the usefulness of Yun's mission to Hawaii depended somewhat on the turning out of a large number of the present Korean cabinet and the substitution of decent men with whom Yun is popular and for whom they have a liking." Stevens also said that Kojong "will promise any cabinet reform Stevens suggests but [he] can only be forced with effecting reforms by 'being taken by the scruff of the neck.' When the war is over and the suzerainty of Japan over Korea is established this will be possible."[39] Swanzy thus left Japan encouraged that it would eventually permit Korean immigration to Hawaii to resume. But this approval hinged upon Yun's investigation, and Swanzy was anxious that he have a favorable impression of the treatment of Koreans in Hawaii.

After a "very pleasant voyage," the two men disembarked at eight o'clock on the morning of September 8, and Swanzy immediately took Yun to the Royal Hawaiian Hotel.[40] Upon his arrival, Yun granted an interview to one of the local newspapers. The planters must have been encouraged, because Yun stated "that there were no stories of ill-treatment of Koreans in Hawaii. He said he heard of ill treatment of Koreans in Mexico and he was going there to investigate."[41] Later that same morning, Swanzy took Yun to meet Governor Carter who "said nice things about Koreans." At 7:30 that evening, Yun met with Saitō, after which he addressed eighty Koreans at the Methodist church on Nuuanu Street and was greeted there by Mrs. Harold Noble who had been a missionary friend in P'yŏngyang.[42]

At ten the following morning, Swanzy took the thirty-four-year-old Yun to meet the HSPA trustees. When Yun "stated that he desired to visit the Koreans here and ascertain their conditions," an itinerary was arranged.[43] And so on the afternoon of Saturday, September 9, 1905, Yun, in the company of the missionary Harold Noble and Hyŏn Sun, the interpreter turned preacher, set out on the Oahu railway for Ewa Plantation, the first of many plantations he would visit during his four-week sojourn in Hawaii.[44]

Because the resumption of Korean immigration was important to the planters, every effort was made to make Yun's trip agreeable. For example, when Yun sailed from Oahu to Kauai, Swanzy arranged for him to occupy the captain's room, and he was escorted by Secretary of Hawaii Atkinson and Immigration Commissioner Bechtel.[45] And a letter to the manager of a plantation Yun was about to visit read: "We beg to impress upon you the necessity of your doing your utmost for this gentleman, as future immigration of laborers from Korea will depend largely upon him. Complaints have reached the Korean Foreign Office that the Korean laborers in Mexico have been maltreated, and as they are not sure about the treatment their people are receiving here, he wants to find out from the men personally as to whether or not they have any complaints to make against the plantations. The resumption of this immigration from Korea will, therefore, depend largely upon this investigation, and for this reason we would ask that every courtesy be shown to Mr. Yun, as their Foreign Office will doubtlessly pay great attention to his statements. It is essential to the welfare of the plantations to have other elements than Japanese here."[46]

The planters were confident that because of Swanzy's apparently successful meetings in Tokyo and the fact that Koreans were not ill-treated in Hawaii, Yun would recommend that immigration resume, the Korean Foreign Office would draw up the necessary regulations, and Japan would drop its objections to Korean immigration to Hawaii. So confident were they that, even while Yun was still making his rounds on the outer islands, the HSPA trustees met to fix the amount they would pay Deshler for boat passages and commissions upon the resumption of immigration.[47]

While Yun was investigating the conditions of the Koreans in Hawaii and the planters were preparing for what they thought would be the imminent resumption of immigration from Korea, unbeknownst to both, certain events and trends during that summer of 1905 had strengthened the determination of Japan to prevent the resumption of Korean immigration to Hawaii.

The first of these trends was the rise of Korean nationalism and anti-Japanese feelings among overseas Koreans in general and those in Hawaii in particular. The event that seems to have galvanized this movement was the appointment of Saitō Miki as honorary consul for Korea in Honolulu. Since the summer of 1904, the Japanese had been pressing the Korean government to allow the Japanese consul-general in Honolulu to care for the Koreans in Hawaii by naming Saitō honorary consul.[48] This was part of a larger effort to induce the Korean government to recall its diplomatic missions abroad and transfer their responsibilities to the respective Japanese diplomatic missions.

After the prohibition on emigration was issued in early April 1905, the pressure to make Saitō honorary consul increased markedly.[49] In early May, the Korean government finally succumbed and Saitō was appointed.[50] The reaction of the Koreans in Hawaii was predictable: they immediately informed the Korean legation in Washington that they desired a consul of their own nationality rather than a Japanese subject.[51] While Saitō did take steps to begin charitable work among the Koreans in Hawaii and persuaded the planters to contribute,[52] the Koreans still insisted on a *Korean* consul and sent a messenger to Seoul to press their claim.[53] The petition to the Korean Foreign Office in early August was so moving that it was reported that people shed tears upon reading it.[54] Calling themselves "sheep without a shepherd and a boat without an oar," the Koreans in Hawaii expressed loyalty to the emperor, chided the government for not sending a consul, refused to accept Saitō as consul, and again offered to raise the money for a Korean consulate.[55]

While the refusal of the Koreans in Hawaii to accept Saitō can perhaps be seen as less anti-Japanese than pro-Korean nationalism, their activities in response to the Portsmouth peace talks were more overtly directed against the increasing Japanese domination of their Korean homeland. In August, Rev. Yun P'yŏng-gu, one of the Koreans in Hawaii, traveled to the mainland to meet with Syngman Rhee, then a student at George Washington University, with most of the expenses contributed by Koreans in Hawaii.[56] The two met with President Roosevelt to plead the case of Korea against Japan and to present him with "A Petition from the Koreans of Hawaii to President Roosevelt," dated July 12, 1905. Roosevelt brushed them off by referring them to the Korean Legation in Washington.[57] Naturally the Japanese were sensitive to the publicity surrounding Yun's departure for the mainland and sought to downplay the trip by announcing in a local Japanese paper: "Korean Going to Mainland Not a Peace Envoy—Goes to Solicit Funds for Korean School and Hospital in Hawaii."[58] There were also rumors that the *Sinminhoe* in Hawaii was setting up a provisional Korean government.[59] It was clear to Japan that as Japanese domination of Korea increased, growing opposition could be expected from Koreans abroad, especially from those in the freer and more affluent surroundings provided by the United States, where even on the mainland, nationalist figures like Syngman Rhee, An Ch'ang-ho, and Pak Yŏng-man were beginning to raise anti-Japanese voices. In order to limit anti-Japanese nationalist activities among Korean emigré communities abroad, it made perfect sense to Japan to continue to ban further emigration from Korea.

An additional reason for keeping the lid on Korean emigration was the revelation in early August that the Koreans in Mexico were in dire straits. This turn of events provided Japan with another reason for preventing further emigration and also for justifying the transfer of their care to the Japanese minister to Mexico. In mid-August, Foreign Minister Yi Ha-yŏng even asked Hayashi's assistance in helping to stop the reported ill-treatment of Koreans in Mexico[60] and three days later asked the American government for similar help.[61] All this, of course, played into the hands of Japan, which immediately urged the Korean government to entrust the protection of the Koreans in Mexico to the Japanese Legation there.[62] While the Korean minister of Foreign Affairs replied that no decision could be made until the completion of Yun's inspection visit, it was clear that the position of the Korean government was extremely weak vis-à-vis Japan on this issue.[63]

A third event that stiffened the resolve of Japan not to give in on the issue of Korean emigration was the conclusion of the Taft-Katsura Agreement in late July, which had the effect of giving American approval for Japan's establishment of a protectorate over Korea in return for Japanese acquiescence in American domination of the Philippines. The United States had taken note of the tremendous increase in Japanese power in Asia and its predominant interest in Korea. In order to protect its own recently acquired colony of the Philippines from Japanese meddling, President Roosevelt was willing to guarantee that the United States would not interfere in Japan's control over Korea. This, then, was the purpose of Secretary of War Taft's trip to Japan mentioned earlier in this chapter.

Finally the continued anti-Japanese agitation in California over the issue of Japanese immigration was another reason for maintaining a strict prohibition on Korean emigration.[64]

Thus, by the fall of 1905 there was little chance that the Japanese were about to relent and allow the resumption of Korean immigration to Hawaii. Yun suspected that this might be so but the planters were still operating under the illusion that immigration would be resumed.

In preventing the resumption of Korean immigration to Hawaii, Japan wanted to tread softly, rather than act as a bully, if at all possible, in order to maintain its image as Korea's benefactor and protector. However, if Yun were to conclude that Koreans in Hawaii were not mistreated, go to Mexico to investigate conditions there, and finally return to Korea to draw up suitable regulations, then Japan would be forced to resort to a heavy-handed approach, which would involve going back on its pledges to Yun and the planters. At the very least, this would cast a shadow on Japanese claims that it desired the reform and the uplifting of Korea—claims which garnered British and American approval for its policy on Korea. Japan needed to prevent Yun's mission from being brought to a successful conclusion.

The opportunity presented itself in late September. While Yun was in Hawaii, he received a telegram from Seoul containing a bank draft for the remainder of his trip. It read: "Get 490 Yen from Specie Bank. Yun Ch'i-ho travelling expenses Mexico. Foreign Office, Seoul." Yun went to the bank with Saitō to cash the bank draft, which came to $242 in American currency. However, Swanzy had told Yun that the trip to the Yucatan would require at least $360.[65] After talking to Saitō, Yun cabled back to the Korean Foreign Office in Seoul the next morning: "490 Yen received. 300 American dollars more for Mexico. Yun." The cable itself cost Yun over eighteen dollars.[66]

This was just the opportunity that Japan was waiting for. When the Foreign Office received the cable, it asked the Finance Department to forward the necessary funds to Yun.[67] Once this request had reached the Finance Department, it now became a matter for the Japanese adviser to that department, Megata Tanetarō, to consider. Not surprisingly, Megata vetoed the additional expenditure.[68] In declining to fund Yun's trip to Mexico, Megata could easily point to the depleted state of Korea's exchequer, which had allowed the Korean Legation in Washington to go several months in arrears.[69] Megata had also recently lambasted the "irresponsible" practices of the Korean Finance Department.[70]

Meanwhile, in Hawaii, Yun returned to Honolulu from the island of Maui at seven in the morning of October 3, after having visited no fewer than thirty-two plantations and making forty-one speeches. At nine that same morning he met with Consul Saitō and learned that his traveling expenses for Mexico had not arrived from Seoul. Having no alternative, Yun made up his mind to return to Korea that afternoon aboard the *Manchuria*, which departed at five.

Before returning to the Orient, his mission only partly accomplished, Yun met one final time with "the members of that solid and able body"—the HSPA trustees—at 1:30 that afternoon.[71] At that meeting, "Yun stated . . . that he found that the Koreans were well treated by the managers; that complaints among the Koreans are not against the plantations or the managers. . . . Yun stated that his business was to find out how the Koreans are doing here and to report what he has seen and heard to his Government; that a renewal or suspension of the immigration to these Islands rests with the Government, but that he would strongly recommend a renewal of the immigration."[72]

And so Yun left Hawaii on October 3 for Japan; Democratic leader William Jennings Bryan was also on board.[73] While Yun was certainly disappointed that he was unable to continue on to Mexico, he had assured the planters in Hawaii that he would recommend resumption of the immigration and would draw up the necessary regulations to satisfy the Japanese conditions. Eagerly, the planters prepared for the arrival of more Korean immigrants.

The optimism of the planters was also buoyed by the arrival of Homer Hulbert on the heels of Yun's departure. Hulbert also investigated the condition of the Koreans in Hawaii whom he pronounced "uniformly happy and successful" and "in great favor with the managers." Commenting on Yun's recent visit, Hulbert said, "I do not see how he can do otherwise than advise that the coming of Koreans to Hawaii be not discouraged. Everything that I heard and saw made me believe that no one who has Korea's welfare at heart can continue to oppose their coming here."[74]

Once again the planters began lavishing praise on the Koreans, telling the editor of the *Des Moines Capital*, who was traveling through with the Taft party, that the Koreans "make excellent laborers."[75] More important, the Koreans were once again proving their worth as a foil to the Japanese by refusing to cooperate with a Japanese strike in Lahaina, Maui, in early October.[76] Rumors began to circulate that Korean immigration had in fact already been resumed.[77]

Others in Hawaii were more realistic. The inspector in charge of immigration, Bechtel, for example, had learned that "the policy of the Japanese government [is] towards the restriction of emigration of the Koreans themselves."[78] This observation was backed up by the fact that the five-month period of August to December 1905 recorded only seven Korean arrivals.[79] And by late November the planters began clutching at straws as the expected arrival of Koreans did not materialize as they had assumed: A local man bragged to the "deeply interested" planters that "I could go to Korea and arrange for any number of Koreans to come here."[80]

As the planters waited in Hawaii in vain for the immigration to resume, Yun had arrived in Tokyo in mid-October and was informed by Korean Minister to Japan Cho Pyŏng-sik that in his absence Pak Che-sun had been named head of the Korean Foreign Office, leading Yun to remark, "The Korean Palace and government [are] too corrupt and imbecile and impotent to enforce laws for the protection of the people while the Japanese prolong and encourage this corruption, imbecility and impotence in order to make [the] Korean government stink."[81] And two days later he observed, "Under the galling slavery of Japan, Koreans will learn that the despotism of their own rulers has been the stepping stone to the despotism of alien masters."[82] It was clear to Yun that the Korean Foreign Office was now in no position to draw up the necessary regulations protecting emigrants and that Japan had prevailed in this issue.

Just as all seemed lost, Yun was surprised to receive a cable from the Korean Foreign Office reading: "Yun's Mexican traveling expenses 600 Yen sent by mail steamer. Start at once." Certainly Megata had not relented, so where had the money come from? It had, in fact, been sent by Emperor Kojong himself. But the 600 *yen*, nearly $300, was not enough now for Yun to get to Mexico; so he cabled back to Seoul: "Round ticket from Tokio to Mexico Yen 1164. Total expenses in Mexico Yen 400. Total Yen 1564. Yen 490 formerly received plus Yen 600 now coming, total Yen 1090. Deficiency Yen 474. Better instruct Korean Legation Washington to investigate and report—reply."[83]

Just when Japan had thought the issue settled, Kojong had intervened, threatening Japan with the renewed prospect that Yun would go to Mexico after all—despite Yun's suggestion that the Korean Legation in Washington handle the issue. Japan had to nip this new initiative in the bud. So when Yun, Stevens, and Hayashi had lunch at the Tokyo Club three days later, Hayashi suggested that Stevens cable the Korean Foreign Office advising against Yun's trip to Mexico.[84]

In a surprising display of independence, however, Korean Foreign Minister Pak Che-sun, deferring to the wishes of Kojong, continued to insist that Yun proceed to Mexico. According to Yun, "Stevens thinks that the Palace is anxious to send me to Mexico not out of any solicitude for the Koreans in Yucatan but of some political motive—to show the foreign nations that the Korean government is managing its own foreign affairs—In either case I do not think the Palace is wrong for this once." Nonetheless, Yun "sent another long message insisting that [he] should be in Seoul."[85] Japan was finding Kojong a difficult sovereign to control.

So serious was the prospect of Kojong sending Yun enough money to go to Mexico that Komura, who had recently returned from the Portsmouth peace talks in mid-October, was forced to intervene, cabling Hagiwara in Seoul to "try to persuade him [the Emperor] to cancel his order" by telling Kojong that Stevens had been in Mexico before and could tell him about the situation there if requested, and therefore Yun's trip to Mexico was unnecessary.[86] Hagiwara's "persuasion" was effective and the next day he informed Komura that Foreign Minister Pak Che-sun had cabled the Korean minister to Japan, Cho, saying, "Inform Yun Ch'i-ho to return."[87] Yun, though, had not yet received this cable, so he cabled Seoul once again: "Traveling expenses for Mexico not come. Shall I return? Answer." He noted in his diary that this was the third message he had sent. Only after dispatching this final cable did he record, "I found a message from Seoul telling me to return."[88]

Thus ended the saga of Yun's proposed inspection trip to the Yucatan. Japan had finally prevailed. Because Yun had been unable to go to Mexico, Japan could continue to argue plausibly that the Korean Foreign Office had not investigated the emigration situation thoroughly and therefore could not possibly draw up suitable rules and regulations to protect emigrants. Japan could still justify its prohibition of Korean emigration. Also precluded was any attempt by Korea to establish diplomatic relations with Mexico and thereby reverse Japan's efforts to force Korea to withdraw its diplomatic missions abroad and transfer all such responsibility to Japan.

Dispirited, Yun left Tokyo by train on the evening of November 2, bitter that Chinda and Ishii had snubbed him during his stay there and pessimistic about Korea's future: "You can no more expect independence and good government from the present generation of Koreans than Moses could have expected from the generation of slaves whom he led into the wilderness. . . . The miserly and unloving authority of [the] Foreign Office, the stinking smells of the House[hold Department], the tyranny and arrogance and oppression of the Japanese all over Korea."[89] Also on the train was D. W. Stevens, whom Yun did not blame for the emigration debacle: "As an individual Korean I thank you as an individual American and friend for the efforts you have been making for the amelioration of the condition of Koreans. But past experience tells me not to entertain too high a hope for your success. . . . If Koreans writhe under the double tyranny now and possibly a worse one hereafter they have none to blame but their own weakness."[90] It was clear that Yun blamed the incompetence of the Korean government, which made possible Japanese imperialism in the issue of emigration particularly and the impending takeover of Korea in general.

After changing trains in Kobe the following morning, Yun arrived in Shimonoseki the next day and, after spending the night, boarded a ship for Pusan, arriving there on the morning of November 6. That same morning he took a train for Seoul and arrived late that evening.[91] Two days later, Yun had an audience with Kojong, who asked him where he had visited and where he lived now, but "not much about the Koreans in Hawaii."[92] This was rather strange, in that a week earlier the monarch seemed vitally interested in the issue. But the fact that Kojong had not sent Yun enough money to go to Mexico and the fact that he consistently neglected to send the additional amount required by Yun suggests that, while the emperor may have resisted Japanese domination of his kingdom, his erratic leadership rendered his efforts ineffective. In fact, the Japanese would find the monarch difficult to control during the remaining two years of his reign.

Ironically, the final entry in Yun's diary relating to Korean immigration to Hawaii is dated November 17, 1905, the very day that Marquis Itō Hirobumi finally forced the Korean government to accede to a protectorate. On that day, he wrote "At 10 A.M. called on Mr. Morgan, the U.S. Minister. He seemed much interested in my accounts of Hawaii as a field for the Korean laborers."[93]

The establishment of the Protectorate once and for all ended the tug-of-war between Seoul and Tokyo over the emigration issue. It was announced that "from now on all passports demanded . . . by Koreans who wish to leave their country . . . will be issued at the office of the Resident General instead of at the Korean Foreign Office as heretofore."[94] Japan had finally taken over full control of Korean emigration.

15

The Fate of Korean Immigration Is Sealed

WHILE the locus of decision making with regard to Korean immigration was definitely in Japanese hands by the end of 1905, the planters still desired the resumption of Korean immigration. Their reason was summarized once again in a report issued at the end of that year: "If the immigration of Koreans continues . . . the Planters will have succeeded before long to a considerable extent in breaking up the solidarity of the plantation labor force and the consequent economic control now held by the Japanese on the plantations."[1] This trend was demonstrated in statistics released after Korean immigration was stopped in the summer of 1905, which showed that Japanese made up 62 percent of the labor force, Koreans 11 percent, and Chinese 9 percent.[2] So Koreans were still needed because, as Giffard put it that December, "We are too much in the hands of the Japanese."[3] Naturally the planters were pleased in mid-December when they received a cable from Deshler in Kobe stating that Korean immigration to Hawaii would resume very soon and requesting a $7,500 loan.[4] Three days later the planters granted the loan and hoped that their long wait was finally over.[5] What had Deshler been doing in the Orient that made him so optimistic?

Deshler had been biding his time since the summer of 1905 waiting for the Korean government to enact emigrant regulations so that he could resume recruiting. When Yun's inspection tour ended in failure, however, and when Japan took control of Korea's foreign relations with the establishment of the Protectorate in mid-November, Deshler knew that Japan would be the final arbiter of Korean immigration to Hawaii. Consequently, he met with American Minister Edwin V. Morgan before the American Legation departed Korea to ask his advice on how to convince Japan to allow the resumption of his work. Morgan's advice to

Deshler was to work with the American chargé d'affaires in Tokyo, Huntington Wilson.

In the first week of January 1906, Deshler wrote a letter to Wilson informing him that he would be arriving in Tokyo on the tenth or eleventh and added, "On my arrival in Tokyo I will have very much pleasure in calling on you to learn the best thing to be done to bring about the desired result."[6] At their meeting, Deshler gave Wilson a copy of Kojong's 1902 decree putting him exclusively in charge of emigration[7] and a document that he had compiled summarizing briefly the history of Korean immigration to Hawaii, including his April meeting with Foreign Minister Yi Ha-yŏng in which he agreed to work under any regulations promulgated, and stating that he represented Hawaii's Territorial Board of Immigration. Deshler's document concluded: "A period of nine months now having elapsed, it would seem that ample time had been had to have investigated emigration conditions and to have enacted suitable laws and regulations by which emigration could be carried on. The delay and interruption that this work has had has been of great financial loss to me and I have the honor to request that you will be kind enough to make such representations to the authorities at Tokyo as may seem best likely to tend to an early revival of this work. . . . It is the writer's firm belief that there is no objection on the part of the Imperial Japanese Government to the emigration of Koreans, properly regulated and the writer will be very glad to comply with any reasonable regulations which the Imperial Japanese Government may see fit to impose."[8]

At Deshler's request, Wilson personally handed a copy of Deshler's document to the new Japanese foreign minister, Katō Takaaki, who promised he would give the matter his attention. The next day, Wilson sent a letter, written in longhand, to Katō in which he enclosed a copy of Kojong's 1902 decree. The letter stated: "Mr. Deshler seems simply to want the embargo on Korean emigration removed, and apparently the date when this shall be done awaits only the promulgation of appropriate regulations. He therefore asks me to try to enlist the cooperation of Your Excellency's Government to hasten the drawing up of emigration regulations and the removal of the embargo. What Mr. Deshler asks seems to me entirely unobjectionable, and so I think Your Excellency's Government may be quite willing to exert its influence in favor of the desired end. I shall be very glad if this matter receives favorable consideration."[9]

Wilson had thus done all that he could to help Deshler and the matter was now in the hands of the Japanese Foreign Ministry. Meanwhile, Wilson dutifully informed Washington what he had done for Deshler, enclosing copies of all the documents Deshler had given him, and telling the State Department that Deshler "was introduced to the legation by Mr. Morgan, lately Minister at Seoul, and has since called several times to seek our good offices, with a view to removing the obstacle to his again engaging in the emigration business. As I understand that Korean immigrants are welcome in the Hawaiian Islands, I felt justified in mentioning the above matter informally to the Minister for Foreign Affairs, in whose hands I placed a copy of the enclosed correspondence."[10] But, by informing Washington what he had done for Deshler, Wilson unwittingly turned the State Department against Korean immigration to Hawaii.

The materials that Wilson had forwarded to Washington represented the first information on this subject that had been received there since Allen's letters to Secretary of State Hay in 1902 and 1903. Now for the first time Washington discovered to its chagrin that the Korean immigration was an organized affair, contrary to Allen's characterization, and that it was headed by, of all people, an American. This was a troublesome revelation because of the political repercussions surrounding Asian immigration in 1906. The fact that Korean immigration was being organized by an American made it that much worse. Perhaps even more damning was the statement made by Deshler in his summary of the history of Korean immigration that he represented Hawaii's Territorial Board of Immigration. Since the Board of Immigration, headed by A. L. C. Atkinson, had been established in April 1905 for the express purpose of encouraging immigration of white European labor into Hawaii, Washington demanded to know why it was apparently encouraging the immigration of Asian labor, a problem that was wreaking so much political havoc for the Roosevelt administration.

As a result, no less a personage than Acting Secretary of State Robert Bacon fired off a letter to Atkinson, who was now also acting governor in Hawaii (due to the illness of Governor Carter) at the end of February, asking why the Territorial Board of Immigration was encouraging Asian labor to come to the United States.

This query placed Atkinson in a most embarrassing position, because when he had recently been in Washington, Roosevelt had told him he wanted fewer Asian immigrants to come to Hawaii, and Atkinson had made strong speeches about "Americanizing" the Islands. Atkinson moved quickly to mollify Washington, writing: "I wish to state, for your information, that our Territorial Board of Immigration has no representative in the Orient and to further state that it is not the policy of this Administration to encourage Oriental emigration."[11] Three months later, in June, Governor Carter reiterated the anti-Oriental immigration policy of the Hawaiian government.[12] Despite these disclaimers from Hawaii, the correspondence was circulated throughout the relevant bureaus in the federal government.[13] And by the summer of 1906 it was clear that Korean immigration to Hawaii had a bad name in Washington and would be unlikely to receive the blessings of the American government if it should resume.

As the federal government in Washington was in the process of turning against Korean immigration to Hawaii during the first half of 1906, a similar process was taking place within the territorial government in Hawaii, but for different reasons. While both Washington and Honolulu espoused an official policy of discouraging immigration from Asia, the Hawaiian government had always shown itself to be relatively more attuned to the labor needs of the planters and had therefore been more tolerant of the large influx of Japanese and Koreans who had come to the Islands since annexation in 1900, as long as it conformed to U.S. immigration laws. This more tolerant attitude on the part of the territorial government came to a sudden halt in early 1906.

The planters and the Hawaiian government had had a serious falling-out in the spring of 1903 when it was discovered that the Koreans aboard the *Nippon Maru* had signed contracts before leaving Korea and had had their passage paid by the planters. The imbroglio had been settled when the planters agreed to mend their ways, and indeed, Koreans no longer signed work agreements until after their arrival in Hawaii. Yet the planters had never stopped paying the passage of immigrants from Korea and, for the next three years, managed to keep the territorial and federal governments ignorant of this violation of U.S. immigration laws. All this came undone in January 1906.

When F. M. Swanzy had been in Tokyo the previous summer, he had granted an interview to a Yokohama newspaper, probably the *Japan Gazette*, in which he stated that the planters provided passage money for Japanese and Korean laborers to come to Hawaii. Swanzy probably thought that his statement that the planters were systematically violating the contract-labor immigration laws of the United States would be confined to Japan. Unfortunately for Swanzy and the planters, however, his interview appeared in the English portion of that Yokohama newspaper and subsequently was reprinted in early January in the *Hawai shinpō*, a paper "which is inimical to planter interests." For the planters, the appearance of Swanzy's interview in a local paper came "as a thunderbolt from the blue."

Governor Carter had been "under the impression that . . . the laborers were coming of their own free will and accord." But when "a copy of the [article] fell into the Governor's hands . . . he got some of the individuals [concerned] into his office and threatened to give the whole matter . . . to the newspaper, . . . the District Attorney, [and] the Immigration Inspector . . . to bring action at once . . . against the HSPA for breaking the federal immigration laws." Citing the promise that "the Planters would no longer assist Asiatic immigration," Carter charged that they were "not honest." As for the effect on immigration from the Hermit Kingdom, "The Korean business was just about being reopened but cable grams are being sent today to suspend it until further orders." Perhaps later, the planters hoped, "we [can] open up matters with the Jap Gov't direct and try to get them to send . . . Koreans."[14]

On January 9 the HSPA trustees met to discuss "what action, if any, should be taken in reference to informing Mr. Deshler that Korean immigration should be suspended."[15] Ironically, this was being done at the same time that Deshler was badgering Wilson in Tokyo to intercede on his behalf with the Japanese government.

In San Francisco, Irwin, who had initiated talks with Horace Allen four years earlier, was not about to give up so easily. In a letter to Giffard, Irwin stated, "I do not see why some new arrangement cannot be made of a secret nature but which would enable the introduction of labor to be carried on the same as it was before. I am sure if the trustees got their heads together in secret session that they can handle the matter notwithstanding the opposition which Governor Carter is assuming towards us at the present time. If the Trustees did not care to handle the question as a body, could they not do it through some individual in whom implicit confidence might be placed?"[16] Irwin clearly did not want to give up, even if it meant finding another way to evade the law.

Giffard, however, remembering the close shave the planters had had in the spring of 1903, disabused Irwin of the notion: "The idea suggested by you in your letter is not feasible at this time in the face of what has transpired in the past as regards assistance in getting these people here." Moreover, "Secret Service men are in town watching developments in this regard and it would be too risky to do anything on the lines you suggest." Needless to say, the planters could no longer pay the passage of Koreans or Japanese. While this situation was currently moot with regard to Koreans, it meant that any future Japanese immigrants would have to pay their own way to Hawaii. And since Japanese immigration was the mainstay of the Hawaiian plantations, this was truly a serious development. It also meant the ruin of the Japanese emigration agents who "are of course disgusted as all the arrangements made with them fall to the ground and their future business is pau [finished]."

As for whom to blame, "It is the opinion of most of the Trustees that the whole trouble has been caused through Swanzy who evidently whilst in Japan gave little heed to the secrecy of his movements and actions, with the result that all he did and all that we had been doing in the past was reproduced. . . . Had Swanzy used better judgment . . . this matter would not have leaked out. . . . I am given to understand that they [Japanese emigration agents] warned Swanzy . . . on several occasions to be more secret in his methods, but without avail.

"[Since] there are enough level heads among the Board of Trustees to grasp and cope with the situation . . . it is no use crying over spilt milk. We will have to do the best we can and trust to Providence and the introduction of Japanese laborers who may come on their own account after paying their own passages. Unfortunately, the exodus to California has again started and this 'Alameda' is taking a full steerage load of them away from here. I presume this will continue for some months yet."[17]

Three weeks later, in early March, the HSPA trustees convened for what would turn out to be the final discussion of Korean immigration to Hawaii. At that meeting, "[E. Faxon] Bishop stated that Mr. Atkinson had received a communication from the Secretary of State Root, enclosing copies of letters which had been written by Mr. Deshler to the United States representative at Tokyo . . . which letters put the State Department into possession of all the facts connected with the Korean emigration." Since "Atkinson is desirous of having advice as to how the communication from Washington should be answered . . . it was the sense of the Trustees that Mr. Bishop should see Mr. Atkinson and state to him the present condition of affairs."[18] Bishop, of course, told Atkinson that the planters could no longer hope to import Korean laborers because they could no longer get away with illegally paying their passage. This allowed Atkinson to state in his letter to Washington two days later that the Territory of Hawaii did not encourage the immigration of Orientals.[19] The planters now were aware that the federal government, as well as the state government, was on their case. It looked as if the planters had finally given up.

Or had they? There are indications that in May the planters were still hoping that Japan would allow Korean immigration to Hawaii to resume. For instance, a small notice appeared in the local Hawaiian press: "Five Koreans are to hang for the murder of one man. The sugar planters are hoping that Gov. Atkinson will commute their sentences for, if they hang, these planters foresee all hope lost for future Korean emigration to Hawaii."[20] It was now up to Japan alone to decide the fate of Korean immigration to Hawaii.

While the planters in Hawaii were forced to give up their efforts in the face of determined opposition from both state and federal governments as the result of Deshler's and Swanzy's indiscretions in violating the planter code of silence, the possibility still existed that the Japanese government might relent in its opposition. If that were to occur, perhaps new and different arrangements could be worked out between Hawaii and Japan to allow the immigration to resume. After all, the new administration in Japan had assured Huntington Wilson that it would consider Deshler's request for a resumption of Korean immigration to Hawaii.

Whether in response to Wilson's request to Foreign Minister Katō Takaaki or as a standard review of foreign policy acompanying a change in government, in early February an unsigned position paper entitled "The Korean Emigrants" was circulated in the Japanese Foreign Ministry. The document reviewed the history of Korean immigration to Hawaii, noting that the Korean workers were less efficient than the Japanese but better liked by the planters because of their docility and stability. As a result, the Koreans represented strong competition to Japanese immigrants and also provoked the opposition of the Japanese emigration companies. Since Korean emigration was now prohibited, Japanese immigrants in Hawaii once again held a monopoly on labor.

The report then made several points that should be considered in setting policy dealing with Korean emigration to Hawaii. First, if Koreans were allowed to go to Hawaii, Korea would become rich when the workers sent back remittances to their families. Second, if Korean workers went abroad, Japanese workers would be in demand in Korea. Third, if Japan allowed its own subjects to emigrate while prohibiting Koreans from doing the same, Japan would be open to criticism from other countries. Fourth, if Japan persisted in prohibiting Koreans from emigrating to Hawaii, Americans involved in the business of importing Koreans [Deshler and the planters] would criticize the prohibition as being against "American vested interests." The policy paper concluded that the Japanese government should permit Korean emigration with some limitations and that Japanese consuls abroad should undertake the protection of Korean emigrants.[21]

Another voice in this debate came from the Japanese resident-general's office in Seoul two weeks later. It would be difficult, in their opinion also, to continue a total prohibition of emigration and that inevitably emigration would have to be allowed, although under Japanese supervision. The letter also stated that the decision should be made only after Resident-General Itō arrived at his post, but that the resident-general's office wanted to know beforehand the opinion of the Japanese Foreign Ministry.[22]

The Japanese vice-minister of foreign affairs, basing his reply on the aforementioned policy paper, informed Seoul that Tokyo also believed that emigration could not be completely prohibited for very long and that it was reasonable to expect that emigration would be permitted "under proper controls and regulations" by Japan. Revealing more of the thinking of the Japanese Foreign Ministry, the document continued that it would be difficult to transplant the discipline of Japan's Emigrant Protection Law, which required that agents be Japanese citizens since, "considering the level of the Korean people, we cannot expect them to act under strict regulations." As a result, Japan should be careful in the choice of emigration agents because, "it is difficult for them [Koreans] to become agents themselves at least for a while." Yet if only Japanese were certified as emigration agents for Korea, "other countries will certainly criticize us for being unfair." One way out of this, the reply continued, was to say publicly that any foreigner with appropriate qualifications could be an emigration agent for Korea, "but in actual fact license only Japanese companies and Japanese." Or, if foreigners were to be licensed, it would be necessary to add some conditions, such as requiring a security deposit and making them responsible to Itō's supervision.[23] Clearly, the resident-general was preparing emigration rules and regulations for Korea which would have the primary purpose of avoiding the criticism of foreign countries, and would severely circumscribe opportunities for Koreans to emigrate.

After receiving this advice from Tokyo in late March, Itō and his staff in Seoul quickly drew up a draft set of rules and regulations governing Korean emigration "after considering the situation of the Korean people and the experience of our own protection law." In mid-April, Itō's office presented the draft to the Korean government and "advised" the Korean government to enact the law. After two months of discussions between the Korean government and the Japanese residency-general, the Korean government agreed to the law and on July 12 the law was passed. This law was supplemented by enforcement regulations passed by the Ministry of Agriculture, Commerce and Industry on July 19. Both laws were scheduled to take effect on September 15, 1906.[24]

Essentially, this new law prohited Koreans from leaving their country without first securing the permission of the minister of Agriculture, Commerce and Industry, who in turn had to seek the permission of Itō and the resident-general's office since emigration involved foreign affairs.[25] Japan had succeeded in enacting emigration rules for Korea that would keep Japan in control. Japan was less successful in blunting foreign criticism, which had been, after all, the primary purpose of the law.

After visiting the Koreans in Hawaii in November of 1905 and approving of their condition, Homer Hulbert continued on to San Francisco where he visited the *Kongnip Hyŏphoe*, a Korean nationalist organization. From there he traveled to Washington bearing a secret letter from Emperor Kojong to President Roosevelt and returned to Korea in

June 1906.[26] Thus Hulbert, a fervent supporter of Korea in its struggle against Japan, was on hand at the promulgation of the Emigration Protection Law in July. Not surprisingly, Hulbert linked the new law with the Japanese domination of the country.

"There is something pathetic in the way Japan is providing 'protection' for Koreans where no protection is required," began Hulbert's caustic account, entitled "The Korean Emigrant Protection Law," in his *Korea Review*. Although "no one has heard that Koreans have suffered because they went abroad to work . . . these laws seem to be simply putting obstacles in the way of emigration." Invoking the idea of fair play, Hulbert continued, "The Korean has as much right to go abroad and work as has the Japanese but these laws practically prohibit this." As an example, Hulbert equated this law with "hold[ing] a man down by the throat while you rifle his pockets and at the same time give him a dose of quinine for fear he will catch cold during the process." Hulbert's article concluded: "As for the emigration laws one is almost forced to believe that successful Korean competition with Japanese labor in Hawaii has much to do with these stringent regulations. We do not affirm this but the fact of such competition combined with the further fact that all so-called reforms in Korea, so far, have looked to the sole benefit of the Japanese themselves make it look very much as if more than mere protection of the Korean were involved."[27]

Hulbert was still complaining about the law in September: "It is difficult to see just the reason for taking from the Korean government the right of giving passports to its people who wish to go abroad and centering it in the Residency General. This is only one more encroachment upon the rights of Korea. If Japan is sincere in her professed desire to see Korea advance the more Koreans go abroad the better, but this change is manifestly for the purpose of restricting emigration rather than for encouraging it."[28]

The law seems to have angered not only Homer Hulbert, an ardent champion of Korean independence, but also some Koreans, as is evidenced by an incident that occurred in December. Two Koreans by the name of Pak Yang-nae and Kim Tŏk-wŏn were arrested for the crime of rebellion, being suspected of trying to abolish the Emigration Protection Law.[29] Whatever their actions may have been, there was no doubt at the end of 1906 that no Koreans were being allowed to emigrate. The final chapter had been written on the subject of Korean immigration to Hawaii. Japan was now legally empowered to prohibit Koreans from going abroad and did not hesitate to exercise this power.

As the year 1907 began, no new Korean immigrants had arrived in Hawaii for a year and a half. For the more than seven thousand

Koreans who had arrived between 1903 and 1905, four choices were open.

One choice was to return to Korea. During the first two years of immigration, 1903 and 1904, 62 Koreans returned to Korea (including some who returned to Hawaii with their families). In 1905, the first year for which separate records were kept, 190 men, 15 women, and 14 children returned to Korea. In the following year, this number increased to 254 men, 29 women, and 43 children. In 1907, the highest number of returnees was recorded—266 men, 39 women, and 44 children. In 1908, 85 men, 9 women, and 11 children went back to Korea. In 1909, 117 men, 8 women, and 9 children returned, and in 1910, the year that Japan annexed Korea, only 36 men, 9 women, and 10 children returned. Therefore, between 1903 and 1910 a total of 1,250 Koreans returned (including those who went back only to bring their families to Hawaii). After 1910, the number returning to Korea was almost negligible—a total of 112 men, 15 women, and 9 children during the years 1911 to 1915.[30] It should be noted that the total number of returnees in all these years (1,386), including those who came back to Hawaii, represented less than 20 percent of the total number of arrivals, far less than similar figures for Chinese (23,000 out of 46,000 or 50 percent), and Japanese (98,000 out of 180,000 or 54 percent).[31]

The fact that a much smaller percentage of Koreans returned to their homeland than Japanese and Chinese is extremely interesting. Unlike the Japanese and the Chinese, Koreans would have to think twice before deciding to return to the domestic chaos they had left behind them in Korea. Moreover, the establishment of the Protectorate in 1905 and annexation in 1910 would mean a return to a Korea that had become a colony of Japan. Therefore, for the overwhelming majority of the Korean immigrants to Hawaii, an early return to Korea was not a practical option. As a result, Koreans were more likely to view living in the United States as a long-term proposition until a drastic change in the East Asian political situation allowed them to return to their homeland. Thus, while many Japanese and Chinese immigrants may have seen themselves as sojourners, who, if not successful in America, could always return to their homeland, this psychological state of mind was not shared by most Korean immigrants. They had little choice but to "make it" in the United States. As members of an immigrant group who for the most part regarded themselves as permanent residents in the United States, the Koreans would be prepared psychologically to adjust rapidly and climb the ladder of social and economic success more quickly than immigrants who regarded themselves as sojourners. Their future lay in their new home rather than in Korea.

A second option for the Korean immigrants in Hawaii was to

move on to the mainland United States. In the years 1903 and 1904, only 19 men, 9 women, and 4 children left for the West Coast. In 1905, this number increased markedly as we have already seen, to 373 men, 16 women, and 10 children. In 1906 this number grew to 428 men, 17 women, and 13 children departing for California and other western states.[32] In 1907, the number dropped sharply, as only 130 men, 12 women, and 6 children made the crossing. And during the years 1908 through 1915 only 50 Koreans went to the mainland United States. Thus in the years 1903 to 1907, 950 men, 54 women, and 33 children went to the mainland, for a total of 1,037, and if we add the 50 who went between 1908 and 1915, we have a grand total of 1,087 Koreans who moved to the mainland United States, chiefly California, between 1903 and 1915, only slightly less than the 1,300 or so who returned to Korea.[33]

The reason for the sharp decline in the number of Koreans going to California in 1907 was the result of an Executive Order issued by President Roosevelt in March of that year. Although only about 1,100 Koreans had gone to the West Coast between the years 1903–1907, more than 27,000 Japanese had done so during the same five-year period. The anti-Oriental pressure from California became so intense that Roosevelt was forced to prohibit Japanese and Koreans in Hawaii and other insular possessions or the Canal Zone from entering the continental United States.[34]

It will be recalled that Japan had been willing to acquiesce in such a ruling (and may even have suggested it) in order to prevent a Japanese exclusion act from being passed, just as it had sought to choke off Korean immigration to Hawaii in order to lessen anti-Japanese sentiment in California. What this ruling meant for Koreans in Hawaii, of course, was that if they chose not to return to Korea, they would have to remain in Hawaii.

Of the approximately 2,500 Korean immigrants who left Hawaii, slightly more than half returned to Korea and slightly less than half moved to California. For the remaining 5,000 Koreans in Hawaii, supplemented by approximately a thousand picture brides who arrived between 1910 and 1924, two additional options were open. One was to remain working on the plantations, and, to be sure, many did just that. As described earlier, though, since most of the Korean immigrants were not from farming backgrounds, they tended to choose the other option and leave the plantations. In fact, Koreans left the plantations most quickly of all the thirty-three immigrant groups in Hawaii.[35] Already by 1906 the number of Koreans in the total plantation work force had dropped to less than 9 percent, the same as the Chinese. By 1907 this percentage had fallen to 6; by 1909 they represented 5 percent; and by

1910, only 4 percent of the total plantation work force.[36] And because of their original urban backgrounds, after leaving the plantations they did not remain in the rural areas of Hawaii, but tended to move to cities such as Honolulu, Hilo, and other smaller urban centers—environments with which they were more familiar. In fact, Koreans were destined to record one of the highest rates of urbanization of any immigrant group in Hawaii.[37]

For all of these reasons, this immigrant group was prepared to conquer the poverty, hardship, and racism of the Hawaiian plantation system and become successful competitors in an increasingly urban American environment.[38] The Korean community in Hawaii would also soon become a leading center of the nationalist movement against Japanese domination of Korea, spawning organizations like the *Kungminhoe* and the *Tongjihoe,* and personalities like Syngman Rhee and Pak Yŏng-man. This important movement would continue uninterrupted for four decades, until Korea's liberation in 1945.

Soon after Roosevelt's Executive Order prohibiting movement of Oriental immigrants from Hawaii to the American mainland had been issued, negotiations between Japan and the United States in 1907–1908 resulted in a settlement known as the Gentlemen's Agreement in which Japan agreed not to issue passports to laborers to come to the United States, including Hawaii. Since Koreans now had to travel with Japanese passports, the Gentlemen's Agreement in effect supplanted the 1906 Emigration Protection Act as far as travel to the United States was concerned. Once and for all, Korean immigration to Hawaii was finished.

For Japan and Japanese laborers, new opportunities for immigration had opened up in the meantime in Korea and Manchuria. Because of nasty imbroglios, such as the San Francisco School Board Incident in the fall of 1906, Japan was relieved that the issue of anti-Japanese agitation in California appeared to have been resolved through the Gentlemen's Agreement rather than by a Japanese exclusion act. After all, it was to prevent such an act Japan had excluded Koreans from Hawaii. Thus it was a terrible shock to Japan when the United States enacted the Asiatic Exclusion Act in 1924, which was in effect aimed against Japan. This Act became one of the signal causes of the worsening of Japanese-American relations which was to lead to the Pacific War less than two decades later.

For the planters, the end of Korean immigration after 1905 meant a return to the relatively more expensive white labor from Portugal as an offset to the Japanese: 17,500 Portuguese arrived between 1906 and 1913. During the same period 8,000 Spaniards also arrived. In 1908–1909 650 Indians arrived and 2,000 Russians in 1910. But when the Japanese stopped coming in 1907, the planters' search for inexpensive immigrant labor took them to the Philippines. Filipino workers began arriving in 1907 and continued coming until 1931, 120,000 of them in all—the last major immigrant group to work in the cane fields of Hawaii. Employment on the sugar plantations was at its height in 1928 with 56,600 jobs. Acreage peaked in the 1930s at 255,000 acres. By the 1940s unionization and mechanization changed forever the character of plantation labor. It was the end of a century of immigrant cycles, grueling manual labor, and plantation paternalism.[39]

For Korea, the Protectorate lasted five years until 1910, when Japan annexed the country and brought an official end to the Yi dynasty and Korean independence. For the next thirty-five years, Korea would remain a colony of the Japanese empire.

As for the individuals involved in Korean immigration, their lives went on, occupied with other projects. Hyŏn Sun, who had been the interpreter for the second boatload of immigrants, became a traveling preacher on the island of Kauai for a couple of years. In 1908 at the urging of his former mentor, the Reverend George Heber Jones, Hyŏn returned to Korea and wrote a memoir of his experiences in Hawaii. He later became an important figure in the Korean nationalist movement.[40]

After the Protectorate was established in 1905, Yun Ch'i-ho became the president of the *Chaganghoe* [Society for Self-Improvement] and was later implicated in the 1911 Conspirators Trial involving anti-Japanese activities. He died soon after the liberation of his homeland in 1946.

Min Yŏng-hwan committed suicide in 1905 after the establishment of the Protectorate.

Emperor Kojong was forced by the Japanese to abdicate in 1907 in favor of his son Sunjong. His death in 1919 became the occasion for the outpouring of nationalist sentiment known as the March First Movement.

Yi Yong-ik died in 1907, but not before founding the school that would later become Korea University.

E. Faxon Bishop was elected president of the Hawaii Territorial Senate in 1907 and succeeded to the presidency of C. Brewer and Company upon the death of C. M. Cooke in 1909.

Horace Allen, who had done so much to promote Korean immigration to Hawaii, returned to Toledo, Ohio, to practice medicine. He died in 1932.

Durham White Stevens was shot and killed in the Ferry Building in San Francisco by Chang In-hwan, a Korean immigrant to Hawaii, in 1908.

In the following year, 1909, Resident-General Itō Hirobumi was shot and killed by another Korean emigrant, An Chung-gŭn in Manchuria.

David Deshler, having previously worked for the Unsan mines in northern Korea, returned briefly to that line of work; the *Korea Review* reported: "It gives us great pleasure to state that Mr. D. W. Deshler is to make his home in Seoul, his interest in the gold mines in Chik-san, forty miles south of Seoul, requiring his presence in this vicinity."[41] He later became the purchasing agent for the Peking Union Medical College of the Rockefeller Foundation at Peking and Shanghai. He retired in 1923 to Nagasaki and in 1926 built a house on Mogi Road in the Tagami section in that city, where he lived with his Japanese wife. He died on November 22, 1927, at the age of fifty-five.[42] The epitaph on his tombstone at the Yokohama Foreign General Cemetery reads: "Who Loved Japan and Her People." His wife, Hideno Honda Deshler, died at the age of sixty-three in 1934, also in Nagasaki. Her tombstone, next to her husband's in Yokohama, reads: "Who helped others with devotion" and "There will be no more sorrow."[43]

16
Conclusion

THE arrival of seven thousand Koreans in Hawaii between 1903 and 1905 had implications far beyond the simple movement of a relatively small number of people from one country to another. Because it was not the spontaneous type of movement that characterized immigration from Europe, but instead involved businessmen and diplomats in Washington, Honolulu, Tokyo, and Seoul, Korean immigration to the United States had far-reaching consequences in a number of key issues.

First was the matter of Korean-American relations. American policy toward Korea at the turn of the century can be described as one of friendly disinterest. When Roosevelt became president in 1901, American policy became aligned with Japan's desire to control Korea. This was frustrating to Horace Allen, America's minister to Korea, who had been in that country for two decades and who, not surprisingly, was sympathetic to Korea's desire for independence. He resolved this contradiction by pursuing an activist role in Korea and ignoring State Department instructions not to interfere in Korea's domestic affairs. This activism usually took the form of attempts to gain American business concessions in Korea in order to attract more political attention from Washington—a classic example of dollar diplomacy. Nowhere was this more evident than in Allen's involvement with Korean immigration to Hawaii.

Evidence abounds that Allen's actions were reprehensible. There is no doubt that he deliberately disobeyed instructions, that he conspired with the planters in Hawaii to violate immigration laws, that he was involved in a cover-up by laundering his correspondence and lying to his superiors, that he put inordinate pressure on, and perhaps even lied to, the Korean government to grant the emigration concession, and that he did so to repay a political debt. Furthermore, his actions tended to give the impression of an activist American policy when no such policy existed.

On the other hand, it can be argued that a number of Koreans wanted to go to America, that they were arguably better off there, that anti-Asian sentiment in America was based on racism, that Roosevelt's and Japan's policy toward Korea was wrong, and that the Korean government needed to be prodded to allow emigration. If we subscribe to this reasoning, Allen becomes a hero single-handedly standing up against three governments for the rights of the individual Korean to emigrate, against racism, against imperialism, and against bad policy.

Clearly then, there is no easy way to evaluate Allen's ethics in the matter of Korean immigration. But we can reach some conclusions about the outcome of his efforts. In the short-run issue of Korean immigration, Allen was successful. Without his active interference and assistance at every stage of development, it is difficult to imagine how emigration could have been brought about. In the long run, however, Allen's policy of garnering American concessions in Korea was a failure, not because of flaws in his use of dollar diplomacy or the lack of concessions, but because it was not backed up by the necessary political will. Washington did not adopt an active policy in Korea, nor did it support the continuation of Korean independence. In the end, Japan was allowed to take over Korea with the tacit approval of the United States.

Allen's actions also suggest that Korean-American relations at the turn of the century must be viewed on two levels. At the policy level was a disinterested and noninterfering United States. At a second level, represented by Horace Allen, was a relationship in which private interest was advanced over public policy and which ran at cross-purposes to official policy. At the very least, then, the Koreans received mixed signals concerning American policy and were encouraged to rely in vain on an America that in the end was unwilling to defend Korean independence against the will of Japan.

A second issue is the implementation of planter policy regarding Korean immigration. The fact that the planters wanted to bring in Koreans as a counterbalance to the more numerous Japanese in the hope of avoiding strikes and thus keeping wages low has long been established. But their methods in attaining this goal are another matter.

We have seen, for instance, that the planters were engaged in a broad-based conspiracy to violate immigration laws, including maintaining informers within law-enforcement agencies, laundering passage money, censoring new reports, bribing federal officials, running opponents out of town, and lying to federal and territorial officials. Were they successful in using these methods to obtain their goals?

In the short run, of course, the planters were unsuccessful. That is, they were unable to maintain Korean immigration long enough to create a genuine offset to the Japanese. Moreover, they were unable to keep their illegal methods secret, bringing down the wrath of both the territorial and the national governments upon them. In the long run, however, one must say that their aims were achieved. After all, none of the planters ever went to jail or paid fines. And eventually they were able to find alternate sources of labor to mix the races and thus to keep wages low.

Examination of the immigration of Koreans to the United States also allows us insights into the issue of conditions in the final decade of the Yi dynasty. Much is already known about this period, and the judgment of historians is nearly unanimous that conditions were very bad. What more can be added to the picture? At the very least, conditions may have been even worse than previously reported, and much of the blame can be laid at the doorstep of the Korean government itself.

The Korean Foreign Office certainly deserves censure. That it allowed a private citizen of a foreign country to assume passporting functions, that it failed to send a consul to Hawaii, that it allowed illegal emigration to a country with which Korea did not enjoy diplomatic relations and which had abysmal working conditions, and that it was unable to enforce its own ban on emigration, indicates a largely incompetent ministry in charge of foreign affairs.

The economic picture is also bleak, made worse by corruption within the government. It has been shown that even steady wage earners felt the necessity to emigrate. Not only does this suggest severe economic dislocation, but also suggests that since tax collectors were opposed to emigration, government oppression added to the worsening of the economic condition of the common people.

Corruption in its own right was yet another hallmark of late Yi Korean government. Opposition to emigration arose in part because the right people were not bribed into compliance. Moreover, revenue from passporting was, at least initially, channeled into the emperor's pocket to prevent opposition from that source.

Late Yi Korean government also suffered from factionalism. While one can cite the poor caliber of public officials in a system of political recruitment that favored traditional learning over modern studies, the fact that the government seemed unable to achieve consensus on the issue left the government essentially with no policy at all.

This overall lack of policy on such an important issue magnified the indicators of governmental weakness and mismanagement. No one seemed to be in charge of emigration and, moreover, emigration regulations were inadvertently legislated out of existence. Perhaps the most obvious sign of weakness, however, was the inability to resist pressure from Japan to halt the outflow of emigrants.

But competence can hardly be expected from subordinates if it is lacking at the top. In searching for reasons for this state of affairs, one must come to grips with the absoluteness of the emperor's power and his leadership. In fact the failure of leadership extends to Emperor Kojong himself. In recent years, scholars have been divided in their evaluation of the emperor. Some give him high marks for his desire to modernize Korea, while others see him as inconsistent and erratic and unable to keep Korea on a steady course. There is no doubt that there were enormous foreign pressures upon Kojong. But his incompetence is amply demonstrated in this study.

Kojong was virtually a captive of his corrupt advisers and was unable to overrule bad advice. He continued to staff his government with conservative, traditionally trained men of Confucian learning. As a result, he changed course on emigration several times. Moreover, he committed a major blunder by failing to realize that his cancellation of the edict creating the Department of Emigration also eliminated emigration regulations. He was even unable to pay enough attention to detail to send the correct amount of passage money for Yun Ch'i-ho to travel to Mexico. While Kojong clearly valued the continued independence of Korea, he was unable to provide the leadership required. Certainly this led to a situation that commanded little respect from Koreans at home or abroad, and even less from Americans and Japanese.

Another issue this study touches on is the relationship between Japan and Korea. Again, there is little disagreement among the scholars about the broad outlines of Japanese imperialistic intentions toward Korea. Examination of Korean immigration, however, provides additional insights into the reasons for Japanese actions and the methods they employed.

There is no doubt that Japan possessed the raw power in 1905 simply to quash Korean emigration. Yet Japan showed itself to be scrupulous in avoiding the appearance of heavy-handed bullying. Still concerned with its image in the world and still orienting its foreign policy within a cooperative mode with the West, Japan wanted to avoid criticism of its actions in Korea. By moving cautiously and surreptitiously, Japan could cloak its actions within the intrigues of late Yi Korean politics, taking advantage of the shortcomings of Kojong's government, rather than risking the unwanted glare of the international spotlight.

For Korean and international consumption, Japan could claim, not without some justification, that its actions were dictated by the failure of the Korean government to oversee the process in a way designed to protect emigrants. Thus, Korea's weakness not only made Japan's imperialism easier to accomplish but also provided a rationale to explain its actions. And both of these, the means and the ends, served to satisfy Japan's international audience.

We should not conclude that it was the immigration issue which led to the establishment of the Japanese protectorate in Korea. It was not. What this study does suggest, however, is that while security was undoubtedly the primary motivation for Japan's actions in Korea, it was not the sole motivation. The affair was more complex than merely a search for security and reinforces the previous conclusion that more attention be paid to the notion of prestige in determining the roots of Japanese foreign policy in the late Meiji era.

We also need to ask if Japan's policy was successful. On one level, the answer is yes. Japan was able to seize Korea without international approbation and halt the flow of Korean immigrants to Hawaii. But on another level, the answer is no. Not only was Japan unsuccessful in convincing Koreans that a Japanese administration was better for them, but Japan was also unsuccessful in stemming the tide of Japanese moving from Hawaii to the mainland United States. Because the planters simply began importing Filipinos to replace the Koreans, the Japanese were prevented from reestablishing a labor monopoly. As a result, wages did not rise fast enough to deter Japanese from moving on to California. While Japan was able to avoid an exclusion act for nearly two decades, its enactment in 1924 led to the deterioration in relations which Japan had hoped to avoid by preventing Koreans from going to Hawaii.

A final consideration is that of Japanese-American relations at the turn of the century. It has already been noted that Japan was successful in getting America's approval for its takeover of Korea, accomplished in part by its ability to convince the United States that it would bring reforms in the management of issues like emigration. A thornier problem, however, was tension over Japanese immigration to the American mainland, a tension which increased between the two nations after 1900. As both sides struggled to contain the problem, the Japanese decision to force a halt on Korean immigration to Hawaii must be seen as their most drastic unilateral step in that campaign. This study establishes a link, therefore, between the two critical issues of the establishment of the Japanese protectorate over Korea and the problems associated with Japanese immigration to the United States. And this linkage allows us to conclude that the tensions over Japanese immigration to the United States were much closer to the surface than previously thought.

All of these issues are connected—Korean-American relations, the aims and methods of the Hawaiian sugar planters, the decline and fall of Yi dynasty Korea, Japanese imperialism and foreign policy toward Korea, and Japanese-American relations at the turn of the century. And they all have as a common thread the immigration of Koreans to the Territory of Hawaii in the United States between 1903 and 1905.

APPENDIX

THE material in the main body of this volume has been constructed mainly from sources generated by elites in Washington, Hawaii, Japan, and Korea. Yet, in the end, immigration is, by its very nature, a mass movement of people who, if they come from the lower segments of their society, are likely to be illiterate or otherwise not attuned to the historical importance of the movement in which they are participating. We are fortunate to have writings which give an individual flavor to the historical events we are recording. They are edited primarily for length or grammar. Variations in spelling or historical accuracy have not been altered. These selections serve as valuable vignettes of what it was like to be an immigrant and to provide further support for the assertions made earlier.

"My father . . . loves to read. My mother can't read or write either Korean or English. She wouldn't learn, but now she desires to be taught to read and write Korean. My father is well educated in Korean. I have heard my mother say that when my father was a young man, he loved to study, and to keep himself awake while studying til way in the night, he would bite his thumb until the blood came."[1]

"My father was one of seven sons of a farmer. He was educated in one of the schools in Pyung Yang, the capital of a state in Korea. There he became a scholar and was ready to become an instructor when duties at home called him back. So he took to be a farmer and had no occasion to be an instructor. My mother was one of four daughters. As it was the custom of the Koreans not to educate women, mother was illiterate until she became a Christian in 1885. After a great many hardships and useless efforts in his farm, in 1904 father left Korea with my mother, two brothers and a sister. He settled in Ewa as an immigrant and became a plantation laborer. . . . A year later my grandmother came and in the following year, 1906, on January 16, I was born."[2]

"My parents were born in Korea and came out to the Hawaiian Islands as immigrants. They were both young and came out with the intention of making money and of living in a better place. My parents had no education whatsoever and they couldn't speak English when they first arrived. The Korean language was spoken in our home."[3]

"The Kim family is one of the proudest Korean families in Hawaii and in the United States. It boasts of a family history that dates somewhere back, about 500 A.D. The renowned ancestor was the prime minister of Korea at that time. He was the duplicate of the King in face and figure. Once when the Korean King was at war with his rebellious lords, the prime minister, seeing the danger that the King was in, quickly changed his garb for the King's, had him taken to a safe refuge, then riding boldly to the front and cheering the soldiers on, he died bravely in the midst of battle, thus saving the King's life and bringing victory for his King. This brave heroism was made renowned in Korean history and every student in Korean history loves and reveres this noble prime minister. His tomb is still standing in Pyueng Son, Whang Hai Do, the family estate of the Kim family or else it has been destroyed by the Japanese government. His descendants all revere him and are proud to call him their illustrious ancestor.

"The present Kim family in Hawaii are the direct descendants of this prime minister. When a young man, Mr. Kim lived in Pyueng Son, Whang Hai Do, the west central province of Korea. His father, called 'The Tiger of Pyueng Son,' through inheritance owned a large family estate, more like a feudal estate with serfs or laborers working in the fields for him. His word was law. No one dared to contradict him. He is a typical patriarch. He has a wife and three concubines. He believes that women are inferior to men. He does not believe in educating the women folk except in the learning of household duties. He was all-powerful. His relatives all respect and obey him. They are afraid to displease him for the 'old tiger' was unmerciful. He would have the servants whipped publicly. The patriarch is a man of strong will power, of a stubborn, steadfast characteristic. He believes in ancestral worship. He offers gifts to the ancestral graves and household gods faithfully. He is a stern old man, very tall and stout. He is fond of drinking but he forbids his son to drink. He is a true patriarch, masterful, and domineering, stern, cruel at times, and the dominant head of the Kim clan.

"The family estate covering many acres of farm lands with a large ancestral burying place, buildings, and forests of pines, herbs and incense still stands in Pyueng Son, Korea and one of the fondest desires of the Kim family in Hawaii is that in the near future, they might be able to return to Pyueng Son and help build the family estate again. . . .

"The older Kim families have been heathens but the present Mr. Kim is a Christian. When a little boy, contrary to his father's teachings, he had attended the Christian mission, and had studied the Bible diligently. He induced his aunts to become Christians but he never could induce the old patriarch to turn to a new life. The old family worship and religion meant more to him than the new faith.

"When the younger Mr. Kim became a Christian he began to think differently, to have a different outlook on life. He began to have a desire to go to new lands, to see new faces, to give his children all the educational advantages there are in America and to live a broader and fuller life. The old life in Pyueng Son with its customs, its restrictions, seemed to cramp his soul, so one night with his wife, a baby girl of a month old, and a few friends, he ran away to Hawaii. His father never forgave him. He would not answer any of the letters of his son's. So, communications stopped and the proud, sensitive Kims in Hawaii do not know what became of the old family in Korea. . . .

"After leaving Korea, Mr. Kim came to Honolulu in 1902 [*sic*]. From here he was sent to Hawaii as a laborer. At first the plantation work was too much for him for he had never worked in the fields, but through sheer determination, he soon became a skilled worker and for his personality and his name, he was respected by all. . . . Mr. Kim, as I have already said, was a Christian and his great ambition was to be a minister. He knew the Bible."[4]

"In a far away country of the East called Korea, there was in the sitting room of the King, a courtier who was noted the country round for his eloquent story-telling. His family came down from a stock of nobles who took part in the affairs of the realm. He was also privileged to have in his ancestral tree a queen of Korea, the wife of one of Korea's ancient kings. That sedate old gentleman lived to see the old kingdom of Korea, the native land of his ancestors and himself, seized and annexed by Japan and its young ruler kept away from his subjects. Soon after this great misfortune he died broken-hearted, leaving two orphan grandsons. These boys were taken care of by their rich uncle, the son of the noble story-teller to the king. They were given the privilege to study the wise sayings of Confucius and the old and ancient classics of Korea under private tutors. As these boys grew to be young men, they established for themselves homes and farms and the younger of the two had the fortune to marry the prettiest and the most-praised girl of the village at the early age of twenty-three years. These young people began to rear a family of a son and two daughters within a period of eleven happy years. The fate of the family was predestined by Dame Fate for something that was beyond human imagination. Hawaii at this time opened her doors to the Orient and this special family, after being deprived of all the fortune since the annexation of Korea left their mother country to come to Hawaii, a land that was new and strange. The experiences undergone are unmentionable. As soon as they arrived in Honolulu, the family was sent to the Ewa Plantation."[5]

"My parents, having met with a reverse in fortune, decided to leave their native land and start life over again in a new land, so they left Korea in the early part of 1903 and came to the Hawaiian Islands. Their intention was to return to their land as soon as they had saved some money. In this hope they were disappointed, for they soon found out that it was not so easy to save money as they thought it would be. However, they became so used to the climate, freedom, and advantages of this land that they no longer desire to leave this land permanently."[6]

"I was born in Korea and came to know the Christian religion through the American missionaries. I am very thankful to them and always will be that they brought Christianity to Korea. I was educated in the mission schools and was ordained in the Methodist Church. I came to Hawaii as the first Christian Korean missionary sent out from Korea. I worked in Hawaii for four years and then around San Francisco with the Methodist Church. I have been in the United States for twenty years. I came into the Presbyterian Church when I came to Southern California and worked among my own people as a preacher but I was not able to support myself and so I have gone into business."[7]

"I was born in Korea and was a Christian before I came to the United States. I was converted to Christianity by the American missionaries. I came to Hawaii first and then to the United States. I have been in the United States fifteen years."[8]

"I was born in Pyeng Yang, Korea, and was converted to the Christian faith through the Presbyterian missionaries. Dr. Moffett is a very special friend of mine. I attended the mission schools. I came to Hawaii first and stayed one year. I have been in the United States eighteen years."[9]

"My parents are Koreans who moved to America before Korea lost her independence, because of the educational and business advantages of America. They are not narrow minded or bigoted in their views holding to customs and habits of the old country, although they revere the old customs. Father obtained all the education possible in Korea, being able to speak, read and write the best Korean. He came to America to obtain a greater education, which he was not able to do."[10]

"During the Yi Dynasty, before Japan cunningly took possession of Korea, a little girl was born in a province called Chung Chun Do in the year 1882. There was not the customary rejoicing and celebration given for the first child in this particular Lee family because she turned out to be a girl. The Lees were especially disappointed, for being Yangbans or aristocrats, they most naturally craved for a boy. They named her Young Hee meaning pure and gentle and without further fuss or thought turned her over to their nursemaid. Young Hee grew up amidst pleasant surroundings and her childhood was carefree and happy. However, this condition did not last long for at the age of seven she was promptly put indoors and was not allowed to go out further than her gate. This was the law in those days. Her time thereafter was spent in learning to embroider. There were no economic problems in this family for the elder Lee owned several pieces of rice fields and employed a great number of men. He could therefore afford to have servants since personal services were so cheap. Life was indeed comfortable. At the age of eleven Young Hee's routine existence was rudely, and perhaps for the better, interrupted by the war between China and Japan. Chung Chun Do was the stamping grounds so the family had to get out fast. The family hastily packed their necessities and hurried inland to Inchon where an aunt lived. There they stayed until it was safe to return. Young Hee, however, did not return with her parents. She stayed on with her wealthy aunt until the age of sixteen when she was given in marriage to a local Kim. Young Hee then went to live with her in-laws. Her manner of living did not change for her father-in-law was also a Yangban and had a good income running a hotel. The Kims were formerly from Seoul (the capital), their birthplace, but for some unknown reason they moved to Inchon. In due time the young bride found out that her husband was a spendthrift. Time and again he would drain his father's pockets without making the slightest attempt to pay his father back. Finally the elder Kim disowned his son and daughter-in-law. The question of finding a job was worrying Kim because he had never worked in his life. Fortunately, just at that time there were notices saying that fortunes could be made in a far-off land called Hawaii. The young couple had no choice but to take this chance. So in 1903 they sailed to Hawaii with some other immigrant groups. The trip was hard but they finally reached Hilo."[11]

"In response to the very attractive advertisements of contract labor to Hawaii, my father and many other migrants in 1906 [*sic*] dispersed to Hawaii chiefly for economic reasons. . . . Not only peasants but professional people were emigrating also. . . . The immigrants were unaware of the kinds of habitude to follow. Therefore, they became fast attached to what little cultural material objects they were able to muster and to bring to Hawaii. My father, being a scholar, treasured his Korean books and silverware. To him, his knowledge of the language must remain intact so that the cultural traits of his people would flourish and remain in the generation to come."[12]

"No one, not even my grandmother, knows with any certainty what my grandfather's background was. One of my uncles said he used to be head gatekeeper for the Korean royal family, and that as a youth he had run away from cruel foster parents. At any rate, he was educated, for he could read, write and speak Japanese, Korean, a little Chinese and English. . . . He is old now, but his features are still impressive. His face is chiseled in proudness, and his hair, crew cut and bristling, surrounds him with an air of military bearing. In another age, perhaps, he would have been an army officer, as his grandfather was. Or a respected yangban, who was a government official-scholar of Korea. But time and circumstances dictated otherwise, and instead, my mother's father became a tailor. He was born Chung Doo Ok on November 21, 1887, in the city of Hayang, twelve miles east of Taegu. His grandfather was a colonel in the Korean army, his father was a secretary for the local city government and his mother was from the distinguished yangban class. 'I came to Hawaii because my grandfather said soon we would get war in Korea,' grandfather said. Arrangements were made for my grandfather, his parents and grandmother, and his younger brother to come to Hawaii on work visas. However, his grandmother and younger brother failed eye examinations and could not leave their country. . . . Although he landed in Honolulu, grandfather and his family were soon shipped to Kealia, Kauai, for plantation work."[13]

"Chi Pum Hong was a manager of a store when the first Christian missionaries came to Korea. It is not known what first attracted him to the white man's religion. Perhaps it was the opportunity to gain an education and to learn to read and write in English that led to his becoming one of the first Korean converts. In time he became a local preacher and traveled all over his province to spread the word. At this time famine was occurring in Korea. Many of his countrymen were migrating to Hawaii to seek better opportunities. The Hawaiian Sugar

Planters' Association needed laborers to work in the fields. Koreans were sought when the Japanese began to demand too much. One hundred dollars was paid to the immigrants to cover their expenses. Since the Organic Act forbade contract labor, a clause in their contract stated that they were to repay the money at a later date. This was only a maneuver to escape the contract labor classification so that no one was really required to return the money. The demand for interpreters was created by the influx of foreign labor so that the Hawaiian Sugar Planters' Association approached the young minister with a job offer. He was to become an employee of the Baldwin family in Maui. So in 1903 he moved to Hawaii. His chores varied from settling labor disputes to serving as interpreter for the court."[14]

"The following is a brief history of one Man Kee Lee. Mr. Lee is my grandfather on my mother's side. He was born on April 23, 1883, in Seoul, Korea. There is nothing known of his father or any other ancestor in Korea. The information obtained here is from what his family in Hawaii remembers, and a few documents. It is said that Mr. Lee was sort of a playboy in Korea. He was married to Si On Paik in Korea on September 24, 1900. There was little or no opportunity for my grandfather to find a job in Korea in those days. The Japanese imperial government was controlling Korea at that time and the outlook toward the future was very poor. The Japanese were cruel oppressors and when it was found that the Japanese government was letting people out of the country to work in Hawaii, Mr. Lee was happy to volunteer. Mr. Lee left his wife and two-year-old daughter, Wan Soon Lee, in Korea and came by himself to Hawaii in 1903. The reason his wife stayed back is said to be that she disapproved of his gambling and would not come with him until he reformed himself. Another factor and maybe the basic reason was that the contract may have been only for men. In any event, he arrived on the vessel *Siberia* on May 19, 1903, at Honokaa, Hawaii. He was contracted to work on a sugar plantation on that island; which one is not known. After he finished his contract on Hawaii, his whereabouts and doings are not clear."[15]

"I was born in Hankyung-do, Kilju, Korea, in 1878. I was the ninth child in a family of ten children. In comparison with our neighbors, our family was well off, for although we had no money as such, we had land, houses, cows, pigs, and chickens. You see, the possession of such goods was considered to be restricted to the wealthy. Thus, I say that we were quite well-to-do. Indeed we had much wealth then, especially with all the grain that we had. I can remember still how we worked in the fields all summer and then harvested the grain in such quantities that the pile would grow higher and higher, and wider and wider around the base. No, we didn't have money but we were well off. Many of our neighbors were not as fortunate as we were, however, and they were forced to send their sons to Russia or to Manchuria to work. Sometimes whole families went to Manchuria to live. Some of them came back and told us wonderful tales of the countries outside our village. Because my family could afford it, I was sent to school instead of working in the fields. I remained in school until the sixth grade. Then one night, twenty-five of us stole away from home to seek our fortunes in Russia and to see some of the wonderful things we had heard so much about. We stayed in Russia for about fourteen years, working as laborers at first, and as contract laborers later. We were engaged in all kinds of work—sometimes in building roads, and sometimes in building railroads. While doing the latter type of work in Vladivostok in 1902 and 1903, the Japanese and the Russians went to war. Many people died. We had to leave or take the chance of being killed. Confusion was everywhere, everybody was in panic, all the roads and railroads were blocked, and there was no place to go. We left all we had earned and fled for our lives. Many merchants and businessmen who stayed back to sell their property lost their lives because of their delay. We couldn't go back to Korea because the roads were blocked. Finally, we were able to get passage on an English ship and sailed for Japan. We were safe on the ship, for the Russians and the Japanese did not dare fire upon it because of the English flag. We stayed in Japan for three months and then were able to get passage to Korea. When we arrived in Korea, we had no money left, and found that there were no opportunities for work of any kind and that conditions were bad. It was then that we heard of a man who was talking a lot about the opportunities in Hawaii. He said that it was a land of opportunity where everybody was rich. He promised to give us work, free houses, and adequate pay. It all looked very lucrative and so after reading the contract, which seemed quite suitable, thirteen of us signed. We were shipped to Mountain View, Hawaii."[16]

"On May 10th of the Year of the Snake [1881], I was born. I studied a little at the So Dang but I was not a diligent student. At Hyang Kyo in the Year of the Snake [1893] I did not feel like studying so I kicked away my desk and played. At that time my father told me that 'You don't want to study now, but you will "pick your own eyes out" so I don't want you to blame me because I didn't make you study.' At that time I felt very sincerely my father's advice so I went to Seoul again to study in December in the Year of the Tiger [1902]. When I went to Seoul I looked at a poster on Namdaemun. According to the poster, anybody could take their family to Hawaii. It said: 'We encourage you to inquire about anybody who want to take their family, we will give them an opportunity. The farms will pay wages, water and hospital, and the government provides free education. The work is ten hours every day and the wages are 58 *chon* [cents] daily, 26 days for fifteen dollars.' After reading this poster, I went to my family home in Chang Dong Na, was welcomed by my family and had a delicious dinner. I told them about the poster and asked them about the world situation. I received permission to go to the far-away country even though they told me, 'Really you are going to America, you are the only male in the family and you will be a stranger in those far-away countries.' But they wished me success. The next day I went to the company and they said to prepare for travel. Returning home, my cousin gave me a Western suit and undershirt and told me to take it and go. I felt embarrassed wearing that suit and only took it in the suitcase when I went to the company in Sodaemun in Seoul. As soon as I arrived at the company I took the train from outside Namdaemun and arrived at the Kaebal Hoesa Company in Inch'ŏn. After arriving at Inch'ŏn, four or five people were waiting and then we took the ship in Inch'ŏn harbor to Hawaii. I took the ship of the Korean Steamship Company named *Ŭiju-hwan*. . . . I would like to record what I have forgotten before: When I left Korea I had one Western suit but because I did not have money to buy shoes and a hat, I had only a Western suit and *chip sin* [shoes made of rice shoots], so I was ashamed to be seen."[17]

"Mrs. Kim Tai-yoon came to Hawaii at the age of eighteen in 1905 as a bride. She and her husband were influenced to come by Korean Methodist missionaries. She said, 'Almost every boatload of Korean immigrants brought their own minister. It was a tremendous help to their morale.' "[18]

"Kim Chan-jay was brought to Hawaii on the *Gaelic* by his brother Yee Chai Kim, a minister, to get an education. They arrived on January 13, 1903. Kim Yee Chai preached the gospel on board ship. The first shipload of immigrants were all Christians."[19]

"Times were hard. The country had been passing through a period of famine years. The emperor needed more money, but my occupation as tax collector barely kept me from starvation's door as I traveled from village to village. More often than not, I would be greeted thusly: 'You are too late. The one before you has already collected the money.' Even now, I've often wondered how your mother got along, but somehow she managed and took good care of your Harabuji [grandfather]. But the little babies—they never lived to be even a year old. We had already lost four, and only one remained. He was about five years old when I heard about Hawaii. I remember as if it were yesterday. It was in Seoul. I had gone there to find out more about this land of opportunity, this land of perpetual sunshine where it is never cold, this paradise across the Tai-Pyong-Yang [Pacific]. I had been directed to go to a certain minister's house, and as I entered the yard, I saw a little girl. She was about five, too. I asked her if her father was in. She stopped her swinging and ran into the house. Soon, Yoon Son-sang-nim came out. We shook hands. 'Is it true—about this land beyond Tai-Pyong-Yang—where one can make a fortune in just a year?' 'Why, most assuredly, yes. Thousands have already gone, and you must not await another day but make preparations immediately. A boat will be sailing in a week from Inchon harbor.' So I returned to Kaisong and spoke to your Mother. It was my intention to go to Hawaii alone. I would be gone for three years at the longest and I would return to the family. You know, your Mother never said a word for a long time. Then she said, 'We'll sell the house to Saam-choon [Uncle]. He'll take care of Kunahboonim [Paternal Father-in-Law].' And she started packing. Your Grandfather had just celebrated his Haangup [sixty-first birthday]. I was sure he should remain at home in Korea. But he would hear nothing of it. 'I am still good for another ten years. Surely we will return long before that. We'll call this a little vacation trip for me. Let's go, Kabojakkuna [we'll go and look],' were his words. You remember him don't you—tall, spry six-footer to his dying day at eighty-six? It was the S.S. *Mongolia* that brought us across the great Tai-Pyong-Yang, and we landed in Honolulu on April 1904. We were a family of four, then—your grandfather was sixty-one, I was thirty-six, your mother was thirty-nine, and your brother was five years old. And now it is 1953."[20]

"Mr. Lim was almost one hundred years old when he died. He arrived in Hawaii in 1904 [*sic*] with the second group of immigrants at the age of thirty. He was accompanied by his wife and two-year-old daughter Julia. Assigned to Ewa Plantation as a laborer, his knowledge of English soon earned him a promotion to foreman. He served as a translator, acted as an aide in the plantation dispensary, assisted with labor negotiations, and it was here he first became a lay pastor."[21]

"I was born on March 30, 1875 in Pyeng-Yang, Korea, and became a baptized Christian in my early days. When I saw my country fall into the hands of the Japanese aggressors, I was filled with sorrow, but, unable to do much to help, I applied for the status of an immigrant and came to Hawaii hoping to learn something in order to help my country."[22]

Joshua Lee's father was born in 1883 and came to Hawaii at the age of 22. His mother was born in 1893 and came to Hawaii at the age of twelve. She spoke "perfect English."[23]

"Our life in the Islands actually was more or less guided by her [my mother's] sad experience she had in Korea when on two occasions she almost starved to death. That sort of left a mark, a scar in her. And when she came to Hawaii, she never did forget that experience. It was all work and trying to save her money, and foremost in her mind was she didn't want her own children to go through that unfortunate experience that she went through in Korea. She came from a family so poor that they never had meat."[24]

"At that time, she was a nineteen-year-old who accompanied her mother, her two brothers, and a sister-in-law. Her mother was a woman of the aristocracy and her husband was a high official which entitled him to acquire a concubine. . . . Her mother was deeply hurt and saddened that her husband would not leave his concubine who was a former gisang girl. One day she defied him and announced, 'I am no longer going to live with you, I am going to take my three children to America and educate them. I shall become a wonderful woman. You shall be disgraced and you will remain as you are.' . . . She now sought means to carry out her threat and got 'free' passage to 'America' for herself, her two sons, a daughter, and a daughter-in-law. We thought Hawaii was America in those days. . . . We were told that money was unnecessary so my mother exchanged the money for gold pieces before we left for 'America'. . . . When we arrived we were immediately sent to a labor camp on a sugar plantation in Maui."[25]

"We left Korea because we were too poor. . . . We had nothing to eat. . . . There was absolutely no way we could survive. . . . I came with a person called my husband, my mother, and a younger brother. We all came to Honolulu as immigrants and were sent to different camps—our group was sent to the Ewa camp. We cut sugar canes. . . . It was better than Korea because in a month we could get rice, soy sauce, and if you needed anything, it eventually could be bought."[26]

"Yang Choo-en was born in Kaesong (Songdo), which was the capital of the old Koryo Kingdom, on May 25, 1879. His father was an *insam* [ginseng] merchant. . . . Unfortunately, because of droughts and floods in 1902, Yang's father lost money and had to give up the *insam* business. Yang studied the Chinese classics at the local Confucian school and helped on his father's *insam* farms. In the autumn of 1902, he met a friend in Seoul who told him that some of his friends were planning to go to Hawaii to work on the sugar plantations. Yang, then twenty-four years old, decided to join the first emigration group, primarily because he believed that he would have an opportunity to learn Western civilization in the United States. So Yang and his friends went to Chemulpo (today called Inchon), submitted the required application forms, and sailed on the first emigration ship. According to Yang, his steamship fare, including meals, was paid by Hawaiian plantation owners with the understanding that the total expense of one hundred dollars would be deducted from his monthly paychecks over a three-year period. He was also told that he was to work at least three years, although he does not recall signing any contract. The first Korean emigration ship left Inchon on December 22, 1902. Yang said: 'I could not sleep a few nights, because so many things were in my mind and I worried so much since I did not know what would happen in the new, strange land in Hawaii. I did not know how to speak English and I did not know anything about sugar plantation work either.' He remembered that about one hundred immigrants, including women and children, landed in Honolulu in January 1903. A few days later he found that he had been assigned to work at a sugar plantation on Oahu Island."[27]

A separate interview of Yang turned up the following additional information: "My family raised ginseng in Kaisung for three generations. We also planted ginseng in Chunui, Choongchun-Do. When we returned to Chunui to harvest three years later (it takes three years to grow ginseng), the ginseng farm was ruined by a heavy rainstorm and flood. We harvested whatever we could and went to Seoul. In Seoul we met Mr. Chang Kam-chul who told us about America and Hawaii. At that time an American white missionary named 'Rev. Cho' [George Heber Jones] encouraged Korean young men to consider going to America for 'training and experience abroad.' "[28]

Kim [Hyung-soon] was eighty-nine years old in 1975 and one of the most successful businessmen in the Korean community. He was born on May 4, 1886, in Tong-gun, Korea. He came to Hawaii in 1903 as an interpreter on a plantation. He had learned English at the American missionary school, *Paejae Haktang*, in Seoul. He worked three years as an interpreter on Maui and was paid well, seventy-five dollars per month.[29]

Yoon Yong-ho, interviewed on November 26, 1975, at the age of ninety-four, was born in P'yŏngan-do and came to Hawaii in 1904 at the age of 23: "During the Russo-Japanese War, I followed the Japanese as far as China. I associated with those that came out of Japan to study. It was through them that I learned of Americans and their habits, as well as of other countries. Other than that, I lived in the country and didn't know much. After a while, I left home and traveled around as I no longer wanted to stay home. One day as I was returning from P'yongyang I noticed posted on the Ch'ilsungmun (Seven Star Gate), an ad about travel to Hawaii. Thus it was, I left for America. . . . I did nothing in Korea. My family is a farming family, but we had money and so I didn't work. . . . My father passed away early; I did have an older brother that passed away and then I came along and father passed away a year after that. Mother had me when she was twenty-three and Dad was twenty-four. She took me and raised me and lived at the same place. When I matured she married me off. My wife died and I left home and wandered. Meantime, the Russo-Japanese War broke out and I continued on to China, then to America. I didn't know how to do a thing, but that wind inside of me brought me to America 'to visit' but I'm living out my life in America."[30]

Paik Meung-son "Jim" was born in P'yŏngyang in 1897 and came to Hawaii in 1905 with his parents and younger sister at the age of eight. He is the oldest of ten children. His mother was born September 9, 1880, and died March 12, 1969, at the age of eighty-nine in Los Angeles. He was interviewed on January 2, 1976, at the age of seventy-nine: "My mother and father got married and had me, the first child, and my sister, the second child. . . . My parents said, 'No more opportunities here, so in order to better ourselves and protect our children's future we will go to a free country.' That is why we left Korea. . . . Our grandparents refused to leave familiar land and go with us. They were too old and they stayed. . . . [B]efore missionaries came to Korea, my grandparents worshipped idols, but after the missionaries converted them, they threw away the idols. My Dad personally studied the Bible and became a Christian. He was one of the early Koreans to teach the Korean language to missionaries; he taught Dr. Underwood. My Dad could've been ordained minister, but he had to make money to support his own family (ten children) as well as all the aunts and cousins, etc. . . . He went up and down Korea with a pack on his back—he was a traveling salesman. He peddled anything that brought cash. He did this for several years—then he wanted to stay home, so he learned to sew and became a tailor. He bought a hand operated Singer machine and opened a tailor shop for a while. It was still not profitable enough so he got the idea to leave the country after the Japanese got control. . . . Because my father had training in the missionary field, they wanted him to be a traveling missionary among the Korean camps in the Islands. Father's name was Paik Sin-ku. For about a year he was paid by the church board. The village where we lived was first contacted by the Presbyterian Church so everybody in that village was Presbyterian. They're Presbyterian to this day. It's in the family."[31]

Mary Kwang-son Paik Lee, sister of the previous interviewee, was interviewed on February 8, 1977, at the age of seventy-six: "When [my grandfather] and my grandmother were converted, my mother was also a minister and a school teacher. . . . Meung and I were baptised by Dr. Moffett. My grandparents were converted by him and she took the teaching of the Bible literally—that you should go out and spread the word. . . . My grandfather taught her because he was a well-educated scholar and knew 'Han Mun' [Chinese characters] and wrote beautifully. He taught her. My mother tells me she went around in her village to all the ladies and converted them, and taught them to read and write. In those days, they didn't have pencil or even a piece of paper. Their kitchen floor was just earth, so, they'd take a stick from the fire and make charcoal marks on the ground. She taught them the Korean alphabet and to read and write, using the Bible as a textbook and preaching at the same time. She told them it's not fair that only boys should be educated. She got them to consent to having a little girls' school. I left Korea when I was five, so I don't even remember her face. The only thing I remember about her is that she carried me piggy back to school and I recall there was a whole roomful of children. I remember that—all girls. They rose up in unison and sang a song of greetings. Then she spoke for a few minutes and class was dismissed. That must have been the last day of school or she wouldn't have taken me to school. I remember that distinctly. I don't remember my grandfather's face either, but he used to leave the house early in the morning and return late in the afternoon. I would sit at the front door and watch for him about three blocks away where he'd turn the corner. I used to run up to meet him and he'd pick me up. I'd search all over his pockets to find that piece of candy he always brought. . . . [W]hen the soldiers came into our village, everybody was scared to death, and my mother told us they told us not to be afraid, they just wanted to have the use of our home and whatever we had there. They walked out as they were, with nothing to take and they walked miles to Inchon Harbor. She said something like a day and a night. 'Luckily,' she said, 'God helped, and it was his blessing.' . . . We had to leave our home empty-handed, no place to go, no money, no jobs. What were we to do? We were lucky to meet somebody who offered them some kind of opportunity. So that's how we came to Hawaii with one year's signed contract. Well, about ten or fifteen families."[32]

Kown Yong-ho was born in Samhan, P'yŏngan-do in 1882 and came to Hawaii in 1905 at the age of twenty-three. He was interviewed on January 9, 1975, at the age of ninety-four: "I finished studying all the classics at age fifteen, but when the Japanese took over and abolished the study of Chinese and replaced it with Japanese, I fled to Hwanghae Province, taught Chinese here and there for a while. I was compensated with grain for teaching and straw shoes in exchange for my poetry. That didn't satisfy me—I was only 17 or 18 years old. . . . I was [married] in Korea, but divorced and left for America. How could I bring in a pregnant woman as an immigrant?"[33]

Ahn Young-ho, cousin of Tosan An Ch'ang-ho, was born in P'yŏngan Province in 1894 and came to Hawaii with his aunt and uncle in March 1905 at the age of eleven. He was interviewed on January 6, 1976, at the age of eighty-two: "Nothing to eat. The reason I left Korea was because I simply couldn't live there. . . . Through letters from my cousin [An Ch'ang-ho], I knew it was a better life in America. . . . I didn't know English."[34]

Chun Ho-taik was born in Kaemyŏng, Haeju, Hwanghae-do in 1885 and came to Hawaii in 1904 at the age of nineteen. He was interviewed on January 31, 1976, at the age of ninety-one: "It was 'young time' so I had a desire to leave. Because I was young, I kept wanting to go somewhere. As a child, I used to wander around a lot too. . . . In my youth, I was always footloose, so I left for Seoul. I left all my family. . . . I left home and lived alone in Seoul. . . . There was nothing much to do in Seoul, so I joined the army and traveled a bit, then Hawaii. . . . When I arrived in Inch'on, I boarded a ship which I thought was headed for America, but later I found it was going to Honolulu. There we were taken to sugar plantations. I then knew I came as an immigrant. . . . I left a wife. . . . I just didn't have the sense to know any better. . . . I recall our family had six daughters and I was the youngest child and only son. I recall that until he passed away when I was eleven years old, [my father] got me everything that was supposed to be good for my health. He knew where to get all the herbs, too. . . . I'm ashamed to tell you [what my father did for a living]. He was 'hajun,' or clerk. You see, Haeju was divided into east and west sections. My father worked in the east section. Mr. Cho, my father's friend, worked in the west section. He visited my father frequently. They were good friends. Hajun means he doesn't qualify to become 'yangban,' or upper class status, as he is equivalent to being a clerk or a secretary. He can't become the mayor of the city. Traditionally he always had to lower his head to others of higher rank."[35]

Dr. Kang Young-sung was born in P'yŏngan-do in 1888 and came to Hawaii in 1905 when he was seventeen. His wife, Kang Won-shin was born also in P'yongan-do in 1887 and came to Hawaii in 1905 when she was eighteen. They were eighty-seven and eighty-eight years old, respectively, when they were interviewed on December 10, 1975: "[We departed from] P'yongyang. Got a boat at Dae-dong River. We should mention our leaving Korea. We were still wearing our long Korean dress and Korean shoes. I still wore a bridal covering, as was traditional. We first walked out to the east gate. No rides. Then we boarded a ship and as the ship sailed further and further out, we felt saddened and tearful. We were about one hundred miles from home and just the distant hills were silhouetted—so sad. . . . Since I was to leave, [my mother and I] had our last meeting and she returned to P'yongyang. I had only been married a year. Soon when I looked home-ward, it was total darkness. The boat sailed on to Inch'on. After a night or so, we boarded a larger Japanese vessel which took us on to Japan. We went on to Kobe, Japan. There's where he failed an eye examination and was detained two to three weeks (at the immigration office). . . . We all waited together: his mother, a seven-year-old brother and my sis-ter-in-law. We were getting impatient for Dr. Kang's recovery. As far as meals went, it was always the same, seaweed soup and rice. Another thing, Dr. Kang was a lad of seventeen and I was eighteen. I'm a year older than my husband. They considered his mother, sister, younger brother and me his dependents. The authorities claimed it was impossi-ble for a seventeen-year-old to care for so many dependents and there was a question as to whether or not we should be permitted to leave the country. . . . Now his mother is excellent in PR. What she did was to bribe the immigration officials with my bridal silks and anything of value that we possessed; and thus, she was able to see to it that we all be released. They couldn't resist her friendliness—that's the way we all entered U. S. together. [Dr. Kang's] mother had a great ambition to see that I got the very best of education. She considered the United States would be most wonderful. In those days, we weren't even sure where America was 'stuck' to. We really didn't distinguish America from Hawaii. None of us knew and my mom decided America would be where I should be educated. I, too, had lust for education. All I could think of was studying in America. (Mrs. Kang): Although this was his ambition, it was all due to his mother's efforts. She arranged everything alone. The fact that we all came as a family was her doing. She didn't want the family to be separated. She had no idea of the suffering that was ahead after leaving Japan. We landed on an island—Kipalu [*sic*], a little island. There was no dock, and each of us was carried aboard a smaller boat and taken ashore. About a dozen of us were let off here. When we got ashore, we were taken to our quarters. It was a rural place. We wondered about it, then realized we had to work. We learned that we had to work for a period of time. We all worked on the plantation. After about four days, we were all ordered to get out to the plantation. Now, we who had just arrived from P'yongyang, were still wearing our long traditional clothes. So, thus dressed and wearing woven shoes of dried grass, we went out to the field to haul huge sacks."[36]

Hei-won Sarah (née Kang) Kim was born in P'yŏngan-do in 1885 and came to Hawaii in 1905 at the age of twenty, with her mother, two brothers (one of whom is the subject of the previous interview), and a sister-in-law. She was interviewed at the age of ninety on December 8, 1975, and again on February 23, 1977: ". . . When we came here, we didn't come to labor. In those days, when we came, we thought Hawaii was America—we didn't know what was there—and that all education was free. That is not true. My older brother (Dr. Kang) attended many schools, including the Chinese classics school. At his age, he probably knew more Chinese characters than anyone else in the country. . . . At first we were unaware that we were 'sold' as laborers. . . . We didn't know how we were going to survive. There were not many Koreans there. We shed many tears. . . . [Some of the Korean immigrants] were bad men. Most of those who came as immigrants are of low class: common laborers, mine workers, ex-service men. Why would better class of people come as laborers? . . . [My mother] was 42 years old and a real beauty, much prettier than I was. Mother was truly beautiful. We were sent to Ewa Plantation. It had the greatest number of Koreans . . . about fifty to sixty. Many were from my hometown, Jung-san, Korea. My father was full of 'hot air' when he became an official, so Mom left him when she was only thirty, and took us three with her. My mother is of "Yang-ban" family (noble—a Whang), and it would look bad for her to return to her Whang village with the kids, so she took us to our father's village, Jung-san. Well, that's past history. When we got to Ewa Plantation, there were quite a number of Korean people from Jung-san, including Kang Yong-so, Kang Yong-mun, Kang Yong-dae, all scholars and classmates of my brother. They all asked us to stay around Ewa and that we'd all take care of each other."[37]

Har, Sang-ok was born in P'yŏngan-do in 1888 and came to Hawaii in 1905 at the age of seventeen. He was interviewed on January 14, 1976, at the age of eighty-eight and again on February 2, 1977. He died in 1980: "I attended school [in Korea]. [I left behind] my mother, an older sister and a younger brother. I felt like leaving Korea to see the outside world. . . . I read in the newspapers and heard that [America] was a good place."[38]

Kim Sung-jin (née Hahn) was born in 1881 in Kaemyŏng, Haeju, Hwanghae-do, and came to Hawaii in 1905 at the age of twenty-four. She was ninety-five when she was interviewed on January 17, 1976, and ninety-six during a second interview on February 1, 1977: "[We left Korea] because we were so poor. So poor we had nothing to eat. There was absolutely no way we could survive. So, during the immigration period, we rode in [with] someone we called 'husband,' my mother, my younger sibling, Young-dae. . . . My age, when I left Haeju, was 22 years old. Then we went to Inch'on. That's where we waited a while at the immigration station until immigrants were summoned to get on board. That's how I came. Mother [was] about 40. I am not sure. My father at the time was about 45. [We arrived at] Honolulu. It was there that all us immigrants were then 'divided' up and sent to various camps. We were sent to Ewa camp [to] cut sugar canes. . . . [Hawaii] was better than Korea. If we worked a month there was rice, soy sauce, and if you needed anything it could be bought. In those days if you worked all day long, you were paid only 54 cents for ten hours of work. Even when we accepted such low paying wages, it was still better than in Tae-han—there was no way to earn money there. [In Korea we engaged in] farming where we planted, milled, weeded and harvested. Those who owned their lands were doing alright but the tenant farmers did poorly. We lived poorly in Korea. In our existence there we had nothing to eat. Just the millet which we tenant farmers shared. That's all."[39]

"My maternal Grandfather, Ekpo Pyun, was born on March 10, 1881, to a teacher-farmer and a housewife in the domain of Buyoe. He was first named Daibok [Great Fortune] and was the eldest of three sons. At the age of eight, he assumed many duties of the household after the untimely death of his mother, a few years after the birth of his youngest brother. As the years went by, he held more responsibilities as he helped his father with the chores and assisted in the management of the rice farm. By his seventeenth birthday, young Ekpo was all alone for his father had passed away, and his brothers all died from a cholera epidemic. Ekpo now held the responsibility of the farm alone: contracting laborers, selling the crops in the market, bartering for supplies, and managing the land. At this early age, Ekpo learned the harsh realities of life, and alone he had to face the world in struggling for survival. Until his twenty-third birthday, Ekpo steadfastly worked and tilled the soil of his father's farm. Finally, under the burdens of a series of famines, another epidemic, and Korea's unstable future, Harabuji decided to seek his fortune elsewhere. On a wintry day in early 1904, Ekpo Pyun boarded a Japanese vessel and became one of the original 7,000 Korean people who emigrated to Hawaii. . . . Ekpo arrived on Oahu in March 1904 and for the next twenty years he labored under Hawaii's hot sun working on the sugar plantations of Maui, Kauai, and Oahu."[40]

"It was during the Sino-Japanese War of 1894, when the battle was being waged in Pyeng-An-Do, the northwestern province of Korea, centering around the ancient capital city of Pyeng Yang, that my father's ancestral home was broken up and scattered. Fleeing the scene of battle between the two contending forces of foreign powers close to this native village, in Sunchun, north of Pyeng-Yang, my father, as a youth, went north to find a temporary shelter there among the strangers. . . . As a refugee among the strangers in the northern-most district on Yalu River, bordering Manchuria, called Kang-gay, or River Border, my father found favor and married my mother who gave me birth to this world. [My uncle said] Americans, who work only six days a week, are the richest people in the world. . . . So my uncle preached Christianity to everybody he met and everywhere he went. And he was not alone in doing that, for I, too, and every Christian, did the same. . . . Yes, I wished that I could go to Me-Gook [America] some day and come back as a missionary to my native country!

"In the fall of our first anniversary here in Jangchun, my father decided to move into the city in order to make a living there, but chiefly to send me to the missionary school in Yang-gwan district. My father bought a small thatch-roofed house just outside the Sang-soo-goo gate, not far from the Rev. Moffett's house. And how happy I was to be in the city and to be right near the American missionaries. I thought I had already come pretty close to Me-Gook where I longed to be some day. My father, in the meantime, was engaged in a small business of his own to earn a living. As a newcomer to the strange city, of course, he could not think of going into a more intricate and dignified business in which he had no experience. He was a dirt farmer, and he knew the value of the dirt. So he went peddling plaster dirt in the streets of Pyeng Yang. . . . 'And, now look' [said my uncle], 'I've got two passports here for you two boys. They are issued by the Foreign Office of His Majesty's Imperial Government of Korea.' On mine, though, he had added a few years to my age in order to make me look more like the able-bodied laborer that I should be. Back in the city that afternoon, the first thing I did was to get a haircut. I had long, straight, raven-black hair over two feet long, braided down on my back, touching my ankles, and the end tied in a bow with maroon-colored Chinese silk ribbon. A haircut was the first requisite on my way to America. My uncle returned from the city office of the 'Hawaii Development Company' or the Hawaii Immigration Agency, with two Koreans who were to journey to Hawaii with us, and one of them was my barber. Using a pair of scissors found in the sewing basket belonging to my cousin's wife, he chopped off my hair as if he were chopping down a tree with a dull pocket knife. Oh, what a horrible-looking haircut I found I had when I looked into the mirror! I was so ashamed of it that I had to cover up my head with an old cap given to me by Preacher Han's son, and pulled it way down to my ears.

"On that bright, sunny morning of October 15, 1904, . . . I left the ancient city of Pyeng Yang. . . . We traveled on foot some twenty miles that day and stopped at an inn for the night, nursing my sore feet, and just before the sunset the next day, we reached Chinnampo on the Yellow Sea coast. . . . Our boat was not there as yet, and we had to wait quite a few days at the lodging place at the expense of the Hawaii Development Company of which we were welcomed guests. . . . A week later, our boat arrived in Chinnampo, and we set sail on a fine sunshiny morning. The boat was called Ohayo Maru, a small Japanese [*sic*] steamer plying between here and Yokohama. Its passengers were made up entirely of the Korean emigrants bound for Hawaii numbering a score or so persons, including two women and a small boy. . . .

"We arrived at Chemulpo, the Port of Seoul, nearly at noon the next day. Here, some more emigrant passengers were picked up, and we proceeded to Pusan, the last seaport to visit before leaving my native land. More than two hundred people got on our boat here at Pusan. They were the natives of this southeastern province of Kyung-sang-do, the seat of the ancient Silla civilization and the most populous of all the eight original provinces. The number of the emigrants alone tell the story. The Korean emigrants now totaled some 350 on the boat, including several women and children. Finally bidding farewell to our native country, we set sail for Kobe, Japan, across the Korean Strait, which was just about a day's journey. . . . Passing through the channel ports of Shimonoseki and Moji, we stopped at Kobe in the late afternoon of the following day to pick up the first batch of Japanese emigrants. At dusk we continued on through the night and arrived at Yokohama early the next morning.

"Here we were transferred to a giant four-stacker American steamer called *Mongolia*, the sister ship of Manchuria. The ship was so large that there was no pier to dock it close to the shore, so the ship was anchored off a mile or so out in the Tokyo Bay. Sampans, or small skiffs, were employed to transfer all the passengers, including the bulk of the

Japanese emigrants that were picked up here. It took them half a day to
get the ship ready for sail. Now, the emigrants of the two nationalities
totalled something like 900 . . . some 350 Koreans and 550 Japanese.
At last, with a thundering blast of whistle from the big ship we were off
again on our last leg of the journey to Honolulu. . . .

"It was just about noon-hour when we were landed and brought
to a large building right by the pier. . . . The first thing we found there
was our lunch, . . . our lunch in red and white which was prepared on
a long table with benches on either side of it in a spacious room, nice
and clean and cool. Yes, that red salmon and white rice tasted mighty
good to me, I should say. That was the first time in my life, like in
almost everything else, I tasted that red fish that was so good that day.
As soon as our repast was over, a roll call was in order. It was reported
'All present and accounted for,' which proved that we arrived there safe
and sound without any untoward happenings on the ship.

"That done, we were now divided up into several groups to be
sent to the several different plantations in the different islands. Some of
them had the preference, and others had none. Most of them were sent
by boat to the biggest island called Hawaii which was some distance
from Honolulu. Myself, my cousin and most of my original company
from Pyeng Yang were most fortunate to be sent together to the Ewa
Plantation on the island of Oahu, the same island on which Honolulu is
located. It was only a few miles west of there. Others got on small boats
to go to the other islands, some big, some small. But we got on the train
bound for Ewa. It was the first time in my life I had ever been on a
train. . . . How fast that train traveled! . . . The train stopped entirely
too soon for me. We had come to the Ewa station.

"From the station I saw the big sugar mill of the plantation a
short distance to the northeast with the sky-high smoke stacks sticking
up. Here we were transferred from the passenger train to the train of
flat cars which was waiting for us. It belonged to the plantation proper,
and those flat cars were used for hauling sugar cane from the fields to
the mill and for transporting the workers to and from the more distant
fields. Now we were bound for the Korean camp just a little ways east
of the mill. The whole plantation was divided into three separate
camps: the Korean camp on the east said; the Chinese camp, some distance north of it; and the Japanese on the west side—all centered
around the mill and the administration buildings adjoining the superintendent's residence and the plantation store. On the ship, *Mongolia*, the
Chinese cooks were quartered in the rear, the Japanese in the front, and
we Koreans were in the middle part of the steerage. . . .

"It took us but a few minutes to get to our camp which was
found right by the railroad tracks and bound by the cane fields on two

sides. I saw the rows of the whitewashed cabins in the camp. Reflected in the later afternoon sun, they looked pretty good to me from the distance. Now when the train stopped, and just as we were alighting from the cars and wondering just which way to turn, looking this way and that, I saw a man, in light brown mounted on a white horse, racing toward us from the direction of the mill which we had just passed. Coming closer, the horseman, waving his hat, greeting us in Korean, saying, 'You are welcome, my fellow-countrymen! I just went to the depot to meet you, but I was a little too late. I'm very sorry!' Weren't we happy to hear a fellow-countryman greeting us in our native tongue in a faraway strange land! And, wasn't I glad to see a fellow-townman who called me by name most unexpectedly! Of course he knew me and I knew him. He was none other than Boss Jung [Chŏng In-su] of the Korean camp here and he had come from Pyeng Yang, too. Several others of my company knew him also. . . . [H]e had learned to speak English well enough to be the Korean interpreter and supervisor of the Korean settlement here. He had come to Hawaii on the first shipload, I believe.

"Now Boss Jung led us into the camp where we were welcomed by our fellow-countrymen who had arrived there one or two shiploads before us. They were glad to see us for they were few in number and were feeling rather lonesome. . . . So, on the morning following, we were gathered in the lobby of Boss Jung's cabin in the heart of the camp, for as yet there was no regular church building in existence, nor a preacher present. So Boss Jung himself preached a sermon. He was an all around man there; he was everything; he did everything. He was the interpreter, camp boss, social leader, preacher, language teacher, mail carrier, and what-not. All in Sunday attire, some in white or brown suits, most still in Korean costume, we men, women, and children were happy to observe our first Sunday service together in a strange land where we had come to stay and to make a living.

"Now, after a couple days of rest and preparation, I went out to work for the first time. I was sent to a place where they were making a new field out of the wasteland full of bramble brushwood. Oh, yes, I had gone out there on a train early that morning, and I thought it was lots of fun to ride to the place of work. A mansize pickaxe was given to me with which to work. I was to cut down the brushwood and to dig up the roots with it. That pickaxe was so big and heavy, and my hands so small and tender, that pretty soon both of my palms blistered and began to bleed. To be sure, I was too small for that kind of work, and my hands were never used to any rough 'stuff' like that. The only things that I was accustomed to were pen and paper, and nothing else. Although my father was a farmer, I had never done any farm work back in the old country. My father had intended me to be a scholar, and scholars' hands should be as soft as silk and fingers as pointed as a brush pen. Athletics were never known until the missionaries came with the modern idea of physical training. All forms of physical exertion were not dignified, nor befitting a scholarly person to indulge in, according to the old Korean conception. My foreman of that first day was a Korean young man named Yun (who lives in Los Angeles now) and who happened to be my next room neighbor and close friend of Boss Jung himself. And he, too, was a Pyeng Yangite, if that means anything."[41]

ABBREVIATIONS

Allen MSS   Horace N. Allen Manuscripts, New York Public
                         Library, New York City

Cooke Papers   Charles M. Cooke Papers, Hawaiian Mission
                         Children's Society, Honolulu, Hawaii

GI   Walter M. Giffard/William G. Irwin Papers,
                         University of Hawaii Archives, Honolulu, Hawaii

HSA   Hawaii State Archives, Honolulu, Hawaii

HSPA or planters   Hawaiian Sugar Planters' Association

Kankoku imin   *Kankoku seifu Hawai oyobi Mokushika yuki Kan-*
                         koku imin kinshi ikken—tsuki hogo itaku kanko-
                         ku no ken [The prohibition of Korean emigration
                         to Hawaii and Mexico by the Korean government
                         —recommendation and protection], Gaimushō
                         gaikō shiryōkan, Tokyo, Japan

NOTES

Chapter 1. The Setting

1. Isamu Yonekura, "Kikajin—The Naturalized Japanese Citizens Who Molded Ancient Japanese Culture," pp. 41–51.

2. Edwin O. Reischauer, *Ennin's Travels in T'ang China*, pp. 281–289.

3. Walter Kolarz, *The Peoples of the Soviet Far East*, pp. 32–42; John J. Stephan, "The Korean Minority in the Soviet Union," pp. 138–150; George Ginsburgs, "The Citizenship Status of Koreans in Pre-Revolutionary Russia and the Early Years of the Soviet Regime," pp. 1–19.

4. Mikhail Putzillo, *Korean Immigration to Manchuria*, 74–77; Isabella Bird Bishop, "Koreans in Russian Manchuria," pp. 41–44; Yi Hun-gu, [Manchuria and the Koreans]. For a more recent study, see Hyŏn Kyu-hwan, [A history of Korean wanderers and emigrants], vol. 1.

5. In 1836 the population of Hawaii was 108,579. By 1860 only 69,000 native Hawaiians remained. During the same period, sugar production rose as follows: 1837, 4,286 pounds; 1847, 594,816; 1857, 700,556; 1863, 5,292,121; 1867, 17,127,161 pounds. See Hilary Conroy, *The Japanese Frontier in Hawaii, 1868–1898*, p. 13; also Katherine Coman, "The History of Contract Labor in the Hawaiian Islands," p. 65.

6. Andrew W. Lind, *Hawaii's People* pp. 8, 19.

7. Hawaii, Territory, Board of Immigration, First Report, 1907.

8. Hawaii, Kingdom, *Penal Code of the Hawaiian Islands*, pp. 174–175.

9. Conroy, *Japanese Frontier*, p. 16. The Chinese had five-year contracts which provided for wages of three dollars per month, with free passage, food, and lodging.

10. Coman, "History of Contract Labor," p. 12; Conroy, *Japanese Frontier*, p. 16.

11. Hawaii, Territory, Bureau of Labor, *Third Report, 1905*. See also William A. Russ, "Hawaiian Labor and Immigration Problems Before Annexation," pp. 207–222.

12. Richard A. Liebes, "Labor Organization in Hawaii," p. 11.

13. Lind, "Economic Succession and Racial Invasion in Hawaii," p. 329. See also Romanzo Adams, *The Peoples of Hawaii*, p. 35.

14. Lind, *An Island Community: Ecological Succession in Hawaii*, p. 309.

15. Liebes, "Labor Organization," p. 12; Conroy, *Japanese Frontier*, p. 82; Lind, *Hawaii's People*, p. 27. For more on the Chinese in Hawaii see Tin-yuke Char, *The Sandalwood Mountains;* also Clarence Glick, *Sojourners and Settlers: Chinese Migrants in Hawaii*.

16. Liebes, "Labor Organization," p. 12.

17. Ibid.

18. The planter policy of mixing the races on the plantations is well known. For an excellent restatement of this policy, see Ronald Takaki, *Pau Hana: Plantation Life and Labor in Hawaii, 1835–1920*, especially pp. 22–27.

19. Conroy, *Japanese Frontier*, pp. 122–123. One shipload of immigrants from Japan arrived in 1868, followed by a seventeen-year hiatus before immigration resumed in 1885.

20. Ibid., pp. 126–127; see also Lind, *Hawaii's People*, p. 26.

21. Lind, *An Island Community*, p. 254.

22. Conroy, *Japanese Frontier*, pp. 145–146; Russ, "Hawaiian Labor Problems," p. 213.

23. Arthur C. Alexander, *Koloa Plantation, 1835–1935*, p. 99.

24. The breakdown of the number of strikes is: 1890 (2), 1891 (5), 1892 (2), 1893 (4), 1894 (4), 1895 (3), 1896 (3), and 1897 (6). See John E. Reineke, "Labor Disturbances in Hawaii, 1890–1925: A Summary."

25. Lind, *An Island Community*, p. 225.

26. *Planters Monthly*, 1894, p. 493; see also Hawaii, Republic, Labor Commission, Report on Strikes and Arbitration, 1895, pp. 23–24.

27. *Hawaiian Star*, February 1, 1895.

28. Ibid., April 9, 1894.

29. C. Bolte to Henry Cooper (Minister of Foreign Affairs), March 28, 1896, Hawaii, Republic, Foreign Office and Executive, Immigration, 1896. See also Hawaii, Republic, Board of Immigration, Minutes, 1879–1899, pp. 321, 326–327; Interior Department, Immigration, 1865–1899. The 10 percent stipulation lapsed in 1898 when it became clear that the planters were unable to induce the requisite number of non-Asian laborers to immigrate to Hawaii.

30. Hawaii, Republic, Executive and Cabinet Council, Minutes, April 16, 1895–December 3, 1896, p. 174 (November 2, 1896), HSA. The idea to import Koreans was suggested to Hackfeld by a Russian, Constantine Grun-waldt. Circumstantial evidence suggests that the proposal had its origins in Russian policy toward Korea in the period immediately following the end of the Sino-Japanese War. For more on this subject see Wayne Patterson, "The First Attempt to Obtain Korean Laborers for Hawaii, 1896–1897," pp. 9–31. See also M. N. Pak, with Wayne Patterson, "Russian Policy toward Korea before and during the Sino-Japanese War of 1894–95," pp. 109–120. It should also be noted that Hackfeld's proposal to import Koreans became known to the other plant-

ers. See the letter on the subject from Theo. H. Davies and Company to C. McLennan, November 19, 1898, Laupahoehoe Plantation Records, quoted in Takaki, *Pau Hana*, p. 26.

31. Hawaii, Republic, Board of Immigration, Minutes 1879–1899, pp. 328–332, HSA. The other companies comprising the Big Five in addition to Hackfeld (Amfac) were Alexander and Baldwin, Theo. H. Davies, C. Brewer, and Castle and Cooke. See Jared G. Smith, *The Big Five;* also William A. Simonds, *Kamaaina—A Century in Hawaii.*

32. Hawaii, Republic, Executive and Advisory Council, Minutes, 1897, July 9, 1897, HSA. This document contains a detailed verbatim account of the meeting. Summaries of the meeting appear in William O. Smith, Correspondence, 1895–1899, July 9, 1897, HSA. See also Hawaii, Republic, Executive Council, Minutes, December 4, 1896–July 19, 1898, pp. 99–100, HSA. Seven weeks later, in August 1897, the Executive Council once again met. The minutes of that meeting record "In the matter of the application of H. Hackfeld and Company to have the Board of Immigration approve the importation of Korean laborers under contract, a motion was made and carried that the Executive do not approve of the granting of such permits at the present time," ibid., p. 115 (August 27, 1897). There is no indication why the proposal was turned down at this time.

33. Walter M. Giffard to H. P. Baldwin, September 27, 1898, GI. Part of that letter read: "I hear that Senator Collum said we (the Planters) were big fools if we didn't get in all the labor we could whilst we had the opportunity, as we certainly would not get it after Congress had adopted for these Islands the U.S. Immigration laws and that the laws of Hawaii were continued as heretofore until Congress decided otherwise. He said further that it was his opinion that Congress would not touch Hawaiian matters for quite a few months yet, giving us ample time to load up with labor. The question however arises, will Mr. Dole and his colleagues look at it in the same light, or will they adopt their usual tactics of cutting us down? It is essential that they should be made to give us all the labor we require if possible, as there is no knowing what may hapen in the labor market later on."

34. The letter was from a G. E. Boardman, Agent for Seaman & Co., Neuchang, China. The circular was dated Honolulu, September 29, 1898. Hutchinson Sugar Plantation Company, Record, 1898.

35. Giffard to the Manager of the Hutchinson Sugar Plantation Company (Naalehu, Hawaii), October 3, 1898, ibid.

36. Lydgate to Davis, October 14, 1898. Quoted in Edward D. Beechert, *Working in Hawaii: A Labor History* (Honolulu: University of Hawaii Press, 1985), p. 116.

37. Passenger Manifests, Inward, May 1896, May 1898, July 1899, and January 1900, HSA. See also United States, Customs Records, Chinese Arrivals from January 1, 1900 to December 28, 1903, HSA; No Chae-yŏn, *ChaeMi Hanin saryak* [A Short History of Koreans in America], vol. 1, p. 2; Hawaii, Territory, Governor, Report to the Secretary of the Interior for the Year 1901, p. 4; Hawaii, Territory, Bureau of Labor, *Third Report, 1905*, p. 14.

Chapter 2. The Planning Begins

1. When the Hawaiian Commission left for Washington on January 18, 1893, to seek annexation, it was instructed to elicit a guarantee that no existing U.S. law, nor any to be made in the future, should prohibit at any time the introduction into Hawaii of laborers to be used exclusively for the purpose of agricultural labor. Hawaiian Historical Society, "Negotiation of the Annexation Treaty of 1893," *Fifty-First Annual Report*, pp. 5–8; see especially Art. 8, Doc. 1. After annexation was finally achieved in 1898 by a joint resolution of Congress, the application of all American laws to Hawaii was legally embodied in the Organic Act which was passed by Congress on June 14, 1900. United States, *Acts of U.S. Congress, 1899–1900*, Chap. 339, Sec. 10.

2. Russ, "Hawaiian Labor and Immigration Problems," p. 212. See also Walter M. Giffard to William G. Irwin, April 30, 1902, GI.

3. Conroy, *Japanese Frontier*, p. 196; Lind, *An Island Community*, p. 227.

4. Coman, "History of Contract Labor," p. 48.

5. Reineke, "Labor Disturbances," p. 8. See also Liebes, "Labor Organization," pp. 19–22; and Lind, *An Island Community*, pp. 229–232.

6. Lind, *An Island Community*, pp. 225–226. In the Report of the Republic of Hawaii Board of Immigration for 1899 (p. 10) these desertions were attributed to debts incurred by laborers, the attractive opportunities offered in the coffee districts, and ill-treatment received from plantation lunas (foremen).

7. Alexander, *Koloa Plantation, 1835–1935*, p. 110.

8. Ernest K. Wakukawa, *A History of the Japanese People in Hawaii*, p. 136.

9. In 1902, white mechanics and workingmen formed an affiliation, the Honolulu Federation of Trades, which drafted a resolution opposing Asiatic immigration. See Hawaii, Territory, Bureau of Labor, Report of the Commissioner of Labor in Hawaii, Bulletin No. 47 (1903), p. 52. Also, in 1903 a Federation of Allied Trades was organized in Hilo with the express object of opposing entry of Asians into skilled trades and mercantile pursuits. See Liebes, "Labor Organization," pp. 72–73; and Lind, *An Island Community*, p. 270.

10. Dole to McKinley, March 10, 1899, Hawaii, Territory, Executive Letterbook, HSA. Dole had been informed during the July 9, 1897, meeting of the Advisory Council that most immigrants did not reship.

11. Hilo Sugar Company, Minutes no. 1, p. 55 (February 15, 1901). Other identical notices appear in the minute books of other sugar companies. See, for example, Honomu Sugar Company Records, vol. 1, p. 171 (January 17, 1901); Onomea Sugar Company Record, vol. 2, p. 43 (January 17, 1901); Wailuku Sugar Company Records, vol. 1, p. 207 (January 24, 1901).

12. Liebes, "Labor Organization," p. 11.

13. *Planters Monthly*, July 1903, pp. 291–293.

14. Ibid., p. 294.

15. Giffard to Irwin, November 18, 1901, GI.

16. Irwin to Giffard, December 5, 1905, GI. See also Charles M. Cooke to Wolters, January 20, 1902, Cooke Papers.

17. "Korean Laborers Immigrate to Japan," *The Independent* (Korea), November 2, 1897. This article commented on the movement of 200 Koreans to work in the mines of southern Japan to replace Japanese who had gone to Hawaii.

18. *Evening Bulletin* (Hawaii), November 23, 1905.

19. Lillias Horton Underwood, *Fifteen Years among the Top-Knots*, p. 214. The author was the wife of Dr. Horace Underwood.

20. "Koreans Are the Best Workers—American Mining Man Prefers Them to Japanese," *Pacific Commercial Advertiser* (Hawaii), July 28, 1906. See also Sŏ Kwang-un, [A Seventy-Year History of Korean-Americans], p. 29.

21. Giffard to Irwin, November 18, 1901, GI.

22. Cooke to Atherton, November 26, 1901, Cooke Papers.

23. Giffard to Irwin, November 25, 1901, GI. The planters were very much concerned over adverse publicity appearing in the newspapers, and there were occasional suggestions that "a censor be appointed [to the *Pacific Commercial Advertiser*] to supervise all reportorial and editorial matter" and that "certainly something will have to be done to make these newspapers get into line, so that they can subserve the interests of the sugar plantations of these Islands, the representatives of which practically keep them alive through their patronage." See Giffard to Irwin, December 18, 1901, GI, and also Irwin's statement that he would "recommend that stringent methods be taken if a control cannot be obtained in any other manner," Irwin to Giffard, January 15, 1902, GI.

24. Giffard to Irwin, November 25, 1901, GI.

25. Irwin to Giffard, December 5, 1901, GI.

26. Giffard to Irwin, November 18, 1901, GI.

27. Giffard to Irwin, November 25, 1901, GI. Emphasis in the original.

28. Cooke to Atherton, November 26, 1901, Cooke Papers.

29. Giffard to Irwin, November 18, 1901, GI. Emphasis in the original.

30. Irwin to Giffard, December 5, 1901, GI.

31. Giffard to Irwin, November 25, 1901, GI.

32. Giffard to Irwin, November 18, 1901, GI.

33. Cooke to Atherton, November 26, 1901, Cooke Papers. See also C. Brewer and Company Record, vol. 2, p. 37 (minutes of meeting of the directors of C. Brewer and Company, November 22, 1901, of which Bishop was an officer, as was C. M. Cooke, and at which meeting the directors also urged Bishop to undertake the mission to Korea).

34. Cooke to Atherton, November 26, 1901, Cooke Papers. Cooke felt that someone from Alexander and Baldwin should go, since that was the company most in need of labor. Moreover, several of Cooke's colleagues advised against his going.

35. Irwin to Giffard, December 5, 1901, GI.

36. Giffard to Irwin, December 18, 1901, GI.

37. Giffard to Irwin, February 25, 1902, GI.

38. Giffard to Irwin, December 18, 1901, GI. The planters were a bit wary at Swanzy's initiative in writing to Hunt because "this matter of Mr. Swanzy bringing up the above letter for verification of the Trustees brings to

mind the Porto Rican question, when in its infancy the name of Mr. McFee was suggested by Mr. Swanzy and the letter written to the former by the latter asking for very similar information to that which he has asked from those new parties in the Orient." Thus, the trustees "did not seem to be particularly enthusiastic in regard to the matter other than to pass a resolution that there were no objections to writing for information on the subject until such a time as parties could be sent there to find out this information for themselves. . . . [Several of the trustees] do not forget that to a great extent Mr. Swanzy is responsible for the suggestion and appointment of Mr. McFee as agent for the HSPA at Porto Rico [and that the disastrous result] is by no means forgotten by members of the Board of Trustees, while some of them as a matter of fact do not forget that his name was suggested and correspondence initiated by Mr. Swanzy. . . . [The trustees] as a matter of course do not wish to hurt his feelings, but are naturally quite lukewarm to any suggestion which he recommends in the way of further appointments with a view to introduction of laborers from new sources." Irwin, in San Francisco, defended Swanzy by writing, "I presume that Swanzy thinks he is doing the best he knows how, in pushing his ideas and opinions, and I must give him credit for being a worker, because you know yourself there are a great many drones connected with the Association, and all the work and ideas emanate from a very few." "For that reason," Irwin continued, "I would not precipitate any quarrel with Swanzy, though naturally it is well to analyze his views before acting on them, and I trust you will not be hasty in opening up any new fields." See Irwin to Giffard, January 3, 1902, GI.

39. Giffard to Irwin, March 4, 1902, GI. For more information on Leigh Hunt see Laurance B. Rand III, "American Venture Capitalism in the Former Korean Empire."

40. Giffard to Irwin, February 11, 1902, GI. See also Giffard to Irwin, February 25, 1902, GI.

Chapter 3. Enter Horace Allen

1. *Hansŏng sinbo*, October 17, 1901.

2. Irwin to Giffard, February 24, 1902, GI.

3. Allen to Morgan, May 21, 1902, Allen MSS.

4. Fred Harvey Harrington, *God, Mammon and the Japanese*, pp. 62, 92n.

5. Ibid., p. 292.

6. Ibid., p. 294.

7. Ibid., p. 133; see also Robert R. Swartout, "United States Ministers to Korea, 1882–1905."

8. Harrington, *God, Mammon and the Japanese*, p. 130.

9. Ibid., p. 153, see also Spencer J. Palmer, *Korean-American Relations*, vol. 2, p. 204.

10. Harrington, *God, Mammon and the Japanese*, p. 185. The Russian minister to Korea as well as Kojong approved of franchise grants to the United States to curb Japanese influence in Korea. See ibid., p. 169.

11. Ibid., p. 225.

12. Ibid., p. 309.

13. Irwin to Giffard, February 24, 1902, GI.

14. Irwin to Swanzy, February 24, 1902, GI. The letter read: "Dear Sir: I take pleasure in introducing to you Dr. Horace N. Allen, Envoy Extraordinary and Minister Plenipotentiary of the United States of America, to Korea. Through a mutual friend I have been favored with an interview with Dr. Allen, and we have had a long conversation together on the subject of Korean labor and the prospects for its introduction to the Hawaiian Islands, which the Doctor's long experience in Korea qualifies him to speak on. Dr. Allen leaves by the Nippon Maru on Tuesday, with his wife, and is returning to his station in Korea. He will, naturally, be only a few hours in Honolulu, but has kindly consented to meet yourself and any other officers of the Planter's Association, and will be pleased to give them what information he can on the subject of Korean labor. The position which Dr. Allen occupies in Korea greatly qualifies him to give the information which we, as planters, are so desirous of getting, in this respect, and I have no doubt that you will be much interested and benefited by the information which [he] will convey to you. If convenient I would suggest that you call a meeting of the Trustees of the Planters' Association and listen to Dr. Allen's remarks, and you will be able then to take up the subject, which may develop into one of vital importance to our Island interests. Asking you to extend to Dr. and Mrs. Allen all the courtesies in your power during his brief stay in Honolulu, I am Yours very truly, W. G. Irwin." This letter arrived on the ship that brought Allen.

15. Irwin to Giffard, March 7, 1902, GI.

16. Allen to Hebe, May 14, 1902, Allen MSS. The *Nippon Maru* would soon figure prominently in Korean immigration to Hawaii.

17. Harrington, *God, Mammon and the Japanese*, p. 164n. For Allen's constant desire to obtain concessions for American business in Korea see ibid., p. 147. This topic will be examined in greater detail later.

18. Ibid., p. 133.

19. F. M. Swanzy Diary, March 4, 1902; Giffard to Irwin, March 4, 1902, GI. Allen's wife, Fannie, had brokern her leg in Ohio and was obliged to stay on board the ship while Allen was meeting with the planters.

20. HSPA, Trustees, Minutes, March 4, 1902.

21. F. M. Swanzy Diary, March 4, 1902.

22. Giffard to Irwin, March 4, 1902, GI. Emphasis added.

23. Allen to Edwin V. Morgan, May 21, 1902, Allen MSS. Emphasis added. There was also the potential for opposition from Washington because of the illegal nature of the proposed operation. Allen wrote that the planters "think they can make some arrangment in Wash. and as Mr. Dole is one of those I saw and he has been on to see the President lately, I suppose the matter has been discussed." At any rate, as we shall see, Allen would also attempt to assist the planters in that direction.

24. Irwin to Giffard, March 12, 1902, GI. Irwin wrote: "I am pleased to hear that you had such a satisfactory meeting with Dr. Allen, and feel confident that his influence and knowledge of Korea will be of great value to the Islands."

25. Giffard to Irwin, March 24, 1902, GI.

26. Giffard to Irwin, April 30, 1902, GI.

27. Irwin to Giffard, May 9, 1902, GI.

28. Giffard to Irwin, April 30, 1902, GI. The remainder of that letter dealt with the possibility of obtaining Portuguese laborers, with Giffard indicating that there was a possibility that Washington would allow the HSPA to prepay the passage of Portuguese immigrants. Although this was against the law, the pressure for obtaining white workers for Hawaii's sugar plantations was growing and Washington naturally was in favor of substituting European laborers for Asian laborers.

29. *Hwangsŏng sinmun*, April 1, 1902.

30. Allen to Fassett, May 4, 1902, Allen MSS.

31. *Hwangsŏng sinmun*, April 1, 1902.

32. Allen to Secretary of State John Hay, December 10, 1902, Allen MSS. This also appears in U.S. Department of State, *Despatches from U.S. Ministers to Korea, 1883–1905*. In the previous year, Korean newspapers had carried a story of American restrictions on the Chinese in America. See *Hwangsŏng sinmun*, July 21, 1901.

33. Allen to Fassett, May 4, 1902, Allen MSS.

34. The Japanese government promulgated an Emigrant Protection Law in 1894 allowing private emigration companies to begin sending laborers abroad. The law required that passports be used, that people go only to countries having relations with Japan, that emigration agents be licensed by the government, and that the agents give a deposit to guarantee the emigrant against financial distress and to provide for return passage. See Conroy, *Japanese Frontier*, pp. 160–161. This law would soon be translated into Korean to become the legal basis for Korean emigration in 1902.

35. Allen to Fassett, May 4, 1902, Allen MSS. It was Hunt who first introduced Allen to Fassett. See Rand, "American Venture Capitalism," p. 10.

36. Allen to Irwin, August 16, 1902, Allen MSS.

37. Allen to Morse (telegram), June 6, 1896; Allen to Hunt, June 6, 1896; Allen to Morse, August 18, 1896. Allen MSS.

38. Allen to Morse and Hunt, June 12, 1896, Allen MSS.

39. For more on Townsend, see Harold F. Cook, "Walter D. Townsend: Pioneer American Businessman in Korea," pp. 74–103, and his book, *Pioneer American Businessman in Korea: The Life and Times of Walter Davis Townsend.*

40. Allen to Mears, September 10, 1896, Allen MSS.

41. *The Biographical Cyclopedia and Portrait Gallery with an Historical Sketch of the State of Ohio*, vol. 5, p. 1236; see also James O. Jones, *Southern Ohio and Its Builders*, pp. 295, 308; James K. Mercer and Edward K. Rife, *Representative Men of Ohio, 1900–1903*, pp. 7–11; *The Columbus Dispatch*, obituaries for October 1886 and October 1904. All of these are located in the Ohio State Historical Society Library in Columbus, Ohio.

42. Robert H. Bremner, "George K. Nash, 1900–1904," in *The Governors of Ohio*, pp. 136–139.

43. Allen to Morse, September 16, 1896; Allen to Prescott, September 17, 1896. Allen MSS.

44. Allen to Everett, September 17, 1896, Allen MSS.

45. Nash to Everett (n.d. but probably in late January 1897), George K. Nash Manuscripts, Ohio State Historical Society, Columbus, Ohio. Hereafter cited as Nash MSS.

46. Allen to Nash, September 19, 1896, Allen MSS. Twenty-five letters of recommendation from influential people were eventually sent. In fact, Allen had so many sponsors that he was accused of conducting a "shotgun campaign." There were religious leaders who valued his missionary background and businessmen who thought Allen "of all men the most important to our interests in Korea." See Harrington, *God, Mammon and the Japanese*, p. 224.

47. Nash to Morse, January 16, 1897, Nash MSS. In that letter Nash also expressed his desire to meet Morse on his way to Asia and hoped that he could stop in at Columbus and "become acquainted with Mr. Deshler's friends."

48. Nash to Allen, January 30, 1897, Nash MSS.

49. Nash to Morse, January 28, 1897, Nash MSS.

50. Nash to Allen, January 30, 1897, Nash MSS.

51. Everett to Allen, February 27, 1897, Allen MSS.

52. [Illegible] to Nash, April 23, 1897, Nash MSS.

53. Allen to Deshler, May 11, 1897, Allen MSS.

54. Deshler to Allen (telegram), June 12, 1897, Allen MSS.

55. Deshler to Allen (telegram), July 15, 1897, Allen MSS.

56. Townsend to Allen, July 15, 1897; Deshler to Allen, July 16, 1897. Allen MSS.

57. Nash to Allen, July 17, 1897, Nash MSS.

58. Allen's Introduction to Press Copy Book No. 7, Allen MSS. Allen continued to be reminded of his debt to Deshler and Nash as seen in his continuing correspondence with Nash even after his appointment until Nash's death in 1904. See Nash to Allen, December 6, 1901; Nash to Allen, December 23, 1901; Nash to Allen, January 23, 1902; Nash to Allen, October 8, 1903; Allen to Nash, May 4, 1904; Nash to Allen, June 11, 1904; Allen to Nash, September 6, 1904; and Nash to Allen, October 18, 1904. Nash MSS. In this last letter written ten days before his death, Nash asked Allen for an appointment as a representative of Korea in the United States. Two weeks after Nash's death, Allen wrote to his brother-in-law, Clayton Everett, in Toledo: "I was very much cut up over the loss of my good friend Gov. Nash. I telegraphed and wrote my condolence, and feel that a great and good man has gone, and I have lost a true friend. Fortunately I had written him two long letters this summer about his step-son Dave Deshler, of whom he thought so much, but who, like other young men here to whose parents I have to write for them, was very negligent in writing home." Allen to Everett, November 10, 1904, Allen MSS.

59. Ibid.

60. After 1897 Allen tried to get Deshler placed with the engineering firm of Collbran and Bostwick. Allen also, at Deshler's request, found a position for Raymond Krumm (also of Columbus) with the firm. Krumm "proved to be a paranoiac and quite impossible" and was dismissed, whereupon Allen "at the request of Deshler . . . got him a civil engineering position with the Korean government for a five year period at a lucrative salary." Later Allen had

to defend Deshler against charges made by Krumm. Allen Press Copy Book No. 7, Introduction and pp. 116–119, Allen MSS.

61. Horace Allen Diary, October 3, 1903, Allen MSS. Townsend also had a Japanese wife.

62. Allen to Deshler, February 21, 1900; Allen to Deshler, October 9, 1902. Allen MSS. See also Harrington, *God, Mammon and the Japanese*, pp. 161, 164.

Chapter 4. Bishop Goes to Korea

1. HSPA, Trustees, Minutes, September 5, 1902.
2. C. Brewer and Company, Record vol. 2, p. 62 (September 6, 1902).
3. Josephine Sullivan, *A History of C. Brewer and Company*, p. 169. Bishop is erroneously identified as his cousin, Charles Reed Bishop, in Koh Seung-jae (Ko Sŭng-ie), [A Study of the History of Korean Immigration], p. 208.
4. C. M. Cooke to Charles J. Welch (in New York), September 9, 1902, Cooke Papers. In another letter, Cooke added, "We hope his mission may be successful, thereby relieving the labor conditions here." Reaffirming the value of using Koreans mainly as an offset to the Japanese, Cooke wrote that "while labor is sufficient just at this time, we fear when grinding commences there may be a combination to put up wages." See Cooke to Rithet, October 14, 1902, Cooke Papers.
5. Bishop's letters were dated September 22 and September 29, 1902 (HSPA, Trustees, Minutes, October 16, 1902). The trustees' response came in a meeting four days later (HSPA, Trustees, Minutes, October 20, 1902). In a letter written on the following day, Cooke elaborated on Bishop's mission: "We hope his mission is to be successful in sending regular installments of labor by each mail steamer but even if he is unable to do this immediately and looks over the situation thoroughly, many of us believe that his mission will not be a failure as we shall then know just what we can expect from that direction." Cooke to Dear Cousin Cooke, October 21, 1902, Cooke Papers.
6. Cooke to Bishop, October 22, 1902, Cooke Papers.
7. Cooke to Rithet, October 14, 1902, Cooke Papers.
8. Bishop to Cooke, November 11, 1902, Cooke Papers.
9. Allen to Fassett, October 9, 1902, Allen MSS.
10. HSPA, Trustees, Minutes, November 4, 1902.
11. Cooke to Bishop, November 6, 1902, Cooke Papers.
12. HSPA, Trustees, Minutes, November 4, 1902.
13. Ibid.
14. Cooke to Wolters, November 7, 1902, Cooke Papers.
15. HSPA, Trustees, Minutes, November 4, 1902.
16. Bishop to Cooke, November 11, 1902, Cooke Papers.
17. Cooke to Bishop, November 6, 1902, Cooke Papers.
18. Bishop to Cooke, November 11, 1902, Cooke Papers.
19. Cooke to Welch, December 4, 1902, Cooke Papers.

20. Cooke to Bishop, December 10, 1902, Cooke Papers.

21. Giffard to Irwin, December 23, 1902, GI.

22. Giffard to Irwin, January 7, 1903, GI.

23. Giffard to Irwin, December 23, 1902, GI.

24. Irwin to Giffard, January 17, 1903, GI.

25. Cooke to Bishop, October 22, 1902, Cooke Papers.

26. Bishop to Cooke, December 13, 1902, Cooke Papers.

27. Cooke to Welch, January 6, 1903, Cooke Papers. Also, C. Brewer and Company Record, vol. 2, p. 70 (January 3, 1903).

28. HSPA, Trustees, Minutes, January 8, 1903.

29. C. Brewer and Company Record, vol. 2, p. 71 (January 10, 1903).

Chapter 5. Allen Deals with Seoul and Washington

1. Harrington, *God, Mammon and the Japanese*, p. 194.

2. Harrington (ibid., p. 311) characterized Allen's actions toward Japan in this way: "Often and in many ways did Allen fight Japan. He defied the Nipponese envoys in Seoul, refusing to concede Japanese 'predominating interests.' He headed off Japanese attempts to get franchises, snatched grants that officials in Tokyo desired. He attacked pro-Japanese natives, built up hostile sentiment in the minds of those Koreans he could reach."

3. Kingsley K. Lyu, "Korean Nationalist Activities in Hawaii and America, 1901–1945," p. 15.

4. Allen to Hay, December 10, 1902, Allen MSS.

5. Allen to Dole, December 10, 1902, Allen MSS.

6. See, for example, Cook, *Korea's 1884 Incident: Its Background and Kim Ok-kyun's Elusive Dream*. For information on the Independence Club see Vipan Chandra, "The Independence Club and Korea's First Proposal for a National Legislative Assembly," pp. 19–35.

7. Keijō-fu, *Keijō-fu shi* [History of Seoul], vol. 1 (1934), p. 551, cited in Koh Seung-jae (Ko Sŭng-je), "A Study of Immigrants to Hawaii," p. 21n. Koh attributes these rumors to the activities of field workers of Japanese emigration companies who, he asserts, may have kidnapped Korean children to Japan to fill their quotas for Japanese labor immigrants to Hawaii when they could not obtain enough laborers in Japan. However, this explanation seems a bit far-fetched. See ibid., p. 22.

8. "Korean Laborers Immigrate to Japan," *Independent*, November 2, 1897.

9. *Hwangsŏng sinmun*, August 24, 1901; see also *Cheguk sinmun*, November 17, 1904.

10. In the fall of 1900, for example, the Foreign Office instructed the *kamni* to issue passports only if the intending emigrant was vouched for by a person agreeing to take responsibility. *Hwangsŏng sinmun*, October 27, 1900. Three months later passport forms were sent by the Foreign Office to all *kamni*. *Cheguk sinmun*, January 21, 1901.

11. Yun Ch'i-ho, *Yun Ch'i-ho ilgi* [Yun Ch'i-ho's diary], 5:371 (Novem-

ber 20, 1902). Hereafter cited as Yun Ch'i-ho *Ilgi*, with volume, page, and date of entry.

12. Allen to Hay, December 10, 1902, Allen MSS.

13. Allen to Dole, December 10, 1902, Allen MSS.

14. Yun Yŏ-jun, [Seventy years of immigration to America]. In *Kyŏnghyang sinmun*, October 6, 1973. See also his abridged article in English, "Early History of Korean Emigration to America (I)," p. 22. This article also appears in Hyung-Chan Kim, *The Korean Diaspora*.

15. Mrs. William L. (Sallie) Swallen to Jennie Ashbrook, October 9, 1903, Swallen, Letters, 1901–1903.

16. Allen to Dole, December 10, 1902, Allen MSS.

17. Yun Ch'i-ho *Ilgi*, 5:371 (November 29, 1902). For more on the Imperial Household Department see *Kuksa taesajŏn* [Dictionary of national history], ed. Yi Hong-jik, p. 200.

18. Giffard to Irwin, March 6, 1903, GI.

19. Allen to Dole, December 10, 1902, Allen MSS.

20. Article Six read: "Subjects of Chosen who may visit the United States shall be permitted to reside and to rent premises, purchase land, or to construct residences or warehouses, in all parts of the country. They shall be freely permitted to pursue their various callings and avocations, and to traffic in all merchandise, raw and manufactured, that is not declared contraband by law." Article Eleven read: "Students of either nationality who may proceed to the country of the other, in order to study the language, literature, laws or arts, shall be given all possible protection and assistance, in evidence of cordial good will."

21. For a comprehensive article on how the Koreans interpreted this clause, see Yur-Bok Lee, "Kojong and Korean-American Relations, 1882–1905," pp. 12–45.

22. This ploy became apparent when Deshler again represented himself as an American official to the Korean Foreign Minister in 1905, but it was revealed only in 1906. See A. L. C. Atkinson (acting governor of Hawaii) to Robert Bacon (acting secretary of state), March 10, 1906, Hawaii, Territory, Governors Files, HSA. In that letter, Atkinson writes: "In the letter from D. W. Deshler to Huntington Wilson, dated January 27th, 1906, a reference is made 'that he knew the management of the Company who represented the [Hawaiian] Territorial Bureau of Immigration in Korea. . . . 'I wish to state, for your information, that our Territorial Board of Immigration has no representative in the Orient. . . . " In fact, until April 27, 1905, no such organization was even in existence.

23. This proclamation, with accompanying English translation, can be found in Hawaii, Territory, Governors Files, HSA. It is also located in Huntington Wilson to Elihu Root, January 27, 1906, U.S., Department of State, *Despatches from United States Minister to Japan, 1855–1906*.

24. *Kwanbo* [Official gazette], November 20, 1902. See also *Hwangsŏng sinmun*, November 21, 1902, and the enclosure with Allen to Hay and Allen to Dole, December 10, 1902, Allen MSS. The *Yuminwŏn* was to have a president, vice-president, and superintendent, all three of whom were to be

appointed by the emperor. Below these were to be one chief or general manager and three secretaries: one private secretary for the president, one corresponding and recording secretary at the chief's office, and the third, a treasurer, also at the chief's office. Below these were to be six clerks, to be appointed by the president, two at each secretary's office. In addition, official agents were to be assigned at all the treaty ports of Korea, appointed on the recommendation of the president for the emperor's approval. In transliterating the Chinese characters which make up the name of this new department, several writers use the sound "su" for the first character. It appears, though, that "yu" is the correct pronunciation since it appears that way in the November 29, 1902, entry in Yun Ch'i-ho's diary. There was a *Suminwŏn* (with the same Chinese characters). See note 25, following.

25. Technically, this was not a new department since there had been a department with the same characters (but read *Suminwŏn*) in the Imperial Household Department from 1896 to 1902 staffed by six people, for the purpose of revenue bookkeeping. See *Han'guk hakdae paekkwa sajŏn* [Encyclopedia of Korean studies], 3:293. See also *Kuksa taesajŏn* [Dictionary of national history], ed. Yi Hong-jik, p. 785.

26. *Kwanbo*, December 10, 1902.

27. *Hwangsŏng sinmun*, November 18, 1902. Previously, Min had served as president of the Board of Courtesy. See *Hwangsŏng sinmun*, December 24, 1900. Min Sang-ho, the vice-president, had formerly been director of the Communications Bureau. The general manager (a sixth-level bureaucrat) was Sŏ Pyŏng-gyu. Others were Song Pyŏng-gyun, Cho Chae-hyŏk, Chŏng Chong-rak, Ko Chong-sik, Cho Tong-yŏn, and Yi Chin-yong. See Yun Yŏ-jun, ["Seventy Years of Immigration"], *Kyŏnghyang sinmun*, no. 2, October 10, 1973. There are indications that the *Yuminwŏn* was not intended to be very active since Min Yŏng-hwan (1861–1905) refers to himself as the vice-president. See his [The Posthumous Works of Min Yŏng-hwan], p. 36. Amendments to the rules and regulations were published in *Kwanbo*, December 10, 1902.

28. William Franklin Sands to Father, January 31, 1903, The William Franklin Sands Papers.

29. Sands to Solicitor for the Department of State, May 10, 1908, ibid.

30. Allen's record of blatant interference in Korean domestic political matters in violation of State Department instructions had earlier been noted with disapproval by Washington. In 1895, for instance, he had violated instructions against neutrality and noninterference by taking an open stand against the new, pro-Japanese Korean government which had been installed as a result of the Japanese victory over China in that year. And when the Japanese murdered Kojong's wife, Queen Min, he demanded an investigation. He also organized a diplomatic united front against the Japanese representative in Seoul while denying recognition of the new government's decrees. In addition, he granted asylum to members of the opposition to the new government. Washington branded these actions on Allen's part "a matter of regret" which was "no part of his duty," and registered its "serious objections." Allen survived this episode in part because, as secretary to the American legation, he was shielded by Minister John Sill; it was Sill who received the message: "Continued intermeddling with

Korean political affairs in violation of repeated instructions noted with astonishment and emphatic disapproval." From that time forward, Allen was more circumspect. While he continued to meddle, he took pains to disguise his actions, as the letter to Hay in December 1902 attests. See Harrington, *God, Mammon and the Japanese*, pp. 275–282.

31. Allen to Hay, December 10, 1902, Allen MSS. His letter included four copies of the November 16 Edict of Emperor Kojong and a copy of a letter to Governor Dole on the same subject written on the same day.

32. Hay to Allen, January 23, 1903, U.S., Department of State, *Diplomatic Instructions, 1801–1906*.

33. L. M. Shaw (Secretary of the Treasury) to Hay, January 19, 1903 (enclosure in Hay to Allen, January 23, 1903), ibid.

34. Allen to Dole, December 10, 1902, Allen MSS.

35. Dole to Allen, January 14, 1903, Hawaii, Territory, Governor, Executive Letterbook No. 5, HSA.

Chapter 6. Deshler Begins to Recruit

1. Lyu, "Korean Nationalist Activities," p. 23.

2. Hyŏn Sun, [A Record of a sightseeing trip to Hawaii], p. 4. See also Yun Yŏ-jun, ["Seventy years"], in *Kyŏnghyang sinmun*, October 10, 1973.

3. Hyŏn Sun, "My Autobiography," p. 59. Deshler's organization has been incorrectly labelled by several other authors, including Koh, Houchins and Houchins, Lyu, No, and Sŏ.

4. *Hwangsŏng sinmun*, May 15, 1902. The Deshler Bank was also known as the American-Korean Bank, or *Bei-Kan Ginkō* in Japanese correspondence. See Saitō Miki (Japanese consul-general in Honolulu) to Komura Jutarō (Japanese foreign minister), April 24, 1905, *Kankoku imin*.

5. Yun Yŏ-jun, ["Seventy years"] in *Kyŏnghyang sinmun*, October 6, 1973.

6. Easurk Emsen Charr, *The Golden Mountain*, pp. 121–122.

7. Yun Yŏ-jun, "Early History of Korean Emigration to America" (I), p. 23.

8. Hyŏn Sun, "My Autobiography," p. 59.

9. They were An Chŏng-su, Chŏng In-su, Kim Chae-ho, Chang Kyŏng-sang, An Pyŏng-su, Yok Chong-su, Song Chin-yong, and Hyŏn Sun. These names come from Hyŏn Sun, "My Autobiography," p. 61, and his [Record of a sightseeing trip], p. 5; also Yu Hong-yŏl, [Koreans in America], p. 39.

10. *Hwangsŏng sinmun*, November 18 and 21, 1902, quoted in Lee Houchins and Chang-su Houchins, "The Korean Experience in America, 1903–1924," p. 552n.

11. Bernice Bong Hee Kim, "The Koreans in Hawaii" (1937), p. 80. See also Hyŏn Sun, [Record of a sightseeing trip], p. 5.

12. Ibid.

13. Bernice Kim, "The Koreans in Hawaii" (1934), pp. 409–413.

14. Sŏ Kwang-un, [Seventy years of America's Koreans], in *Han'guk ilbo*, May 1, 1971.

15. No Chae-yŏn, [A short history of Koreans in America], p. 2.

16. Hyŏn Sun, "My Autobiography," p. 61.

17. No Chae-yŏn, [Short history], p. 2.

18. *The Korea Methodist* 1, no. 11 (September 1905): 146. This journal was later renamed *Korea Mission Field*.

19. Allen to Harris, February 12, 1903, Allen MSS.

20. Interview with Yang Chu-un, February 27, 1974, by Bong-Youn Choy. Yang was one of the original immigrants and was ninety-six at the time of the interview.

21. Bernice Kim, "Koreans in Hawaii" (1937), pp. 80–81.

22. Hyŏn Sun, [Record of a sightseeing trip], p. 5. Bernice Kim says that most of the first group were farmers; see her "Koreans in Hawaii" (1937), p. 82.

23. Rev. John W. Wadman, "Educational Work Among the Koreans," p. 146. Jones retained an interest in Korean immigration to Hawaii even though he was transferred to southern Japan in 1903. On August 12, 1906, Jones preached the first sermon at the official opening of a new Korean church on Punchbowl Street in Honolulu. In that sermon he attacked the public statements of one Judge Robinson that Koreans, as well as Portuguese and Puerto Ricans, were of low character, being spiritual, moral, and social misfits. The following day Jones expressed his satisfaction at the general progress and welfare of the Koreans in Hawaii. See No Chae-yŏn [Short history], pp. 33–34. In November 1906, in an article in the *Korea Review* (pp. 401–406) entitled "The Koreans in Hawaii," Jones commented favorably on the progress of the Koreans in Hawaii.

24. Katō Motoshirō (Japanese consul in Inch'ŏn) to Komura Jutarō, January 24, 1903, *Kankoku imin*. Pup'yŏng is presently a subdivision of Inch'ŏn.

25. HSPA, Trustees, Minutes, January 15, 1903.

26. Sŏ Kwang-un, in *Han'guk ilbo*, April 21, 1971.

27. Katō to Komura, January 24, 1903, *Kankoku imin*.

28. Yun Yŏ-jun, in *Kyŏnghyang sinmun*, October 6, 1973.

29. Allen to Townsend, January 3, 1903; also Allen to My Dear Boys, January 18, 1903. Allen MSS.

30. Hyŏn Sun, "My Autobiography," pp. 61–62, and his [Record of a sightseeing trip], p. 5.

31. HSPA, Trustees, Minutes, January 15, 1903.

32. George Heber Jones, *Korea—The Land, People and Culture*, p. 108. One of those who preached the gospel on that first voyage was Kim Yee Chai. See Ella Chun, "Korean Golden Jubilee."

33. *Evening Bulletin*, January 13, 1903.

34. Wadman, "Educational Work," p. 146.

35. *Evening Bulletin*, January 13, 1903.

36. HSPA, Trustees, Minutes, January 15, 1903.

37. HSPA, Trustees, Minutes, December 22, 1902; also, December 30, 1902.

38. Cooke to Welch, January 6, 1903, Cooke Papers.

39. Deshler to Allen, February 6, 1903, Allen MSS.

40. These were the sentiments of Bishop in a letter to Deshler. See Deshler to Allen, February 6, 1903, Allen MSS.

41. *Evening Bulletin*, January 13, 1903. Fifty years later, Francis Kang, in his article, "Korean Milestone," quotes directly from this 1903 article but adds, "No work contracts were signed." This sentence does not appear in the original article.

42. HSPA, Trustees, Minutes, January 15, 1902.

43. Allen to My Dear Boys, January 18, 1903, Allen MSS.

44. Deshler to Allen, February 6, 1903, Allen MSS.

45. Giffard to Irwin, January 19, 1903, GI.

46. HSPA, Trustees, Minutes, January 8, 1903.

47. Cooke to Rithet, February 6, 1903, Cooke Papers.

48. *Hwangsŏng sinmun*, February 9, 1903; also, February 12, 1903.

49. Hyŏn Sun, [Record of a sightseeing trip], p. 5.

50. Hyŏn Sun, "My Autobiography," pp. 61–62.

51. Deshler to Allen, February 6, 1903, Allen MSS.

52. Hyŏn Sun, [Record of a sightseeing trip], p. 5.

53. Deshler to Allen, February 6, 1903, Allen MSS; also Suhu Kohei (governor of Kanagawa prefecture) to the Home Minister (no name), March 11, 1903 (enclosure with Suhu to Sugimura [section director of Trade and Commerce in the Japanese Foreign Ministry], March 14, 1903), *Kankoku imin;* and, Hyŏn Sun, [Record of a sightseeing trip], p. 5.

54. Deshler and the planters agreed on 500 immigrants per month at the rate of 150 per steamer. HSPA, Trustees, Minutes, February 28, 1903; also Cooke to My Dear Dora, March 9, 1903, Cooke Papers. Although the flow of Korean immigrants increased somewhat, it never reached these proportions.

55. Giffard to Irwin, February 13, 1903, GI.

56. Katō to Komura, August 31, 1903, *Kankoku imin.*

57. Suhu to the Home Minister, March 11, 1903, *Kankoku imin.* This case of smallpox may have resulted in a tightening of the medical inspection of Korean immigrants in Japan, because a Hawaiian newspaper carried a report that steamship companies were threatening not to carry any more Koreans because of this incident. See *Pacific Commercial Advertiser*, April 18, 1903, quoting from the *Hawaii shinpo*, no date given.

58. Manager of the Hawaiian Agricultural Company to Deshler, April 23, 1903, Hawaiian Agricultural Co., Letterbook, 1903–1906.

59. Katō to Komura, August 31, 1903, *Kankoku imin.* This source also states that eighteen emigrants left on February 17, but no other source verifies this report. If there was such a group, it may have left from Kunsan. See Deshler to Allen, February 6, 1903, Allen MSS. At any rate, there is often no one-to-one correspondence between departures from Korea and arrivals in Hawaii, since several groups from Korea may have been combined in Japan for one shipment to Hawaii.

60. Cooke to My Dear Dora, March 9, 1903, Cooke Papers.

61. Katō to Komura, August 31, 1903, *Kankoku imin.* This group may

have made up part of the group that arrived on the ill-fated (as we shall see) *Nippon Maru*, which landed on April 30, 1903, with 113 adult Koreans abroad.

62. Katō to Komura, August 31, 1903, *Kankoku imin*.

63. *Hansŏng sinbo*, May 7, 1903.

64. Katō to Komura, August 31, 1903, *Kankoku imin*.

65. *Hansŏng sinbo*, May 7, 1903.

66. Ibid., May 7, 1903.

67. The four sources and their figures are: (1) the Third Report of the Commissioner of Labor, Territory of Hawaii, 1905, which lists a total of 515 (454 men and 61 women) but which apparently does not include children; (2) Morioka Makoto, Hyūga Terutake and Tomiochi Chūtarō to Komura, February 4, 1905, reporting the number as 514; (3) Katō to Komura, August 31, 1903, giving a total of 586; and (4) from Deshler who was interviewed by Katō and reported in Katō to Komura, August 31, 1903 (the last three sources all from *Kankoku imin*). Other figures are available from secondary sources, including Koh and No.

68. Giffard to Irwin, February 3, 1903, GI.

69. Cooke to Rev. Walter Frear, January 27, 1903, Cooke Papers. Giffard to Irwin, January 28, 1903, GI. Giffard to Irwin, March 31, 1903, GI. Cooke to Rithet, February 6, 1903, Cooke Papers. Annual Report of the Waialua Agricultural Company for 1902, p. 8. S. F. Moore, "One Night with the Koreans in Hawaii," pp. 529–532. *Maui News*, March 7, 1903. Giffard to Irwin, March 10, 1903, GI. "Koreans Are Good Labor," *Pacific Commercial Advertiser*, June 6, 1903. Bishop to Cooke, April 4, 1903, Cooke Papers. Horace Allen Diary, October 29, 1903, Allen MSS.

70. Cooke to Rithet, November 7, 1902, Cooke Papers.

71. Cooke to Bishop, November 6, 1902, Cooke Papers.

72. Giffard to Irwin, January 28, 1903, GI.

73. Cooke to Bishop, November 6, 1902, Cooke Papers.

74. Cooke to Rithet, December 18, 1902, Cooke Papers.

75. Cooke to Bishop, November 6, 1902, Cooke Papers.

76. Giffard to Irwin, January 19, 1903, GI.

77. Giffard to Irwin, December 31, 1902, GI.

78. Giffard to Irwin, January 19, 1903, GI. Emphasis in the original.

79. Giffard to Irwin, March 6, 1903, GI.

80. Giffard to Irwin, April 7, 1903, GI.

81. Cooke to My Dear Dora, March 9, 1903, Cooke Papers.

82. Allen to Fassett, February 7, 1903. Allen was accustomed to operating secretly, having told Leigh Hunt in a letter concerning a possible mining concession dated March 22, 1899, to "please burn it [the letter] up." Allen MSS.

Chapter 7. Troubles in Korea

1. Cooke to Bishop, October 22, 1902, Cooke Papers. The planters informed Vice-Consul Okabe Saburō since Consul General Saitō Miki was temporarily in Japan.

2. Giffard to Irwin, April 13, 1903, GI.

3. No letter from Japanese emigration companies to the Foreign Ministry concerning Korean immigration was sent until 1904, and that letter was opposed to Korean immigration to Hawaii.

4. Okabe Saburō to Komura, January 26, 1903, *Kankoku imin.*

5. Hagiwara Moriichi to Komura, January 17, 1903, *Kankoku imin.*

6. Hagiwara to Komura, January 17, 1903 (no. 1146). Distinguish this document from the communication cited in note 5, above. It appears also in folder 143, reel 18, of Correspondence of the Japanese Legation in Korea with the Home Office, 1903, Hoover Institution for War, Peace and Revolution.

7. Katō Motoshirō to Komura, January 24, 1903, *Kankoku imin.*

8. *Hwangsŏng sinmun,* February 9, 1903.

9. Bishop to Cooke, March 19, 1903, Cooke Papers.

10. Ibid.

11. Giffard to Irwin, April 13, 1903, GI.

12. Irwin to Giffard, May 1, 1903, GI.

13. Irwin to Giffard, April 1, 1903, GI.

14. HSPA, Trustees, Minutes, March 24, 1903.

15. Irwin to Giffard, April 1, 1903, GI.

16. Bishop to Cooke, March 19, 1903, Cooke Papers.

17. Irwin to Giffard, April 1, 1903, GI. Emphasis in the original. Allen had accepted gifts from Leigh Hunt and J. Sloat Fassett in 1898. See Harrington, *God, Mammon and the Japanese,* pp. 157–159.

18. Giffard to Irwin, April 13, 1903, GI.

19. Giffard to Irwin, December 12, 1902, GI.

20. Giffard to Irwin, February 13, 1903, GI.

21. Giffard to Irwin, December 23, 1902, GI.

22. Giffard to Irwin, March 6, 1903, GI.

23. William F. Sands, *Undiplomatic Memories: The Far East, 1896–1904,* pp. 202, 220. While the observations concerning Hayashi's overriding aim of annexation must be used with caution, there is little doubt that Hayashi disliked the United States. See his autobiography, [My Seventy Years], especially pp. 271–273, 352–354.

24. The role of the American minister to Korea, Horace Allen, is detailed in chapter 3. See also Patterson, "Sugar-Coated Diplomacy," pp. 19–38.

25. *Korea Review,* January 1903, p. 30.

26. *Korea Review,* February 1903, p. 79.

27. *Korea Review,* January 1903, p. 30.

28. Allen to Moffett, February 25, 1903, Allen MSS.

29. *Korea Review,* August 1903, pp. 365–366.

30. Allen to Moffett, February 25, 1903, Allen MSS.

31. *Korea Review,* August 1903, pp. 365–366.

32. William M. Baird to Frank Ellinwood, March 21, 1903 (Monthly Station Letter, P'yŏngyang), Presbyterian Church in the USA, Korean Letters, vol. 233, reel 280.

33. Sallie Swallen to Jennie Ashbrook, October 9, 1903, Swallen, Letters, 1901–1903.

34. William M. Baird to John Baird, May 19, 1904, in Samuel H. Moffett, Documents, no. 6 (1890–1903). (Used with the permission of Rev. Samuel A. Moffett, Seoul.)

35. Rev. Charles F. Bernheisel Diary, November 9, 1904, ibid. (Used with the permission of Rev. Samuel A. Moffett, Seoul.

36. Charr, *The Golden Mountain*, p. 113.

37. Jones, *Korea*, p. 33.

38. Rev. S. F. Moore, "One Night with the Koreans in Hawaii," pp. 529–532.

39. *Korea Review*, January 1904, p. 31.

40. Underwood, *Fifteen Years Among the Top-Knots*, p. 174.

41. Tai Sung Lee, "The Story of Korean Immigration," pp. 47–49.

42. Deshler to Wilson (chargé d'affaires, American Legation in Tokyo), undated, enclosure in Huntington Wilson to Elihu Root, January 27, 1906, Hawaii, Territory, Governors Files, Carter-U.S. Departments, State (October 1905–June 1907). HSA.

43. Moffett to Brown, October 20, 1904, Presbyterian Church in the USA, Korean Letters, vol. 234, reel 281.

44. Allen to Hunt, January 14, 1903, Allen MSS.

45. Allen to Townsend, January 8, 1903, Allen MSS.

46. Ibid.

47. Deshler to Allen, February 6, 1903, Allen MSS.

48. Hagiwara to Komura, January 17, 1903, *Kankoku imin.*

49. *Hwangsŏng sinmun*, May 15, 1903.

50. Hagiwara to Komura, January 17, 1903, *Kankoku imin.*

51. Harrington, *God, Mammon and the Japanese*, p. 304.

52. Ibid., p. 311. While we do not know exactly why Yi was so anti-American, there seems to be no doubt about his feelings toward the United States; according to William Sands: "He has been the consistent enemy of everything American for five years that I know of, and is the cause of the present complications with the American capitalists in Korea." Sands to Father, January 31, 1903, William Franklin Sands Papers.

53. Harrington, *God, Mammon and the Japanese*, p. 190.

54. Allen to Bostwick, May 17, 1903, Allen MSS.

55. Allen to Fassett, May 17, 1903, Allen MSS. That American was Raymond Krumm.

56. Correspondence of the Japanese Legation in Korea with the Home Office 1903, folder 143, reel 18, January 13, 1903, Hoover Institution for War, Peace and Revolution.

57. Homer B. Hulbert, *The Passing of Korea*, pp. 171–182.

58. *Kojong sidaesa*, vol. 5 (February 21, 1903).

59. *Hwangsŏng sinmun*, April 8, 1903.

60. *Cheguk sinmun*, May 12, 1903. A translation of the entire editorial appears in Yun Yŏ-jun, "Early History of Korean Emigration to America" (II), p. 44.

61. Allen to Fassett, May 17, 1903, Allen MSS. *Hansŏng sinbo*, May 19, 1903. See also Sin Il-ch'ŏl, [A seventy-year chronicle of Korea University], pp. 4–19.

62. Allen to Hay, May 17, 1903, Allen MSS.

63. *Korea Review*, May 1903, p. 223.

64. *Hansŏng sinbo*, November 30, 1903.

65. *Kwanbo*, October 13, 1903, no. 2640. It was Edict Number 90, Article 26.

66. Ibid., no. 2642.

67. *Korea Review*, June 1903, p. 269.

68. Ibid., February, 1904, p. 82.

Chapter 8. Troubles in Hawaii

1. McLean to Hill, Assistant Secretary of State, November 15, 1902, U.S., Department of State, Despatches from United States Consuls in Yokohama, Japan, 1897–1906. I am indebted to Deborah Church for this reference. See her "Korean Emigration to Hawaii, 1902–07."

2. *Pacific Commercial Advertiser*, May 1, 1903.

3. Giffard to Irwin, May 12, 1903, GI. That $25 was the going rate for Korean interpreters was confirmed in Illegible to C. Brewer and Co., LTD, March 31, 1903, Hawaiian Agricultural Company, Letterbook to C. Brewer and Co., LTD, 1903–06.

4. HSPA, Trustees, Minutes, May 4, 1903.

5. Giffard to Irwin, May 12, 1903, GI; see also HSPA, Trustees, Minutes, May 7, 1903.

6. Giffard to Irwin, May 12, 1903, GI.

7. No, [Short history], p. 4.

8. Giffard to Irwin, May 12, 1903, GI.

9. "To Study Labor—Mr. Sargent Arrives in City of Peking to Look into Labor Problems," *Pacific Commercial Advertiser*, May 9, 1903.

10. Irwin to Giffard, May 22, 1903, GI.

11. "What Sargent Says," *Hilo Tribune*, June 12, 1903.

12. *Evening Bulletin*, June 15, 1903.

13. Irwin to Giffard, May 22, 1903, GI.

14. HSPA, Trustees, Minutes, May 12, 1903.

15. *Pacific Commercial Advertiser*, May 23, 1903.

16. Giffard to Irwin, May 22, 1903, GI.

17. Irwin to Giffard, May 22, 1903, GI.

18. Giffard to Irwin, May 22, 1903, GI. Emphasis in the original.

19. Giffard to Irwin, May 19, 1903, GI.

20. Giffard to Irwin, May 12, 1903, GI.

21. "Investigated the Koreans," *Pacific Commercial Advertiser*, May 23, 1903.

22. U.S. Congress, *Statutes at Large*, 57th Cong., 2nd Sess., part 1, pp. 1213–1222; see also U.S. Commissioner-General of Immigration, Annual Report for 1903 p. 41.

23. Giffard to Irwin, May 22, 1903, GI.

24. Irwin to Giffard, June 3, 1903, GI.

25. "Judge Estee's Address on Future of Hawaii," *Pacific Commercial Advertiser*, May 2, 1903.

26. Giffard to Irwin, May 22, 1903, GI.

27. Ibid.

28. Irwin to Giffard, June 11, 1903, GI.

29. Giffard to Irwin, May 22, 1903, GI.

30. Ibid.

31. Irwin to Giffard, June 3, 1903, GI.

32. *Pacific Commercial Advertiser*, May 26, 1903; "One Hundred Pleas Filed," *Pacific Commercial Advertiser*, June 4, 1903; "Korean John Does," *Evening Bulletin*, June 3, 1903; *Evening Bulletin*, June 10, 1903; "Berger's Attack on Korean Labor," *Pacific Commercial Advertiser*, June 13, 1903; "Judge Estee Will Not Give Snap Judgment," *Pacific Commercial Advertiser*, June 16, 1903; "Hartwell's Brief in the Korean Immigrant Cases," *Evening Bulletin*, June 16, 1903; "May End Korean Case," *Evening Bulletin*, June 18, 1903; "Plea Is Overruled," *Evening Bulletin*, June 22, 1903. The names of those 113 immigrants aboard the *Nippon Maru* are given in Hawaii Korean Golden Jubilee Celebration Committee, *Fifty Years of Progress*.

33. Giffard to Irwin, July 20, 1903, GI.

34. Giffard to Irwin, July 14, 1903, GI.

35. "Korean Detective Comes to Bribe Countrymen and Lands in Jail," *Hilo Tribune*, July 17, 1903; see also No, [Short history], pp. 5–6.

36. "Law Was Not in Effect—A New Demurrer Filed in the Korean Cases," *Pacific Commercial Advertiser*, July 25, 1903.

37. Berger departed on July 30 aboard the *Aorangi*. *Pacific Commercial Advertiser*, July 31, 1903. Judge Estee and his wife departed six days later. *Pacific Commercial Advertiser*, August 2, 5, and 6, 1903.

38. "Labor Unionists Want to Change Island Labor," *Pacific Commercial Advertiser*, September 17, 1903.

39. Giffard to Irwin, May 22, 1903, GI.

40. "A Commissioner of Immigration," *Pacific Commercial Advertiser*, June 3, 1903.

41. *Pacific Commercial Advertiser*, July 30, 1903; see also "Lansing Is Commissioner," *Evening Bulletin*, July 29, 1903; and F. M. Husted, *Directory and Handbook of Honolulu and the Hawaiian Islands, 1900–01*, p. 287.

42. "Lansing's Plans—Will Advertise for Labor in Korea and Portugal," *Hilo Tribune*, August 21, 1903. His advertisement, dated August 6, was soon in circulation in Korea.

43. "Lansing Says Koreans Are Good Laborers," *Evening Bulletin*, August 25, 1903.

44. *Pacific Commercial Advertiser*, September 12, 1903; "Korean Cases Thrown Down," *Pacific Commercial Advertiser*, September 30, 1903. For secondary accounts of the trial see No, [Short history], pp. 8–9; Sŏ, ["Seventy years of America's Koreans"] nos. 4 and 5 (May 8, 1971 and May 11, 1971); Francis Kang, "Korean Milestone"; R. C. Lydecker, "Memorandum on the Introduction of Foreign Laborers"; Hawaii Korean Golden Jubilee Celebration Committee, *Fifty Years of Progress*.

45. *Hwangsŏng sinmun*, August 28, 1903.
46. Horace Allen Diary, October 29, 1903, Allen MSS.
47. Allen to Nash, May 4, 1904, Allen MSS.

Chapter 9. Systematic Immigration Is Established

1. Katō Motoshirō (consul in Inch'ŏn) to Komura, August 31, 1903, *Kankoku imin*. That the Japanese government kept an eye on Korean immigration to Hawaii would prove to be significant in less than two years.
2. *Hwangsŏng sinmun*, May 22, 1903.
3. *Hansŏng sinbo*, July 3, 1903.
4. Kawakami Tatsuichirō to Komura, December 22, 1903, *Kankoku imin*.
5. *Hwangsŏng sinmun*, April 25, 1904. For a personal experience, see Morris Pang, "A Korean Immigrant," pp. 117–123.
6. Inch'ŏn, Seoul, Wŏnsan, Sŏngjin, Chinnamp'o, Mokp'o, Manbokku, Kunsan, Kanggyŏngp'o, P'yŏngyang, Pusan, and Chinjungp'o.
7. In Kunsan, Mokp'o, and Pusan, for example, the recruiting offices were managed by Japanese. See Yokota Saburō (chief of the branch in Kunsan) to Komura, March 27, 1905; and Wakamatsu Kisaburō (consul in Mokp'o) to Komura, April 13, 1905. *Kankoku imin*. See also Allen to Swanzy, February 5, 1905, Allen MSS.
8. Lyu, "Korean Nationalist Activities," p. 15.
9. Sŏ, ["Seventy years of America's Koreans"], No. 3 (May 5, 1971).
10. Bernice Kim, "The Koreans in Hawaii," p. 80.
11. Charr, *The Golden Mountain*, p. 105.
12. Yun Ch'i-ho *Ilgi*, 6:167–168 (October 3, 1905).
13. Bernice Kim, "The Koreans in Hawaii," p. 80.
14. Yun Ch'i-ho *Ilgi*, 6:168 (October 3, 1905).
15. L. George Paik, *The History of Protestant Missions in Korea*, p. 282, which quotes from p. 312 of the Methodist Episcopal North *Report* for 1904. See also the statement by Mrs. Bernice Kim Park that Korean Methodist missionaries influenced her parents to come to Hawaii, in "Korean Women Toiled in Camps," *Honolulu Advertiser and Star-Bulletin*, January 7, 1973, and *Han'guk ilbo*, January 10, 1973.
16. Lyu, "Korean Nationalist Activities," p. 14.
17. Katō to Komura, March 29, 1905, *Kankoku imin*.
18. Bernice Kim, "The Koreans in Hawaii," p. 86.
19. Ibid., pp. 86–87.
20. Wakamatsu to Komura, April 13, 1905, *Kankoku imin*.
21. Lyu, "Korean Nationalist Activities," p. 15.
22. Hyŏn Sun, [Record of a sightseeing trip], p. 4. While the *Yuminwŏn* was still in existence in 1903 the passports were written in Korean, English, and French and bore the signature of Min Yŏng-hwan, the president of the *Yuminwŏn*. After Yi Yong-ik engineered the demise of this department, passports were issued by the Foreign Office, written in English, French, and

Chinese and bearing the seal of the Korean Foreign Office. See Lyu, "Korean Nationalist Activities," p. 16.

23. Lyu, "Korean Nationalist Activities," pp. 15, 17; see also Hattori Ichizō (governor of Hyōgo Prefecture) to Ishii Kikujirō (director of the Commerce Bureau in the Foreign Ministry), June 14, 1905, *Kankoku imin.*

24. Lyu, "Korean Nationalist Activities," p. 15.

25. Underwood, *Fifteen Years among the Top-Knots*, p. 2. The train reputedly ran at 15 miles per hour.

26. Robert T. Oliver, *Syngman Rhee: The Man Behind the Myth*, pp. 76–77.

27. Allen to Harris, May 18, 1904, and August 4, 1904; Allen to Nash, September 6, 1904. Allen MSS.

28. Oliver, *Syngman Rhee*, pp. 76–77. Judging from the price that Rhee paid for his trans-Pacific ticket (126 *yen*), he did not ride in steerage with the rest of the immigrants, as Oliver claims, but must have occupied a stateroom.

29. Charr, *The Golden Mountain*, p. 116.

30. Hattori Ichizō to Ishii Kikujirō, June 14, 1905, *Kankoku imin*. See also Dr. J. Bucknill Fowler (acting assistant surgeon, Public Health and Marine Hospital Service) to Hunter Sharp, (American consul at Kobe), December 31, 1905, U.S., Department of State, Despatches from United States Consuls in Osaka and Hiogo (Kobe), Japan, 1868–1906, roll 13.

31. Katō to Komura, March 29, 1905, *Kankoku imin*. Also Hyŏn Sun, [Record of a sightseeing trip], p. 6.

32. Hyŏn Sun, [Record of a sightseeing trip], p. 6; also, Lyu, "Korean Nationalist Activities," p. 19.

33. Bernice Kim, "Koreans in Hawaii," (1937), p. 87.

34. Ibid., pp. 86–87; see also the interview with Mrs. Kim Tae-yun who came to Hawaii at eighteen as a bride in 1905: "Korean Woman Toiled in Camps," *Honolulu Advertiser and Star-Bulletin*, January 7, 1973, and "Imin ilse," *Han'guk ilbo*, January 10, 1973.

35. HSPA, Trustees, Minutes, February 4, 1904.

36. HSPA, Trustees, Minutes, January 26 and February 20, 1905.

37. Yi Chŏng-gŭn, *Insaeng p'alsipe chŏngbyŏn manhwa* ["Great changes in the eighty years of my life"].

38. *Maui News*, February 13, 1904. See Husted's *Directory and Handbook of Honolulu, 1900–01*, p. 28, for the names of the barkentines and schooners plying the interisland routes.

39. HSPA, Trustees, Minutes, February 4, 1904; see also Hyŏn Sun, "My Autobiography," pp. 63–66.

40. HSPA, Trustees, Minutes, August 4, 1904.

41. Ogg (manager of the Hawaiian Agricultural Company) to C. Brewer and Company, March 31, 1903, Hawaiian Agricultural Company, Letterbook, 1903–1906.

42. Ogg to David Deshler, April 23, 1903, ibid.

43. Ogg to Bishop and Company, Bankers, November 14, 1903, ibid.

44. Morioka Makoto, Hyūga Terutake and Tomiochi Chūtarō to Komu-

ra, February (n.d.), 1905, *Kankoku imin*. See also Hawaii Territory, Bureau of Labor, *Third Report, 1905*, which gives a breakdown by men, women, and children; and F. M. Bechtel, Chinese Inspector in Charge of Immigration, to Acting Governor Carter, n.d., Hawaii, Territory, Governors Files, Carter–U.S. Departments, Immigration, HSA.

45. Bechtel to Atkinson, Acting Governor, July 25, 1905, Hawaii, Territory, Governors Files, Carter–U.S. Departments, Immigration, HSA. See also No, [Short history], pp. 5–17; Hawaii, Territory, Bureau of Labor, *Third Report, 1905*, p. 14; and Hawaii, Territory, Board of Immigration, First Report, p. 24. During the period of Korean immigration, about 18,000 Japanese arrived, compared with about 7,000 Koreans. A small number of Koreans were not admitted because of disease, and the figures also include a small (undetermined) number who returned to Korea to bring relatives back to Hawaii.

46. *Hwangsŏng sinmun*, May 22, 1903.

47. Arakawa Gitarō, Governor of Nagasaki Prefecture, to Komura, June 2, 1903, *Kankoku imin*.

48. Harrington, *God, Mammon and the Japanese*, pp. 133, 164; "Koreans Are the Best Workers—American Mining Man Prefers Them to Japanese," *Pacific Commercial Advertiser*, July 28, 1906; "Korean Laborers Immigrate to Japan," *Independent*, November 2, 1897; Hawaii, Territory, Bureau of Labor, *Third Report, 1905*, p. 117.

49. HSPA, Trustees, Minutes, February 28, 1903.

50. HSPA, Trustees, Minutes, September 14, 1905.

51. HSPA, Trustees, Minutes, April 18, 1905.

52. Katō to Komura, January 24, 1903; also Yokota Saburo to Komura, March 27, 1905, *Kankoku imin*.

53. Hyŏn Sun, [Record of a sightseeing trip], p. 5.

54. S. F. Moore, "One Night with the Koreans in Hawaii," *Korea Review*, December, 1903, pp. 531–532.

55. Interview with Yang Chu-un (age 97) conducted by Bong-Youn Choy, February 27, 1974. This interview was later transcribed and appears in Choy, *Koreans in America*, pp. 293–300.

56. Yi Hong-ki, quoted in Sŏ, ["Seventy years"], No. 5 (May 11, 1971).

57. See ibid., and Lyu, "Korean Nationalist Activities," pp. 44, 44n.

58. No, [Short history], pp. 10–11.

59. HSPA, Trustees, Minutes, February 4, 1904.

60. Kim Wŏn-yong, [A Fifty-Year History of Koreans], pp. 85–86; see also Lyu, "Korean Nationalist Activities," p. 37.

61. Lyu, "Korean Nationalist Activities," pp. 44, 44n.

Chapter 10. Characteristics of the Immigrants and Why They Came

1. Bernice Kim, "Koreans in Hawaii" (1937), pp. 85–86.

2. Katō to Komura, March 29, 1905, *Kankoku imin*. See also Japanese

Consulate in Honolulu, [Korean Registration Cards], n.d., which lists date of arrival in Hawaii and birthplace. Additional information can be found in U.S. Immigration and Naturalization Service, Port of Honolulu, *Inbound Vessels, Passenger Manifests*. This finding is also suggested by the results of a survey done in 1970 by three graduate students (Oh In-hwan, Park Pyoung Wha Kim, and Kim Seun-ung) who interviewed 84 elderly Koreans. Of the 84, 13 came as young men, 23 came as children, and the remaining 48 were women who came either between 1903 and 1905 or as picture brides between 1910 and 1924. This survey, which will be referred to as the Oh Survey, is only suggestive because of the small sample and the length of time since emigration. It is used with the permission of the instructor involved, Herbert Barringer of the Sociology Department of the University of Hawaii. See Appendix A of my dissertation, "The Korean Frontier in America: Immigration to Hawaii, 1896–1910," pp. 701–702. The Oh Survey found that about half of the emigrants came from cities, one-third from towns, and only about one-tenth from rural areas. In addition, a review of seventy-seven obituaries or articles about elderly Koreans in Hawaii during the period 1950–1985, when a birthplace is mentioned, Seoul appears most frequently (about 10 percent). These obituaries are listed in Appendix B (pp. 703–705) of my dissertation. Moreover, the Oh survey found that 18 percent came from Seoul, 10 percent from Kyŏnggi-do, 8 percent from P'yŏngan-do, 5 percent from Chŏlla-do, 4 percent from Ch'unch'ŏng-do, 2 percent from Hwanghae-do, and 1 percent from Hamkyŏng-do. The remaining 52 percent were from Kyŏngsang-do, an indication of the large number of picture-bride respondents.

3. The small number of farmers is mentioned by Kim Hyŏng-sun in an interview given to Bong-Youn Choy on March 26, 1974, in San Francisco. The transcribed interview appears in Choy's book *Koreans in America*, pp. 303–305, but this particular remark was edited out.

4. Bernice Kim, "Koreans in Hawaii" (1937), pp. 85–86; see also her 1934 article "The Koreans in Hawaii," pp. 409–413.

5. Kim Hyŏng-sun interview.

6. According to Bernice Kim (1937, p. 78), "During those years [1898–1901], starving farmers moved away [from Hwanghae Province] to other cities in the north in the hope of finding a means of allaying their hunger." In addition, the responses in the Oh Survey indicate that the parents of immigrants were much more generally farmers than were their offspring, indicating a move to the city soon before emigration. The Oh Survey found that 37 percent of those interviwed answered that their fathers or their husbands' fathers had been farmers, while 31 percent indicated that their fathers had been engaged in non-manual labor, and 7 percent that their fathers had been engaged in commerce. When the Oh Survey asked about their own (or husbands') occupation in Korea before emigrating, 15 percent said they had been soldiers or governmental officials, 9 percent said they had been in business or commerce, and 30 percent responded "other." These last responses may mean occupations of common laborer or simply unemployment. Finally, the fact that many of the immigrants were Christians and/or had left their native villages and ancestral graveyards is

an important factor, in that a truly Confucian Korean would never have been so unfilial as to abandon the graves of his ancestors or parents for a destination thousands of miles overseas.

7. "Koreans Are the Best Workers," *Pacific Commercial Advertiser*, July 28, 1906.

8. Rev. Henry B. Restarick, *Hawaii, 1778–1920*, p. 322.

9. Wadman, "Educational Work among the Koreans," p. 146.

10. Moffett to Brown, October 20, 1904, Presbyterian Church in the USA, Korean Letters.

11. Rev. G. L. Pearson quoted in *Korea Review*, January, 1904, p. 31.

12. *Hawaiian Church Chronicle*, September, 1908, p. 12. This publication is the successor to the *Anglican Church Chronicle*.

13. Warren Y. Kim [Kim Wŏn-yong], *Koreans in America*, p. 11.

14. In the Oh Survey, of the thirteen male workers who came as adults between 1903 and 1905, one had 10–12 years of education, one had 7–9 years of education, three had 4–6 years, four had 1–3, and 4 had no education. To a slightly differently worded question, responses indicated that of the eighty-four, one had been to college, six had had middle school training, six had attended elementary school, twenty-six said that they had studied *hanmun* (Chinese characters), sixteen had studied *hangŭl* (the Korean alphabet), and twenty-one had no education. Obviously it is difficult to define "literacy" accurately. In addition, some of the immigrants knew some English from their association with missionaries and mission schools.

15. Eum Shi Moon (Ŏm Si-mun) of P'yŏngan-do, for example, was of *yangban* stock; he was employed as a scribe in Korea before coming to Hawaii. Because he was literate, Eum was a letter-writer for the illiterate Korean immigrants who wanted to write home. See Eum Shi Moon Family Papers. *Yangban* from the northern part of Korea might have been more likely to emigrate since they were permanently blocked from access to political power in the Yi court.

16. See U.S. Commissioner-General of Immigration, Annual Report for 1906, p. 6; see also the reference to seventy-seven obituaries in note 2 (above), which gives an average age of 27; finally, see Bernice Kim, "The Koreans in Hawaii" (1934), pp. 409–413.

17. See Tin-yuke Char, *The Sandalwood Mountains;* also Clarence Glick, *Sojourners and Settlers.*

18. *Hwangsŏng sinmun*, December 22, 1900.

19. Wadman, "Educational Work among the Koreans," p. 146.

20. Dick Gima, "Marriage to a Cobbler Really Lasts."

21. Kang, "Korean Milestone."

22. Of 46,000 Chinese immigrants to Hawaii, 23,000 returned to China; of 180,000 Japanese immigrants to Hawaii, 98,000 returned to Japan. Romanzo Adams, *Interracial Marriage in Hawaii*, pp. 31–32. I will also argue later that some changed their minds about returning after having lived in Hawaii for a few years, during which time Japan took over Korea.

23. Allen to Hay, December 10, 1902, Allen MSS.

24. Lyu, "Korean Nationalist Activities," p. 20.

25. Oh Survey.

26. Tai Sung Lee, "The Story of Korean Immigration," pp. 47–49. This article was published in Kim and Patterson, *Koreans in America, 1882–1974*, pp. 106–108. Lee served as executive secretary of the Korean Student Christian Movement in Hawaii in the 1930s.

27. The visit of Vice-Foreign Minister Yun Ch'i-ho to the Islands in the fall of 1905 was attributed in part to an attempt on the part of the Korean government to investigate the antigovernment activities of the Koreans in Hawaii who were associated with the *Sinminhoe*.

28. Chōsen sōtokufu [Government-General of Chosen], *Annual Report on the Administration of Chosen*, p. 17.

29. For a statement from nationalist figures, see "850 Attend Korean Golden Jubilee," *Honolulu Advertiser*, November 21, 1953. For a statement from a missionary, see Alice R. Appenzeller, "A Generation of Koreans in Hawaii," pp. 81–83.

30. Oh Survey. For information on the methodology of this survey, see my dissertation, Appendix A, pp. 701–702.

31. While there have been numerous references to the heavy influence of Christianity among the Korean immigrants, consider the following additional indications of that predominant influence: Bishop Restarick (*Hawaii, 1778–1920*, p. 322) noted the influence of different Protestant denominational influences among the arriving Koreans; Rev. Pearson stated, "I am pleased to say that the loyalty, zeal, spiritual power, observance of the Sabbath, etc., on the part of the Koreans who are here testify to the thorough work of the Missionaries in Korea" (*Korea Review*, January, 1904, p. 31); among the seventy-seven obituaries mentioned earlier, about one-third indicated a strong affiliation with Christianity; finally, it might be noted that in October 1904, Ewa Plantation contributed $750 to build a church for their Korean laborers (in Ewa Plantation Minute Books, cited in E. Leigh Stevens, Assistant Secretary, Castle and Cooke LTD, to Wayne Patterson, May 7, 1976, and June 1, 1976).

32. See, for example, Rev. C. E. Sharp, "Reasons for Seeking Christ," p. 182.

33. Quoted in Harrington, *God, Mammon and the Japanese*, p. 58.

34. Tai Sung Lee, "Story of Korean Immigration," pp. 47–49.

35. Paik, *History of Protestant Missions*, pp. 205, 248–249. By 1905 there were 174 missionaries representing fourteen denominations. Of these, 80 were Presbyterian.

36. *The Korea Methodist* 1, no. 7 (May 10, 1905): 82.

37. "The Korean Abroad," Letter 1, translated by Yun Ch'i-ho, the *Korean Repository*, May 1897, p. 107.

38. Oh Survey.

39. Sin Hŭng-u, ["The present situation of our eight thousand countrymen"], pp. 287–290.

40. Chōsen sōtokufu, [Concerning the annexation of Korea], pp. 290–292; Japanese Consulate in Honolulu, ["The general condition of the Koreans in Hawaii"], 1925, (in Kim Chŏng-ju, [Political studies of Korea], vol. 7, p.

930); and, Chōsen sōtokufu, *Keimu kyoku* [The situation of insubordinate Koreans in the United States and the Territory of Hawaii], p. 1. One might argue, of course, that Japanese accounts are unreliable and would tend to downplay the nationalist impulse for emigration and instead emphasize nonpolitical factors, such as poverty, as the primary cause. This may be true. However, other Japanese reports on Korea used in this study have been found to be, for the most part, accurate. Moreover, other evidence about to be introduced essentially corroborates these accounts of poverty and bad conditions in Korea.

41. Hulbert, *The Passing of Korea*, p. 173; see also Yun Yŏ-jun, "Early History of Korean Emigration," in *The Korean Diaspora*, pp. 34–35.

42. No Chae-yŏn writes in his [Short history], p. 2: "All of Hwanghae-do was in a state of famine and the people were moving out. Since the government had no specific relief policy, the people were encouraged to emigrate as a means of making a suitable living." See also Bernice Kim, "The Koreans in Hawaii" (1937), p. 79; and Lyu, "Korean Nationalist Activities," p. 14.

43. *Hwangsŏng sinmun*, December 29, 1902.

44. Allen to Dole, December 10, 1902; also Allen to Hay, December 10, 1902. Allen MSS.

45. Tai Sung Lee, "Story of Korean Immigration."

46. Allen to Hay, December 10, 1902, Allen MSS.

47. Baird to Ellinwood, March 21, 1903, Presbyterian Church, Korean Letters, reel 280, 69–5, no. 37 (monthly station letter).

48. Sallie Swallen to Jennie Ashbrook, October 9, 1903, Swallen Letters, 1901–1903.

Chapter 11. Koreans As Workers

1. "President's Address," *Planters Monthly*, December 1903, p. 525.

2. Giffard to Irwin, December 15, 1903, GI.

3. C. Wolters (manager of Hutchinson Sugar Plantation Company) to William G. Irwin and Co., LTD, December 16, 1903. See also his letters of December 29, 1903, and April 6 and 11, 1904. One year later Wolters would have a negative opinion of Korean workers. Hutchinson Sugar Plantation Co., Letterbook, 1903–1904.

4. HSPA, Trustees, Minutes, November 16, 1903.

5. Giffard to Irwin, December 29, 1903; see also Irwin's response to Giffard dated January 8, 1904. GI.

6. HSPA, Trustees Minutes, May 5, 1904.

7. *Pacific Commercial Advertiser*, July 30 and August 1, 1904. See also Reineke, "Labor Disturbances," p. 11.

8. *Pacific Commercial Advertiser*, June 6, 1905; Reineke, p. 12.

9. Hawaii, Territory, Bureau of Labor, Third Report of the Commissioner of Labor, 1905, p. 144.

10. *Pacific Commercial Advertiser*, December 9, 10, 11, and 12, 1904; see also Reineke, "Labor Disturbances," p. 11; No, [Short history], p. 14; and Third Report (see note 9, above), pp. 136–137.

11. C. M. Cooke to R. P. Rithet, May 17, 1905, Cooke Papers, Rithet was the president of the California and Hawaiian Sugar Refining Company based in San Francisco.

12. C. M. Cooke to George [illegible], September 23, 1904, Cooke Papers.

13. Hawaii, Territory, Third and Fourth Reports of Commissioners of Labor; Fifth Report, p. 14 (cited in Hawaii Korean Golden Jubilee Committee, *Fifty Years of Progress*,); Board of Immigration, First Report, 1905–1907, p. 24, table (statistics of immigration—arrivals and departures of immigrants at Honolulu).

14. U.S. Commissioner-General of Immigration, Annual Report 1906, pp. 66–67.

15. No [Short history], p. 15.

16. C. M. Cooke to C. B. Wells, April 3, 1905; see also Cooke to [illegible], April 11, 1905, concerning the two-dollar per month raise, Cooke Papers.

17. Swanzy to Allen, March 14 and May 18, 1905, Allen MSS. The latter communication was the last letter Swanzy wrote to Allen.

18. Saitō Miki to Komura, April 24, 1905, *Kankoku imin*.

19. HSPA Labor Committee, Territory of Hawaii Report, 1905, HSA.

20. E. Faxon Bishop to C. M. Cooke, November 11, 1902, Cooke Papers.

21. For a fuller discussion of these implications see Patterson, "Upward Social Mobility of the Koreans," pp. 81–92.

22. C. Wolters to William G. Irwin and Co., LTD, March 1, 1905, Hutchinson Sugar Plantation Co., Letterbook to William G. Irwin and Co.

23. C. Wolters to William G. Irwin and Co., LTD, April 11, 1905. Ibid.

Chapter 12. Japanese Opposition Resurfaces

1. George Heber Jones, "The Koreans in Hawaii," pp. 401–406.

2. Sin Sŏk-ho, et al., [History of modern Korea], vol. 9, p. 213. The newspapers learned of the prohibition on the third of April. See *Hwangsŏng sinmun*, April 3, 1905. The prohibition was publicly announced on the fourth. See Wakamatsu Usaburō, Consul in Mokp'o, to Komura, April 13, 1905, *Kankoku imin*.

3. Irwin to Giffard, April 1, 1903, GI.

4. Allen Diary, no. 4, October 29, 1903, Allen MSS.

5. Allen to Swanzy, February 20, 1905. The two men exchanged nine letters between July 1904 and May 1905. Allen MSS. Swanzy's daughter, Mrs. James P. Morgan of Honolulu, still has this chest in her possession.

6. Allen to Swanzy, April 8, 1905, Allen MSS.

7. HSPA, Trustees, Minutes, May 10 and June 1, 1905.

8. Allen to Swanzy, April 8, 1905, Allen MSS.

9. Allen to Harris, March 9, 1905, Allen MSS.

10. Harrington, *God, Mammon and the Japanese*, pp. 314–318.

11. Ibid., p. 330.

12. Deshler to Allen, April 13, 1905, Allen MSS.

13. Allen MSS, no date. (Insert in Allen MSS.)

14. Takahira to Komura, March 20, 1905. Gaimushō gaikō shiryōkan. *Zai Bei ryōji rai* [Incoming from America], p. 3094.

15. Swanzy to Allen, May 18, 1905, Allen MSS.

16. Allen to Morgan, May 16, 1905, Allen MSS.

17. Allen to Swanzy, April 8, 1905, Allen MSS.

18. Allen to Underwood, December 6, 1905, Allen MSS. Kennan's article was reprinted in Japan in the *Japan Weekly Mail*, November 4, 1905.

19. F. M. Swanzy Diary, May 23, 1905.

20. *Cheguk sinmun*, May 3, 1905.

21. F. M. Swanzy Diary, May 29, 1905.

22. HSPA, Trustees, Minutes, June 2, 1905.

23. F. M. Swanzy Diary, June 2, 1905.

24. *Hwangsŏng sinmun*, April 5, 1905.

25. Hayashi Gonsuke to Komura, April 5, 1905, *Kankoku imin*.

26. *Hwangsŏng sinmun*, April 5, 1905.

27. Allen to Swanzy, April 8, 1905, Allen MSS.

28. Hayashi to Komura, April 5, 1905, *Kankoku imin*.

29. Bill Hosokawa, *Nisei: The Quiet Americans*, p. 96.

30. Roger Daniels, *The Politics of Prejudice*, pp. 22, 27.

31. Payson J. Treat, *Diplomatic Relations Between the United States and Japan, 1895–1905*.

32. Daniels, *Politics of Prejudice*.

33. A. M. Pooley, ed., *The Secret Memoirs of Count Tadasu Hayashi*, p. 248.

34. Hanihara Masanao (Japanese ambassador to the United States) to Secretary of State Hughes, April 10, 1924, U.S. Department of State, *Foreign Relations of the United States, 1924*, pp. 372–373. Quoted in Daniels, *Politics of Prejudice*, p. 101.

35. Hosokawa, *Nisei*, p. 46.

36. Takahira Kogorō to Komura, March 18, 1905, Gaimushō, *Nihon gaikō bunsho*, [Documents on foreign policy], vol. 38, no. 2, p. 308. See also Gaimushō, *Nihon gaikō bunsho: Tai Bei imin mondai keika gaiyō fuzokushō* [Documents on Japanese Foreign Policy: Annexes to . . .], pp. 117–118.

37. Ronald Takaki, *Pau Hana*, p. 70.

38. Giffard to Yamaguchi, June 27 and July 7, 1902, GI. Giffard also wanted the Japanese Diet to pass a law forbidding Japanese to go to the mainland, but this was not acted upon.

39. Ishii Kikujirō (director of the Commerce Bureau of the Foreign Ministry), to Saitō Miki, August 28, 1905, *Kankoku imin*.

40. Gaimushō, *Nihon gaikō bunsho: Tai Bei imin . . .* , p. 119. See also Saitō Miki to Chinda Sutemi, April 22, 1905, in *Nihon gaikō bunsho*, vol. 38, no. 2, pp. 317–318.

41. Saitō to Chinda, April 24, 1905, Gaimushō, *Nihon gaikō bunsho*, vol. 38, no. 2, pp. 318–319.

42. Cooke to Rithet, June 5, 1902; Cooke to Alexander, July 7, 1902. Cooke Papers. Hawaii, Territory, Bureau of Labor, *Third Report, 1905*, p. 40. Cooke also hoped that ill-treatment in California would dissuade Japanese from going there.

43. Takahira to Komura, March 18, 1905, Gaimushō, *Nihon gaikō bunsho*, vol. 38, no. 2, p. 308.

44. Pooley, *Secret Memoirs*, p. 248.

45. Giffard to Irwin, December 12, 1902, GI.

46. Morioka Makoto to Komura, July 5, 1904. Komura did send a copy of the letter to Hayashi in Seoul. See Komura to Hayashi, July 26, 1904. *Kankoku imin.*

47. See Yuji Ichioka, "Recent Japanese Scholarship on the Origins and Causes of Japanese Immigration," pp. 2–7. See also Alan Moriyama, *Imingaisha.*

48. Daniels, "Japanese Immigrants on a Western Frontier," p. 91.

49. Morioka Makoto, Hyūga Terutake and Tomiochi Chūtarō to Komura, February 5(?), 1905, *Kankoku imin.* Hyūga was the director of the Dairiku Shokumin Kaisha [Continental colonization company] which had recruited the 1,033 Koreans for Mexico.

50. Ueno to Komura, March 3, 1905. Gaimushō, *Zai Bei ryōji rai*, nos. 8 and 9. Ueno confirmed this news by letter as well. See Ueno to Komura, March 7, 1905 (also March 25 and June 28), Gaimushō, *Nihon gaikō bunsho*, pp. 297–298, 300, 302.

51. Komura to Saitō, March 9, 1905 (drafted March 3, 1905), *Kankoku imin.* The Japanese ambassador in Washington, Takahira, also immediately recognized the seriousness of the action taken by the California legislature and wrote to Komura: "You are no doubt fully informed by our Consul-General at Honolulu impossibility of preventing Japanese immigrants to Hawaii from coming to the United States and also by our Consul at San Francisco, of passage through State Senate and Assembly of California of resolution to take necessary measure to restrict Japanese immigration. In my opinion it is important that our position regarding the matter should be clearly defined, informally communicated to the United States Government, and if needs be, American public by means of press." In this letter Takahira suggests to Komura that he might propose to Washington that a law be passed prohibiting Japanese from going from Hawaii to the mainland United States. See Takahira to Komura, March 18, 1905, Gaimushō, *Nihon gaikō bunsho*, p. 308.

Chapter 13. Japan Brings Emigration to a Halt

1. Komura to Katō Motoshirō, March 7, 1905; Komura to Wakamatsu Usaburō, March 7, 1905; Komura to Ariyoshi Akira, March 7, 1905; and Komura to Yokota Saburō, March 7, 1905. All these letters were drafted on March 3 and accepted on March 6. *Kankoku imin.* Komura also knew a little about the pending emigration of a thousand Koreans to Mexico, having read an article on the subject in the previous day's issue of *Asahi shinbun.*

2. Komura to Hayashi, April 5, 1905, *Kankoku imin.*

3. Hayashi to Komura, April 5, 1905, *Kankoku imin.* He did not mention the report in the newspaper that one reason for the prohibition was that many Korean immigrants in Hawaii could not adjust and were prohibited from returning to Korea because of the difficulty in accumulating enough money for boat passage.

4. Komura to Hayashi, April 6, 1905. On the following day he informed Takahira in Washington and Saitō in Honolulu of his policy to make permanent the temporary ban on Korean emigration. See Komura to Takahira, April 12, 1905 (drafted April 7), and Komura to Saitō, April 12, 1905 (drafted April 7). *Kankoku imin.*

5. Deshler to Huntington Wilson (chargé d'affaires, American Legation in Tokyo), January, 1906 (undated), an enclosure with Wilson to Elihu Root, secretary of state, January 27, 1906, U.S. Dept. of State, Despatches from U.S. Ministers to Japan, 1855–1906. This document can also be found in Hawaii, Territory, Governors Files, Carter–U.S. Departments, State (October 1905–June 1907), HSA. Also Wilson to Katō Takaaki (foreign minister), January 19, 1906, *Kankoku imin.*

6. Yokota Saburō to Komura, March 27, 1905, *Kankoku imin.*

7. Wakamatsu Usaburō to Komura, March 16 and April 13, 1905, *Kankoku imin.*

8. Katō to Komura, March 29 and April 4, 1905. The consul in Pusan, Ariyoshi Akira, replied in a letter dated March 14, 1905, and Saitō Miki replied on March 29, 1905. *Kankoku imin.*

9. *Hwangsŏng sinmun,* April 17, 1905.

10. *Hwangsŏng sinmun,* April 21, 1904. He replaced Cho Pyŏng-sik who had served only one month.

11. *Ilsŏngnok, Kojong-p'yŏn, 42* [Royal annals, 42nd year of Kojong (1905)], p. 74.

12. Press Copy Book No. 8, p. 447, Allen MSS.

13. Deshler to Wilson, January, 1906 (undated), in Wilson to Root, January 27, 1906 (see note 5, above).

14. *Hwangsŏng sinmun,* April 7, 1905.

15. Ibid., April 6, 1905.

16. Ibid., April 10, 1905.

17. A clipping from the fourth page of an unidentified Japanese newspaper dated April 17 telling of Deshler's threat to sue the Inch'ŏn *kamni* Ha Sang-gi for (now) 70,000 *yen* was included in the *Kankoku imin* documents, indicating that the Japanese Foreign Ministry was aware of Deshler's actions.

18. Komura to Hagiwara Moriichi, April 28, 1905, *Kankoku imin.* Minister Hayashi left for Tokyo after forcing the Korean government to quash the new emigration regulations on April 17 and did not return to Seoul until May 13, *Hwangsŏng sinmun,* May 13, 1905.

19. Hagiwara to Komura, April 28, 1905. On the following day, Hagiwara learned from the consul at Chinnamp'o that Deshler's claim for damages probably resulted from the fact that the *kamni* there refused to allow Deshler to send those emigrants issued passports before April first, even though the Korean

Foreign Office had made an exception for such cases. See Someya Nariaki to Hayashi, April 22, 1905, enclosure with Hagiwara to Komura, April 29, 1905, *Kankoku imin*.

20. Komura to Hayashi, April 13, 1905, *Kankoku imin*.

21. Hayashi to Komura, April 14, 1905, *Kankoku imin*.

22. Wakamatsu to Komura, April 13, 1905, *Kankoku imin*.

23. Komura to Someya Nariaki, April 29, 1905; enclosed was a similar message to Katō in Inch'ŏn, *Kankoku imin*.

24. Komura to Hagiwara, May 6, 1905, *Kankoku imin*.

25. Hagiwara to Komura, May 8, 1905, *Kankoku imin*.

26. *Ku Han'guk oegyo munsŏ, Ilan* [Documents Relating to the Foreign Relations of Old Korea, Japan], vol. 7, (hereafter cited as *Ilan*), p. 549, no. 8646 (May 8, 1905).

27. Ibid., p. 552, no. 8651 (May 9, 1905).

28. *Hwangsŏng sinmun*, May 10, 1905.

29. *Cheguk sinmun*, May 16, 1905.

30. Someya Nariaki to Komura, May 8, 1905. Someya also indicated to Komura that some two to three hundred Koreans had been recruited before April 1 and were thus in a similar situation. *Kankoku imin*.

31. *Ilan*, p. 580, no. 8696 (May 31, 1905).

32. *Ilan*, pp. 588–589, no. 8708 (June 3, 1905).

33. *Hwangsŏng sinmun*, June 9, 1905.

34. Suhu Kohei to Ishii Kikujirō, director of the Commerce Bureau, May 27, 1905, *Kankoku imin*.

35. Ishii Kikujirō to Hattori Ichizō, governor of Hyŏgo Prefecture, June 1, 1905; Ishii to Hattori, June 14, 1905, *Kankoku imin*.

36. Hattori to Ishii, June 14, 1905, *Kankoku imin*.

37. *Hwangsŏng sinmun*, October 14, 1903. See also *Kwanbo*, October 11, 1903.

38. *Korea Review*, March 1905, p. 116.

39. C. Kenneth Quinones, "The Impact of the Kabo Reforms upon Political Role Allocation in Late Yi Korea, 1884–1902," pp. 1–18.

40. Jae Schick Pae, Nam-Yearl Chai, and Choon-ho Park, *Korean International Law*, p. 32.

41. *Hwangsŏng sinmun*, November 21, 1902.

42. Allen to Hay, May 17, 1903. See also Allen to Fassett, May 17, 1903, in which Allen wrote that he "suggested the appointment to report on the situation and to draw some revenue from visaing passports, etc." Allen MSS.

43. HSPA, Trustees, Minutes, May 19, 1904.

44. Press Copy Book No. 8, p. 451, Allen MSS.

45. Yun to Dr. Young J. Allen, June 16, 1904, quoted in Robert Hyung-Chan Kim, *The Collected Letters of Yun Tchi Ho*, pp. 147–148.

46. Interview with Yang Choo-eun, in Sonia Shinn Sunoo, *Korea Kaleidoscope*, p. 11.

47. Yun Ch'i-ho *Ilgi*, 6:45 (July 4, 1904).

48. Ibid. (July 9, 1904).

49. Ibid., p. 46 (July 10, 1904).

50. *Hwangsŏng sinmun*, July 11 and 12, 1904. See also *Korea Review*, July 1904, p. 314. Rumors persisted that Yun would be appointed to a diplomatic post in the United States, perhaps even the post of minister in Washington. See Yun Ch'i-ho *Ilgi*, 6:49–50 (August 3, 1904), and *Hwangsŏng sinmun*, August 17, 1904. Throughout, Yun remained pessimistic, writing at this time that "the affairs in Korea are worse than ever." Yun to Dr. Young J. Allen, August 5, 1904, in Robert Hyung-Chan Kim, ed., *The Collected Letters of Yun Tchi Ho*, pp. 150–151. While Yun was in favor of emigration and study abroad, Hayashi Gonsuke let him know in no uncertain terms what he thought about overseas Koreans: "Those who have been abroad are ten times worse in corruption than home-staying Koreans." Yun Ch'i-ho *Ilgi*, 6:61 (September 4, 1904).

51. Allen to Hay, September 10, 1904, Allen MSS; see also *Korea Review*, September 1904, p. 415.

52. *Hwangsŏng sinmun*, September 6, 1904.

53. Allen to Gallaudet, August 25, 1904, Allen MSS; see also *Korea Review*, August 1904, p. 366.

54. *Hwangsŏng sinmun*, November 3, 1904. Six days later the newspapers reported a rumor that Americans had requested permission to allow the emigration of eight thousand Koreans to Panama. Had the rumor been true, Korea would have been obligated to station a diplomatic representative in yet another country. *Taedong sinbo*, November 9, 1904.

55. HSPA, Trustees, Minutes, December 15, 1904. Swanzy would also write to Allen in the spring of 1905 about the need to have a good Korean consul to advise Koreans not to go to California, but by that time it was too late. See Swanzy to Allen, May 18, 1905, Allen MSS.

56. *Hwangsŏng sinmun*, January 25, 1905; see also *Korea Review*, January 1905, p. 35.

57. *Hansŏng sinbo*, March 1, 1905; see also, *Korea Review*, March 1905, p. 115.

58. The imperial decree of November 15, 1902, read: "The control of the laborers of Great Korea to be employed abroad is hereby given to Deshler, an American citizen." Hawaii, Territory, Governors Files, Carter–U.S. Departments, State, HSA.

59. *Hwangsŏng sinmun*, December 17, 1904, to January 13, 1905.

60. Warren Y. Kim, *Koreans in America*, p. 15.

61. Books such as *Barbarous Mexico* by John K. Turner could have provided the necessary information.

62. *Ilsŏngnok: Kojong p'yŏn*, 42 [Royal annals: 42nd year of the reign of Kojong], p. 74.

63. George Trumbull Ladd, *In Korea with Marquis Ito*, pp. 252, 365.

64. Nakai Kinjō, *Chōsen kaikoroku* [Memories of Korea], pp. 185–186. On the occasion of a dinner for a visiting legislator from Japan, Nakai, whose company was responsible for sending the thousand Koreans to Mexico, complained to Hayashi about the Korean ban on emigration. Hayashi answered that the prohibition had been the idea of the Japanese emigration companies. In this way, Hayashi could blame Nakai's colleagues rather than a more

abstract appeal to the national interest of Japan in preventing the United States from enacting a Japanese exclusion act.

65. *Kojong shidaesa*, [History of the Kojong Era], vol. 6, pp. 218–219; Gaimushō, *Nihon gaikō bunsho*, p. 250.

Chapter 14. The Planters and Korea Fight Back

1. Bechtel, Inspector in Charge of Immigration, to Acting Governor Atkinson, July 25, 1905, Hawaii, Territory, Governors Files, Carter–U.S. Departments, Immigration, HSA.

2. Hawaii, Territory, Bureau of Labor, *Third Report, 1905*, p. 14.

3. HSPA, Trustees, Minutes, June 2, 1905.

4. F. M. Swanzy Diary, June 14, 1905.

5. Ibid., June 15, 1905.

6. Ibid., June 17, 1905.

7. C. M. Cooke to Rithet, May 17, 1905, Cooke Papers.

8. F. M. Swanzy Diary, July 6, 1905.

9. Cooke to Rithet, July 18, 1905, Cooke Papers.

10. Cooke to Rithet, August 8, 1905, Cooke Papers.

11. *Pacific Commercial Advertiser*, July 8, 1905.

12. Cooke to E. E. Olding, August 14, 1905, Cooke Papers.

13. *Kwanbo*, September 9, 1904.

14. *Cheguk sinmun*, September 21, 1904.

15. Ibid., December 8, 1904.

16. *Hwangsŏng sinmun*, January 15, 1901.

17. Allen to Swanzy, April 8, 1905, Allen MSS.

18. *Japan Weekly Mail*, July 29, 1905.

19. F. M. Swanzy Diary, July 26, 1905.

20. Yun Ch'i-ho *Ilgi*, 6:118 (June 20, 1905).

21. Ibid., 6:139 (August 12, 1905).

22. Ibid., 6:128–130 (July 17–22, 1905).

23. *Japan Weekly Mail*, August 5, 1905.

24. F. M. Swanzy Diary, August 9, 1905.

25. Ibid., August 10, 1905.

26. Yun Ch'i-ho *Ilgi*, 6:139 (August 12, 1905).

27. F. M. Swanzy Diary, August 11, 1905.

28. Yun Ch'i-ho *Ilgi*, 6:143 (August 30, 1905). The agent, Ōba Kannichi, offered to pay Yun's expenses if he would visit the Yucatan to correct the false reports about the treatment of the Korean laborers.

29. Yun Ch'i-ho *Ilgi*, 6:202 (November 29, 1905).

30. Ishii Kikujirō to Saitō Miki, August 28, 1905; see also Chinda Sutemi to Tsuruhara Jyōkichi, Director General in the Governor-General's Office, March 20, 1906. *Kankoku imin*.

31. Yun Ch'i-ho *Ilgi*, 6:140 (August 28, 1905).

32. *Hwangsŏng sinmun*, July 29, 1905 (letter), and August 1, 1905 (article).

33. *Kojong sillok*, [The veritable record of Kojong], August 1, 1905; *Hwangsŏng sinmun*, August 3, 1905.

34. Yun Ch'i-ho *Ilgi*, 6:141 (August 28, 1905).

35. Yun Ch'i-ho *Ilgi*, 6:141 (August 30, 1905); F. M. Swanzy Diary, August 30, 1905; *Japan Weekly Mail*, September 2, 1905.

36. Chinda Sutemi to Saitō Miki, August 29, 1905, *Kankoku imin*.

37. Ishii Kikujirō to Yun Ch'i-ho, August 30, 1905, *Kankoku imin*.

38. Ishii Kikujirō to Saitō Miki, August 28, 1905, *Kankoku imin*.

39. F. M. Swanzy Diary, August 28, 1905.

40. Yun Ch'i-ho *Ilgi*, 6:143–145 (September 7 and 8, 1905). See also F. M. Swanzy Diary, September 8, 1905.

41. *Pacific Commercial Advertiser*, September 9, 1905.

42. Yun Ch'i-ho *Ilgi*, 6:146 (September 8, 1905).

43. HSPA, Trustees, Minutes, September 9, 1905; Yun Ch'i-ho *Ilgi*, 6:147 (September 9, 1905).

44. Hyŏn Sun, "My Autobiography," p. 66; Yun Ch'i-ho *Ilgi*, 6:147 (September 9, 1905).

45. "Atkinson Went Away with Yun," *Hawaiian Star*, September 13, 1905; Yun Ch'i-ho *Ilgi*, 6:148–149 (September 13, 1905).

46. [Illegible], Director, H. Hackfeld and Company, to W. Weber, Manager, Lihue Plantation Company, September 12, 1905, HSPA Library, Aiea, Hawaii.

47. HSPA, Trustees, Minutes, September 14, 1905.

48. The earliest reference I can find is *Ilan*, pp. 161–162, no. 8160 (June 23, 1904); also pp. 278–279, no. 8294 (August 2, 1904).

49. See, for example, *Ilan*, pp. 515–516, no. 8595 (April 21, 1905).

50. *Ilan*, pp. 540–541, no. 8632 (May 5, 1905); also pp. 552–553, no. 8652 (May 9, 1905). See also, *Hansŏng sinbo*, May 5, 1905; *Hwangsŏng sinmun*, May 6, 1905; and, Teh Moo Sin, Korean Chargé d'Affaires in Washington, to Hubert H. D. Pierce, June 29, 1905, U.S., Department of State, Notes from the Korean Legation, roll 1 (September 18, 1883–April 24, 1906).

51. *Hwangsŏng sinmun*, May 17, 1905; see also *Korea Review*, May 1905, p. 194.

52. HSPA, Trustees, Minutes, August 10 and 17, 1905; *Yamato shinbun*, September 11, 1905; No [Short history], pp. 19–20. The favorable response by the planters to Saitō's request for charitable aid to the Koreans may have been made partly as a signal to the Japanese that the planters were concerned about the welfare of Koreans and thus to help persuade the Japanese government to permit the resumption of Korean immigration.

53. *Korea Review*, August 1905, p. 318. The messenger's name was Yi Tong-ho.

54. *Hwangsŏng sinmun*, August 10, 1905.

55. *Hwangsŏng sinmun*, August 15 and 17, 1905. See the translation of the petition by Yun Yŏ-jun in Hyung-Chan Kim, *The Korean Diaspora*, pp. 67–68.

56. *Korea Review*, September 1905, p. 351.

57. No [Short history], p. 18; see also Henry Chung, *The Oriental Policy of the United States*, pp. 241–245.

58. *Yamato shinbun*, July 17, 1905.
59. Lyu, "Korean Nationalist Activities," pp. 37, 40–41; see also Yun Ch'i-ho *Ilgi*, 6:154 (September 18, 1905).
60. *Ilan*, no. 8848 (August 14, 1905).
61. *Hwangsŏng sinmun*, August 17, 1905.
62. *Ilan*, no. 8865 (August 22, 1905). Hayashi repeated his request a month later. See Ibid., vol. 7., No. 8930 (September 26, 1905).
63. Ibid., no. 8948 (October 2, 1905). See also *Korea Review*, September 1905, p. 359.
64. Gaimushō, *Nihon gaikō bunsho*, pp. 297–317; see also *Nihon gaikō bunsho: Tai Bei imin* . . . [Documents on Japanese Foreign Policy: Annexes of . . .], pp. 117–134.
65. Yun Ch'i-ho *Ilgi*, 6:154 (September 18, 1905).
66. Yun Ch'i-ho *Ilgi*, 6:154–155 (September 19, 1905); see also *Korea Review*, September, 1905, p. 351.
67. *Korea Review*, September 1905, p. 354.
68. *Hwangsŏng sinmun*, October 2, 1905; see also *Korea Review*, October 1905, p. 393.
69. *Korea Review*, October 1905, p. 395.
70. *Japan Weekly Mail*, August 12, 1905.
71. Yun Ch'i-ho *Ilgi*, 6:166–170 (October 3, 1905); see also *Korea Review*, October 1905, p. 397.
72. HSPA, Trustees, Minutes, October 3, 1905.
73. Yun Ch'i-ho *Ilgi*, 6:170–171 (October 14, 1905).
74. Hulbert, "Koreans in Hawaii," pp. 411–413.
75. *Evening Bulletin*, September 14, 1905.
76. *Pacific Commercial Advertiser*, October 9, 1905.
77. C. M. Cooke to P. C. Jones, October 14, 1905, Cooke Papers.
78. Bechtel to Acting Governor Atkinson, July 25, 1905, Hawaii, Territory, Carter–U.S. Departments, Immigration, HSA.
79. Hawaii, Territory, Bureau of Labor, *Third Report, 1905*, p. 14.
80. *Evening Bulletin*, November 23, 1905.
81. Yun Ch'i-ho *Ilgi*, 6:172 (October 14, 1905); see also *Ku Han'guk oegyo munsŏ*, vol. 12, pp. 782, 785, and 788, which detail the shakeup of the Foreign Office.
82. Yun Ch'i-ho *Ilgi*, 6:174–175 (October 16, 1905).
83. Yun Ch'i-ho *Ilgi*, 6:174–176 (October 16 and 25, 1905); see also *Ku Han'guk oegyo kwangye pusok munsŏ*, vol. 7, *Kyosŏpguk ilgi* [Record of negotiations], (hereafter cited as *Kyosŏpguk ilgi*), pp. 802–803 (October 17, 1905).
84. Yun Ch'i-ho *Ilgi*, 6:175 (October 19, 1905); see also *Kyosŏpguk ilgi*, pp. 803–804 (October 20–21, 1905).
85. Yun Ch'i-ho *Ilgi*, 6:177 (October 25, 1905); see also *Kyosŏpguk ilgi*, p. 805 (October 25, 1905).
86. Komura to Hagiwara, October 25, 1905, *Kankoku imin*.
87. Hagiwara to Komura, October 26, 1905, *Kankoku imin*.
88. Yun Ch'i-ho *Ilgi*, 6:180–181 (October 28, 1905).
89. Yun Ch'i-ho *Ilgi*, 6:186 (November 2, 1905).
90. Yun Ch'i-ho *Ilgi*, 6:178–179 (October 25, 1905).

91. Yun Ch'i-ho *Ilgi*, 6:184–189 (November 2–6, 1905).

92. Yun Ch'i-ho *Ilgi*, 6:184 (November 8, 1905). On the same day, Yun reported on his trip to the Korean Foreign Office. See *Kyosŏpguk ilgi*, p. 810 (November 8, 1905).

93. Yun Ch'i-ho *Ilgi*, 6:194 (November 17, 1905).

94. *Korea Review*, February 1906, p. 79.

Chapter 15. The Fate of Korean Emigration Is Sealed

1. Hawaii, Territory, Bureau of Labor, *Third Report, 1905*, p. 19.

2. Hawaii, Territory, Board of Immigration, First Report, 1907, p. 26.

3. Giffard to Irwin, December 19, 1905, GI.

4. HSPA, Trustees, Minutes, December 11, 1905.

5. HSPA, Trustees, Minutes, December 14, 1905.

6. Deshler to Wilson, January 6, 1906, enclosure no. 1 in Wilson to Elihu Root, Secretary of State, January 27, 1906, U.S. Department of State Despatches from U.S. Ministers to Japan, 1855–1906. This document can also be found in Hawaii, Territory, Governors Files, Carter–U.S. Departments, State, October 1905–June 1907, *HSA*.

7. Enclosure no. 2 in Wilson to Root, January 27, 1906; see note 6 above.

8. Enclosure no. 3 in Wilson to Root, January 27, 1906; see note 6 above.

9. Huntington Wilson to Katō Takaaki, January 19, 1906, *Kankoku imin*.

10. Wilson to Elihu Root, January 27, 1906, see note 6 above.

11. Acting Governor A. L. C. Atkinson to Robert Bacon, Acting Secretary of State, March 10, 1906, Hawaii, Territory, Governors Files, Carter–U.S. Departments, State (October 1905–June 1907), HSA. Bacon's letter to Atkinson is dated February 21, 1906, in ibid. Root acknowledged Atkinson's letter in early April. See Root to A. L. C. Atkinson, April 3, 1906, ibid. Despite Atkinson's statement that he did not encourage immigration from the Orient, November found him in Tokyo encouraging the continuation of Japanese immigration to Hawaii. See *Japan Weekly Mail*, November 4, 1905. Atkinson's reply to Washington of March 10 reflected the fact that the planters themselves knew that they could no longer illegally pay the passage for Koreans. In fact, as we shall see, Atkinson consulted the planters before drafting his response to the acting secretary of state.

12. Carter to Elihu Root, June 6, 1906, Hawaii, Territory, Governors Files, Carter–U.S. Departments, State (October 1905–June 1907), HSA.

13. Lawrence O. Murray, Acting Secretary of the Department of Commerce and Labor, to Elihu Root, April 5, 1906, ibid. See also Bacon to Atkinson, April 14, 1906, ibid.

14. Giffard to Irwin, January 7, 1906, GI. No copies of the *Hawaii shinpo* or the *Japan Gazette* exist for that year, making it impossible to track down the text of the interview. It will be remembered, however, that Swanzy had said the same thing to Japanese Foreign Ministry officials in Tokyo. Since

this letter was handwritten, some portions are illegible, necessitating the addition of the approximate word in brackets.

15. HSPA, Trustees, Minutes, January 9, 1906.
16. Irwin to Giffard, January 20, 1906, GI.
17. Giffard to Irwin, February 13, 1906, GI.
18. HSPA, Trustees, Minutes, March 8, 1906.
19. Acting Governor Atkinson to Robert Bacon, Acting Secretary of State, March 10, 1906, Hawaii, Territory, Governors Files, Carter–U.S. Departments, State (October 1905–June 1907), *HSA*.
20. *A Setta*, May 18, 1906.
21. The report was dated February 6, 1906, and bore the seal of the minister and vice-minister of Foreign Affairs. The phrase "American vested interests" was written in English. *Kankoku imin.*
22. Tsuruhara Jyōkichi, Director General in the Resident-General's Office, to Chinda Sutemi, Vice-Minister of Foreign Affairs, February 19, 1906, *Kankoku imin.*
23. Chinda to Tsuruhara, March 20, 1906, *Kankoku imin.*
24. Tsuruhara to Chinda, July 16, 1906, *Kankoku imin; Kojong sillok,* June 29, 1906; *Kwanbo,* July 12, 1906; *Hwangsŏng sinmun,* July 13–14, 1906. The law, entitled *Imin pohopŏp* [Emigration Protection Law], was signed by Prime Minister Pak Che-sun and Minister of Agriculture, Commerce and Industry Kwŏn Chung-hyŏn. The supplementary law was *Imin pohopŏp sihaeng sech'uk.* See Hyŏn Kyu-hwan, [A History of Korean wanderers and emigrants], vol. 2, pp. 808–810. See also *Japan Weekly Mail,* July 14, 1906.
25. Chōsen sōtokufu [Government-General of Chosen], *Annual Report on Reforms and Progress, 1910–1911,* pp. 36–37. This is sometimes referred to as the *Chosen Report.*
26. *Korea Review,* June, 1906, p. 238; see also No, [Short history], pp. 20–21, 26, 29, 32; also Warren Y. Kim, *Koreans in America,* pp. 51–52.
27. *Korea Review,* July, 1906, pp. 256–258.
28. Ibid., September, 1906, p. 356.
29. *Kojong sillok,* December 28, 1906.
30. Hawaii, Territory, Board of Immigration, First Report, 1907, pp. 24–26, and Second Report, pp. 18, 24, 38, 39. Also U.S. Department of Labor, Bureau of Labor Statistics, *Labor Conditions in Hawaii: Fifth Report,* p. 45.
31. Romanzo Adams, *Interracial Marriage in Hawaii,* pp. 31–32.
32. Hawaii, Territory, Board of Immigration, First Report, "Statistics of Immigration," p. 24.
33. Ibid., Second Report, pp. 18, 61. See also U.S. Department of Labor, Bureau of Labor Statistics, *Labor Conditions in Hawaii,* p. 45. For a list of the individual departures, including the names of the ships and the number of Koreans aboard see No, [Short history], pp. 21–37 passim.
34. Hawaii, Territory, Governors Files, Carter–U.S. Departments, State (October 1905–June 1907), HSA.
35. Lind, *An Island Community,* p. 254.
36. Hawaii, Territory, Board of Immigration, First Report, 1907, p. 26; Bureau of Labor, *Fourth Report, 1910,* p. 23.
37. Lind, *Hawaii's People,* p. 50.

38. Patterson,"Upward Social Mobility of the Koreans in Hawaii," pp. 81–92.

39. Liebes, "Labor Organization in Hawaii," p. 11.

40. No, [Short history], pp. 28, 34–35; Hyŏn Sun, "Autobiography," pp. 67–68, 73, and [Record of a sightseeing trip], passim; George Heber Jones, "Koreans in Hawaii"; *Korea Review*, November 1906, pp. 401–406. See also the book written by Hyŏn's son, Peter Hyun, entitled *Man Sei! The Making of a Korean American.*

41. *Korea Review*, December 1906, p. 478.

42. *The Nagasaki Press*, November 23, 1927.

43. This writer personally visited the cemetery where the Deshlers are buried in May of 1985. The information comes from the records of the caretaker, Mr. Andō Torazō.

Appendix

1. "Life History of E. S." This piece was written in the 1920s by a female who has four sisters and three brothers. Her father, about whom she writes, was a Methodist minister in Hawaii. William C. Smith Documents, Special Collections, University of Oregon Library.

2. "A Life History." A handwritten account by a female in the 1920s. Ibid.

3. "The Story of Life." A handwritten account by a female in the 1920s. Ibid.

4. "The Kim Family." Author unknown. Typewritten in the 1930s. The writer is a Methodist. Ibid.

5. "Life History." A handwritten account by a female in the 1920s. The author was born in 1907. Ibid.

6. "The History of My Life." A handwritten account written in the late 1920s. The writer was born on June 5, 1905, in Kahuku, Oahu, where the father was a plantation laborer. Ibid.

7. "Life History of Mr. Hong." At the time of this writing, Mr. Hong had a large store and market near 80th and Moneta in Los Angeles. He was forty-four years old and spoke good English and some Spanish. No date. This piece is the result of an interview. The interviewer, who is not identified, has also done the two following pieces. Ibid.

8. "Story of Mrs. Chong." Ibid.

9. "Life Story of Mr. Lee." At the time this was written, Mr. Lee was forty-five years old, spoke good English, and had a boy and girl in high school. Ibid.

10. "Life History of J. Lim." Ibid.

11. Lila K. Lee, "The Way Migrations Have Played a Role in My Family" (November 2, 1943).

12. Lind/Hormann Student Paper Files, University of Hawaii. Changsook Kim, "Migrations in May Family" (November 2, 1943).

13. Douglas Woo, "The Story of the First Two Generations of My Fam-

ily in Hawaii" (Summer 1972). Donald Johnson Student Paper Files, University of Hawaii. The eye disease referred to was probably trachoma, which had reached epidemic proportions in Korea at the turn of the century and which was grounds for rejection.

14. Clifford Hong, "A Korean Grandfather" (ca. 1960s). Ibid.

15. Duke Moon, "A Korean Pioneer" (1973). Ibid. Mr. Lee was ninety years old at the time this paper was written.

16. Morris Pang, "A Korean Immigrant," *Social Forces in Hawaii* 12 (1949): 19–24; reprinted in Hyung-Chan Kim and Wayne Patterson, eds, *The Koreans in America, 1882–1974.*

17. Yi Chŏng-gŭn, *"Insaeng p'alsipe chŏngbyŏn manhwa"* [Great changes in the eighty [years] of my life], pp. 1–4. n.d., but probably 1950s.

18. *Honolulu Advertiser and Star-Bulletin,* January 7, 1973. This article also appeared in *Han'guk Ilbo* on January 10, 1973.

19. Ella Chun, "Korean Golden Jubilee," *Honolulu Advertiser,* November 8, 1953; Margaret Meyers, "Korean Immigrant's Story of Advancement Is Told," *Honolulu Star-Bulletin,* November 20, 1953.

20. Hawaii Korean Golden Jubilee Celebration Committee, *Fifty Years of Progress.* The speaker was eighty-five years old in that year.

21. "Services Set Saturday for Choon Ho Lim," *Honolulu Star-Bulletin,* April 24, 1974.

22. Statement made in court in 1908 by Chang In-hwan during his trial for the murder of Durham White Stevens in San Francisco. Warren Y. Kim, *Koreans in America,* p. 82.

23. Ethnic Studies Oral History Project, *Waialua and Haleiwa: The People Tell Their Story,* pp. 1–24. The interview occurred on May 27, 1976.

24. Ibid., pp. 30–32. The interviewee was fifty-five years old at the time of the interview on June 14, 1976.

25. Harold Hakwon Sunoo and Sonia Shinn Sunoo, "The Heritage of the First Korean Women Immigrants in the United States: 1903–1924," pp. 152–153.

26. Ibid., pp. 155–156. The interviewee was from Hwanghae-do and was ninety-five at the time of the interview.

27. Bong-youn Choy, *Koreans in America,* pp. 293–294. The interview with Yang took place on February 27, 1974. Yang died on August 30, 1981, at the age of 102.

28. Sonia Shinn Sunoo, *Korea Kaleidoscope: Oral Histories,* pp. 7–20.

29. Choy, *Koreans in America,* p. 303. In an interview with Sonia Sunoo (*Korea Kaleidoscope,* pp. 22–27), Kim revealed that he was baptized by a Methodist missionary in Korea, attended the Paejae school in 1901, and became an interpreter at the Inch'ŏn Customs Office before leaving for Hawaii. That interview was conducted on December 19, 1975. Kim died on January 25, 1977.

30. Sunoo, *Korea Kaleidoscope,* pp. 53–72.

31. Ibid., pp. 73–87.

32. Ibid., pp. 89–109.

33. Ibid., pp. 111–121.

34. Ibid., pp. 123–131.
35. Ibid., pp. 133–137.
36. Ibid., pp. 139–154.
37. Ibid., pp. 155–167.
38. Ibid., pp. 169–181.
39. Ibid., pp. 191–208.
40. Ahn [Andrew H. N.] Kim, "A Homeward Journey," pp. 22–27.
41. Charr, *The Golden Mountain*, pp. 15–124.

GLOSSARY OF PARTICIPANTS AND PLACES

AGRICULTURE, COMMERCE AND INDUSTRY MINISTRY 農商工部. The department that shared responsibility for emigration with the Privy Council and the Foreign Office of Korea after the demise of the *Yuminwŏn* in 1903.

ADAMS, ANDREW. Manager of Kahuku Plantation where the second group of Korean immigrants was taken.

ALLEN, HORACE N. (1858–1932). American minister to Korea (1897–1905). Known in Korea as 前顧口.

AMERICAN TRADING COMPANY. An importing firm operating in Inch'ŏn, Korea, and Kobe, Japan, in which Everett, Townsend, Morse, and Deshler were involved.

ATKINSON, A. L. C. Secretary of the Territory of Hawaii and director of the Territorial Board of Immigration in 1905.

ARIYOSHI AKIRA 有吉明. Japanese consul in Pusan.

BAIRD, WILLIAM. Presbyterian missionary stationed in P'yŏngyang who opposed Korean immigration to Hawaii.

BEI-KAN GINKŌ 米韓銀行, KOREAN-AMERICAN BANK. Alternate name for the Deshler Bank.

BERNHEISEL, CHARLES F. Presbyterian missionary stationed in P'yŏngyang who opposed Korean immigration to Hawaii.

BIG FIVE. The five large financial concerns in Hawaii with major interests in the sugar industry: Alexander and Baldwin, C. Brewer, Theo. H. Davies, American Factors, and Castle and Cooke.

BISHOP, E. FAXON (1863–1943). A trustee of the HSPA who went to Korea in the fall of 1902 to initiate Korean immigration.

BRECKONS, R. C. U. S. district attorney in Hawaii and friend of the planters.

BROWN, J. D. Commissioner of immigration for Hawaii who was involved in the *Nippon Maru* investigation of 1903.

CARTER, GEORGE R. Successor to Sanford B. Dole as governor of the Territory of Hawaii who learned about the illegal importation of Koreans in 1906.

CHEMULP'O 濟物浦. Alternate name for Inch'ŏn.

CHINDA SUTEMI 珍田捨己. Vice-foreign minister of Japan.

CHINESE EXCLUSION ACT (1882). An act of Congress prohibiting Chinese from coming to the United States; it began to apply to Hawaii in 1900 with the passage of the Organic Act.

CHO PYǑNG-SIK 趙秉式. Minister to Japan, foreign minister, and later prime minister of Korea in 1905.

CONTINENTAL COLONIZATION COMPANY 大陸植民會社. Known in Japanese as *Tairiku shokumin kaisha* and in Korean as *Taeryuk sikmim hoesa;* a Japanese emigration company involved in sending approximately 1,000 Koreans to Mexico in April 1905.

COOKE, CHARLES M. (1849–1909). President of C. Brewer and Company from 1899 to 1909, one of Hawaii's "Big Five" Corporations.

CHINNAMP'O 鎭南浦. A city where a branch office of Deshler's company was located, on the northwestern coast of Korea in Hwanghae Province.

CHUNGCH'UWǑN 中樞院. Privy Council which shared responsibility for Korean immigration, after the demise of the *Yuminwǒn* in 1903, with the Foreign Office and the Ministry of Agriculture, Commerce and Industry.

COOPER, HENRY E. Foreign minister of the Republic of Hawaii (1895–1899) and later secretary of the Territory of Hawaii. Succeeded by A. L. C. Atkinson.

DEPARTMENT OF EMIGRATION. See *Yuminwǒn.*

DESHLER, DAVID W. (1872–1927). Recruiter of Korean immigrants to Hawaii as head of the *Tongsǒ kaebal hoesa* [East-West Development Company]. Known in Korea as 大是羅.

DESHLER, HIDENO HONDA (1871–1934). Japanese friend and later wife of David W. Deshler.

DESHLER BANK. The bank created by Deshler to lend passage and pocket money to Korean immigrants going to Hawaii. Headquartered in the same building as Deshler's East-West Development Company. Known in Korea as 大是羅銀行. See also Bei-Kan Ginkō.

DOLE, SANFORD B. President of the Republic of Hawaii (1894–1900) and first governor of the Territory of Hawaii (1900–1903). Succeeded by George R. Carter.

DUNN. Assistant district attorney in Honolulu and an opponent of the planters.

EAST-WEST DEVELOPMENT COMPANY. See *Tongsǒ kaebal hoesa.*

EMIGRATION PROTECTION ACT 移民保護法 [*Imin pohopǒp*]. Enacted by the Korean government at the insistence of Itō Hirobumi in July 1906 as a means of preventing Koreans from emigrating to Hawaii.

ESTEE, MORRIS M. (1834–1903). Federal judge in Honolulu who heard the lawsuit against the planters in 1903 and who may have been bribed by the planters. He died a month after the trial ended on October 27, 1903.

EVERETT, CLAYTON. Horace Allen's brother-in-law in Ohio. He held an interest in the American Trading Company.

FASSETT, J. SLOAT. Co-owner of the Unsan Gold Mines and the go-between for correspondence between Allen and the planters. He resided in Elmira, New York, where he was a congressman.

Gaelic. The ship that carried the first group of Korean immigrants from Japan to Hawaii on January 13, 1903.

Genkai Maru. The ship that carried the first group of Korean immigrants from Inch'ǒn to Nagasaki in December 1902.

GENTLEMEN'S AGREEMENT. The series of protocols of 1907–1908 by which Japan promised not to issue passports to Japanese (and Korean) laborers to come to the United States.

GIFFARD, WALTER M. (1856–1929). Vice-president and manager of W. G. Irwin and Company. A co-trustee of the HSPA and a member of the HSPA Labor Committee.

GOODALE, WILLIAM W. Manager of Waialua Plantation where the first group of Korean immigrants were sent to work.

H. HACKFELD AND COMPANY. One of the "Big Five" corporations in Hawaii, later known as American Factors or Amfac.

HACKFELD, J. F. Director of H. Hackfeld and Company and the first person formally to propose the introduction of Korean labor, in 1896.

HAGIWARA SHUICHI 萩原守一. Japanese chargé d'affaires in Korea, subordinate to Minister Hayashi Gonsuke.

HAGUE. Deshler's liaison with the planters in Honolulu in 1903 whose job it was to sign up Korean immigrants to work on the plantations. Succeeded in 1904 by J. D. Julian.

HAWAIIAN SUGAR PLANTERS' ASSOCIATION (1895–PRESENT). The representative body of the companies that owned sugar plantations and whose trustees made decisions affecting immigrant labor. Known variably as the HSPA or planters in this study.

HAY, JOHN. U.S. secretary of state (1898–1905). He was kept in the dark by Allen concerning the true nature of Korean immigration to Hawaii.

HAYASHI GONSUKE 林權助. Japanese minister to Korea who opposed Korean immigration to Hawaii.

HULBERT, HOMER B. Editor of the *Korea Review* in Seoul, who approved of Korean immigration to Hawaii.

HUNT, LEIGH S. J. Co-owner with J. Sloat Fassett of the Unsan Gold Mines in northern Korea.

HYEMINWŎN 惠民院. "Bureau to Benefit the People" created in 1901 to assist in famine relief. Possible prototype of the *Yuminwŏn* created the following year.

HYŎN SUN (1879–1968) 玄楯. The interpreter who accompanied the second group of Koreans to Hawaii in February 1903. He later became a minister and a leader in the Korean provisional government in Shanghai.

HYŪGA TERUTAKE 日向輝武. Director of the Continental Colonization Company who opposed Korean immigration to Hawaii.

IMIN POHOPŎP. See Emigration Protection Law.

IMPERIAL HOUSEHOLD DEPARTMENT. See *Kungnaebu*.

INCH'ŎN 仁川. Port city 28 miles west of Seoul, the capital of Korea, where Deshler had his headquarters and from whence the first group of Korean immigrants to Hawaii departed in 1902. Also known as Chemulp'o.

IRWIN, W. G., AND COMPANY. A major sugar company headed by William G. Irwin and Walter M. Giffard, with headquarters in San Francisco.

IRWIN, WILLIAM G. (1843–1914). Founder of W. G. Irwin and Company and co-trustee of the HSPA.

ISHII KIKUJIRŌ 石井菊次郎. Director of the Commerce Bureau of the Japanese foreign ministry.

Itō Hirobumi 伊藤博文. Resident-general of Korea from 1905 until 1909, when he was assassinated by a Korean nationalist, An Chung-gŭn, in Manchuria.

Jaisohn, Philip [Sŏ Chae-p'il] (1863–1951) 徐載弼. One of the first immigrants to the United States. He became a medical doctor and an American citizen. Founder of the Independence Club and the newspaper *Independent*.

Jones, George Heber. Methodist minister in Inch'ŏn who persuaded some of his congregation to join the first group to go to Hawaii. Known in Korea as Cho Wŏn-si 趙元時.

Julian, J. D. Successor to Hague in 1904 whose job it was to act as a liaison between Deshler and the planters and to sign up Koreans to work on the plantations.

Kahuku Plantation. Located on the north shore of Oahu, this plantation, managed by Andrew Adams, was the destination for the second group of Koreans in February 1903.

Kamni 監理. Port officials assigned to the Korean foreign office who issued passports to Korean emigrants after the demise of the *Yuminwŏn* in 1903.

Kanatani Kaichi 金谷嘉一. One of Deshler's employees in Yokohama engaged in Korean immigration to Hawaii.

Kanggyŏngp'o 江景浦. A city where a branch office of Deshler's East-West Development Company was located, in Ch'ungch'ŏng Province in southwestern Korea.

Katō Motoshirō 加藤本四郎 Japanese Consul in Inch'ŏn.

Katō Takaaki (Kōmei) 加藤高明. Japanese minister of foreign affairs in 1906.

Katsura Tarō 桂太郎. Prime minister of Japan, 1901–1906.

Kawakami Tatsuichirō 川上立一郎. Japanese consul in Sŏngjin.

Kim Tŏk-wŏn 金德元. Arrested for opposing the Emigration Protection Law in December 1906.

Kojong (1852–1919) 高宗. King and, later, emperor, of Korea, reigning from 1864 to 1907, when he was deposed by Japan in favor of his son, Sunjong.

Komura Jutarō 小村寿太郎. Japanese foreign minister during the Katsura Tarō government (1901–1906) who decided that Korean immigration to Hawaii must be stopped.

Korean Foreign Office 外部. Shared responsibility for Korean emigration with the Ministry of Agriculture, Commerce, and Industry and the Privy Council after the demise of the *Yuminwŏn* in 1903.

Kungnaebu 宮内府. Imperial Household Department, under which was placed the *Yuminwŏn*. Directed by Yi Yong-ik.

Kunsan 群山. A city where a branch office of Deshler's company was located, in Chŏlla Province on the southwestern coast of Korea.

Lansing, Theodore F. Commissioner of immigration in Hawaii beginning in 1903.

Manbokku 万福旧. Location of a branch office of Deshler's East-West Development Company. Exact location undetermined.

Megata Tanetarō 目賀田種太郎. Japanese adviser to the Korean Finance Department who vetoed funds for Yun Ch'i-ho to go to Mexico in the fall of 1905.

Min Yŏng-hwan 閔泳煥. President of the *Yuminwŏn* who committed suicide when Japan established a protectorate over Korea in 1905.

MOFFETT, SAMUEL H. A Presbyterian missionary stationed in P'yŏngyang who opposed Korean immigration to Hawaii.

MOKP'O 木浦. A city where a branch of Deshler's East-West Development Company was located, in the southwestern part of Korea in Chŏlla Province.

MOORE, S. F. Presbyterian missionary in Korea who approved of Korean immigration to Hawaii.

MORGAN, EDWIN V. Successor to Horace Allen as American minister to Korea in 1905.

MORSE, JAMES R. American investor in Korea in mining and railroad concessions and head of the American Trading Company.

MORIOKA MAKOTO 森岡真. Director of a Japanese emigration company who complained to Foreign Minister Komura about Korean immigration to Hawaii.

NASH, GEORGE K. Republican governor of Ohio from 1900 to 1904, step-father of David Deshler, and personal friend of Secretary of State John Sherman and President William McKinley, who successfully urged that Allen be appointed minister to Korea in 1897.

Nippon Maru. The ship containing 143 Korean immigrants which arrived in Honolulu on April 1, 1903, and whose interpreter told the truth about their illegal importation.

OKABE SABURŌ 岡部三郎. Japanese vice-consul in Honolulu (1902–1905), subordinate to Consul General Saitō Miki.

ORGANIC ACT (1900). The Act passed by the U.S. Congress by which all U.S. laws became applicable to Hawaii after its annexation in 1898, including immigration laws, contract labor laws, and the Chinese Exclusion Act.

PAK CHE-SUN (1858–1916) 朴齊純. Became foreign minister of Korea while Yun Ch'i-ho was in Hawaii in the fall of 1905.

PAK YANG-NAE 朴樑來. Arrested for opposing the Emigration Protection Law in December 1906.

PAK YŎNG-HWA 朴鏞和. Vice-foreign minister of Korea in 1903 who opposed Korean immigration to Hawaii.

PEARSON, GEORGE L. Methodist minister in Hawaii who met the first group of Koreans and who concerned himself with the welfare of Koreans in Hawaii. Succeeded by the Reverend John Wadman.

PUSAN 釜山. A city where a branch office of Deshler's company was located, on the southeastern coast of Korea in Kyŏngsang Province.

P'YŎNGYANG 平壤. A city where a branch office of Deshler's company was located, in northwestern Korea in P'yŏng'an Province.

REMEDIOS. A Portuguese employee of Deshler whose job it was to accompany Korean immigrants on the trip between Korea and Japan.

RESIDENT-GENERAL OF KOREA 統監. The office headed by Itō Hirobumi which controlled Korea during the protectorate, 1905–1910. Known in Korea as *t'onggam*.

RHEE SYNGMAN [YI SŬNG-MAN] (1875–1965) 李承晚. Korean nationalist leader who went to the American mainland at the same time that Korean workers were going to Hawaii.

ROOT, ELIHU. Secretary of state (1905–1909) in the Theodore Roosevelt administration.

ROYAL HAWAIIAN AGRICULTURAL SOCIETY (1850–1882). The predecessor of the Planters' Labor and Supply Company (1882) and the Hawaiian Sugar Planters' Society (1895).

SAITŌ MIKI 斎藤幹. Japanese consul general in Honolulu (1898–1908).

SANDS, WILLIAM FRANKLIN. American adviser to the Korean Imperial Household Department from 1900 to 1904 and formerly secretary to the American Legation in Seoul.

SAN FRANCISCO SCHOOL BOARD INCIDENT. In October 1906, Japanese students were lumped together with Chinese and Koreans and ordered to attend a segregated Oriental school. The order was rescinded after strong pressure by President Roosevelt.

SARGENT, J. P. U.S. immigration inspector-general (commissioner) who investigated Korean immigration in 1903 and again in 1905.

SEOUL 서울. Capital of Korea and location of a branch office of Deshler's company.

SHERMAN, JOHN. Secretary of state during the McKinley administration who recommended Allen's appointment as minister to Korea at the urging of Governor Nash of Ohio, the step-father of David Deshler.

SINMINHOE 新民会. One of the first Korean nationalist organizations with roots in both Korea and Hawaii. The name means "New Peoples' Society" or "Society to Renovate the People."

SMITH, WILLIAM O. (1848–1929). Attorney-general of the Republic of Hawaii (1893–1899).

SOMEYA NARIAKI 染谷戒章. Japanese vice-consul in Chinnamp'o.

SŎNGJIN 城津. A city where a branch office of Deshler's company was located, on the northeastern coast of Korea in Hamgyŏng Province.

STACKABLE, E. R. Collector of customs for Hawaii.

STEVENS, DURHAM WHITE. An American employed by the Japanese government as an adviser to the Korean Foreign Office and a friend of Horace Allen. Assassinated by a Korean nationalist, Chang In-hwan, in San Francisco in 1908.

SWALLEN, WILLIAM L. Presbyterian missionary in P'yŏngyang who opposed Korean immigration to Hawaii.

SWANZY, F. M. (1850–1917). Director of Theo. H. Davies and Company, one of Hawaii's "Big Five" corporations, and a trustee of the HSPA. He was president of the HSPA in 1905 when he revealed in Japan that the planters were importing Japanese and Koreans illegally to Hawaii.

TAERYUK SIKMIN HOESA See Continental Colonization Company.

TAFT, WILLIAM HOWARD. Met with Swanzy before leaving for Japan to sign the Taft-Katsura Memorandum in the summer of 1905 giving Japan free rein in Korea in return for assurances of American free hand in the Philippines.

TAIRIKU SHOKUMIN KAISHA. See Continental Colonization Company.

TAKAHIRA KOGORŌ (1854–1926) 高平小五郎. Japanese ambassador to the United States who proposed that the United States prohibit Japanese from moving from Hawaii to the mainland.

TOMIOCHI CHŪTARŌ 富落忠太郎. Director of a Japanese emigration company who opposed Korean immigration to Hawaii.

T'ONGGAM. See Resident-General of Korea.

TONGSŎ KAEBAL HOESA 東西開發会社. Deshler's East-West Development Company, which was the recruiting agency for Korean immigration to Hawaii. Headquartered in Inch'ŏn with branch offices in Seoul, P'yŏngyang, and major port cities.

TOWNSEND, WALTER D. (1856–1918). Co-owner with James R. Morse of the American Trading Company in Inch'ŏn and Kobe who refused to become involved with Korean immigration to Hawaii.

TRUSTEES OF THE HSPA. The decision-making body of the sugar planters, composed mainly of the directors of the large financial houses having substantial sugar interests.

TSURUHARA JYŌKICHI 鶴原定吉. Director-general under Itō in the resident-general's office in Seoul.

ŬLSA TREATY 乙巳保護條約. November 17, 1905. See Resident-General of Korea.

UNSAN GOLD MINES. An American concession obtained by Horace Allen in northern Korea for Leigh S. J. Hunt and J. Sloat Fassett with which David W. Deshler was affiliated.

WADMAN, JOHN W. Successor to the Reverend George Pearson who ministered to Korean immigrants in Hawaii.

WAIALUA PLANTATION. Located on the north shore of the island of Oahu where the first group of Korean immigrants were sent in January 1903. Managed by William W. Goodale.

WAKAMATSU USABURŌ 若松免三郎. Japanese consul in Mokp'o.

WILSON, HUNTINGTON. American chargé d'affaires in Japan in 1906 who tried to intervene on Deshler's behalf with the Japanese foreign ministry.

WŎNSAN 元山. A city where a branch office of Deshler's company was located, on the northeastern coast of Korea in Kangwŏn Province.

YANGBAN. Elite class in Yi dynasty Korea, usually conservative, who made up the civil service, the scholarly ranks, and the landed gentry.

YI CHI-YONG (1870–?) 李址鎔. Korean foreign minister in 1903.

YI HA-YŎNG (1858–1919) 李夏榮. Korean foreign minister, 1904–1905.

YI YONG-IK (1854–1907) 李容翊. Head of the Imperial Household Department and an opponent of Korean immigration to Hawaii. Trusted adviser to Emperor Kojong.

YOKOTA SABURŌ 横田三郎. Japanese representative in Kunsan.

Yuminwŏn 綏民院. The Korean Department of Emigration (literally, "People-easing bureau") from November 1902 to October 1903 which issued passports for Koreans going to Hawaii. Min Yŏng-hwan was its president.

YUN CH'I-HO (1864–1946) 尹致昊. Vice-foreign minister of Korea (1904–1905) who went to Hawaii in 1905 to investigate the conditions of Koreans there.

BIBLIOGRAPHY

Adams, Romanzo. *The Peoples of Hawaii*. Honolulu: Institute of Pacific Relations, 1933.

———. *Interracial Marriage in Hawaii*. New York: Macmillan Co., 1937.

Alexander, Arthur C. *Koloa Plantation, 1835–1935: A History of the Oldest Hawaiian Sugar Plantation*. Honolulu: Honolulu Star-Bulletin, Ltd., 1937.

Allen, Horace N. Correspondence. Allen MSS.

———. Diary. Allen MSS.

———. Introduction to Press Copy Books. Allen MSS.

Appenzeller, Alice R. "A Generation of Koreans in Hawaii." *Paradise of the Pacific* 56, no. 12 (December 1944).

Baird, Reverend William. Correspondence. Samuel H. Moffett Documents, no. 6 (1890–1903). In the possession of the Reverend Samuel A. Moffett. Seoul, Korea.

Beechert, Edward D. *Working in Hawaii: A Labor History*. Honolulu: University of Hawaii Press, 1985.

Bernheisel, Reverend Charles F. Diary, 1900–06. Samuel H. Moffett Documents, no. 6 (1890–1903). In the possession of the Reverend Samuel A. Moffett. Seoul, Korea.

Berton, Peter A., and Andrew C. Nahm. *Japanese Penetration of Korea, 1894–1910: A Checklist of Japanese Archives in the Hoover Institution*. Palo Alto: Hoover Institution of War, Peace and Revolution, 1959.

Biographical Cyclopedia and Portrait Gallery with an Historical Sketch of the State of Ohio. Cincinnati: Western Biographical Publishing Co., 1891.

Bishop, Isabella Bird. "Koreans in Russian Manchuria." *The Korea Repository* 4 (1897).

Bremner, Robert H. "George K. Nash, 1900–1904." *The Governors of Ohio*. Columbus: Ohio State Historical Society, 1969.

Brewer, C., and Company. Record. Vol. 2 (January 12, 1901–December 4, 1905). Honolulu.

Chandra, Vipan. "The Independence Club and Korea's First Proposal for a National Legislative Assembly." *Occasional Papers on Korea*, no. 4 (September 1975).

Char, Tin-yuke, ed. *The Sandalwood Mountains*. Honolulu: The University Press of Hawaii, 1975.

Charr, Easurk Emsen. *The Golden Mountain*. Boston: Forum Publishing Co., 1961.

Chōsen sōtokufu 朝鮮總督府 [Government-General of Korea]. *Chōsen no hogo oyobi heigo* 朝鮮ノ保護及併合 [Concerning the annexation of Korea], 1918.

————. Keimu kyoku 警務局 [Bureau of Police Affairs]. *Beikoku oyobi Hawai chihō ni okeru futei Senjin jokyō* 米國及布哇地方ニ於ケル不逞鮮人狀況 [The situation of insubordinate Koreans in the United States and the Territory of Hawaii], 1921.

————. *Annual Report on Reform and Progress in Chosen (Korea), 1910–11*. Keijō [Seoul], December 1911.

————. *Annual Report on the Administration of Chosen*. Keijō [Seoul], 1924.

Choy, Bong-Youn. *Koreans in America*. Chicago: Nelson-Hall, 1979.

Chun, Ella. "Korean Golden Jubilee," *Honolulu Advertiser*, November 7, 1953.

Chung, Henry. *The Oriental Policy of the United States*. New York: Fleming H. Revell, 1919.

Church, Deborah. "Korean Emigration to Hawaii, 1902–1907: An Aspect of American Diplomacy." Unpublished seminar paper. University of Hawaii, 1971. In the possession of Professor Donald Johnson, University of Hawaii Department of History.

————. "Korean Emigration to Hawaii: An Aspect of U.S.–Japanese Relations." Unpublished paper. University of Hawaii, April 19, 1971. In the possession of Professor John Stephan, University of Hawaii Department of History.

Coman, Katherine. "The History of Contract Labor in the Hawaiian Islands." *Publications of the American Economic Association* 4, no. 3 (1903).

Conroy, Hilary. *The Japanese Frontier in Hawaii, 1868–1898*. Berkeley: University of California Press, 1953.

————. *The Japanese Seizure of Korea, 1868–1910: A Study of Realism and Idealism in International Relations*. Philadelphia: University of Pennsylvania Press, 1960.

Cook, Harold F. *Korea's 1884 Incident: Its Background and Kim Ok-kyun's Elusive Dream*. Seoul: Royal Asiatic Society, Korea Branch, 1972.

————. "Walter D. Townsend: Pioneer American Businessman in Korea." *Transactions of the Korea Branch of the Royal Asiatic Society* 4 (1973).

————. *Pioneer American Businessman in Korea: The Life and Times of Walter Davis Townsend*. Seoul: Seoul Computer Press, 1981.

Cooke, Charles M. Papers. Hawaiian Mission Children's Society, Honolulu.

Daniels, Roger. *The Politics of Prejudice: The Anti-Japanese Movement in California and the Struggle for Japanese Exclusion*. Berkeley: University of California Press, 1962.

————. "Japanese Immigrants on a Western Frontier: The Issei in California, 1890–1940." In *East Across the Pacific: Historical and Sociological Studies of Japanese Immigration and Assimilation*, edited by Hilary Conroy and T. Scott Miyakawa. Santa Barbara: ABC Clio Press, 1972.

Ethnic Studies Oral History Project. *Waialua and Haleiwa: The People Tell Their Story.* Vol. 2. Honolulu: University of Hawaii Ethnic Studies Program, 1977.

Eum Shi Moon [Ŏm Si-Mun 嚴時文] Family Papers. Bishop Museum, Honolulu.

Ewa Plantation. Minute Books. Castle and Cooke, Honolulu.

Gaimushō 外務省. *Kankoku seifu Hawai oyobi Mokushika yuki Kankoku imin kinshi ikken—tsuki hogo itaku kankoku no ken* 韓國政府布哇及墨西哥行韓國移民禁止一件附保護委託勸告之件 [The prohibition of Korean emigration to Hawaii and Mexico by the Korean Government—recommendation and protection]. 3-9-2-18. It is dated Meiji 38 nen [1905], but there are some items dated 1906 and 1907. The collection is divided into two subgroups: *Mokushika ni okeru Kankoku imin kankei zakken* 墨西哥ニ於ケル韓國移民關係雜件 [Miscellaneous items relating to Korean immigration to Mexico], and *Hawaikoku e Kankokujin dekasegi ikken* 布哇國へ韓國人出稼一件 [The matter of emigration of Koreans to Hawaii]. Gaimushō gaikō shiryōkan 外務省外交史料官 [Diplomatic Records Office], Tokyo.

———. Correspondence of the Japanese Legation in Korea with the Home Office, 1903. Folder 143, reel 18. Hoover Institution of War, Peace and Revolution, Palo Alto.

———. *Zai Bei ryōji rai* 在米領事來 [Incoming from the United States] (Consuls, January–June 1905). Gaimushō gaikō shiryōkan.

———. *Nihon gaikō bunsho* 日本外交文書. [Documents on Japanese foreign policy]. Vol. 38, no. 2 (1905).

———. *Nihon gaikō bunsho: Tai Bei imin mondai keika gaiyō fuzokushō* 日本外交文書：対米移民問題經過概要附屬書 [Documents on Japanese foreign policy: Annexes to summary of the course of negotiations between Japan and the United States concerning the problem of Japanese immigration to the United States]. Tokyo: Gaimushō, 1973.

Gardner, Arthur L. *The Koreans in Hawaii: An Annotated Bibliography.* Honolulu: Social Science Research Institute, University of Hawaii, 1970.

Giffard, Walter M. Papers. University of Hawaii Archives, Sinclair Library, Honolulu.

Gima, Dick. "Marriage to a Cobbler Really Lasts." *Honolulu Star-Bulletin*, June 17, 1964.

Ginsburgs, George. "The Citizenship Status of Koreans in Pre-Revolutionary Russia and the Early Years of the Soviet Regime." *Journal of Korean Affairs* 5, vol. 2 (1975).

Glick, Clarence. *Sojourners and Settlers: Chinese Migrants in Hawaii.* Honolulu, The University Press of Hawaii, 1980.

Hackfeld, H., and Company to W. Weber, Manager, Lihue Plantation Company, September 12, 1905. HSPA Library, Aiea, Hawaii.

Han'guk hakdae paekkwa sajŏn 韓國學大百科事典 [Encyclopedia of Korean studies]. Seoul: Sin'gu munhwasa, 1972.

Harrington, Fred Harvey. *God, Mammon and the Japanese: Dr. Horace N. Allen and Korean-American Relations, 1884–1905.* Madison: University of Wisconsin Press, 1944.

Hawaii Korean Golden Jubilee Celebration Committee. *Fifty Years of Progress.* Honolulu, 1953.

Hawaii, Kingdom. *Penal Code of the Hawaiian Islands.* Honolulu, 1850.

Hawaii, Republic. Labor Commission. Report of the Labor Commission on Strikes and Arbitration. Honolulu, 1895.

———. Executive Council. Minutes, December 4, 1896–July 19, 1898. HSA.

———. Executive and Advisory Council. Minutes, 1897. HSA.

———. Executive and Cabinet Council. Minutes, April 16, 1895–December 3, 1896. HSA.

———. Foreign Office and Executive. Immigration, 1896. HSA.

———. Board of Immigration. Minutes, 1879–1899. HSA.

———. Interior Department. Immigration, 1865–99. Miscellaneous. File 51. HSA.

Hawaii, Territory. Board of Immigration. First Report of the Board of Immigration of the Territory of Hawaii to the Governor of the Territory of Hawaii (Under Act of April 24, 1905) for the Period April 27, 1905, to January 31, 1907. Honolulu, 1907.

———. Board of Immigration. Second Report of the Board of Immigration of the Territory of Hawaii. Honolulu, February 28, 1909. HSA.

———. Bureau of Labor. Report of the Commissioner of Labor in Hawaii. Bulletin no. 47 (1903). HSA.

———. Bureau of Labor. *Third Report of the Commissioner of Labor in Hawaii, 1905.* Washington: Government Printing Office, 1906. HSA.

———. Bureau of Labor. *Fourth Report of the Commissioner of Labor in Hawaii, 1910.* Washington: Government Printing Office, 1911. HSA.

———. Executive Letterbook, 1899. HSA.

———. Governor. *Report of the Governor of the Territory of Hawaii to the Secretary of the Interior for the Year 1901.* Washington: Government Printing Office, 1901.

———. Governor. Governors Files. Carter–U.S. Departments. State (October 1905–June 1907). HSA.

———. Governor. Governors Files. Carter–U.S. Departments. Immigration—Honolulu and Washington, D.C. Offices. HSA.

———. Governor. Executive Letterbook no. 5. Dole–Foreign Officials, Including Consuls A–M. HSA.

Hawaiian Agricultural Company. Letterbook to C. Brewer and Co., LTD, 1903–1906. In the possession of Professor Edward Beechert, University of Hawaii Department of History.

Hawaiian Historical Society. "Negotiation of the Annexation Treaty of 1893." Fifty-First Annual Report. September 1943.

Hawaiian Sugar Planters' Association. Trustees. Minutes, 1902–1906. Aiea, Hawaii.

———. Labor Committee. Territory of Hawaii Report, 1905 (Books 1 and 2). HSA.

Hayashi Gonsuke 林權助. *Waga shichijūnen o kataru* わが七十年を語る [My seventy years]. Edited by Iwai Sonjin. Tokyo: Daiichi shobō, 1935.

Hilo Sugar Company. Minutes. No. 1 (September 11, 1884–December 2, 1915). C. Brewer and Company, Honolulu.

Honomu Sugar Company. Records. Vol. 1 (August 13, 1883–April 23, 1904). C. Brewer and Company, Honolulu.

Hosokawa, Bill. *Nisei: The Quiet Americans.* New York: William Morrow and Co., 1969.

Houchins, Lee, and Chang-Su Houchins. "The Korean Experience in America, 1903–1924." *Pacific Historical Review,* November 1974.

Hulbert, Homer B. "The Koreans In Hawaii." *Korea Review,* November 1905.

———. "The Korean Emigrant Protection Law." *Korea Review,* July 1906.

———. *The Passing of Korea.* Seoul: Yonsei University Press, 1969.

Husted, F. M. *Directory and Handbook of Honolulu and the Hawaiian Islands, 1900–01.* Sacramento: News Publishing Co., 1901.

Hutchinson Sugar Plantation Company. Record, 1898. In the possession of Professor Edward Beechert, University of Hawaii Department of History.

———. Records; Letterbook, 1903–1904; Miscellaneous. In the possession of Professor Edward Beechert, University of Hawaii Department of History.

———. Letterbook to William G. Irwin and Co., LTD, 1904–1905. In the possession of Professor Edward Beechert, University of Hawaii Department of History.

Hyŏn Kyu-hwan 玄圭煥. *Han'guk yuiminsa* 韓國流移民史 [A history of Korean wanderers and emigrants]. Vol. 1. Seoul: Ŏmungak, 1967. Vol. 2. Seoul: Ŏmungak, 1976.

Hyŏn Sun 玄楯. *P'owa yuram ki* 布哇遊覽記 [A record of a sightseeing trip to Hawaii]. Seoul: Hyŏn Kong-yŏm, 1909.

———. "My Autobiography." Typescript. Center for Korean Studies, University of Hawaii, n.d.

Hyun, Peter. *Man Sei! The Making of a Korean American.* Honolulu: University of Hawaii Press, 1986.

Ichioka, Yuji. "Recent Japanese Scholarship on the Origins and Causes of Japanese Immigration." *Immigration History Newsletter* 15, no. 2 (November 1983).

Ilsŏngnok, Kojong-p'yŏn, 42日省錄, 高宗編 [Royal annals, 42nd Year of Kojong (1905)]. Seoul: Sŏul taehakkyo, kojŏn kanhaenghoe, 1968.

Irwin, William G. Papers. University of Hawaii Archives, Sinclair Library, Honolulu.

Japanese Consulate in Honolulu. *Kankoku tōroku kaado* 韓國登錄カード [Korean Registration Cards]. n.d.

———. "Hawai Chōsenjin jijō." 布哇朝鮮人事情 [The general condition of the Koreans in Hawaii]. Honolulu, 1925. Kim Chŏng-ju, 金正柱 ed. *Chōsen tōchi shiryō* 朝鮮統治史料 [Political studies of Korea]. Tokyo: Kankoku shiryō kenkyūjo, 1971.

Jones, George Heber. "The Koreans in Hawaii." *Korea Review,* November 1906.

———. *Korea—The Land, People and Culture.* Cincinnati: Jennings and Graham; New York: Easton and Manis, 1907.

Jones, James O., comp. *Southern Ohio and Its Builders.* Cincinnati: Southern Ohio Biographical Association, 1927.

Kang, Francis. "Korean Milestone." *Honolulu Advertiser,* November 7, 1953.

Kim, Ahn [Andrew H. N.]. "A Homeward Journey." *75th Anniversary of Korean Immigration to Hawaii, 1903–1978*. Honolulu, 1978.

Kim, Bernice Bong Hee. "The Koreans in Hawaii." *Social Science* 9, no. 4 (October 1934).

———. "The Koreans in Hawaii." Master's thesis, University of Hawaii, 1937.

Kim, C. I. Eugene, and Han-Kyo Kim. *Korea and the Politics of Imperialism, 1876–1910*. Berkeley and Los Angeles: University of California Press, 1967.

Kim, Christopher. *Annotated Bibliography on Koreans in America*. Los Angeles: Asian American Studies Center, University of California at Los Angeles, 1976.

Kim, Hyŏng-sun. Interview. March 26, 1974. Interview conducted by Bong-Youn Choy in San Francisco.

Kim, Robert Hyung-chan. *The Korean Diaspora: Historical and Sociological Studies of Korean Immigration and Assimilation in North America*. Santa Barbara: ABC Clio Press, 1977.

———, ed. *The Collected Letters of Yun Tchi Ho* 尹致昊書翰集 Seoul: Kuksa p'yŏnch'an wiwŏnhoe, 1980.

Kim, Hyung-chan, and Wayne Patterson, eds. *The Koreans in America, 1882–1974: A Chronology and Fact Book*. Dobbs Ferry, New York: Oceana Publications, 1974.

Kim, Warren Y. [Kim Wŏn-yong]. *Koreans in America*. Seoul: Po Chin Chai Printing Company, 1971.

Kim, Wŏn-yong [Warren Y. Kim] 金元容. *ChaeMi Hanin osimnyŏnsa* 在美韓人五十年史 [A fifty-year history of Koreans in America]. Reedley, California: Charles Ho Kim, 1959.

Koh, Seung-jae [Ko Sŭng-je] 高承濟. *Han'guk iminsa yŏn'gu* 韓國移民史研究 [A study of the history of Korean immigration]. Seoul: Changmungak, 1973.

———. "A Study of Immigrants to Hawaii." *Journal of Social Sciences and Humanities*, no. 38 (June 1973).

Kojong sidaesa 高宗時代史 [History of the Kojong Era]. Vol. 5 and 6. Seoul: Kuksa p'yŏnch'an wiwŏnhoe, 1971–1972.

Kojong sillok 高宗實錄 [The veritable record of Kojong]. Seoul: T'amgudang, 1970.

Kolarz, Walter. *Peoples of the Soviet Far East*. New York: Praeger, 1954.

KuHan'guk oegyo munsŏ 舊韓國外交文書 [Documents relating to the foreign relations of Old Korea]. Vol. 12. Seoul: Koryŏ taehakkyo, Asea munje yŏn'guso, 1965.

———. *Ilan* 日案 [Documents relating to the foreign relations of Old Korea, Japan]. Vol. 7. Seoul: Koryŏ taehakkyo, Asea munje yŏn'guso, 1970.

KuHan'guk oegyo kwangye pusok munsŏ 舊韓國外交關係附屬文書 [Documents relating to the foreign relations of Old Korea, Foreign Affairs Division]. Vol. 7. *Kyosŏpguk ilgi* 交涉局日記 [Record of negotiations]. Seoul: Koryŏ taehakkyo, Asea munje yŏn'guso, 1974.

Kuksa taesajŏn 國史大事典 [Dictionary of national history], edited by Yi Hong-jik 李弘植. 2 vols. Seoul: Chimungak, 1962.

Ladd, George Trumbull. *In Korea with Marquis Ito*. London: Longmans, Green and Co., 1908.

Lee, Chong-Sik. *The Politics of Korean Nationalism*. Berkeley: University of California Press, 1965.

Lee, Tai Sung. "The Story of Korean Immigration." Korean Student Association Annual. Honolulu, 1932.

Lee, Yur-Bok. "Kojong and Korean-American Relations, 1882–1905." In *One Hundred Years of Korean-American Relations, 1882–1982*, edited by Yur-Bok Lee and Wayne Patterson. University, Alabama: University of Alabama Press, 1986.

Liebes, Richard A. "Labor Organization in Hawaii: A Study of the Efforts of Labor to Obtain Security Through Organization." Master's thesis, University of Hawaii, 1938.

Lind, Andrew W. "Economic Succession and Racial Invasion in Hawaii." Ph.D. dissertation, University of Chicago, 1931.

———. *Hawaii's People*. 3rd ed. Honolulu: University of Hawaii Press, 1967.

———. *An Island Community: Ecological Succession in Hawaii*. Chicago: University of Chicago Press, 1938.

Lydecker, R. C. "Memorandum on the Introduction of Foreign Laborers into the Hawaiian Islands." Typescript. Honolulu, 1910. HSA.

Lyu, Kingsley K. "Korean Nationalist Activities in Hawaii and America, 1901–1945." Typescript. Hamilton Library, University of Hawaii, 1950.

Mercer, James K., and Edward K. Rife. *Representative Men of Ohio, 1900–1903*. Columbus: James K. Mercer, 1903.

Meyers, Margaret. "Korean Immigrant's Story of Advancement Is Told." *Honolulu Star-Bulletin*, November 20, 1953.

Min Yŏng-hwan 閔泳煥. *Min Ch'ungjŏng kong yugo* 閔忠正公遺稿 [The posthumous works of Min Yŏng-hwan]. Seoul: Kuksa p'yŏnch'an wiwŏnhoe, 1958.

Moffett, Samuel H. Documents, no. 6 (1890–1903). In the possession of the Reverend Samuel A. Moffett, Seoul.

Moore, S. F. "One Night with the Koreans in Hawaii." *Korea Review*, December 1903.

Moriyama, Alan Takeo. *Imingaisha: Japanese Emigration Companies and Hawaii, 1894–1908*. Honolulu: University of Hawaii Press, 1985.

Nakai Kinjō 中井錦城. *Chōsen kaikoroku* 朝鮮回顧錄 [Memories of Korea]. Tokyo: Tōgyō kenkyūkai shuppanbu, 1915.

Nash, George K. Manuscripts. Ohio State Historical Society, Columbus.

No Chae-yŏn 盧載淵. *ChaeMi Hanin saryak* 在美韓人史略 [A short history of Koreans in America]. Vol. 1. Los Angeles: America Printing Company, 1951.

Oh, In-hwan, Park Pyoung Wha Kim, and Kim Seun-ung. Survey of 84 Korean Immigrants in Hawaii. University of Hawaii, 1970. In the possession of Professor Herbert Barrington, University of Hawaii Department of Sociology.

Oliver, Robert T. *Syngman Rhee: The Man Behind the Myth*. New York: Dodd, Mead and Co., 1954.

Onomea Sugar Company. Record. Vol. 2 (January 17, 1899–December 26, 1905). C. Brewer and Co., Honolulu.

Pae, Jae Schick, Nam-Yearl Chai, and Choon-ho Park. *Korean International Law*. Berkeley: Institute of East Asian Studies, University of California, 1981.

Paik, L. George. *The History of Protestant Missions in Korea.* P'yŏngyang: Union Christian College Press, 1929.

Pak, M. N., with Wayne Patterson. "Russian Policy toward Korea before and during the Sino-Japanese War of 1894–95." *Journal of Korean Studies* 5 (1984).

Palmer, Spencer J., ed. *Korean-American Relations: Documents Pertaining to the Far Eastern Diplomacy of the United States. Vol. 2, The Period of Growing Influence, 1887–1895.* Berkeley and Los Angeles: University of California Press, 1963.

Pang, Morris. "A Korean Immigrant." In *The Koreans in America, 1882–1974: A Chronology and Fact Book,* edited by Hyung-chan Kim and Wayne Patterson. Dobbs Ferry, New York: Oceana Publications, Inc., 1974.

Passenger Manifests. Inward. 1896–1900. HSA.

Patterson, Wayne. "The First Attempt to Obtain Korean Laborers for Hawaii, 1896–1897." In *The Korean Diaspora: Historical and Sociological Studies of Korean Immigration and Assimilation in North America,* edited by Hyung-chan Kim. Santa Barbara: ABC Clio Press, 1977.

———. "The Korean Frontier in America: Immigration to Hawaii, 1896–1910." Ph.D. dissertation, University of Pennsylvania, 1977.

———. "Horace Allen and Korean Immigration to Hawaii." In *The United States and Korea: American-Korean Relations, 1866–1976,* edited by Andrew C. Nahm. Kalamazoo: Center for Korean Studies, Western Michigan University, 1979.

———. "Sugar-Coated Diplomacy: Horace Allen and Korean Immigration to Hawaii, 1902–1905." *Diplomatic History* 3, no. 1 (Winter 1979).

———. "Upward Social Mobility of the Koreans in Hawaii." *Korean Studies* 3 (1979).

———. "Chōsenjin no Hawai iju to Nihon" 朝鮮人のハワイ移住と日本 [Japan and Korean immigration to Hawaii]. *Sanzenri* 三千里 22 (May 1980).

———. "Japanese Imperialism in Korea: A Study of Immigration and Foreign Policy." In *Japan in Transition: Thought and Action in the Meiji Era, 1868–1912,* edited by Hilary Conroy, Sandra T. W. Davis, and Wayne Patterson. London and Toronto: Fairleigh Dickinson University Press, 1984.

Patterson, Wayne, and Hilary Conroy. "Recent Studies of Korea." *Pacific Affairs* 45, no. 3 (Fall 1972).

Patterson, Wayne, and Hyung-chan Kim. *The Koreans in America.* Minneapolis: Lerner Publications, 1977.

"Pioneering in Korea with George Heber Jones." Mission Research Library, New York City. n.d.

Pooley, A. M., ed. *The Secret Memoirs of Count Tadasu Hayashi.* New York and London: Putnam and Sons, 1915.

Presbyterian Church in the USA. Board of Foreign Missions. Korean Letters. Presbyterian Historical Society, Philadelphia.

Putzillo, Mikhail. *Korean Immigration to Manchuria.* St. Petersburg, Russia: Hogenfeld and Company, 1874. Translated from Russian to English by William Rozuchi in *Ronin* 16 (1975).

Quinones, C. Kenneth. "The Impact of the Kabo Reforms upon Political Role Allocation in Late Yi Korea, 1884–1902." *Occasional Papers on Korea* 4 (September 1975).

Rand, Laurance B. III. "American Venture Capitalism in the Former Korean Empire: Leigh S. J. Hunt and the Unsan Gold Mines." Unpublished paper presented at the Columbia University Seminar on Korea, May 18, 1984.

Reinecke, John E. "Labor Disturbances in Hawaii, 1890–1925: A Summary." Typescript. Honolulu, 1966. University of Hawaii Library.

Reischauer, Edwin O. *Ennin's Travels in T'ang China*. New York: Ronald Press, 1955.

Restarick, Rt. Rev. Henry B. *Hawaii, 1778–1920 from the Viewpoint of a Bishop*. Honolulu: Paradise of the Pacific, 1924.

Rhodes, Harry A. *History of the Korea Mission, Presbyterian Church, USA, 1884–1934*. Seoul: Chosen Mission Presbyterian Church, USA, 1934.

Russ, William A., Jr. "Hawaiian Labor and Immigration Problems Before Annexation." *Journal of Modern History* 15, no. 3 (1943).

Sands, William Franklin. The William Franklin Sands Papers. St. Charles Seminary, Philadelphia.

———. *Undiplomatic Memories: The Far East, 1896–1904*. New York: McGraw-Hill, 1930. Reprinted Seoul: Royal Asiatic Society, 1975.

Sharp, Reverend C. E. "Reasons for Seeking Christ." *Korean Mission Field* 2 (August 1906).

Simonds, William A. *Kamaaina—A Century in Hawaii*. Honolulu: American Factors, Ltd., 1949.

Sin, Hŭng-u 申興雨. "Miju ŭi p'alch'ŏn tongp'o kŭnhwang" 美州의八千同胞近況 [The present situation of our eight thousand countrymen in the United States]. In *P'yŏnghwa wa chayu* 平和와自由 [Peace and freedom], edited by Kim Tong-hwan 金東煥. Seoul, 1932.

Sin Il-ch'ŏl 申一澈. *Koryŏ taehakkyo ch'ilsimnyŏnji* 高麗大學校70年誌 [A seventy-year chronicle of Korea University]. Seoul: Koryŏ taehakkyo, 1975.

Sin Sŏk-ho, et al., eds. *Han'guk hyŏndaesa* [History of modern Korea]. Vol. 9, *Nyŏnp'yoro ponŭn hyŏndaesa* [A chronological look at the history of the modern period, 1863–1945]. Seoul: Sin'gu munhwasa, 1972.

Smith, Jared G. *The Big Five*. Honolulu: Advertiser Publishing Co., 1944.

Smith, William O. Correspondence, 1895–1899. Miscellaneous. File 133. HSA.

Sŏ Kwang-un 徐光云. *Miju Hanin ch'ilsimnyŏnsa* 美州韓人70年史 [A seventy-year history of Korean-Americans]. Seoul: Haeoe kyop'o munje yŏn'guso, 1973.

———. "Miju ŭi Hanin ch'ilsimnyŏn." 美州의韓人70年 [Seventy years of America's Koreans]. *Han'guk ilbo*, 韓國日報 April 21, 1971–September 1, 1971. 26 installments.

Stephan, John J. "The Korean Minority in the Soviet Union." *Mizan* 13, no. 3 (1971).

Sullivan, Josephine. *A History of C. Brewer and Company, Limited: One Hundred Years in the Hawaiian Islands, 1826–1926*. Edited by K. C. Leebrick. Boston: Walton Advertising & Printing Co., 1926.

Sunoo, Harold Hakwon, and Sonia Shinn Sunoo. "The Heritage of the First Korean Women Immigrants in the United States: 1903–1924." *Korean Christian Scholars Journal,* no. 2 (Spring 1977).

Sunoo, Sonia Shinn. *Korea Kaleidoscope: Oral Histories. Vol. 1, Early Korean Pioneers in USA: 1903–1905.* Davis, California: Korean Oral History Project, 1982.

Swallen, Mrs. William L. (Sallie). Letters, 1901–1903. In Samuel H. Moffett, Documents, no. 6 (1890–1903). In the possession of his son, the Reverend Samuel A. Moffett, Seoul.

Swanzy, F. M. Diary. In the possession of his daughter and grandson in Honolulu, Mrs. James P. Morgan and Francis Morgan.

Swartout, Robert R., Jr. "United States Ministers to Korea, 1882–1905: The Loss of American Innocence." *Transactions of the Royal Asiatic Society, Korea Branch* 57 (1982): 29–40.

Takaki, Ronald. *Pau Hana: Plantation Life and Labor in Hawaii, 1835–1920.* Honolulu: University of Hawaii Press, 1983.

Treat, Payson J. *Diplomatic Relations between the United States and Japan, 1895–1905.* Stanford: Stanford University Press, 1938.

Turner, John K. *Barbarous Mexico.* Austin: University of Texas Press, 1969.

Underwood, Lillias Horton. *Fifteen Years Among the Topknots, or Life in Korea.* New York, Boston, and Chicago: American Tract Society, 1904.

U.S. Customs Records. Chinese Arrivals from January 1, 1900, to December 28, 1903. HSA.

U.S. Commissioner-General of Immigration. *Annual Report of the Commissioner-General of Immigration for the Fiscal Year Ended June 30, 1903.* Washington: Government Printing Office, 1903.

U.S. Commissioner-General of Immigration. *Annual Report of the Commissioner-General of Immigration to the Secretary of Commerce and Labor for the Fiscal Year Ended June 30, 1906.* Washington: Government Printing Office, 1906.

U.S. Congress. *Acts of U.S. Congress, 1899–1900.* Washington. Government Printing Office, 1900.

U.S. Congress. *Statutes at Large of the United States of America.* 57th Cong., 2nd Sess., 1901–1903. Washington: Government Printing Office, 1903.

U.S. Department of Labor. Bureau of Labor Statistics. *Labor Conditions in Hawaii: Fifth Report on Labor Conditions in Hawaii.* Senate Document 432, 64th Cong., 1st Sess. Washington: Government Printing Office, 1916.

U.S. Department of State. *Despatches from United States Ministers in Korea, 1883–1905* (File Microcopies of Records in the National Archives, Washington, D.C.: no. 134), Roll 19.

———. *Despatches from United States Ministers to Japan, 1855–1906* (File Microcopies of Records in the National Archives, Washington, D.C.: no. 133), Roll 81.

———. *Despatches from United States Consuls at Yokohama, Japan, 1897–1906* (File Microcopies of Records in the National Archives, Washington, D.C.: no. 136), Roll 3.

———. *Despatches from United States Consuls in Osaka and Hiogo (Kobe),*

Japan, 1868–1906 (File Microcopies of Records in the National Archives, Washington, D.C.: no. 460), Roll 13.

———. *Notes from the Korean Legation in the United States to the Department of State* (File Microcopies of Records in the National Archives, Washington, D.C.: no. 166), Roll 1 (September 18, 1883–April 24, 1906).

———. *Diplomatic Instructions of the Department of State, 1801–1906* (File Microcopies of Records in the National Archives, Washington, D.C.: no. 77), Roll 109 (Korea, March 2, 1883–December 4, 1905).

U.S. Immigration and Naturalization Service. Port of Honolulu. Inbound Vessels, Passenger Manifests. HSA.

Wadman, Reverend John W. "Educational Work Among the Koreans." Report of the Supervisor of Public Instruction to the Governor of the Territory of Hawaii, December 31, 1910 to December 31, 1912. Honolulu: Hawaiian Gazette Co., 1913.

———. "The Koreans in Hawaii." *Korea Review,* November 1906.

Waialua Agricultural Company. Annual Report of the Waialua Agricultural Company for the Year 1902. Submitted February 16, 1903. In the archives of Castle and Cooke, Inc., Honolulu.

Wailuku Sugar Company. Records. Vol. 1. C. Brewer and Co., Honolulu.

Wakukawa, Ernest K. *A History of the Japanese People in Hawaii.* Honolulu: Toyo shoin, 1938.

Yang Chu-un. Interview, February 27, 1974, by Bong-Youn Choy, in Washington, D.C.

Yi Chŏng-gŭn 李正根. "Insaeng p'alsipe ch'ŏnbyŏn manhwa" 人生八十에千変萬化 [Great changes in the eighty (years) of my life]. Unpublished manuscript. Center for Korean Studies, University of Hawaii, n.d. Appears to have been written in the 1950s.

Yi Hong-gi 李鴻起. "Autobiographical Sketch." (In Korean.) Manuscript. Center for Korean Studies, University of Hawaii.

Yi Hun-gu. *Manju wa Chosŏnin* 滿州와朝鮮人 [Manchuria and the Koreans]. P'yŏngyang: Union Christian College, 1932.

Yonekura Isamu. "Kikajin—The Naturalized Japanese Citizens Who Molded Ancient Japanese Culture." *East* 11, no. 1 (1975).

Yu Hong-yŏl 柳洪烈. "Mi'guk e innŭn Hanindŭl" 美國에있는韓人들 [Koreans in America]. *Sasang-gye* 6, no. 4 (April 1958).

Yun Ch'i-ho 尹致昊. *Yun ch'i-ho ilgi* 日記 [Yun Ch'i-ho's diary]. Edited by Kuksa p'yŏnch'an wiwŏnhoe [National History Compilation Committee]. Seoul: T'amgudang, 1973–1976.

Yun Yŏ-jun 尹汝儁. "Miju imin ch'ilsimnyŏn" 美州移民70年 [Seventy years of immigration to America]. *Kyŏnghyang sinmun* 京郷新聞, October 6, 1973–December 31, 1973. 28 installments.

———. "Early History of Korean Emigration to America." *Korea Journal.* Part I: vol. 14, no. 6 (June 1974); Part II: vol. 14, no. 7 (July 1974).

———. "Early History of Korean Immigration to America." In *The Korean Diaspora: Historical and Sociological Studies of Korean Immigration and Assimilation in North America,* edited by Hyung-chan Kim. Santa Barbara: ABC Clio Press, 1977.

Newspapers

Cheguk sinmun 帝國新聞
Columbus Dispatch (Ohio)
Evening Bulletin (Hawaii)
Han'guk ilbo 韓國日報
Hansŏng sinbo 漢城新報
Hawaiian Church Chronicle
Hawaiian Star
Hilo Tribune
Honolulu Advertiser
Hwangsŏng sinmun 皇城新聞
The Independent [*Tongnip sinmun*] (Korea) 獨立新聞
Japan Weekly Mail
Korea Methodist
Korean Repository
Korea Review
Kwanbo 官報
Maui News
Nagasaki Press (Japan)
Planters Monthly (Hawaii)
Taedong sinbo 大東新報
Tongnip sinmun [see *The Independent*]
Yamato shinbun

INDEX

ABOUT THE AUTHOR

Wayne Patterson received his Ph.D. in international relations at the University of Pennsylvania in 1977. Currently associate professor of history at Saint Norbert College in Wisconsin, he has been visiting professor of Japanese history at Vanderbilt University and visiting professor of Korean history at the University of Chicago, the University of Wisconsin-Madison, and Korea University. Among his publications are *The Koreans in America* and *One Hundred Years of Korean-American Relations, 1882–1982*.

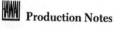 **Production Notes**

This book was designed by Roger Eggers.
Composition and paging were done on the
Quadex Composing System and typesetting
on the Compugraphic 8400 by the design
and production staff of University of
Hawaii Press.

The text typeface is Compugraphic Caledonia
and the display typeface is Caslon.

Offset presswork and binding were done by
Vail-Ballou Press, Inc. Text paper is
Glatfelter Offset Vellum, basis 50.